The Brothers Grim

The Films of Ethan and Joel Coen

Erica Rowell

THE SCARECROW PRESS, INC.
Lanham, Maryland • Toronto • Plymouth, UK
2007

SCARECROW PRESS, INC.

Published in the United States of America
by Scarecrow Press, Inc.
A wholly owned subsidary of
The Rowman & Littlefield Publishing Group, Inc.
4501 Forbes Boulevard, Suite 200, Lanham, Maryland 20706
www.scarecrowpress.com

Estover Road
Plymouth PL6 7PY
United Kingdom

British Library Cataloguing in Publication Information Available

Library of Congress Cataloging-in-Publication Data

Rowell, Erica, 1965–
  The brothers grim : the films of Ethan and Joel Coen / Erica Rowell.
    p. cm.
  Includes bibliographical references and index.
  ISBN-13: 978-0-8108-5850-3 (pbk. : alk. paper)
  ISBN-10: 0-8108-5850-9 (pbk. : alk. paper)
  1. Coen, Joel—Criticism and interpretation. 2. Coen, Ethan—Criticism and
interpretation. I. Title.
PN1998.3.C6635R69 2007
791.4302'33092273—dc22
                                                              2006100168

Ethan (left) and Joel Coen (center), on the set of *The Ladykillers* with Tom Hanks. (Credit: Touchstone/Photofest © Touchstone Pictures)

Contents

Acknowledgments

$\mathcal{W}$riting a book is like climbing a mountain. As you get closer to the destination, you keep thinking you're about to reach the summit only to find that it's merely the next peak. When you finally do get to the top, it's high time to take a breather and enjoy the view. Almost there. Before making the descent, I would like to offer a hearty thanks to the support of family and friends to whom I owe a mountain of gratitude. Whether it was fact-checking help, a word of encouragement, a celebratory drink, or editing assistance, I am profoundly grateful to everyone who helped me.

First and foremost is Annette Insdorf, my thesis adviser at Columbia University, whose deep film knowledge, dynamic teaching, and mentorship (both during graduate school and beyond) were guiding lights for completing this project. Her Post-it note with the phrase "eminently publishable" stuck on my graded dissertation kept me working toward making this book a reality. I'd also like to thank Richard Pena for his discerning comments on my early drafts. Both Annette and Richard introduced me to a wide range of cinema and film criticism, which were essential resources for this analysis.

I also wish to acknowledge Jennifer Levesque, whose consistent encouragement, especially when I most needed it, meant more than she probably realizes (except that now I've told her). I also extend warm gratitude to Cheryl McGillivary for her generosity of character; she came through in the clutch when the project was just barely off the ground and demonstrated that there are good, kind souls out there. Special thanks go to my parents, Bob and Peg Rowell. Time and again my mother leant an ear and gave good editorial advice when everyone else was off the clock. And my father's good humor and storytelling made for well-needed diversions at break time.

Great appreciation goes to those whose keen insights and comments enhanced the manuscript. I thank my sister, Lisa Preney, for good direction on an early draft of *Fargo*. Her suggestions helped me find a new approach to the book as I transformed an academic paper to a general reader title. Pam "Eagle-eye" Egan was also instrumental at various stages of the writing and editing, most recently as copy editor when the summit was almost in sight. I also extend a hearty thanks to many colleagues, former and current, who leant their top-notch editing skills and offered astute observations: Allison Cobb, Jennifer Coleman, Tim Connor, Kirk Davis, Peter Klebnikov, John Lewin, Margo Melnicove, Lisa Moore, Leslie Valentine, Leila Walker, and James Wang.

A very special thanks goes to David Stuart and David Morgan, who went above and beyond to help me through the manuscript's many revisions and bring this project to a successful conclusion. Their knowledge and love of film were inspiring and enlightening. I look forward to many more collaborations and hope I can repay the favor as we move forward in our careers.

Finally, I'd like to thank Scarecrow Press, Niki Guinan, and especially my editor Stephen Ryan, for his critiques, his keen understanding of the process, and his utterly professional guidance. I owe him a debt of gratitude.

Introduction

*V*iewer beware.

To casual observers, the films of Ethan and Joel Coen notoriously confound audience expectations. Refusing to adhere to genre conventions or movie-marketing ploys, the Coens' cinema can leave even professional journalists like Charlie Rose searching for a common denominator. Viewers who try to locate a common theme, directorial signature, or political streak may only see technical bravura, sly cinema in-jokes, or sidesplitting gags. But the depth and breadth of the Coen brothers' body of work—one of the most impressive and, strangely, influential in independent cinema today— bespeak an intelligence and cultural acuity that is rich, highly topical, and certainly hard to pigeonhole. Audiences may be excused for missing the obvious point of the Coens' work. It's not about the message; it's the medium. Or so these high priests of the lowbrow art of moviemaking would have you think.

But think again. The fraternal filmmakers' eleven movies to date not only upend expectations but also show how our view of the world profoundly affects what we accept as "reality." The Coens' cinema dresses up belief to look like knowledge, testing the viewer's perspicacity or, at the very least, jolting us out of our escapist comfort zone. While watching a Coen movie, it's a good idea to keep in mind the warning of *Blood Simple's* narrator, "Nothing comes with a guarantee." Their self-conscious movies all implicitly carry a similar message: *caveat spectator*.

TRICKSTER MYTHMAKING

Like the West African trickster god Eshu, the Coens and their films encour-
age us to leave our assumptions at the theatre door. Eshu is a provocateur who
dons a two-colored hat, revealing only the red side to one man and the white
side to his friend, to show that people can be simultaneously right and wrong.
Like this mischievous but benevolent god of the crossroads, the Coens,
through their films, show how perspective is key to one's perception of reality. Exposing the Coens as prankster mythmakers, who create nebulous,
dreamlike story universes, this book anatomizes a body of work that both
draws on and subverts storytelling techniques. Part of the Coens' subversion
and artistic agenda is to make you laugh. And laugh you will, perhaps without
noticing the potent lessons of perception woven into each work. But giving
their films a second look with new eyes rarely hurts.

 Coen films often make us rethink our roles as observers, telegraphing intrinsic dualities of human nature, such as truths and lies, the revealed and the
hidden, male and female, and dreams and reality. *Barton Fink* with its horror-
movie feel not only mordantly razzes Hollywood's slavelike studio system of
the 1940s; it also suggestively and slyly warns against an informer—a "fink"—
who trusts his chummy neighbor, only to discover he has given information
to a murderous madman. All the while, the astute *Fink* viewer may wonder if
these things are really happening or if the contents of Barton's head are
spilling onto the cinematic canvas. *Fink* is a surreal journey into the imagination and a sardonic exploration of how art is made, experienced, and contemplated.

 In an age saturated by moving images, the Coen brothers consistently test
our mettle as observers while holding a mirror up to society to show us its
cracks. *Fargo*'s title cards advertise deception from the get-go, but the signs are
so cryptic that many an astute viewer is fooled. Trucking in trickery, *Fargo*
hides its true lies. As confounding as that might seem, such a tactic shows
Fargo, and the Coens' cinema more broadly, as a line of progression from the
films of Alfred Hitchcock, whose thrillers not only shocked viewers but also
probed their role. Alongside implicating the bad guys, Hitchcock's and the
Coens' movies indict gullible viewers. The message hidden in *Fargo*'s bloody
crime story? Check your·source and be skeptical of surface images. The Academy Award–winning *Fargo*, in pretending to be real, makes watching a fictional
film murky territory for the unsuspecting.

 Then there are sociopolitical aspects of their films that amplify universal
struggles even as the plots take mystifying turns. Vietnam War talk and
glimpses of Saddam Hussein in *The Big Lebowski*, for example, might give momentary pause, but their consideration is soon eclipsed by the guffaws trig-

gered by the idiosyncratic, lovable, bowling-enamored Dude. Yet, behind the comic curtain of this odd, entertaining crime story lies a powerful statement about the absurdity of war and an exhortation against the threat of nihilism.

Raising Arizona's Hi, whose apocalyptic showdown with his alter ego is rife with sociological implications during the cold war, really undergoes a coming of age. The disheveled, late bloomer Hi must grow out of his bad-boy self and into his manhood, a common motif in the Coens' cinema. Imagination sets him free.

O Brother, Where Art Thou? boldly looks at race, crime, and punishment like few of its contemporaries. The film takes on not the overt slavery of *Roots* but the virtual slavery institutionalized by Depression-era penal systems. With the odd duo of the Greek poet Homer and filmmaker Preston Sturges as their primary muses, the Coens mine history and art—especially music—to float racial harmonies into the discord of racist rant. The result is a cinematic hymn to the common man, the musical man, the democratic man.

MOVIES THAT HELP US REDISCOVER MOVIES

Most of the Coens' films find the "little man" going toe-to-toe with powerful fat cats to grab—or steal—a piece of the American Dream pie. Norville Barnes (from *The Hudsucker Proxy*), Ed Crane (from *The Man Who Wasn't There*), and H. I. McDunnough (from *Raising Arizona*) struggle to get ahead, by hook or by crook, in a capitalistic system designed to keep them down. They are caricatured little guys unempowered but inspired to buck the system. The result is a set of quirky morality tales about capitalism, family, and social institutions. The Coens' movies are modern folk tales. They are parables embedded in plots turning on the odd, the hilarious, and the absurd. In probing the Coens' art, this book uncovers the filmmakers' pas de deux with the film-going public—the moves the Coens use to tease and braintease the viewer, the styles they borrow and newly fashion to let us see familiar genres in a totally new light, and the music and language they choose to render their bizarre film worlds, all the while moving to a beat of cultural relevancy. Coen films may be subtle in their shared themes, but more than just diversions, they open a window onto a panorama of American foibles.

• 1 •

Blood Simple: A Photo

John Getz and Frances McDormand "pose" for a surreptitious photo taken by an unscrupulous private eye. (Credit: Circle Films/Photofest © Circle Films)

"Nothing comes with a guarantee."

—Narrator/Loren Visser (M. Emmet Walsh)

"If I could do it, I'd do no writing at all here. It would be photographs; the rest would be fragments of cloth, bits of cotton, lumps of earth, records of speech, pieces of wood and iron,

1

phials of odors, plates of food and excrement . . . a piece of the
body torn out by the root might be more to the point."

—James Agee, *Let Us Now Praise Famous Men,*
Preamble (1946)

PREVIEW

In 1984, Ben Barenholtz, the father of the midnight movie, took a gamble
on a debut film.[1] Ethan and Joel Coen's small gothic thriller *Blood Simple* had
generated a big buzz at the Toronto Film Festival, impressing the indie dis-
tributor so much so that he bought it the day after it screened. "I've seen a lot
of first films, and there was something about this film that was so good and so
natural," said Barenholtz. "The only other first film that impressed me as much
was David Lynch's *Eraserhead,*" the creepy, intellectual horror movie he also
helped put on the map.[2] Barenholtz and brothers Ted and Jim Pedas, his partners at Circle Releasing (formed just months earlier), guided the Coens over
the tall hurdle independent features face: distribution.

More success followed. *Simple* earned kudos at the New York Film Festival and won the Jury Prize at the U.S. Film Festival, the precursor to Robert
Redford's Sundance. After a one-week run at Manhattan's Cinema I, the Coens' film and Circle's gamble on it began to pay off. "*Blood Simple* had made
the most spectacular debut for a film of its kind that anyone could remember—the grosses totaled $62,000 . . . and the reviews were uniformly ecstatic."[3]
Hailing its "abundant originality" and "brilliant visual style," the *New York
Times* called it "a directorial debut of extraordinary promise."[4] The *Los Angeles Times* dubbed it "a dazzling *comedie noire*, a dynamic, virtuoso display."[5] By
the end of 1985, it "had earned over $2 million in domestic rentals, easily re-
couping its [$1.5 million] production costs and more."[6]

Falling somewhere between a comic thriller and a revisionist film noir,
Simple deftly blends light and dark tones—a fusion that will become a Coen
trademark. The violent tale, complete with latent and blatant horror-film
snatches, pulses to an off-beat rhythm that cleverly pumps new blood—sometimes literally—into old genres. Its conventional roots stem from the hard-
boiled novels of Dashiell Hammett, to whom the brothers pay tribute in the
title. Taken from his 1929 novel *Red Harvest*, the term "blood simple" describes the panic and fear that visit a killer in the wake of a murder—a phenomenon the movie demonstrates in spades along with its close cousin
"money simple."[7] Such gritty inspiration is a springboard into a neo-noir landscape where requisite double-crossing, treachery, and corruption ooze into a

story of mixed signals that shock (and shockingly delight) with self-conscious flair and over-the-top gore, Texas-style.

REVIEW

Tracing a labyrinthine crime scheme gone awry, the story revolves around a love triangle between wife/lover Abby (Frances McDormand), husband/boss Julian Marty (Dan Hedaya), and lover/employee Ray (John Getz). This romantic arrangement erupts into a violent *ménage a quatre* when Marty engages the help of an obnoxious private detective, Loren Visser (M. Emmet Walsh). Never mentioned by name (like Hammett's nameless Continental Op), Visser is the one-time narrator whose short, strange voice-over starts things off with talk about whiners, Russian collectivism, and Texas loners. After his brief mood-setting monologue the story gets under way with a road trip in a fierce rainstorm. The unhappy wife is leaving her louche husband, and his employee drives her getaway car. As she blandly outlines her marital strife, he laconically mentions his romantic interest in her. In no time their mutual attraction leads to a night of passion, her solo flight becoming their shared plight. She was on her way to Houston, but they detour to a no-tell motel and then head back to Podunk.

It turns out that Marty had put a tail on his wife. After learning of her infidelity—which appears to be a fluke—he hires the same man to commit a double murder. The detective "proves" his homicidal handiwork to the vengeful, paranoid husband with a doctored photo of the betrayers' bodies presumably dead from gunshot wounds. Actually, the two lovers were just sleeping and the blood in the picture is Visser's photographic art, but Marty takes the visuals as proof, pays Visser for the job, and then pays with his life for dealing with such a nasty fellow. Visser double-crosses Marty with Abby's gun—apparently in the throes of being "money simple."[8] Nevertheless, he has the wherewithal to plant the murder weapon.

That night, Ray discovers Marty's body and Abby's gun and falls irrevocably into Visser's trap. Assuming that Abby shot her husband, Ray cleans up the bloody mess and tries to dispose of the body. Upon realizing Marty isn't quite dead yet, he finishes him off—in a move out of character. Afterward, suffering from a bad bout of the "blood simple" blues, he returns scared and confused to Abby with whom he believes he has forged a tighter "blood" bond. Yet, unaware that Marty is dead, she doesn't get his enigmatic confession and grows increasingly wary of his strange behavior. Their mutual distrust mounts and climaxes with estrangement.

In the penultimate bloody face-off, Ray, who has finally figured out that Marty's real killer framed Abby, duped him, and is now out to get them both, tries to relay this information to Abby. Visser kills him before he can clarify their strange circumstances. In the gruesome climax, Abby kills her unseen stalker, believing him to be her husband. The film goes out on Visser, the smirking victim of his own double cross lying beneath sweaty toilet pipes.

A PRIVATE EYE

The wordless ending is a visual punch line to the prologue's koan teased by a sneering voice. Over seven shots of a Texas wasteland, the speaker describes an unpredictable world:

> The world is full of complainers, but the fact is nothing comes with a guarantee. And I don't care if you're the Pope of Rome, President of the United States, Man of the Year, something can always go wrong. Go ahead, complain, tell your problems to your neighbor. Ask for help and watch him fly. Now in Russia, they got it mapped out so that everyone pulls for everyone else. That's the theory, anyway. What I know about is Texas, and down here you're on your own.[9]

We don't yet know the monologuist is Visser, the jolly, nefarious private eye, who dabbles in photography and hit-man activities if the price is right. But by the final scene we know that this one-time narrator with a twisted take on partnerships and a penchant for bad jokes and storytelling is the bad guy who winds up dead. As predicted, things went wrong.

This private dick, to cop a Hammett phrase, who shoots with his camera before his gun, is a surrogate filmmaker. He is the one who utters the phrase "money simple"—the closest thing to a title scene—and he is the hinge on which so many of the plot twists turn and bang. He is both part of convention and an exception to it. Guide to *Simple*'s duplicitous world, Visser is also the de facto emcee of the Coens' cinema. His message? Watch out—or *caveat spectator*. It's a caution that can be applied to their entire oeuvre.

In *Simple*'s neo-noir territory, the Coens make their first villain a messenger, a storyteller-cum-story maker who is destroyed by his greed—and art. Early on, his photos put viewers on notice of his deviously authorial role, and belatedly Ray catches on, too. A master manipulator, Visser is a bit like Hammett's Continental Op, who gets pulled into the dirty allegorical city of Personville (which he dubs Poisonville), but Visser is far less scrupulous. The Coens' dick is more a descendant of Orson Welles's crooked Captain Quinlan in *Touch of Evil* (1958), who also fakes evidence and whose dirty work ultimately backfires. But the Coens' crooked cop is not just any corrupt authority figure; he is *the* corrupt authority figure, a narrator who tells his listeners and viewers to beware. In short, he's something of an ill-intentioned trickster.

Not merely a fact finder, Visser is a "fact" creator. He is a power hungry, godlike manufacturer of reality with baleful, even sadistic tendencies who rules his world as long as he can. In this respect, Visser is of the same stock as Fritz Lang's mad scientist Rotwang in *Metropolis* (1922), who builds machines that allow the elite class to exploit the enslaved working class. His grand plan is to wipe out the workers by fooling them with a robot that looks like their leader and will guide them to their deaths. Characters like Rotwang and Visser, in the words of film historian Leo Braudy, "create the order of objects; much like a director, they are masters of inner space, Gods within the film."[10] However, because Visser and Rotwang are ultimately at the mercy of the film's true "God"—the directors—theirs is an asymptotic power drive.

Visser is the first in a long line of Coen characters who let their greed make them both money and blood simple. Hardly a straight shooter, he is a photographer and gunslinger—thus, he is both creator and destroyer, and his roles help sculpt a parable about visual perception.

Visser's calamitous monitions ring true for all concerned, including the viewer. Throughout, movie elements look exceedingly familiar in one view but utterly strange in another. From the daylight drive-in shot to the climactic shafts of light piercing the bullet-holed wall, self-conscious details percolate into the plot, to the point that the action of watching becomes vital to the characters' well-being, whether they know it or not. Looking is a constant in the movie's no-guarantees equation; characters behold, observe, and spy but don't always see beyond false appearances, and devices meant to preserve and magnify actions (a camera) are distorted by the perverse use of other devices (a developer, dark room). Through cinematic metaphors and an indeterminate ending—another Coen trademark—the film wryly suggests that looking and understanding are not mutually inclusive and that ignorance is bliss (or at least for Abby a lifesaver).

The movie takes off from Visser's forty-six-second introduction. Like lines from a Greek chorus or a Shakespearean sprite, the stormy petrel's voice-over is for the audience's ears only. It establishes a rural Texas in decline. In the midst of the cold war at the height of the arms build-up, a voice pays Russia a backhanded compliment while the screen shows a grim portrait of Reagan's America. The initial blown-out tire suggests waste and decay—a fresh artifact. The following five landscapes show wide swaths of mostly empty land. Three of these are dotted with oil machinery and point to a paradox of a bountiful land: when constantly sucked, oil-rich earth dries up, becoming oil poor. The empty drive-in fits the "album" of nihilistic "snapshots" showing the downside of supply-side economics—a topsy-turvy view of American capitalism. These seven still lifes set up a decayed world where the seedy side of human nature roosts. Enter the adulterers, the revenger, and the not-to-be-trusted hired help.

With an undercurrent of the Me Generation's greed and its ill effects, the expressionistic opening shows traces of film noir, the French term (literally "black film") describing a class of dark American movies that emerged in the 1940s. Borrowing aesthetically from German Expressionism, these dark, moody movies reflected disillusionment, anxiety, and paranoia. They grew out of hardboiled detective fiction and crime novels by writers like Dashiell Hammett (*The Glass Key*), Raymond Chandler (*The Big Sleep*), and James M. Cain. The World War II and postwar eras spawned such dark classics as Billy Wilder's *Double Indemnity* (1944), Michael Curtiz's *Mildred Pierce* (1945), and Tay Garrett's *The Postman Always Rings Twice* (1946)—offshoots of Cain's crime novels that exposed an ailing society caught in moral entanglements.[11] Along with Hammett's crackling pulp, Cain's slice-of-life stories were on the Coens' minds when penning *Simple*. "We especially liked *The Postman Always Rings Twice*," said Joel Coen. "We liked his hard-boiled style, and we wanted to write a James M. Cain story and put it in a modern context."[12] Part of this modernizing is arrived at through tone.

Painted onto the movie's cynicism is a cartoon veneer with absurdist touches. When down-home jealousy begets down-and-dirty murder, planted lies, wrong assumptions, and miscommunication lead to a slow burn. Marty assumes Visser's photo proves the murders and trusts far too much the slug he hires as a hit man ("If I need you again I know which rock to turn over").[13] Ray misreads the crime scene, finishes a murder he thinks Abby began, and believes Marty's lies about her. The movie shows emphatically that seeing should not be believing—the "eyes" don't always have it. Visser is a sarcastic spokesman of a reconfigured Lone Star State, a place burnt by the sun and plagued by the lure of false profits and, it turns out, a dead-right prophet: Visser. What the dick predicts comes true. Things go wrong—for *himself.*

Perhaps the opening's most striking feature is its conundrum: although a prologue, it acts curiously like an epilogue, defying placement in time. Is Visser speaking from the grave at the start like the dead body in Billy Wilder's *Sunset Boulevard* (1950)? Or is he simply prescient—a not-so-omniscient narrator who is done in by his own story, his own setup even? Like a warped Shakespearean Puck introducing troubles that set the story in motion, the private eye draws viewers into a twisted world, sets a dubious tone for doom, and then manufactures false pictures that ironically lead to his own demise. Thus, in a bit of bizarre, almost prophetic logic, the film comes full circle and the premise is fulfilled. Things can go wrong for anyone, including the "Man of the Year," the phrase inscribed on Visser's lighter.

Playing with form and expectation, the Coens reshuffle the familiar love triangle for the Me Generation. It's every man for himself in this stylized Texas; the woman is clueless. Visser's twisted commentary on American ideals is like a slap in the face to the patriotism of fear that reigned in 1984. With the country locked in a potentially apocalyptic arms race with Russia, the first voice casually praises socialism and casts a shadow on American individualism. In the end, one Lone Star character does manage to ride out the dark Texas miscues while none of the partnerships endure, but Abby's survival is hardly a victory for rugged independence.

Marty's attempts to break things off with Visser fail miserably, first when he rehires him and then when Visser ends the relationship with a gun blast to Marty's chest. Visser's violent breakup with uber sleazebag Marty does not yield many benefits either, for soon Visser is the recipient of gunshot wounds intended for Marty. Ray should have trusted Abby or learned how to communicate or at least avoided windows. Abby, the one most on her own, is unmindful of what is happening around her. Her lone survival suggests that escape—especially internal flight—can be a potent anodyne.

What saves Abby is her look in, not out. She is blind to Visser's plotting, but she is wary of Marty and attuned to her inner self, to which she keeps retreating. As Marty and Visser try to outdo each other with double crosses, the film riffs on the theme of the double. This literary motif, which the Coens will layer into a number of their films, explores the divided self. It is a longstanding narrative device that looks at hidden forces that break with "norms" of self and even culture. Sometimes it examines contrasted traits between two opposing (or sets of opposing) characters to point to desires unarticulated, unseen, even unknown, but influential far below the surface. Think Fyodor Dostoyevsky's *The Double* or Robert Louis Stevenson's better known *The Strange Case of Dr. Jekyll and Mr. Hyde.*

Primed by Visser's puzzling prelude, the film presents two couples breaking up. In one, a woman leaves her spouse, but her tango with his employee stumbles thanks to an outsider's interference. Second, the husband and his gun-for-hire engage in an illicit affair that is driven apart by avarice and double crosses. Solo, Visser shows how easily false images can fool gullible eyes. Together, from spying to killing, the men's tag team shows how jealousy and greed spawn corruption. The focus on this other "couple" helps prefix *neo* to this noir. Scheming men (not a femme fatale) create the mayhem. By the end, Visser's words come true: neither partnership remains intact—proving his theory that in the film's Texas locale "you're on your own."[14]

The seven-shot opening is an ostensibly orphic prelude that lays the groundwork for inversions. Specifically, light—such as the daylight in which Visser delivers his initial warnings—will signal misfortune. Such inversion is key to *Simple's* noir world, where light is menacing and darkness a safe haven. As Visser dies in the harsh light of Abby's bathroom, a lone star burnt and burnt out by his own intrigues, Abby in the unlit room next door is at last out of harm's way in the dark. Structurally, the final images of Visser cramped in the bathroom are inversions of the prelude's wide landscape shots carried by his voice. Rarely is one given so much up-front information to be so surprised by the ending. The film is structured like a joke that starts with a cryptic punch line that doesn't pay off for an hour and a half. The Coens show from this debut a nimbleness for surprises and arch deceptions. "Viewer beware" features will become a hallmark of their work—something they take to the limit in *Fargo,* their Oscar-winning, "film blanc" counterpart to this neo-noir.

SHEDDING LIGHT

Simple has essentially two introductions. The first is all about point of view and stasis. A rural road—normally a spot for movement, arrivals, and escapes—appears here as empty space, and the blown-out tire represents foiled motion. The odd low angle opens up a disorienting view that suggests perspective holds sway. The images that follow expand on the locale's etiolated quality. The empty drive-in anticipates the self-consciousness to come, while lever heads pumping up and down for oil complete the picture of a southwest wasteland unlikely to grace a tourist brochure. Sapped by capitalistic sucking, this is anti-Russian, solo, Me-Generation country, so couples beware. These ideas take off in the next intro, a tableau of Abby's futile escape turning into a long goodbye.

In the second beginning, day shots turn to night, and stasis is replaced by attempted flight and false starts. A speck of light grows rapidly from the black screen's far background into a full beam, mimicking for an instant the band of light that throws movies onto screens. Visually, this escape scene is the short intro's negative: pitch-black moving shots on a blacktop split by a broken white line versus sunny stills and a road striped by a solid yellow line. The rest of the scene plays out inside a car instead of outdoors. Within its first two minutes, the film intimates a primary visual conceit: side-by-side opposites. A pair of intros establishes an initial duality through sharp contrast—the prologue's daylight "snapshots" versus the title sequence's night shots in motion. The disorienting views and strained minimalist talk prime the plot for something to go wrong. A raft of self-conscious elements soon expands on this scheme.

Darkness becomes a key to understanding the discomfiting visuals. Though Abby cannot completely flee her creepy husband here, she starts to locate the part of herself that can do to him what he tries to do to her. That is, she taps into her dark side that allows her flight. In this way, the movie explores the literary double, which is often, as writer Karl Miller notes, "about running away, and revenge, when these pursuits are enjoined and prevented, when they are left to the imagination. One self does what the other cannot; one self is meek while the other one is fierce."[15] Abby's instinct toward dreams and sleep is emblematic of her need for escape, and they help safeguard her from the abominable plotting that is going on around and against her.

The double, a favorite theme of Alfred Hitchcock, is used to externalize dark impulses in *Shadow of a Doubt* (1942), *Strangers on a Train* (1951), and *Vertigo* (1958). *Psycho* (1960) also employs the motif, and its visuals too are dotted with opposite pairs. Marion Crane (Janet Leigh) sports a black then a white bra, and her image is duplicated in a mirror before she steals money. Both portrayals symbolize her as someone with the capacity for good and bad. Norman Bates (Anthony Perkins) is also multiplied in a mirror to visualize his split personality.

Simple's double motif is a bit subtler, but it too hews to psychological exploration. Abby wants out of her marriage and her first observations stir up some pop psychology amid deadpan humor. "Sometimes I think there's something wrong with [Marty]. Like maybe he's sick? Mentally? . . . Or is it maybe me, do you think?"[16] This comes after her first line about the pearl-handled .38 he gave her: "Figured I better leave before I used it on him."[17] Despite her self-restraint, Anton Chekhov's pithy gun theory—that a gun introduced in a drama must be fired—will apply, thanks to trigger-happy Visser. Soon her psychological meanderings find visual form in mirror shots.

Abby's need to escape informs her personality, and it's not just Marty she flees. She retreats from her waking world. She sleeps and dreams and sleepwalks in her dreams. In this way, Abby, who is often lit half in darkness, half in light, becomes the unlikely killer who stops the sleazy, murderous PI. But she thinks he's Marty, a misconstruction that induces fits of laughter from Visser who is dying under the sink, which is where the movie ends, not with Abby and her reaction to the PI's voice. The ending delivers a postmodern twist of humor. The final shot's bead of water falls toward Visser—and the viewer, as if to say the joke's on us. Twists like these become a Coen signature.

At the end, along with Visser's view of the sink, Abby's mistaken belief that she is finally safe from Marty underlines perspective. Disorienting compositions are part of the cinematic landscape, and if they help indicate fuddled minds, the movie's oft-inverted world shows that this can be a good thing. For example, the viewer watches most of the title sequence from Ray's backseat.

Often shot half in shadows and half in light, the mostly innocent Abby (Frances McDormand) is not a typical femme fatale. (Credit: USA Films/Photofest © USA Films)

For nearly two minutes with no cuts, the focus is on the backs of two heads. As with the opening's low-angle shot of the road, this view is strange. The subject is familiar, but the take on it is different and off-putting—classic film noir tactics. One effect of the long shot is that the more we look at their backs, the more we want to see their fronts. Ironically, the alienating view becomes engrossing the longer it lasts.

The backward view is reminiscent of the opening scene in Jean-Luc Godard's *Vivre sa Vie* (*My Life to Live*). This 1962 film of the French New Wave, an iconoclastic filmmaking style from 1950s–1960s France that often delivered blistering social commentary packaged in self-consciousness and jarring visuals, starts on an unedited long take on a couple. Like Ray and Abby, they discuss the dissolution of a relationship (theirs, in this case) with their backs to the camera. The movie goes on to show how the main character's conditions essentially force her into prostitution. Similarly, for almost two minutes with no cuts, the Coen pair conducts an unemotional postmortem on Abby's marriage with their backs to the camera. The movie goes on to show that Abby's and Ray's lives are influenced by their surrounding conditions, though the forces are more personal than sociological. Both openings subvert tradition and expectations.

In some areas, *Simple* pushes boundaries. In others, it adheres to movie norms. The credit sequence is traditional enough to inform us how to read the movie. The light flares blazon each credit signal to the viewer that light will be important. Establishing the main metaphor of photos and picture taking, the oncoming headlights illuminate the car for brief moments like camera flashes. In addition to invoking photographic phenomena, such intermittent lighting says something about their world, too. Unseen forces beyond their control are at work. Ray and Abby only appear when their whimsical world allows—suggesting that their fate, too, might be determined by circumstance. In this way, a tension between light and darkness is established and the opening's dubious warning about things going wrong is echoed visually.

Awash in visual impressions that prompt reconsideration of how images are processed, the film tests the viewer's ability to gain knowledge through sight. Resembling a movie projector shutter that inserts black frames between still images, the windshield wipers swish away the actors' names to clear the rain-pelted glass, creating a pattern: vision obscured, then cleared. This oscillation between clarity and opacity visualizes the Coens' modus operandi: their camera obfuscates and then enlightens. The analogue for the viewer is that seeing what is directly in one's sight is not easy; vision is not always clear. Photos, we learn shortly, can also make things clear or garble them. (The blades also recall Hitchcock's *Psycho* and its portentous drive through a rainstorm. In *Psycho*, the moving wiper blades foreshadow a slashing knife. *Simple*'s moving wipers are self-conscious emblems of a film that often reminds viewers they are watching a film.)

Within the first three minutes, the filmmakers launch the viewer on a cinematic journey evocative of the past through familiar crime story and film noir conventions—a dark, stormy night, a wife leaving her husband. At the same time, unusual camera angles and Visser's prefatory, enigmatic tease insert hairline faults along the road of recognition. And then there is the odd sense of humor. As a backseat passenger practically inserted *in* the action—not unlike forced viewer complicity in *Gun Crazy* (1949) just before the robbery— viewers are drawn toward the characters' point of view. Along with such compositional complicity is the strangely humorous visual metaphor that the Coens are taking the audience for a ride.

The viewer manipulation—or inclusion—of the opening drive is most palpable when the dark scene is suddenly lit. After Abby senses they are being followed, Ray slams on the brakes and turns to look out the rear window. Finally, we see his face full-on, lit by the headlights behind them. The change disrupts the shared character-audience point of view, at first triggering a response to a question of identity posed by the darkness. There's a fleeting feeling of awareness on the viewer's part as Ray looks in our direction toward

Visser's VW, shown in the following shot. More important, after a moment Ray's fully lit face is too bright and the hold on it too long, as if suggesting that even when things are revealed, they are not always pleasing. The rupture keys in on the film's treatment of light: light can be beneficial or perilous depending on one's vantage point, and what is not revealing to Ray and Abby is revealing to the viewer.

The thematic upshots here highlight the importance of reading visual clues—something at which Ray and Abby prove inept. They draw no conclusions about the prying headlights and dismiss the car behind them. Their ignorance of Visser's intrusion forebodes their response to the rest of his predatory actions. At the end, when Ray finally has an inkling about what is going on, he gives more thought to the VW Bug still trailing him. In Abby's apartment, aware he is being tracked, he tries to stay out of the light. But it's too little, too late. If only he had seen before how a malicious force—usually preceded by invasive light—had infringed on his and Abby's privacy with increasing insidiousness all along. Ray comes to the realization too late that light can be hazardous. Abby never fully understands, and ironically such ignorance works in her favor.

ART OF DARKNESS

Ray and Abby's first—and only—sex scene is neither steamy nor perfunctory, but it is expressionistic, and its self-conscious lightshow hints at a peek-a-boo voyeurism. As we watch their intercourse—and thus engage in cinematic voyeurism—Visser takes pictures. So in a strange way, as much as Visser mimics the role of storyteller (filmmaker), he also dons the mantle of viewer. But he is no idle observer; he is someone who watches with an agenda. Money seems to be his ultimate goal—killing gets him a better day-rate than Russia's fifty cent per diem. As in the car, Ray and Abby at the motel are alternately lit and shaded by forces beyond their control and awareness. Passing headlights shadow dance through the window and keep pace with the lovers' sexual rhythm. Though they have managed to escape into each other for the moment, their freedom of motion will soon be limited and Visser's camera is about to put an even bigger squeeze on them. When he shows Marty photos of Abby and Ray in bed, we learn that another force had been exerting control over them: Visser and his camera. Here again we see that the light play suggests post facto an authorial presence.

In short order, a strong, inimical connection between Visser and light materializes. From his pessimistic prelude to his tailing headlights and camera flash of the lovers in flagrante delicto, light indicates both Visser's presence and bad news, especially for Marty and Ray. Like a film director, the PI creates a pictorial fiction by shooting pictures and tinkering with images. Ultimately, although his photographs, which are dependent on light, allow him to trump Marty's sadistic hand and a well-lit window gives him a clear shot of Ray, Visser's twisted scheme boomerangs. Abby, in the literal and metaphoric dark, triumphs.

As *Simple's* world mimics the forces of film in general and film noir specifically—expressionistic lighting, shadows, a cheating wife, a vengeful husband, a PI, a murder or two—the treatment of light and the roles of detective and would-be victim stand out as reversals—or photographic negatives?—to tradition. This neo-noir's private eye—a particularly apt synonym for this crackshot photographer—trades the usual image of a cynical tough guy who gives the story a moral backbone for that of a smug, mocking, spineless bad guy. He's a modern Quinlan outfitted with a camera and an obnoxious laugh. So, into the dark unknown, where lightness comes to symbolize evil and darkness good, the Coen brothers blaze new paths. In this revisionist noir, Visser and Marty, a male "couple," scheme; Ray, a name that plays on the word *light*, is doomed by illumination; and Abby, the victimized woman, survives in the dark.

NEGATIVES AND REVERSAL FILM

For all the deliberate symbolism coloring their lighting scheme, the Coens rarely deliver a story in black and white. Steering clear of absolutes, their cinematic canvas prefers gray tones, where a jumble of good and evil forms a dense morality tale while their wild camera warns against taking anything too seriously. *Simple* begins the Coens' long tradition of infusing their films with a prankster sensibility—including some in-jokes so well hidden that they don't surface until well after the movie is over, if then. One such Easter egg is hidden in the radio announcer's name: Mike Lievsay is a hybrid of the movie's sound editors, John "Skip" Lievsay and Mike Miller.[18] An even more oblique prank comes from a practice, started here, of casting actors whose names create wordplays with their roles. Nancy Finger is among the teens who mock Marty's broken "pussy finger."[19] Then there's Roderick Jaynes, credited as the film editor. An old-time British editor hailing from England's Haywards Heath, Jaynes is as invented as Ray, Abby, or Visser. He is the pseudonym for Ethan and Joel at the editing bay.

The Coens' flair for invention isn't limited to in-jokes. Highly stylized shots wed thriller and horror elements to burlesque, coloring the inscribed world part everyday life, part cartoon. Even some of the scarier moments are lightened by a bold visual style. The resulting feel distances the plot from verisimilitude and careens it toward a kind of "pure cinema" that indulges in movie magic. Critics such as the *Chicago Tribune*'s Gene Siskel found the Coens' bravura style refreshing: "If there is a more interesting way to look at a door, a bar, a drop of water, a soiled jacket, a plowed field, bullet holes or even a bunch of dead fish, Coen finds it."[20]

The drunken barfly is a prime example. The shot glides along the bar toward the scene's main action until it encounters a passed-out patron. Drawing attention to the camera instead of masking it, the shot lifts over the drunk and continues. Such a self-conscious style, captured with élan by tyro cinematographer Barry Sonnenfeld—who eventually left his shooting career for directing— is like a tap on the shoulder that we're watching a movie. At other times, such campy shots ratchet up the violence.[21] When Marty tries to rape Abby, a super fast-paced camera jars and jolts, heightening the attack by upending expectation. Abby's self-preservation also stuns.

Other stylistic standouts unlock the psychological by delving into the dream sphere and unveiling Abby's confusion and subconscious. When Ray finally confesses to her that he buried Marty alive, a newspaper slowly hurtling end over end bangs onto the front door and snaps her out of her usual minimalist stance. The gunshotlike thud against the screen cues her back to reality, where her instinct is to flee. The "wrong" or misplaced audio that marks her grasp of the murder rhymes with the actual gun blast that accompanies Ray's discovery of the body when he accidentally kicks her revolver. The sound in his scene is real; in hers it's illusory.

The play with reality continues to visualize Abby's mind's eye, blurry with confusion, apprehension, and disbelief, as she runs away. She rushes out of Ray's house and glances in his car, and through a moving subjective camera we see spots of blood seep from the backseat. Is this real or a figment of her imagination—or a bit of both? The following shot pans from left to right, maintaining her frantic moves. Suddenly, she is at the barkeep Meurice's (Samm-Art Williams) house. Forgoing reality to extend her experience, the Coens cast off standard film grammar to heighten the tension and fear factor and boost the comical and ironic. Here, Abby's fog seems to trap her like so many women of film noirs past. Yet in the end, she survives her miasma of misunderstanding.

When she goes to the bar to try to figure out what's going on, precisely what she takes away from the visit is unclear because, as the camera captures so well, her world is mapped by dreams. Here, as they will do throughout their other work, the Coens show a European film sensibility in posing questions that don't always get answered. Her arrival at the office interrupts Visser's frantic search for the incriminating photo. He hides and spies on her as she surveys evidence of the break-in: scattered papers, a smashed window, and the banged-up safe. When she grabs a towel off the safe, the hammer wrapped inside slips out in slow motion. The tool should indicate an outsider's involvement, because Marty, Meurice, and Ray all know the combination. But she seems to absorb nothing from her find. After a last, cursory look, she falls backward and suddenly is no longer in the bar but back in her apartment.

The transition is momentarily confusing. Did she faint? Or was there a time ellipsis between the bar and her home? The montage conveys surreal intake to sync us to her fuzzy "reality." Then her return home opens a window into her dreams when she falls into sleep. But again her dreams and waking states collide. After a fade-out followed by a fade-in, she gets up, splashes water on her face, and looks in the mirror. When Marty appears in the other room, we see she has woken up within her dream. Again, we are whisked into her viewpoint and bewildered mind-set.

Just as the plot turns on a photo doctored to falsify reality, the Coens play with the film's "real" world. Electrifying camera moves and miscues short circuit our expectations and knowledge. Cinematic allusions and self-conscious artistry weave thematic threads of perception into the narrative fabric while inverted genre conventions and a host of image doubles play up themes predicated on, wrapped up in, and flummoxed by the visual. What we see is not always what we know—we see what we believe. The Coens hang this theme on most of their films.

Simple's themes reveal an essential, if obvious, truth about visual media— things aren't always what they appear and in films anything goes. Faked pictures are key to a crime scheme (frames are the basic building blocks for motion pictures). Shadows dance on ceilings; headlights light up walls (images projected on a "screen" mimic a movie). Windows become frames within frames, limiting the world the viewer is exposed to (the camera's lens—its eye—bounds its subject within a frame). "The result is to peel back our eyes and see movies again," to quote film critic Siskel again on the Coens' filmmaking style.[22]

Puckish camera work dips into philosophical realms as it recalibrates visual knowledge. Recognizable forms and genres lure the viewer into false recognition—the setup—and then subversions generate unexpected payoffs and propel us into a new level of understanding. Just as Visser clouds perceptions with visual deceptions, his creators also pull a wooly veil over the viewer's eyes. So, contrary to Joel Coen's claim that "the audience knows every step of the way what's happening," there are important moments when the Coens crop the full, true picture, just like their photo-loving villain, with a goal of misleading the eye.[23] For example, during Ray and Abby's sex scene, we don't know until afterward the private eye was spying.

While genre films trade off between convention and newness, *Simple* tips the scales toward novelty, subverting the noir with comedy and augmenting it with self-conscious themes of perception. When the PI rhetorically asks, "Who looks stupid now?" we think the answer is him.[24] But the extent of his stupidity is not known until later though those who recognize the allusion might get an early picture of the irony. The "stupid" line is borrowed from Alexander Mackendrick's *The Ladykillers* (which the Coens remake in 2004), a 1955 black comedy in which a thug glibly asks that very question when he thinks he has cornered an adversary, only to discover the gun he fires at him is not loaded. Moments later, his stupidity is made more apparent when an arm from the train trestle knocks him over the wall to his death.

As in *The Ladykillers*, *Simple* leads us to assume the joke is on Visser, but the visuals do not tell the whole story and the fact that he leaves his lighter at the crime scene is distended. (This is the inverse of the lighter's role in Hitchcock's *Strangers on a Train*, in which the lighter is intentionally planted at a scene.) To begin their meeting, Marty showily plops fish onto his desk in a bonding gesture with the PI. He's just back from his fishing-trip alibi to *Corpus* Christi—a name resounding with the idea of bodies, with which Marty thinks they've both been dealing. Visser smokes as more carcasses bury the lighter. After he shoots Marty, Visser watches the body a long time. When he finally leaves, the camera shoots the forgotten lighter under the rotting fish, dead on.

What seems like a black-and-white clue, though, is, humorously enough, largely a red herring. By framing an important snippet that crops out the larger truth, the filmmakers successfully misdirect attention away from the dick's *really* stupid move—leaving behind a dying man instead of a *dead* one. The final high-angle shot of the body expands on the title sequence's metaphoric wipers. Like a camera shutter (or a film projector's gate), the blades of the ceiling fan expose, then block, Marty. Thematically, they speak to the duality of visual information. Photographic images, which are limited to moments in time, are also bound by their frame. In other words, they reveal a partial view that may or may not tell the whole story.

"The script," says Joel, aims to "circumvent the audience's expectations. . . . Characters operate out of misapprehension, but by the end of the movie the characters are still in the dark."[25] The chief villain is the only one in the know at the close, but he expires. The viewer gathers that he killed for money—and possibly vengeance—and tried to frame and kill off those in the lovers' triangle, thus erasing his own hand in his murders-for-hire. But his scheme, which involves crafting a lie from a falsified image, backfires. It turns out ignorance and darkness are survival tools here, and Visser operates with too much knowledge and its visual counterpart, light.

Marty, Visser's partner in crime and the other "bad guy," is also too much in the know. Yet, he is too inept—or, as Abby might say, anal—to succeed. As a betrayed spouse, he typifies a film noir staple but only in part. Ultimately, he is all bark and no bite. He's the kind of person Visser thinks fills the world: complainers. Marty talks big and tells folks his problems, but they aren't much help. Like sending Abby to a psychiatrist instead of seeing one himself, he hires Visser to exact revenge on his wife. Marty is a bad guy by proxy.

The infelicitous Visser, marvelously portrayed by Walsh, is the real villain and a comedic varmint to boot. At first, he doesn't seem to fit any particular bad-guy mold, and for some time, his almost congenial persona, at least compared to Marty's, hides his true venal, homicidal self. If it's hard to tell at first who is more obnoxious, their second meeting erases any doubts. Where Marty barks, Visser is all bite.

While Marty cannot articulate that he wants Visser to kill, the dick agrees to the implicit job offer, altering his conditions from "if it's legal and the pay is right" to just the pay bit.[26] Visser, who wants to make a quick buck in Reagan's America, might have benefited from a cooperative system, but the Lone Star setting dooms his partnership with Marty to the fate of star-crossed lovers. In Texas, says Visser, partnerships are anathema. Marty betrays Visser by stealing the photo. Visser double-crosses him with a taste of Marty's own murderous medicine.

Visser is the first in what becomes a Coen character type: a large, seemingly jovial man with a decadent taste for blood and money. Those who follow include John Goodman's Charlie Meadows and Big Dan, David Huddleston's Big Lebowski, and James Gandolfini's Big Dave. Often exhibiting jolly exteriors that belie core wickedness, these large men have big appetites for food and money and are often dead by the closing credits. They are fat cats ever grabbing for a bigger slice of American pie, elbowing out—or destroying—the competition.

Visser is the movie's ganglion of evil. Although Marty puts him up to the killing, the detective causes mayhem largely by concocting reality from manipulated images, like a film director. First, he shows photos documenting the affair the cuckold doesn't want to see. Then, he commits fictional murder, gets paid, and kills his de facto producer. Visser's web of deceit goes on to catch Ray who misreads why Abby's gun is at the crime scene. False appearances keep working in Visser's favor, destroying the film's unwitting internal viewers. As witnesses to various parts of Visser's deviousness, Ray and Abby are first imperceptive viewers and then unwitting actors driven to murder. Thrown into Visser's homegrown "play," Ray kills Marty.

Creator then destroyer, Visser plays the threesome like pawns in a chess game—until Abby. Though Ray's shooting tips her to something dreadfully

Veteran character actor M. Emmet Walsh plays Loren Visser, a venal detective and photography buff whose lighter distinguishes him as "Man of the Year." (Credit: USA Films/Photofest © USA Films)

awry, she never realizes she has entered Visser's web. In a complete reversal of the thriller genre, the stereotypically cornered girl finds an outlet. The detective follows her into the bathroom only to find an empty tub and an open window. (*Fargo's* chased female, who chooses the tub over the window, will not be so lucky.) Visser continues the hunt until she stops him short with a knife to the hand. Maimed but not out, he pursues her, blindly emptying his gun into the wall in hopes of hitting her. When he runs out of bullets, he picks up the knife and, like many a horror villain, keeps on after his prey. Going against the genre's grain, she does not panic. She stares in disbelief at the light streaming through the pockmarked wall and takes her gun mentioned in the opening. She aims and shoots at the door between them. The responding thud indicates her on-target hit.

Her whispered, misplaced defiance of Marty amuses Visser. After a hearty laugh, he says he will pass on her information if he sees Marty again. Then Visser, who introduced *Simple* aurally, gives it visual closure. While the opening describes his point of view, the parting shot shows it, and as predicted, things sure went awry. After outlining the drawbacks of a Texas "Me Country," where solo acts are the norm, Visser ditches his narrator role but retains the mantle of storyteller. He uses Ray and Abby's affair to swindle Marty. Then he kills him. When he turns his sights to the couple, he achieves half his goal, but Abby bollixes the full realization of his get-rich-quick plans. He is undone with severe irony beneath a sweating sink.

On top of being a victim of his own tale, strangely, after all his machinations and spying, his final view is of the quotidian bathroom sink. The dripping pipes are not just justice for Visser's mercenary pursuits. The sink is a parting shot at the viewer, reminding us there are no guarantees. Hardly what we expect to wrap up a crime story cum thriller, the final image is a wink to the viewer. Adding to the futility of crime encapsulated in the odd view is a critique of visual consumption: Trust your eyesight only so much. More devious is the conclusion that staying in the dark can offer a superior vantage point. Rather than close on a presumably stunned Abby, who hears not Marty's voice through the wall but a complete stranger's, the ending bilks a revelation for a joke. Unlike the resolution of finally seeing Ray's face at the start, this deliberate lack of a payoff buoys the idea that darkness, the unknown, is the better vantage point. That's where the Coens leave the viewer—in the dark with the sole survivor.

Abby is not the typical hunted female exploited in horror movies, nor is she the typical femme fatale of film noirs like *Double Indemnity* (1944) and *Body Heat* (1981)—a villainous seductress who lures men into deep, deadly trouble. Abby remains, in Joel Coen's words, "relatively innocent throughout."[27] But her innocence seems to come at the price of sight. Rather than peering out at the world, she looks inward, as if gazing into her psyche's mirror. Along with sleeping and dreaming, regarding her physical form in mirrors is something she does a lot. Abby has limited sight outside herself. As the movie cuts to black, she remains in a visual and conceptual limbo, her saving grace. Refracted through the film's self-conscious mode, her proclivity for the dreamworld and her subconscious points to inner powers. Her imagination is her weapon—it saves her even though she hasn't a clue as to what—or whom—it has saved her from.

THROUGH THE LOOKING GLASSES

Simple suggests that how we see the world can impact our fate. Building from the premise of light connoting danger and darkness safety, the film depicts each character to varying degrees as an observer with characteristic "looking glass." With Ray it is windows. Camera and rifle lenses distinguish Visser. Husband and strip-club owner Marty is characterized by a two-way mirror, and fed-up wife Abby by a regular mirror. These glasses give us insight into their radically different worldviews. As Ray, Abby, Marty, and Visser stumble through their ménage a quatre, seeking refuge or revenge, they look, self-retreat, and spy. These glasses help reveal what makes them tick. The most self-reflexive least observant who is most in the dark survives.

Ray: Light at the Window

Abby and Ray's strange courtship begins behind a windshield speckled by raindrops and intermittent bursts of light. From this first scene, light at the window augurs danger. Visser's headlights compromise privacy; then a camera flash outside Ray's bungalow jeopardizes his safety. Relatively safe in the dark, Ray darts many a close call by extinguishing lights. For instance, when Meurice and his date enter the bar right after Ray finds Marty's body, Ray takes cover by switching off the light. Once the jukebox starts in, signaling the coast is clear, he flips the switch on to clean up the murder scene. Saved by the dark, he can now work in the light.

The efficacy of each character's glass depends on varying degrees of light. As his name suggests, light is particularly significant for Ray. His second appearance behind a windshield is like a negative of the opening—the night is clear and Marty's body, not Abby's, is in his car and on his mind. The low-pitched radio ratchets the creep factor up a notch. Cranking up the horror is the discovery that Marty is still alive. Ray bolts out of the car into a dark field. He calms down and returns to find an empty backseat. In a visual echo of George Romero's *Night of the Living Dead* (1968) Marty crawls along the road. Ray grabs and drags him when a truck's lights threaten to expose him, but he ducks out of the beam just in time. The next morning, his burning headlights put him at risk again by drawing a truck driver's attention. This oversight does no harm, but a failure to dim the lights at Abby's—and step away from the window—does.

Ray controls lights in a nonstop quest to escape detection and gain understanding. When he flips on the lights at Marty's office and finds the photo of the faux corpses, he gets a sketchy view of the encroaching danger. But as the figurative light dawns on him, a literal one is about to furnish his murder. Peering out Abby's window, he hides in the dark until she gets home and misreads his behavior as a threat. She defies him and turns on the lights, thus squelching the dark's safety and granting entry to Visser's incandescent violence. Again *Simple*'s skewed worldview is exposed: Light and transparency—and all that they symbolize, such as understanding, elucidation, clarity, knowledge, consciousness—prove sinister. As if doomed by his very name, which means stream of light, like a moth too close to the flame Ray is again lit up for Visser's gain. Confused by Abby's rebuff, after all he (thought he) did for her, Ray says he loves her, unwittingly reprising another phrase from her nightmare. Before he can explain further, a powerful blast kills him. In the end, Ray can't find safety in the literal dark perhaps because he has become too enlightened—literally and figuratively. Viewed and shot twice with a camera, Ray is finally caught in Visser's crosshairs through a window and malevolent luminosity.

Visser: Private Eyes

Visser's "private eyes" are his camera lens and riflescope. The most active looker of the four main characters, Visser requires stealth and deception for success. His spyglasses need a clear view and light source. Without these, he and his instruments prove powerless. Inside his VW Bug, he tails Ray and Abby until they sense his presence. Ray's gaze in his direction exhausts Visser's advantage and he drives off. Later, with more surreptitiousness, his flash outside Ray's place indicates a successful shooting.

Things start to go wrong for Visser and his carefully crafted visual fiction when he turns money—and blood—simple. Like Ray unable to kill the lights in a crucial moment, the private eye loses control. Visser's losses occur bit by bit. First Marty steals his photo; then Visser forgets his lighter and, worse, fails to kill Marty. As the PI desperately tries to regain his master-creator role, darkness starts to tip the scales against him. He is, after all, a photographer whose craft needs light and darkness in the right balance. When he thinks he kills Marty, Visser has a hidden agenda, a clear view, and a light source. To get Ray, he has a clear view and well-lit target. But with Abby he lacks both light and a clear sightline.

After taking out Ray, Visser breaks into her apartment to get his final victim, but she hides and then plunges a knife into his groping hand. He blindly, impotently shoots at her through the wall separating hunter and hunted but misses his unseen mark. The beams of light piercing Abby's dark hideaway recall movie projectors, a self-conscious detail that highlights Visser's waning role as creator. His destroyer side has taken over, a role that ironically does himself (not Abby) in. He fumbles in the dark—everyone else's safe haven—and his unwitting prey beats him. With no clear view and not enough light, the private eye is halted.

Marty: Watching Out

Before discussing Abby, a look at her husband is in order. Though he hires Visser to spy on his wife, Marty has his own voyeuristic tendencies. His bar, for instance, is a part-time strip club, a place where ogling for pleasure is de rigueur. Not only that, but his office sports a two-way mirror through which he can watch his patrons watching strippers. The mirror dominates the background of his introduction in which he and Visser discuss his wife's infidelity. At their meeting's end, the camera moves toward the glass and the hopping bar beyond it, where Meurice in his Chuck-T high-tops jumps onto the bar. A match cut to his move from the barroom side reveals a mirror where the window was. The duplicity of the glass—it's at once opaque and transparent—gives us a taste of Marty's nature. A combination of both Ray's and Abby's glasses, Marty's two-way mirror strips him of his own strength of character. He watches the world instead of participating in it and prefers clandestine looks. The dual glass also characterizes his double-crossing nature. And when Abby talks of his paranoia, she isn't joking.

His two-way mirror is an appropriate symbol for a paranoid who lacks people skills and, to an extent, manhood, a recurring Coen theme. He gets Visser to do his dirty work with his wife and fails to pick up a patron (Deborah Neumann), suggesting that Marty has problems when it comes to the opposite sex. In a way, he is a kind of *homme fatale*, updating a noir staple with a scheming, dodgy male instigator rather than the typical femme agitator. Though Abby's adultery is the putative inciting incident, it is his paranoia that initially shakes up their world. When Visser shows him pictures of Abby and Ray's spontaneous tryst, Marty doesn't want to look, implicitly acknowledging the effect seeing can have on a situation. He does end up looking and becomes infuriated at Abby and Visser. His fleeting notion to kill the messenger backfires in part because he trusts his business partner, like his eyes, too much.

Abby: A Looking Glass

Abby is the most self-reflexive and the only character who spends any time in front of a mirror—which ultimately doubles as a weapon. Marty re-

Instead of a femme fatale stirring up trouble, in *Blood Simple*'s neo-noir the stormy petrels are Dan Hedaya's Julian Marty (left) and the M. Emmet Walsh's private eye. (Credit: USA Films/Photofest © USA Films)

flects on this metaphor in a dream when he tosses her a mirror, the figurative representation of her double, and says, "You left your weapon behind."[28] The phrase echoes Ray's advice about what not to do when committing a crime, referring to her pistol and a murder she knows nothing about. Dream-Marty refers to her compact. In the end a combination of her weapon and psyche saves her. Earlier, Abby tells Ray that her psychiatrist called her "the healthiest person he'd ever met. So Marty fired him."[29] Unlike Marty, who passes the buck when it comes to direct action and self-reflection, Abby takes action, but for her this usually means some sort of retreat. Her very first act is to escape Marty, and that instinct of flight will not just be an ongoing theme; it will be her lifesaver.

Where Marty demonstrates nasty, duplicitous tendencies, Abby shows a healthy duality. The way she is lit—half in shadow and half in light—reflects her psychology. In the final scene, she cuts the light that allowed for Ray's death with a shoe, a move that cloaks her in life-saving darkness. Throughout *Simple*'s bewildering, oft-inverted rules, her inclination toward the dark and escape is unwitting self-preservation. It's as though her two halves—her waking life and dreams—make her whole. Abby doesn't just physically escape—running from her husband and seeking refuge in Ray's arms—she withdraws from her external world, preferring slumber. More than anyone else, Abby is shown in a state of unconsciousness. She is asleep when Marty calls the motel. Ray returns from disposing Marty's body to find her asleep. She is seen sleeping in his apartment more than he. When she goes to Meurice for help the second time, he tells her to rest. Sleep and dreams will become oft-visited realms of the Coens. With direct dialogue references to psychology and alter egos, it is fitting that her glass be *the* looking glass, a mirror, the common symbol for the psychological double in its ability to effectively show two versions of one person.

Abby's double is her dream self, and her compact helps visually delineate her duality. Her first mirror shots lead into Marty's attempted rape. She drowsily pads to find her purse. Opening her shell-shaped mirror, she gazes at her doubled, bifurcated reflection but her look is cut short. Panting lures her eyes from the mirror to the source of the sound: Marty's dog Opal. A groggy Abby is surprised to see the Alsatian when Marty grabs her from behind, causing her compact to fall to the floor. Two quick cuts show it rocking back and forth, giving it narrative weight. He whispers, "Lover-boy oughta lock his door . . . lotta nuts out there."[30] This line will be reshuffled in her dream, highlighting her knack for melding reality and her subconscious.

The second mirror sequence meshes her inner and outer worlds. Examining the evidence of the office break-in, she reacts by falling . . . into sleep. Here, the Coens effectively communicate her psyche by shaping the viewer's experience after hers. Without an obvious cut, the office setting where she starts to fall backward suddenly becomes her apartment and she lands on the bed. The fall that fantastically begins in one location and ends in another jars the viewer's sense of reality, making us keenly aware of the movie's dreamworld. Light outside her bedroom bathes part of her in brightness, leaving the rest of her shaded. After a complete fade to black—a time ellipsis that also occurs in the compact scene—she appears to wake up. She checks the time—an action suggesting she is awake—and walks to the bathroom. There, she looks in the mirror before splashing her face with water when again a noise gives her pause. This time, instead of Opal's panting, it is the sound of footsteps, breaking glass, and a door squeaking open. Earlier she had told Ray that if Marty were to sneak in, he would be perfectly quiet because he is anal, but this doesn't stop her from thinking it still might be Marty. She cautiously peeks out of the bathroom, tentatively and hopefully calling out for Ray. A shaft of light moves over the bedroom floor to reveal Marty on her bed.

Most likely a dream, for we saw Ray bury Marty, there is ambiguity—he came to life once before. The scene again shows Abby's intertwined waking and sleeping modes with unclear boundaries between the two (a technique ramped up in *Barton Fink*). When he repeats his earlier lover-boy line and then echoes Ray's words about her weapon, we can be more sure she is dreaming, for he repeats a line he didn't hear. The cap comes when he throws Abby not her gun but her compact, slyly suggesting that her psychological exploration is her true liberator.

DOUBLE TAKE

In exploring the double, *Simple* uses narrative déjà vues and rhyming scenes that lend new meaning to the double take.[31] These dramatic pairs point to a key question about visual understanding: Does recognition lead to better understanding? The answer in Coen worlds is often "not necessarily so." This exploration of viewer—and to an extent, character—perspicacity runs through much of the Coens' work and shows up in spades in *Barton Fink*, a murky dreamscape of a writer wrestling his soul, and *Fargo*, a pure piece of fiction housed in a movie posing as fact. *Simple* first challenges the viewer's deftness at solving narrative puzzles formed by misleading clues. We might miss this clever "test" of our visual faculties by being so absorbed in recognition—and laughter. The upshot is that what we think we understand doesn't always lead to veracity or a better understanding, even if we think it might.

As both *Shadow of a Doubt* and *Strangers on a Train* do, *Simple* employs a series of doubles. But instead of forging an association between two characters who represent good and evil (but who could go either way), *Simple's* doubles tend to offer up two alternate views of "reality." Here are just some of the pairs. Two sets of photos depict Ray and Abby (their motel tryst and their faked corpses). There are two sets of fish, two jobs for Visser and two gun kicks (Visser's plant and Ray's discovery). Marty leaves two messages on Meurice's machine.[32] There is a pair of "confessional" phone booth scenes: Visser's false murder call and Ray's real one. Two discoveries of the office break-in produce different reactions: Abby erroneously pins the crime on Ray; Ray finds the photo and realizes something strange is going on. Two comments contrast Russia and the United States: the first is Russian collectivism versus American individualism; then comes an economic comparison and the insinuation that American greed produces Visser's downfall.

Often these doubles use the mechanics of a joke. An initially false appearance sets up an ironic payoff. These doubles keep the viewer in an active role through recognition and laughs, making it a comic chiller and leading us astray. Perhaps we're so busy (or lazy?) recognizing that we fail to see the reality behind the appearance. The characters certainly fall prey to this. Twice, Marty's employees find him in his office in the same position: feet on his desk, hands behind his head, and staring into space. On the first occasion, Meurice approaches his immobile boss and comments, "I thought you were dead. Going home?" Marty answers, "I'm staying right here in hell."[33] Both comments about dead and hell would be more appropriate in the rhyming scene in which Ray discovers Marty's bloody body. However, when Ray calls out to his motionless boss, he asks if he's deaf. The inversion of *dead* and *deaf* provide morbid humor. His accidental kick of the gun triggers, or at least coincides with, the realization that something's amiss and he inspects the scene more closely. But the pools of blood by Marty's limp body beside Abby's gun cause him to draw wrong conclusions, and he enters Marty and Visser's devious "hell." Then another comic double occurs, whose setup takes place in the first bar scene.

When the camera catches Meurice hurdling the bar, he is on his way to charming a patron out of his jukebox money. The smooth-talking Meurice asks the Man From Lubbock (Van Brooks) what night it is and then offers his own answer with what we soon take to be a standard line: "Friday night is Yankee night."[34] He then identifies himself as a northerner, takes the stumped man's quarter, and plays The Four Tops' "It's the Same Old Song" (or Neil Diamond's "I'm a Believer" in the original video version). When Ray finds Marty's "dead" body in the bar, the scene and song are reprised, but the vastly different circumstances make for biting irony.

As Ray processes the scene of Marty's (mostly) lifeless body, holding the proverbial smoking gun, Meurice enters the bar. Ray rushes to lock the door and turn off the lights. From the bar comes a familiar voice and question. Meurice again answers himself, with a more flirtatious line and the same (old) song from the previous scene. With music as his cover, Ray begins furiously cleaning up the murder, assured that Meurice is busy on his date.

Though different in many respects, the clean-up scene's viewer manipulation works on a level similar to Hitchcock's in *Psycho*, another film that uses the double motif. When Norman Bates washes his "mother's" murderous activities, the viewer in part pulls for Norman even though he is aiding a horrific crime. Only later do we realize how duped we were into rooting not for a loyal son but for the actual killer who was in fact covering his own bloody tracks.

In *Simple*, we pull for Ray but in a different way. Though we are much more informed than the *Psycho* viewer—we know that Ray mistakenly believes he is tidying up Abby's mess—we still hope he doesn't get caught. Much of the scene's tension derives from the frustration between our knowledge and his lack of it and from its black comedic sensibility. Meurice's peppy jukebox choice adds irony: Ray, smitten by love and dripping with blood, believes Abby has committed the crime. Indeed, it's the same old scene, observed in countless movies before, one character cleaning up after another. But there's an inversion, too. Ray does not realize he is trying to hide Visser's, not Abby's, handiwork. Plus, the viewer's knowledge of his mistake plays into the song's "different meaning" line.[35] (The video's "I'm a Believer" lyrics also mockingly critique his predicament: Ray too easily becomes an ill-informed "believer" when he sees Marty's body.)[36]

DOUBLE CROSSES AND CROSSED SIGNALS

Simple and its Texas hell are very much concerned with perception. Discerning the truth is difficult because signals are crossed—or double-crossed. Abby and Ray's relationship breaks down thanks to rampant miscommunication, fallacious assumptions, and outside forces that bank on their unsuspecting reactions. Ray, Abby, and Marty, the movie's internal viewers, take for granted that what they see reveals reality rather than the trickery of a man whose existence is unknown for the most part to two of them. Abby only learns of Visser at the end when his voice, not Marty's, responds to her defiance.

To hold our attention, then, since we often know much more about what's going on than the characters, the movie depends a lot on the way the story is told. As much as Visser takes Marty, Ray, and Abby on a ride with his cooked-up murder scheme—which is never explicated to the viewer—the Coens play with plot twists, form, and style to shake up the viewer. Some startling techniques call attention to the cinematic apparatus, rather than hide it, thus subverting established cinematic rules. Ordinary objects and sounds are rendered extraordinarily. Incongruities sit side by side. In short, the atmosphere is often a hyperreality where cinematic trap doors can catch us up, just like Visser's traps trick Ray and Marty.

For instance, take the movie's ceiling fans. These mundane objects, reminiscent of film noirs and their preair-conditioning origins, slice heavy, broody air with their shutterlike blades. They slow the passage of time. Unlike the ubiquitous blower in Lawrence Kasdan's more straightforward noir *Body Heat* (1981), where perspiration visibly marks both clothing and naked skin, *Simple*'s fans have little to do with cooling sweaty bodies. Instead, they add texture, becoming metaphoric barometers of thoughts and emotions. During Marty's meditative moments, the murmurs of his fan externalize his mind's inner whirrings. Its low-pitched hum and slightly uneven cadence evocatively represent Marty's malice.

The fans can also misinform. Twice, in fact, the fans lead to false assumptions. One instance relies on acoustics and falsely supports Marty's lie that Abby will double-cross Ray; the other is visual and tricks the audience. The first misleading fan scene begins with Marty deep in thought at his desk. The low-angle shot, full of visual tension from the angles created by his bent elbows and the crisscrossed ceiling beams, shoots up toward the fan. After a different shot of Marty straight on, there's a cut to the fan and then another cut to, surprisingly, Abby. The jump in settings makes sense but thwarts expectations. We expect to see Marty after the second fan shot until we realize we're looking at a different one—white and plastic instead of tan and wood. What at first appears to be a deceptive camera trick is simply a new view that links Marty's thoughts to Abby and, we find out later, probably murder.

In the second misleading fan scene, the turning blades emit ominously low-pitched tones. Not only do the whirs create a charged soundtrack, but they also create an acoustic miscue that bollixes the characters. When Abby hears the familiar whoosh through the phone line, she mistakes the familiar background sound for Marty's office and thinks he is checking up on them again. When she hangs up and tells Ray it was Marty, he assumes she is lying—he knows Marty is dead and thinks Abby killed him—and Marty's warning seeds about his wife's untrustworthiness begin to bloom for Ray. Sound—both in scene and on just the soundtrack—can help create false pictures like Marty's message heard on Meurice's machine after he is dead, and it can intensify the noir ambience. (*Simple*'s 2000 rerelease includes a full sound remix to add Dolby, stereo effects, and restore the original music, as well as reedited scenes.)

Panting, for example, occurs in two different places to heighten the tension during acts of violation and violence. When Marty ambushes Abby, just as she feared, he sneaks into Ray's unobtrusively, but Opal's panting is less devious. The dog's breathing precedes the assault, stops when she notices him in the apartment, and then begins again as Marty drags her from the bungalow. Outside, the camera, in sync with the mounting panting, speeds across the yard toward their struggle. The orchestrated sound becomes less of a canine noise and more of a soundtrack element that intensifies the attack through dynamic changes in tempo and loudness. Suddenly the sound of bones cracking signals that the attacker has become the attacked. In Freudian terms, by breaking what is later termed his "pussy finger," Abby symbolically castrates him. Though he winds up to hit her, she beats him to the punch with a kick to the groin. With this evisceration of his masculinity, the soundtrack goes silent. He falls to retch—a gesture doubled in her dream—and he regurgitates. (Vomiting is to become a recurring Coen motif.) Score one for Abby.

Frantic breathing occurs again in Marty's burial scene where it bends reality and heightens Ray's physical and moral struggle. The scene begins like Abby's assault scene, with a body being dragged from behind and heels scuffing along the ground. The panting starts after Marty tries shooting Ray from his shallow grave using the gun that was in his pocket. A fly buzzes as he clicks through empty chambers; its disappearance punctuates his failure. Ray takes the gun and resumes the burial more briskly. Shovel scrapes and the brush of dirt mix into the heavy panting.

Sometimes the way sound is layered into a scene accentuates the overriding mood. Carter Burwell, whose first film-composing job on *Simple* would lead to a long partnership with the Coens, explains, "There's something about the human voice that tickles the brain. . . . [Manipulated], it would just be a little bit discomfiting."[37] The human voice just below the threshold of hearing has an especially chilling effect. Thus, the radio playing as Ray searches for a place to dump Marty's body adds prickly tension to an already creepy atmosphere. A radio evangelist (voiced by Rev. William Preston Robertson, a habitual voice in the Coens' films) delivers a quiet doom-and-gloom sermon. Apocalyptic themes titivate many Coen films, but here in their debut the apocalypse is directly announced. Bubbling up into this Texas hell are choice phrases like "this Antichrist is alive today"—a fitting prelude to the burial of a living man.[38]

Sometimes the juxtaposition of horror and comedy jumbles audience cues. When gurgles from the backseat spook Ray, he slams on the brakes. Just then, the DJ ironically talks about having to dig for the next tune. As a buoyant melody kicks in, Ray bolts out of the car and into a furrowed field, where he will dig Marty's grave. The incongruous music plays against Ray's fears and the scene's mood. Again, the mix of upbeat music over the hell that Ray has stepped into works off inversion. Peppy music plays while Ray decides to bury his boss alive.

Music and sounds add bizarre touches of humor to the macabre climactic scene, too. The first inversion is Abby's fear of Ray. He is on the lookout for the person trying to hurt them, but she thinks he is the one to be careful of, so she warns him that people will hear if he does anything to her. But when a deafening gun blast shatters her window, followed by heavy footfalls on her stairs and more gunshots in her apartment, there is not a single response from her neighbors. Ironically, instead we hear a radio being turned on, as if in an attempt to drown out the disturbance. The radio's cheerful melody plays during much of the grisly showdown—adding an ironic dimension to an apartment the landlady advertised as a place where no one will bother her and reinforcing the notion of neighbors flying from others' problems.

Music and sound are used to punch up ironic elements and create incongruities that editorialize on the drama at hand. For instance, the subject of "He'll Have to Go," the country-western song that bridges Marty's phone call to the motel and his first scene with Visser, is another inversion. In the song, a man calls his lover and asks her to make a choice between himself and another man. In the film, instead of speaking to his lover, as the song's singer does, Marty speaks to his *wife's* lover, twisting the song's message and the metaphoric knife she has stuck in his back. Also interesting is the fact that the song is sung by a woman, which muddles the song title's meaning: Is the singer calling her husband's male lover? Though a country hit for Jim Reeves, the song used in the movie is a recording by Joan Black. While commissioning a recording for the movie could have saved the filmmakers money, changing the gender of the singer is still puzzling and seems to speak to the men's subverted role as the instigators of the mayhem. It's one of many touches of the burlesque in the Coens' bloody crime story.

Representations of hell will become fixtures in the Coens' allegories, where fire imagery usually denotes the bad guys. Here, Visser's name is etched on his cigarette lighter, and he not only takes photos but he also burns them. It is during his conflagration session that he discovers the incriminating picture and his lighter are missing. Fearing that these mistakes will lead to his undoing, he frantically searches for both items to no avail. They turn out to be MacGuffins, for Abby gets him in the end with no knowledge of these mistakes. In the end he looks stupid. The final water droplet that falls from the pipe onto him symbolically cleanses his hell.

Another of *Simple's* visual subversions is the incinerator behind Marty's bar, the symbol of perdition Marty and Visser rule over and concoct. Visser, who proves to be not squeamish when it comes to murder, feigns disgust when Marty suggests using the incinerator for dumping the bodies. It is an obvious depository for such a dirty deed, and yet Ray overlooks it when looking for a place to dump Marty. As in *Psycho* when the viewer pulls for Norman to sink the incriminating car in the pond, *Simple's* viewer wants Ray to dump Marty's body in his own incinerator—a desire that implicates the viewer in the dirty deed. Ironically, Ray tosses his jacket into the fire but not the body. This is one of two de facto title scenes, the first one being Visser's admission of going "money simple." Suffering from Hammett's condition, Ray is nervous and fidgety back at Abby's apartment, as if he has lost something. "Is it cold in here?" he blurts out, then, "Where the hell's my windbreaker?"[39] The simple response is "blood simple." Ray suffers from the condition. Could the viewer, too?

NEO-NOIR: TAKEN FOR A RIDE

Central to the movie is a doubled pair of partnerships: Abby and Ray versus Marty and Visser. This centerpiece, in a kind of "boys will be girls" reversal of noir conventions, gives *Simple* one of its most modernizing effects. As predicted in Visser's opening monologue, both relationships melt down, but it is not the typical pair of adulterers who spin a web of duplicity, double-crossing, and deceit. Though Ray and Abby's affair feeds Marty's scheming and his revenge crushes their twosome, it is his and Visser's partnership that actually colors the film red and noir. The men's illicit soured romance carries the de rigueur distrust and treachery that lead to murder.

The notable shift away from the typical femme fatale scenario pushes the blame for all the destruction onto the two men. Typically, it is a female who stirs trouble in film noirs. For example, in Billy Wilder's classic *Double Indemnity*, Barbara Stanwyck is a two-faced wife who seduces and dupes insurance man Fred MacMurray into killing her husband before dumping him for a different lover. Cain's *The Postman Always Rings Twice* employs a similar storyline in which a woman bored with her husband convinces her young lover to help kill him. Needless to say, things do not end happily ever after in either tale, which both degenerate from women's double-crossing schemes. *Simple* atypically posits that a platonic male partnership gone bad can explode just as violently.

Simple inaugurates subtle gender subversions that will become a common practice in the films that follow. Names, often allegorical in Coen land, here hint at the play with sex and surface meaning. Marty is a misleading name, for it is used as if it were his first when in fact his given name is Julian. Not just a Roman emperor cognomen, Julian is also a feminine appellation from medieval Britain. Visser's name, never spoken but still telling, is more illuminating. His lighter, engraved with the phrase "Man of the Year," spells trouble (think of the opening narration), and the name next to this distinction is the feminine-sounding Loren.

The men are catty. Marty wanted neither photos nor a blow by blow of his wife's sexual encounter, but Visser insists on giving him both. Going tit for tat, Marty idly threatens decapitation and throws Visser's payment onto the floor. The PI's initial response to such treatment is to laugh it off. Despite their mutual distaste for each other, Marty reengages the PI with a new proposition.

Simple's amorous language surrounding the business partnership comes after the men's rocky start. Part two of their relationship begins with striking parallels to the other couple's romantic foray. Indeed, the meeting at the overlook is in many ways a mirror opposite of Ray and Abby's opening ride. Instead of movement at night, there is stasis in daylight, and in both scenes the

viewer is a backseat passenger. Replacing Abby's real complaints about her awful husband are Marty's paranoid gripes about his wife. And instead of a
blooming romance between the two in the car, it's a business plan. Yet, romantic tropes fill the air.

When Marty gets to the meeting place, the dick facetiously apologizes to
the woman by his car telling her, "My date is here."[40] Then, in an odd but interesting move, Visser opens his driver's side door and lifts the seat, as if inviting Marty to get in the back. Visser could be making a power play, offering
Marty the VW Bug's tiny backseat as belated retaliation to Marty's treatment
of him on payday. But, alongside all the double-entendres pertaining to their
"affair," it could also be perceived as a sort of sexual advance. Marty doesn't
acknowledge the gesture, yet Visser keeps the door open and the seat up until after Marty gets into the front passenger side. Once Visser joins him, the
camera moves inside and we witness the scene from a familiar backseat angle.
Perhaps, then, the backseat overture is a facetious invitation to the viewer to
step in and get taken for a ride.

From this point on in the scene, the men's transaction is ironically both a
mirror opposite and a recapitulation of Ray's and Abby's introduction. In the
opening scene, the soon-to-be lovers drive in a heavy rainstorm laconically
discussing her bad marriage. It may look like the clichéd "dark and stormy
night," but the brooding atmosphere is merely a setup to a spontaneous tryst.
By contrast, since this is a world where darkness connotes safety, the scene
where the proposition is murder takes place on a bright, sunny day. Sonically,
instead of the windshield wiper's desultory rhythms, the reggae bounce of
"Louie, Louie" accompanies the deed. Despite such opposites, both scenes begin with disorienting angles, set in motion acts of disloyalty, and involve
viewer complicity.

There's little subtlety regarding the romantic language of the men's relationship. One of the first subjects they tackle is trust—something of a sticking issue
in this place: "I'm supposed to do a murder—two murders," says Visser, "and just
trust you not to go simple on me and do something stupid. . . . Now why should
I trust you?"[41] Money is the answer. At the mention of the $10,000 commission,
Visser remarks on Russia's fifty-cent day rate, as if to quell any doubt that he was
the story's emcee. At this point, he obviously prefers capitalism—and its profit
margins—to socialism and goes "money simple."

In examining the men's relationship vis-à-vis the prologue, we see that
Visser's Russian theory where people pull for each other is not his cup of
Texas tea, and the prospect for their continued partnership looks bleaker and
bleaker. After the faux murder job, Marty gives the PI the envelope with a
bathroom sign instead of Visser's photo in it and pays him, reciting the "for

Barbara Stanwyck in a typical role for the film noir "dame": a femme fatale. In *Double Indemnity* she plots against her husband with her lover Fred MacMurray before she double-crosses him. (Credit: Paramount Pictures/Photofest © Paramount Pictures)

richer, for poorer" part of the wedding vow. Visser continues the theme with: "Don't say that. Your marriages don't turn out so hot."[42] With major trust issues between them, Marty tells him to count the cash and leave. But it's not the money that concerns Visser. He wants to be sure that Marty has kept their relationship a secret. When he feels assured in this regard, he shoots Marty. The blood from Marty's chest resembles the faux splotches on Ray and Abby's picture. Both images visualize the double cross.

For a movie with adultery as its inciting incident, *Simple* doesn't exactly drip with sex, a film noir standard. Only two of the four motel shots deal with the lovers' lovemaking, and these are hardly steamy. There's no nudity, no urgency, no seduction, no passion, no sweat. There is just rhythmic moving in bed shot from across a room that is lit to promote a mood not of lust or titillation but of self-consciousness. The other scenes of the two in bed are devoid of sex, too, yet the suggestive picture of their corpses in bed is a major plot component. As part of its film noir modernization, *Simple* substitutes violence and murder for sex.

Both car scenes climax with double crosses. Where Abby takes Ray to bed after their initial drive, thus cheating on her husband, Marty taps his wife for murder. After Visser double-crosses the cuckold, Ray tries to forge a tighter bond with Abby by finishing what he thinks is her dirty work. He has a long night of disposing Marty's body, and when he finishes he enjoys a smoke, the subtext of which strikes of a postcoital cigarette. As the camera pulls out into a high-angle wide shot of him still at the burial site, we see the crisscrossed tire tracks leading directly to Marty's grave, symbolizing the many double crosses on which the tale hangs—and archly denoting a blood simple move.

Taking on the fatale role normally reserved for women, Marty schemes with his partner then double-crosses him. Next, the image manipulator Visser, also something of a *homme fatale*, goes after Ray, whom he gets. Abby, however, eludes him. In a reversal of the genre, the cornered woman fights back and survives her attackers. True to Visser's warnings, things here have no guarantees.

WRAP: OVER AND UNDER EXPOSED

In *Simple*'s Texas hell where money lust is more prevalent than sexual desire, tensions arise between loyalty and corruption on the one hand and reality and appearance on the other—ideas that will thread through many of the Coens' movies to come. Melding psychology, latent wishes, and dreams into a self-conscious style, the film agilely moves between familiar film noir territory and brand new ground. Odd humor, strange camera tricks, and reversed gender roles subvert expectation for a fresh look. And doubles and double crosses abound.

Visser shoots and forges pictures. Later, when he burns the incriminating photos, he learns one is missing. Thus, his creativity precipitates his own destruction, along with Marty's and Ray's. It's as though the light that allows for his early success with Marty flickers out, and his camera and gun—instruments that require light—prove useless. While the venal murderer falters, overexposed in the harsh bathroom light, Abby sits safely in the dark, having beaten the man she doesn't even know existed, thinking he's Marty. He might as well be—he hired Visser. And so the scheming men are done in, and the femme is none the wiser. Replacing the femme fatale noir staple with corrupt males, and making the ending a revelation for the viewer instead of a character, the Coens affix the neo to their noir. *Simple* fulfills its no-guarantees promise, delivering a story at once familiar and new that both embraces and subverts conventions.

NOTES

1. Ben Barenholtz created a phenomenon in the 1970s with midnight screenings of cult films like *El Topo* (1970) and John Waters's *Pink Flamingos* (1973) at New York City's Elgin Theatre. Barenholtz also distributed John Sayles's *Return of the Secaucus Seven* (1980).

2. Judy Klemesrud, "The Brothers Coen Bow in With *Blood Simple*," *New York Times*, January 20, 1985, 2–17.

3. Paul Attanasio, "Brothers in Film *Noir*; The Complicated Joys of Making *Blood Simple*," *Washington Post*, February 3, 1985, D1.

4. Janet Maslin, "*Blood Simple*, A Black-Comic Romp," *New York Times*, October 12, 1984, C10.

5. Kevin Thomas, "*Blood Simple* Is Dark Comedy," *Los Angeles Times*, February 28, 1985, 6–1.

6. Manohla Dargis, "Too Simple," *LA Weekly*, July 7–13, 2000, www.laweekly.com/ink/00/33/film-dargis.php (accessed December 30, 2005).

7. *Red Harvest* first appeared in 1927 in the mystery magazine *Black Mask* under the title "The Cleansing of Poisonville." Soon after, Hammett's fiction hit the screen. *The Thin Man* came out in 1934. *The Maltese Falcon* (1941), with Humphrey Bogart as antihero Sam Spade, earned three Oscar nods and became a classic. Hammett's screenwriting never measured up to his novelist success, and a twenty-six-year writer's block crippled him.

8. *Blood Simple,* DVD, directed by Joel Coen (1985; Universal City, Calif.: Universal Studios Home Entertainment, 2001).

9. *Blood Simple*, DVD.

10. Leo Braudy, *The World in a Frame* (Chicago: University of Chicago Press, 1976), 86.

11. The movies are based on Cain novels published in 1936, 1934, and 1941, respectively.

12. Klemesrud, "The Brothers Coen Bow in With *Blood Simple*," 17.

13. *Blood Simple*, DVD.

14. *Blood Simple*, DVD.

15. Karl Miller, *Doubles* (New York: Oxford University Press, 1985), 416.

16. *Blood Simple*, DVD.

17. *Blood Simple*, DVD.

18. At first glance, the Texas radio station's call letters sound inauthentic, but the Coens got it right. When the "K"/"W" geographical boundary was established in 1928, only stations west of the Mississippi River seeking new broadcast grants had to comply with the "K" prefix. Existing stations in the new "K" area could retain their existing handles.

19. Other actors whose names make sport of a main theme or motif in the films in which they appear include Marcia Gay Harden's moll in *Miller's Crossing*, which has a homosexual subtext, and Richard Wood's mayor in the same movie that makes much ado about forests; David von Bargen's devilish Sheriff Cooley and Ed Gale's "Little

Man" in *O Brother, Where Art Thou?*, which works in folklore about devil bartering and nods to *The Wizard of Oz*.

20. Gene Siskel, "*Blood Simple* Is Shocking, But With Style," *Chicago Tribune*, March 1, 1985, A. Note that while Joel Coen is credited with directing and Ethan with producing, the brothers share responsibility in both areas. Thus, some critics treat Joel (incorrectly) as the sole director.

21. Sonnenfeld shot three Coen films, as well as *Big* (1988) and *When Harry Met Sally* (1989). His directing credits include *The Addams Family* (1991) and *Men in Black* (1997).

22. Siskel, "*Blood Simple* Is Shocking, But With Style."

23. Gary Stern, "The Brothers Coen: Two *Noir*-Do-Wells Score With Original *Blood Simple*," *Chicago Tribune*, February 3, 1985, 20.

24. *Blood Simple*, DVD.

25. Stern, "The Brothers Coen."

26. *Blood Simple*, DVD.

27. Stern, "The Brothers Coen."

28. *Blood Simple*, DVD.

29. *Blood Simple*, DVD.

30. *Blood Simple*, DVD.

31. Starting with *Blood Simple,* Coen films incorporate details that become signature jests. Visser's screaming during the grisly window scene becomes the "large man yelling" motif echoed in *Raising Arizona* when the Snopeses escape from prison, *Miller's Crossing* when a wrestler is tortured, *Barton Fink* when Charlie returns to the Earle a la madman, and *The Hudsucker Proxy* when Waring commits suicide.

32. The voice of Holly Hunter, who was wanted but unavailable for the Abby role, can be heard on Meurice's answering machine.

33. *Blood Simple*, DVD.

34. *Blood Simple*, DVD.

35. Eddie Holland, Brian Holland, and Lamont Dozier, "It's the Same Old Song" (Motown Record Corporation and Jobete Music Co., Inc.: 1965, 1993).

36. Neil Diamond, "I'm a Believer" (1966).

37. David Morgan, *Knowing the Score* (New York: HarperEntertainment, 2000), 60.

38. *Blood Simple*, DVD.

39. *Blood Simple*, DVD.

40. *Blood Simple*, DVD.

41. *Blood Simple*, DVD.

42. *Blood Simple*, DVD.

· 2 ·

Raising Arizona: A Baby

Tykes like Nathan Junior (T.J. Kuhn) are at the center of *Raising Arizona*'s madcap crime caper into which an infernal alterego (Randall "Tex" Cobb) roars.
(Credit: 20th Century Fox/Photofest © 20th Century Fox)

"I didn't know if he was dream or vision, but I felt that I myself had unleashed him for he was The Fury That Would Be as soon as Florence Arizona found her little Nathan gone."

—H. I. McDunnough (Nicolas Cage)

"Having children makes you no more a parent than having a piano makes you a pianist."

—Michael Levine, *Lessons at the Halfway Point* (1995)

PREVIEW

*A*fter *Blood Simple*, the Coen brothers wanted "to make a film as different from [it] as possible—galloping instead of languorous, sunny instead of lurid, genial and upbeat instead of murderous and cynical."[1] So they shifted gears and spawned *Raising Arizona*, a full-blown satire that spins the American Dream on its head. Focusing on warped attempts at parenthood, the brothers' second cinematic brainchild turns loopy compulsions into devilish fun. A roughly $6 million budget (four times *Blood Simple*'s shoestring) bankrolled the film's surreal Wile E. Coyote look and frenetic plot in which oddball characters chase dreams that are just beyond reach.[2] Though different in tone, feel, and genre, like its predecessor, the film was a hit—one of the Coens' biggest—pulling in $22.8 million in the United States by 1990.[3]

The idea for *Raising Arizona* evolved from Holly Hunter's obsessive character Edwina (Ed).[4] Her mad maternal desire sparks Hi's (Nicolas Cage) madcap kidnapping adventure, which helps him lose his bad-boy yens and find his crime-free self. Hi is hounded by a bogeyman, part-real, part-nightmare. Dreams and stories are key to Hi's quest to find himself and happiness, and a farrago of narratives tie into Hi's double vision of himself: a man coping with an inner child and infernal beast. Subscribing to *and* making fun of pop psychology, the movie is comedic fantasia, replete with cactus collisions, procreative quandaries, and a screwy desert metaphor for Ed's infertility. *Raising Arizona* examines crime, punishment, and class in its allegory of the American Dream detoured.

REVIEW

Raising Arizona pursues the story of Hi McDunnough, a disheveled petty crook, who wants to kick his habit of robbing stores with an unloaded gun. He thinks he finds a way when he marries police photographer Edwina, whom he routinely encounters in central booking. But after a short stretch, their marital bliss founders, thanks to Ed's irrepressible baby obsessions. When she discovers she is infertile (and adoption is out because of Hi's criminal past), she decides they must kidnap one. And so Hi ends up right back where he started, in outlaw territory, where their troubles multiply much faster than their family.

Hi purloins a newborn quintuplet from well-known furniture tycoon Nathan (Trey Wilson) Arizona and his wife Florence (Lynne Dumin Kitei). Soon after, Hi's convict friends, brothers Gale (John Goodman) and Evelle Snopes (William Forsythe), escape from prison and show up at Hi's door. They try to lure him back into the crime business with a lucrative bank job. Little do they know he's a born-again criminal, already back in business as a kidnapper. Hi refuses the offer at first but changes his mind when he is fired for declining his boss Glen's (Sam McMurray) proposal to wife-swap his spouse Dot (Frances McDormand) for Ed. On top of all this, Hi is tormented by the apparition of a noxious biker, who steals into his dreams and launches attacks on everything from desert lizards to helpless bunnies—and ultimately Hi.

When the Snopes boys discover Nathan Jr. is a "hot" tot with reward money on his head, they cut Hi out of the bank deal, nab the babe, and proceed to rob the bank with the toddler in tow. Their plan to return the tyke for the reward is unexpectedly thwarted when they become so taken with the little guy that they decide to keep him. Wanting to raise the little Arizona fast becomes a trend: the Snopeses, Glen and Dot, and, of course, the Arizonas all want a piece of the parenting action. The original kidnappers aim to stop all this and reclaim "their" baby.

Their hot pursuit of the infant culminates in fireworks when Hi confronts the biker, a real bounty hunter named Leonard Smalls (Randall "Tex" Cobb) who has grabbed young Nathan from the Snopeses. In a hybrid of a cartoon battle, a *Mad Max* fight, and the conventional Western standoff, Hi and Smalls fight to the finish with fists, knives, guns, and hand grenades. Hi wins and rescues "Junior." Having learned their lesson about looting a little one, the McDunnoughs return the Arizona to his rightful crib only to be caught in the act. Instead of turning them in, the short-fused Nathan Sr., who has found his softer side, gives some fatherly advice to the couple, who are on the verge of breaking up over the parenting fiasco. The furniture king advises them to work things out, or at the very least to sleep on it. That night, Hi has a vision of the future. He dreams that a litter of grandchildren visits him and Ed in their old age.

IMAGINE THAT

The kidnapping of the Arizona baby is spurred by Ed's unfettered family planning. She wants a baby, bad. From this germ of an idea sprouts a film preoccupied with procreation, creativity, and fixations, with biblical flourishes. Ed's infertility might destroy her biological shot at motherhood, but it cannot tamp down her avidity for a child. So rabid are her maternal desires, that, to her mind, stealing a tyke is not a crime but a blessing, and never mind that her kidnapping plan reawakens her ex-con hubby's illegitimate cravings. After they steal a baby, Hi lets loose his own idée fixe: being an outlaw. And while Ed's obsession sparks the plot, Hi's yens drive the story and fuel the hellfire. His journey into parenthood by way of theft is no joy ride. Nightmare visions addle him, his marriage is put to the test, and he must face down his darker impulses. In short, the Arizona baby-snatching sets Hi on a hero's course. Fortunately, his fertile imagination goes from being a chief liability to his best weapon.

Hi is a late bloomer, stunted by immature notions of being a fancy-free gunslinger. His tale recounts his parting ways with crime. Hi starts out as a babe, drawn to the prison womb, a conceit most powerfully visualized by Gale's and Evelle's "birth" into the world beyond the prison. After returning to the penitentiary twice, Hi grows tired of bars and cells—and men!—and pictures a better life with Ed. Her image flashes before him in a vision on his bunk's mesh underbelly: freedom superimposed on representational imprisonment. To end his crime cycle, he thus imagines a way out. Dreaming of liberating solutions becomes his modus operandi, which broadens to include memory and literature.

Imagine things the way you want them, the film suggests, and your wishes can come true. After Smalls arrives, a caveat is added: Be careful what you wish for. Hi's kidnapping caper is the subconscious writ large on the big screen. Opening with a memory and ending on a vision, his story is a recollection—a tale told by a man looking backward. His picaresque yarn yokes together Hi's immature and mature selves: Weaving past and present are narrator Hi (representing freedom, experience, and the present) and physical Hi (representing the captive man of the past who dramatizes events). One has control; the other is completely out of it.

Hi's recidivism, encapsulated in the eleven-minute sequence preceding the titles, establishes the personal demons that continue to plague him after he exchanges the criminal life for marriage. One of these foibles, evident from his first appearance, is a lack of self-dominion. Rather than being master of his own destiny, Hi is acted upon by others. The movie opens on the sound of prison doors slamming shut—a sonic punctuation of his upcoming, all-consuming imprisonment. In the first shot, Hi is propelled in front of a wall of hash marks, where he takes orders from Ed, turning left and right on command. She snaps his picture, capturing him on film. At the scene's end, a man drags him away. In the following shot, a guard leads him by the arm into the prison proper. This opening picture of Hi is many actions, little free will.

Hi's prison stints are actual and metaphorical, for his confinement represents his frame of mind as well as his legal punishment. He is the first of several Coen characters whose internal worlds are represented by external space. In *Miller's Crossing*, the circular, capacious apartment of perpetual thinker Tom Regan is like a residential thinking cap. *Barton Fink* features a seedy, amenity-free hotel room emblematic of the writer's seemingly empty head. The penitentiary to which Hi keeps returning symbolizes the thinking that locks him into the cycle of crime. The prison metaphor also indicates Hi's psychological framework: Prison can be freeing or restricting. Early on, since Reagan's economics have not trickled down into his pockets, Hi sees incarceration as an economic sanctuary with free room and board.

Hi's lens on his felonious tendencies is conflicting, with his narration often clashing with the images. For instance, during his first two returns to prison, while his voice-over waxes nostalgically about the feeling of camaraderie and homecoming, on screen the Sisyphean mopping con (Henry Tank) growls at him hostilely. Such disjuncture paints Hi's tale as a nebulous recollection, partly recalled, largely felt, endowing his first-person narrative with a playful disingenuousness. Hi looks at the past through a hazy filter that supports William Faulkner's idea that "memory believes before knowing remembers." Hi's past and present language is also terribly disjointed. Narrator Hi speaks in profuse, mock grandiloquent prose and is partial to biblical tropes ("Her insides were a rocky place where my seed could find no purchase").[5] Past Hi has a style that is sparse and provincial ("That's one boneheaded word," Hi says about *recidivist*), his language as delimiting as the prison bars.

During his first trip back to prison, Hi ironically talks of the cons bettering themselves by being "forced to meet with a counselor who tried to help us figure out why we were the way we were."[6] Despite the joke that coerced counseling could hardly expel any of the cons from the vortex of recidivism, the session is a harbinger of Hi's inner journey and opens wide the floodgates of pop psychology. Dotting Hi's physical landscape are totems of his internal quest. For example, the message on the counselor's chalkboard—"What we say in this room, let it stay in this room"—highlights the no-escape texture of Hi's life. As his literal incarceration finds figurative form, Hi's criminal leanings are shown to be symptoms of internal issues.

Adding to visual externalizations of his problems are myriad allusions that cleave to and amplify the film's medley of themes that swirl around babies, family, jobs, social climbing, and dreams. One of the more recondite of these is the counselor's fleeting reference to "Bonsche 'the Silent' Schweig," at the start of the first group session. "And all Bonsche wanted was a hot roll and butter," the counselor (Peter Benedek) concludes as the camera glides past the bored cons toward the speaker.[7] To be sure, the snippet of I. L. Peretz's short story is funny in the context of the prisoners on whom the unrecognized story's point is lost. Yet its inclusion fits beyond this joke. Bonsche is like a prisoner trapped by a life of suffering and loss, so much so that when he makes it to heaven, all he asks for is a modest snack. More than the fatalistic moral about human suffering, Bonsche the Silent is an apt warning to Hi. Both are hampered by their thinking. Hi's romance for the outlaw life grips him like a vise. He must loose himself from such mental manacles and embrace a better life or end up like Bonsche, perpetually suffering. Bit by bit, Hi becomes free through wishful thinking, memories, and stories—psychological breakthroughs that tease out, then stomp out, his demons.

By Hi's third trip to the pen, visions of family life change his attitude. When past Hi chides the mopper for missing a spot, he reveals his prison romance is dead. Having turned a corner on his personal freedom trail, he focuses now not on what he returns to but what he leaves behind: Ed. Convict Hi concurs with his narrative counterpart here, tuning out his bunkmate's food stories and tuning into a "brighter future" with a flash of the prison photographer's picture.[8] When Hi is paroled, he returns to the booking room toting a bought-and-paid-for wedding ring.

Intimately tied to Hi's cycle of crime is his social standing. Finding it difficult to get ahead or go legitimate "with that sumbitch Reagan in the White House," the have-not Hi rebels against Reaganomics through a losing routine: He robs a store (with a somewhat Freudian empty gun), locks himself out of his getaway car, and winds up behind bars.[9] But his wants are not purely economic. Part of the allure, Hi suggests, is the company of men. The counselor points out further that his prison spells are protests to growing up: "Most men your age, Hi, are marrying and raising up a family. They wouldn't accept prison as a substitute."[10] When Hi falls for Ed, he overcomes his first hurdle. Love and family put him on the straight and narrow, for a time anyway.

But even as he embraces a new life and wife, there are strong indications from the moment they meet that Ed will be a different kind of ball and chain for Hi. When he first sets eyes on her, he is smitten—caught in her camera lens as much as by the legal system. When she snaps his photo, she effectively traps him inside a frame. Such visuals suggest she cannot release him. The wedding ceremony also hammers this home: The "OK, then!" sanction of their vows is a direct echo of the prison officer's approval for parole.[11] This does not bode well for the repeat offender who sees a lot of similarities between the daily routine of marriage and the strict prison regimen. For example, his new coworker (M. Emmet Walsh) regales him with strange tales as his cellmate used to. But his new life isn't bad. He gets paid, and he's happy with

Ed. Soon, some Freudian imagery foreshadows that their joy is about to run dry. After hosing their dirt yard in the Arizona desert, Hi learns of Ed's infertility.

Ed is not limited only by her body. Like Hi, she becomes trapped in her thinking when she learns of her biological impediment. She stops doing housework, quits her job, and stares at a shrine of baby photos. Again Hi's recollection does not jibe with the onscreen image. As he solemnly states, "Our love was stronger than ever," a removed Ed stares out the car window lost in her one-track mind.[12] Her depression ends when her mind wanders where her body cannot go, and she conceives an idea. In a one-shot deal, she will play Bonnie to Hi's Clyde (minus the blood), and they will steal a child. As their prayers' hoped-for answer becomes a "be careful what you wish for" decision, biblical references percolate into the film, tying into themes of family, outcasts, and desert journeys. The crime refuels Hi's criminal hankerings, and Smalls, his villainous alter ego, is born.

THE SHADOW SELF

Hi's personal demons are embodied in the enigmatic Smalls, a perverted inflation of Hi's criminal yens. Smalls first appears in a nightmare triggered by guilty feelings. Not okay with stealing a baby, Hi, who robbed with an unloaded gun so as not to hurt anyone, rouses an outlaw with severe bloodlust. His dream figure represents everything that he is not—except that Hi has fathered him. Psychologist James Hillman explains the implicit tension in dream construction.

> The ambiguity of dreams lies in their multiplicity of meanings, their inner polytheism, the fact that they have in each scene, figure, image "an inherent tension of opposites," as Jung would say. The tension is more than that, however, it is the tension of multiple likenesses, endless possibilities.[13]

Though perplexing, Hi's dream character represents his own "multiple likenesses"—in other words, his double. The Coens fold the dreamscape so neatly into the cinemascape that it is difficult if not impossible to see the seam, submitting in the process the idea that stories and dreams—products of the mind's eye—are the stuff of life and films. Smalls signifies a duality that will lead to Hi's ultimate freedom. Hi's deeds break the codes of the society in which he lives, but they have a moral rightness. Smalls's actions are illegal and pernicious. There is nothing redeeming about him. Hi, by contrast, repents his offenses and becomes heroic.

Ed first spies Smalls through a puff of black smoke. As the McDunnoughs speed down the rural highway in pursuit of Nathan, a mystified Edwina wonders what the biker is. When Hi realizes Ed can see Smalls, we, along with Hi, again try to make sense of his dream figure. Such processing is a usual part of the reading experience of stories involving the double, a "twin" self with opposite traits. The nebulous portrait that Hi draws of Smalls derives from an interlacing of dream, memory, and literature. Earlier, Hi describes the chimerical, nightmare creature as a product of his own thoughts and deeds. "I didn't know where he came from or why. I didn't know if he was dream or vision. But I feared that I myself had unleashed him for he was The Fury That Would Be as soon as Florence Arizona found her little Nathan gone."[14] Thus, by Hi's own admissions, Smalls is part of himself—his dark side.

From the German phrase "doppelgänger," meaning "double-goer," the literary double refers to a character's ghost, a shadow "twin" who signifies another part of one's self, often a sinister or malicious side. Coined by the German writer Jean Paul Friedrich Richter in his novel, *Siebenkas*, the doppelgänger is what "people who see themselves are called."[15] In his "Dear John" letter to Ed, Hi's "wild man from Borneo" description fits himself and Smalls, who lurks in the desert near his trailer as Hi writes. Smalls represents the flip side of the imagination coin—the "be careful what you wish, for it may come true" half. He's a Mr. Hyde to Hi's Jekyll. "If I leave," he writes, as if he controls the beast, "hopefully, it will leave with me."[16]

Authors from Heinrich Heine (*Ratcliff*, 1822) to Mary Shelly (*Frankenstein*, 1845) and Fyodor Dostoyevsky (*The Double*, 1846) have employed the doppelgänger motif. In an essay on the meshing of dreams and reality, Robert Louis Stevenson, who explored the double in *The Strange Case of Dr. Jekyll and Mr. Hyde* (1886), homes in on part of what the Coens explore in *Raising Arizona*: "There is no distinction on the face of our experiences; one is vivid indeed, and one dull, and one pleasant, and another agonising to remember; but which of them is what we call true, and which a dream, there is not one hair to prove" (Robert Louis Stevenson, *Across the Plains*, 1892). Where Hi's dreams end and his reality begins is difficult to tell—but they both make up his life experience. Put differently, thoughts can appear to be as real as physical experiences, like Smalls's mystifying duality.

Hi's uneasy kinship with Smalls is intimated throughout. In stealing Nathan Jr., though intending him no harm, Hi picks on a helpless, little creature, as does Smalls. Ed calls Hi a "mad dog" while Smalls describes himself as "part hound dog."[17] Nathan Sr. comes closest to spelling out their relationship. When Nathan meets Smalls, the businessman deduces that the biker must be the kidnapper since he is so fixated on "fair market price."[18] He thinks that Smalls stole the baby as a scam to get the reward money. He surmises: "I think you're an evil man. . . . I think it is a shakedown."[19] On one hand, we know he is wrong: Hi took the baby. But in the context of the double, in which Smalls symbolizes Hi's outlaw desires, Nathan is dead-on, and by the end, Smalls does kidnap the baby from the Snopeses. Nathan's appraisal also prophesizes that Smalls will get "his butt kicked"—Hi drop kicks him to tarnation when he finally conquers his bad-boy side.[20]

The subtext of Nathan and Hi's final conversation resounds with double entendres. When Nathan asks if Hi and Smalls are in cahoots, Hi denies the partnership but not the connection. He explains that Smalls is who they saved Nathan Jr. from, adding, "It's a long story."[21] Nathan requests the details, but Hi, borrowing a page from the mercantile Smalls, requests the reward with no further ado. A contrite Ed refuses money, which, ironically, if Hi were to accept would help to perpetrate the "screw job" that Nathan had envisioned earlier. Even though Hi's "screw job" would pack much less ammo and villainy than Smalls's, despite his denials and evasions, Hi and Smalls both stole the toddler and then Hi rescued Nathan from both Smalls and himself.

Though *Arizona* is much jauntier and lighter in tone than *Blood Simple*, Hi's shadow self plunks dollops of darkness onto the larger comic score. The sinister motif derives from the fertile American Gothic tradition, from which springs Edgar Allan Poe's eponymous "William Wilson" (1839), a man at war with a shadow self. In the gothic story, the evil twin prevails, whereas the comical Hi takes the victory lap after his showdown. *Arizona's* rendering of the double is a classic American battle between good and evil. Set in the desert, the fight plays out like a modern Western, complete with special effects and an apocalyptic climax, a befitting end to the "Lone Biker from Hell."[22]

As the prison psychologist suggests, Hi is fighting himself. His internal struggle is manifested physically when he goes toe-to-toe with the apocalyptic biker—a man armed to the teeth and gunning to hurt little things (like babies and scrawny Hi). Their showdown pits Hi's good, decent, unloaded personage against the heavily armed Smalls. His entrance into the film's "reality," in a low-angle, upward-looking shot of his leather-and-boots stride, suggests something wicked this way comes. At least part of this is allusive. His regalia recall the couture of *Mad Max* (1979) movies while the cluster of ceiling fans above him may jog a memory or two of *Blood Simple*. Inside Nathan's office, Smalls introduces himself to the store owner as an outlaw (like Hi), a bounty hunter who "occasionally tracks babies" (as Hi does after marrying Ed), and "a shakedown artist" who wants more money than offered in the reward.[23] In essence, these are exaggerated descriptions of Hi himself. Their shared Woody Woodpecker tattoo, along with Hi's apology before blowing Smalls to smithereens, helps forge the connection.

At first, the doppelgänger connection between Smalls and Hi is merely a wisp, a story strand hanging in the wind, blowing through Hi's dreams. But his strange transformation from a creature racking Hi's mind to a bounty hunter confronting "real" characters puts us on notice of the double theme. Leaning away from reality and toward an allegorical fantasia, *Arizona* cavorts through the possibilities of cinema. The biker, after all, is quintessentially oneiric and cinematic with literary roots. Leonard "my friends call me Lenny" Smalls has a name resonant of John Steinbeck's Lennie Small character, the mentally slow giant with a penchant for hurting small critters in *Of Mice and Men*, a novel about a dashed American Dream.[24] As we watch the sartorially staid Nathan match bravado and toughness with the rock star–clad biker, we're not sure where to place Smalls.[25] We may wonder if he belongs to the dreamscape or reality. Slowly, we realize it is both, and what allows him to straddle these two worlds is the same force that lets him snatch a fly out of thin air: the movies or, more broadly, fantasy.

Seemingly a random dramatic beat, Smalls's extraordinary fly nab speaks to the strange, fictional plane in which he resides. When they meet, Smalls matter-of-factly tells Nathan he has flies. The businessman scoffs at the idea, explaining that sealed windows and climate control would not let them in. Moments later, the languid biker shoots his hand out with lightning speed, stopping short of Nathan's face. The next shot shows a fly squirming between Smalls's digits. Smalls is like the fly. He is not supposed to be there, but he is. And his ability to catch the insect in such a manner shows how "real" we should take him. This is a film, the Coens remind us, and faith in the logical, rational world of technology does not always apply.

The other important piece of such details is that everything we see is subjective. The entire movie is a rummage through Hi's somewhat disjointed memories often reminisced through verbal embroideries that belie onscreen images. The viewer is at the mercy of Hi's two perspectives, his highfalutin narrator's and his gangster wannabe's. And though he extricates himself from his dark side, in the end he is still bound by his limited horizons: "It seemed like us . . . our home . . . If not Arizona, then a land not too far away. I dunno. Maybe it was Utah."[26] The viewer takes this final line with a wink, but Hi, as hapless and sincere as ever, imagines a paradise out there, somewhere, perhaps across the Arizona border.

Hi's penchant for storytelling and his ability to dream, regardless of how narrow, inform amorphous connections. Our knowledge of Hi and Smalls's backgrounds is small, but details such as their uncanny, matching tattoos hint at a twin or brotherly connection, as brothers and family are a running theme.[27] Hi, unsure if Smalls is a vision or dream, opens up the possibility that Smalls could be a manifestation of his former outlaw self or a figure from his memory. Bolstering the idea they share a history are Hi's musings about Nathan Jr. After he is returned, Hi talks about lingering impressions forming from imprecise memory: "Wondering if he ever thought of us . . . and hoping that maybe we'd broadened his horizons a little, even if he couldn't remember just how they'd got broadened."[28] The murkiness of where precisely Smalls fits into the story plays into the psychology of memory. Smalls is akin to Hi's lingering call of the wild.

Borrowing from the psychological double born of myth and literature, the Smalls-Hi relationship also reaches further back to the hero myth that psychologist Carl G. Jung called the "Twins cycle."[29]

> In these two children we see the two sides of man's nature. One of them, Flesh, is acquiescent, mild, and without initiative; the other, Stump, is dynamic and rebellious. In some of the stories of the Twin Heroes these attitudes are refined to the point of where one figure represents the introvert, whose main strength lies in his powers of reflection, and the other is an extravert, a man of action who can accomplish great deeds.[30]

Enter Hi and his prolix narrator, a twosome doubled when Smalls arrives on the scene. That is, it's just not Hi of the past and his narrating present. There's Hi and Smalls, too.

One particular transition visually synthesizes the close affiliation between Hi and Smalls. It comes as Hi contemplates his worsening domestic situation and the Snopes brothers try to enlist him for their bank robbery. Gale appeals to Hi's outlaw side, which he insists is Hi's "true nature."[31] As Gale's words sink in, the Lone Biker gradually appears, superimposed on Hi's image. Mid-dissolve, flames sprout from either side of Hi's head before the biker's visual overtakes the frame. Appearing in shadow, Smalls is like a transient complement to Hi's solid-form half—the true nature to which Gale refers—and Hi's outlaw-dream come true.

Pairs and doubles dapple the plot. Besides packing dual shotguns in his bandolier, Smalls rides a motorcycle with twin exhaust pipes. Then there are the matching Woody Woodpecker cartoons, the strangest evidence of their kindred spirit, discovered just before Hi blows Smalls to kingdom come. This connection in part points to the cartoon sensibility infusing the entire comedy and its population of flat, one-dimensional characters, despite the Coens' statements to the contrary. "We like those cartoons but we never decided, 'Let's make a live-action cartoon,'" said Ethan Coen. "Even what seems like a typical *Roadrunner* shot, like the desert scenes with the big saguaro cactus, was done simply to establish the place at once as classic Arizona desert."[32] Yet, when Hi violently shows his displeasure over Glen's wife-swapping proposition, punching him in the face and sending him running, Glen runs smack into such a saguaro—a live-action stunt mimicking a classic cartoon joke.

Hi and Smalls in particular, with their distinct criminal, tough-guy manners, are cartoonish. With reddish hair, a beard, and a pair of guns at the ready, Smalls even resembles a calmer, darker version of Yosemite Sam, a cartoon character who happens to have a long-lost twin. The resemblance could be a stretch, but then Hi himself, with his own at-times cocked hairdo, has a Woody Woodpecker look to him. Their fight too is cartoonlike, as when Hi comes out relatively unscathed after being dragged behind Smalls's motorcycle.

On top of the film's over-the-top humor combining surreal elements and gags associated with animation are the snippets of Freudian psychology. The anxiety dream that gives birth to Smalls is clearly a product of Hi's palpable uneasiness with stealing a baby—a point rather ludicrously made during the first, unsuccessful kidnapping. From the look of it, toddler-snatching is more difficult for Hi than robbing a convenience store, which only requires dealing with a logy, hormonal teenager armed with a gun, a security buzzer, and a *Juggs* mag. When kidnapping, Hi must contend with not just one child but a seeming legion of unpredictable, diapered adversaries—innocent reminders that Hi isn't grown up enough to handle them.

Life's a drag for Nicolas Cage when his anxieties over fatherhood manifest themselves in a "Biker from Hell" whom he must battle. (Credit: 20th Century Fox/Photofest © 20th Century Fox)

In the nursery, which is strewn with toys that look like cutouts from a pop-up storybook, Hi's kidnapping soft-shoe gives us a taste of his unease at entering parenthood. Hi's difficulty wrangling such a strange creature as a baby is amplified by the two-chord vamp reminiscent of the theme to *Jaws*. The nursery represents unknown waters for the would-be father, whose initially fruitless abduction tacitly acknowledges the moral peril kidnapping puts him. An exasperated Hi reports back to Ed, defeated and empty-handed, calling the experience horrifying.

Ed will have none of that. Too monomaniacal to consider ramifications of their theft, she sends him back to the nursery. He successfully nabs a babe, but the new family's happiness is short lived. The strains of "Home on the Range" have barely faded out when the thunder rolls in. The swift change occurs as they capture the moment in pictures, in a bid to frame their sin as "decent and normal."[33] Punctuating the extraordinary circumstances of how this new mother and father came to be, an ominous, low rumble begins to gather, as if Mother Nature is declaring her disapproval. Familial bliss vanishes in a flash. Hi's imagination will shortly summon Smalls. But first, a simulated birth brings a different bundle of double trouble to Hi's door.

"I DIDN'T KNOW IF HE WAS DREAM OR VISION"

With the snap of the family photo Hi's happy-go-lucky marriage ends. Taking its place are parental responsibilities and concomitant stress, not to mention the guilt of pilfering a child. About to add to these are the twin problems of the seemingly friendly Snopes brothers and the menacing Smalls. First, a cut to the mud bowl outside the prison graduates the thunder from the picture-taking session into a full-blown storm, both literal and figurative. Under pelting rain, a head bursts through the mucky ground. With much effort, Gale extracts himself from the earth's belly, wailing like a newborn. He then reaches into the hole and pulls Evelle out by the leg, effecting a breach birth. The two men bellow together in triumph—a gesture they will repeat later on when they experience failure, kicking off what will become a Coen motif: large men screaming.[34] Then they head for Hi's trailer to bunk up with their prison pal and stir up trouble for the already troubled family. Complaining that the fugitive Snopes brothers will cramp their new life, Ed reluctantly lets them stay for a spell.

That night, Nathan's first at his new abode, more difficulties arrive. Now that Ed has what she wants in terms of a critter to cuddle, Hi is about to have his dreams come true: a rekindling of his criminal fire. Both Nathan Jr. and

Smalls manifest Ed's and Hi's wanton desires, respectively, and both miscarriages of gratification symbolize the wife's and husband's misplaced yearnings. Smalls comes alive in Hi's dream, butting into and edging out his pleasant thoughts about the new baby. Spawned from his anxieties, the biker appears in quick bursts of hellfire. A minor theme escalates into a cacophony befitting the beast's nature, and Hi's conceptual evil "twin," through which he can find redemption, is born.

Gazing out the window after waking from this nightmare, Hi mutters, "Sometimes it is a hard world for little things."[35] The sun's fiery red glow recalls the biker's fiery bike and gun blasts while Hi's words stretch beyond his dream into cinema past. The line about the "little things" is an allusion to *The Night of the Hunter* (1955), a surreal movie about a terrifying, wicked man (Robert Mitchum) posing as a preacher. Though his tattooed knuckles feature the word *love* across one set and *hate* across the other, his psychotic actions clearly show his lodestar is hate. First he preys on a woman, marrying her then killing her for money, but when her children outwit him, he terrifyingly goes after them.

Hi's comment that "it's a hard world for little things" echoes a line from former silent film star Lillian Gish in Charles Laughton's eerie fairy tale *The Night of the Hunter*. (Credit: Paul Gregory Prods/UA/Photofest © Paul Gregory Prods/United Artists)

Charles Laughton's movie, his only directorial effort, has a dark, eerie fairy-tale quality about it. It depicts a nightmare world where a monstrous man spurns the responsibilities of adulthood and society to satisfy his greed. His ill-doings are far more depraved than either Ed's or Hi's, for no deed is too heinous for him. Fortunately, the children find a protector, Mitchum's saintly nemesis (played by silent film star Lillian Gish), whom Hi echoes. Guarding the siblings against the preacher, she comments that "it's a hard world for the little things," as she watches an owl swoop down on a bunny. In his dream, Hi cites the line as Smalls blasts a bunny. Thus, the allusion forges connections between Hi and Gish's character on the one hand and Smalls and Mitchum's on the other. Smalls is a toned-down version of the preacher's evil, but the reference and its initial iteration in a dream help place the biker character in the realm of Jungian collective unconsciousness, a hodgepodge of recognizable character types—a bogeyman under the bed. The dreamworld is an important locus in *Arizona*. It's where things are born and thrive. And it's a place connecting experiences to memories and past tales. The *Night of the Hunter* is one of a number of allegorical stories furthering *Arizona*'s themes.

Another allusion is more surprising but no less revelatory. Within its opening lines, *Arizona* harks back to a classic American tale in which a wise narrator matured by experience, like Hi, tells the adventures of his former self. Following Hi's "Alcoholic's Anonymous"-like introduction—"My name is H. I. McDunnough"—he continues, "Call me Hi."[36] This greeting, along with the larger narrative frame, is tantalizingly reminiscent of *Moby-Dick* and its famous overture "Call me Ishmael." Like so many Coen references, the line is a tease, a suggestion, an impression, an imprecise though utterly possible reference. As the narration continues and we see the gaping distance between Hi's physical and verbal selves, a division marking *Moby-Dick*'s Ishmael, the allusion becomes less and less equivocal.

On a macro level, the parallels between the Coens' movie and Melville's classic are solid. First is the germinating idea of monomania. Captain Ahab, the novel's dark protagonist, will stop at nothing to get the great white whale, just as Hi is dead set on an illicit lifestyle and Ed is on a collision course with motherhood. Like *Moby-Dick*, *Raising Arizona* ponders age-old religious questions about creation, goodness, and evil, and both turn many a religious phrase. More distinctly, Hi and Ishmael (who is modeled after the biblical outcast) appear in two forms: as characters acting out past events and narrators in the present sifting through memories of their adventures. Both also deal with phantoms: Though Moby Dick crests the waters in dramatic appearances, he just as powerfully stalks the sailors' minds. Similarly, Smalls skulks about Hi's head before surfacing in his waking life. Ultimately, the guiding light for both works is, as literary critic Walter Bezanson points out, the imagination "through which all matters of the book pass"—the movie, too.[37]

Both Hi and Ishmael's double characters allow psychological probing through their before and after selves. The two narrators have the advantage of experience, perspective, and wisdom over their more active, bygone counterparts. As with Hi, whose younger identity is adrift in the Arizona desert, in Melville's novel, Bezanson explains:

> We hear the voice, always the magic voice, not of the boy we watch with our eyes, but of one long since went aboard the *Pequod*. . . . This voice recounts the coming adventures . . . as a story fully experienced . . . but not fully understood. . . . Narrator Ishmael is sifting memory and imagination in search of the many meanings of the dark adventure he has experienced.[38]

In the end, both Ishmael and Hi are liberated by their ordeals and, in a way, reborn. Ishmael, who had never been to sea but becomes the only survivor of a tragic whale hunt, relates his story as a man philosophically enlightened by his ocean adventures. Similarly, Hi, who had never navigated the turbulent seas of fatherhood, survives his kidnapping caper. For Hi, trouncing Leonard Smalls is pivotal to his enlightenment.

Woven tightly into both narratives is an ambiguity between the fiction's "reality" and its dreamworld. Hi's reaction to Leonard ("I didn't know if he was dream or vision") closely resembles Ishmael's description of a childhood experience: "Whether it was a reality or a dream, I never could entirely settle." In both cases, the authorial powers (the Coens and Melville) amplify the indeterminate—a realm probed in *Blood Simple*, *Barton Fink*, *Miller's Crossing*, *The Big Lebowski*, and *The Man Who Wasn't There*. In all these movies, dreams and uncertainties spill and blend into the fictional reality, thus vexing the audience. Through the confusion emerges the power of the imagined. In *Arizona*, we never do find out if Hi actually lives happily ever after; we simply know he envisions a happy life with Ed filled with children.

Rather than embarking on an ocean journey like Melville's Ishmael, Hi takes to the desert's sea of sand, a perfect setting for a story that hinges on infertility and a place that harks back to the original Ishmael's turf. Babies, parenting, and problems conceiving are prominent features in *Arizona* and essential details from the biblical Ishmael's story. Hi seems to refer indirectly to Ishmael, the father of Islam, when he subtly counsels Ed on one of the religion's five pillars: charity. "You gotta have a little charity," he says when she is rude to his escape con friends, continuing, "In Arab lands, they'd set out a plate."[39] Earlier he ascribes their childlessness to "biology and the prejudices of others"—two of the main reasons Ishmael is cast into the desert.[40] The "H," we learn, stands for "Herbert." Could the initial "I" stand for "Ishmael"? Similarities between Hi and Ishmael make a compelling argument for the possibility.

In Hi's final dream, he is the progenitor of a clan of rug rats who resemble his neighbor Dot. As with *Moby-Dick*'s wispy allusions, the ending ambiguously connects to the Bible's Ishmael who is the product of prophecy and old-fashioned wife-swapping. In Genesis, though God promises Abraham a son who will become a great ruler, he and his wife Sarah cannot conceive because she is infertile. So, to give her husband a baby the only way possible—it being in the days long before fertility pills—she offers him her slave, Hagar. Their coupling results in Ishmael, meaning "God hears." After Ishmael's birth, though, Sarah miraculously conceives Isaac. After he is born, she has Abraham send Hagar and Ishmael away. They retreat to the desert.

Hi ("I come from a long line of frontiersmen . . . and outdoor types") and Smalls ("part Hopi Indian part, hound dog") both resemble the biblical Ishmael, "a true child of the desert, wild and wayward."[41] Smalls, who is essentially a part of Hi, tells Nathan that his parents sold him on the black market. Such parental abandonment puts him in league with Ishmael. The twist of Hi's final vision of a happy future is that his children and grandchildren look a lot like Dot, whose husband had earlier offered up a vaguely Hagar-like wife-swapping arrangement.

Arizona's ending suggests that Dot plays a Hagar-like role for the McDunnoughs to give them the gift of family. The closing punch line about Utah could be sardonically playing up the possibility, thanks to the state's history of Mormonism, whose early practice tolerated a legitimized form of "swinging" called polygamy that can lead to lots of kids. Either way, the Ishmael-Isaac story presents two possibilities for Hi and Ed to raise a family: through a Hagar-like arrangement or a biological turnaround like Sarah's. Such connections fit into the locus of dreams—imprecise but strongly suggested ideas.

The Bible is ever present in *Arizona*'s Looney Tunes satire. After all, Ed's infertility and her fanatic maternal desire are one of the oldest sources of conflict on record, and procreating and begetting fill many a biblical page. Accordingly, Bible references relating to reproduction, creation, and storytelling make a strong showing, verbally and thematically.

Glen pitches his mischievous, sexual curveball to Hi with religiously tinged phrasing: "Doctor Glen is tellin' ya you can heal thyself."[42] On one level Glen's wife-swapping suggestion hooks into Hi's psychological need to fix himself and is offered as a means to de-stress Hi rather than populate the McDunnough's trailer. But later, with a host of stories springing Hi from his trapped situations, a little bit of old-fashioned swinging in the name of procreation—as practiced in the Bible—seems a likely possibility, especially after characters' names and biblical allusions are considered.

Narrator Hi recounts his desert journey in a lofty patois that is at times more appropriate to a minister than an ex-con. Hi tells us he and Ed tried to conceive when she was "most likely to be fruitful," working in a slice of God's "be-fruitful-and-multiply" command in Genesis.[43] Later, as a tease to his kidnapping exploits, he quotes one of Jesus's parables that instruct against judging others: "Now y'all who're without sin can cast the first stone."[44] His earlier description of Ed's infertility ("Her insides were a rocky place where my seed could find no purchase") recalls the parable of the sower, a story whose moral underscores the importance of story comprehension.[45] Seeds falling on a rocky place are the very subject of Matthew 13.

> Behold, a sower went forth to sow. . . . Some fell upon stony places where they had not much earth. . . . The disciples came and said unto him, Why speakest thou unto them in parables? He answered, . . . I speak to them in parables: because they seeing see not; and hearing they hear not, neither do they understand. . . . When anyone heareth the word of the kingdom, and understandeth it not, then cometh the wicked one and catcheth away that which was sown in his heart. (Matt. 13: 3–19)

Not getting it, the story implies, invites the "wicked one"—which is just what happens when Hi doesn't heed his misgivings about stealing a child. Smalls shows up, and all hell breaks loose.

WHAT'S IN A NAME

Smalls, whose name echoes a literary character's, enters the picture on the heels of Nathan Jr.'s kidnapping. After appearing in Hi's anxiety dream, the biker then meets with Nathan Sr. to try to raise the finder's fee for the baby who people believe is Nathan Jr., though no one knows for sure. His cognomen, along with his dad's, provides some thematic clues to the allegorical satire. Just as the title "Arizona" refers to the stolen baby and beyond, names, whether biblical or secular, provide layers of insight.

Nathan is distinct from his brothers from the get-go. The crib's headboard reads from left to right, *Larry, Harry, Barry,* the oddly spelled *Garry,* and then *Nathan,* which sticks out like a sore thumb. Throughout, his name speaks volumes and like so much of the story it is emblematic of forces at work. For instance, just as things are murky in this Arizona desert, Nathan Sr. is not even sure if it was Nathan Jr. who was stolen. The baby's name is a gift that keeps on giving.

When Dot calls Nathan an "angel straight from heaven," it is as if she knows his real name: "Nathan" means "gift of heaven."[46] Certainly, both Nathans turn out to be gifts to Hi. Senior does not turn him in at the end, and in addition to satisfying Hi's wife's obsession, Junior gives him his greatest "gift": the means through which Hi can find—and cure—himself. Dot's name also supports the theory that she gives the McDunnoughs their children. Dot, as a shortened form of Dorothy, is Greek for "gift from God."

Dot, who is always full of tips, suggests that Ed call the baby Jason. The recommendation cunningly if unwittingly echoes Glen's wife-swapping cure, for the name Jason means "to heal."[47] Her explanation behind her choice ("I just love biblical names") also hints at the allegorical nature of the characters' names, which add to the film's animated word play.[48]

If daddy Nathan is unsure which child was actually nabbed, Ed and Hi are even less in the know. Plus, as if to show their rampant irresponsibility, despite some good intentions, Ed and Hi forget to rename him. When the

Frances McDormand, left, hints at the importance of names when she comments how she loves biblical ones. Here, she calls Holly Hunter's new son "a gift from heaven." (Credit: 20th Century Fox/Photofest © 20th Century Fox)

Snopeses inquire about the child's name, they think quickly and call him "Junior," lopping off Nathan so as not to rouse suspicions about the lad's origins. Reinforcing their parental lack is their response to Glen's and Dot's separate queries into the baby's name. Ed tells Dot it's Hi Jr. and Hi tells Glen it's Ed Jr., as if each is pawning off the baby and his responsibility onto the other parent. This mix-up expands the gender play in the allegory, where names burnish the satirical desert romp that pokes fun at prisons, getting ahead, and parenting.

The androgynous *Ed,* as Hi's quick colloquy with Glen on the subject indicates, is another telling name. In response to hearing that the baby's name is Ed Jr., Glen says, "I thought you said it was a boy."[49] Hi explains the name as the short form of Edward. Part of the movie's comical attack on Americana is gender bending, a frequent monkey-wrenching tool in the Coens' screenwriting kit. The Coens tend to create mixed-up worlds in settings that resemble real-world locales to illustrate the kind of challenges the main characters must overcome. *Arizona* with its desert setting throws in some androgyny in its send-up of social "norms."

If Hi's attraction to Ed is a case of opposites attracting, they are a pair of inverted opposites. When they first meet, he eyes her coyly, almost demurely, while she barely notices his presence. She is rigid and keeps to her tasks of a police officer. Again, his words (this time coming from his physical form) are disjointed from what we see. When he wonders how such a "sweet desert flower" can be an *Ed,* the unemotional taskmaster interjects a "short for *Edwina*" into her commands.[50] Where Ed is characterized with manly traits, Hi is feminized. He wears colorful, flowered Hawaiian shirts and is associated with a bird.

His second trip to central booking finds Edwina distressed over man trouble. Though she tries to perform her police duties as dispassionately as before, tears break through and she confesses that her "fiants" ditched her. Narrator Hi fills in the details. Her "fiancé" (Hi corrects her mispronunciation) chose a "cosmetologist who knew how to ply her feminine wiles" over the not-so-feminine, uniformed, make-up free officer.[51] In other words, Ed's beau found a more womanly mate. Questions concerning Ed's femininity continue to crop up, as in response to her unilateral demand that the Snopes brothers leave when Gale rides Hi about who wears the pants.

It's a good question to pose because Hi too goes against the gender grain, even opting for a pair of nylons at one point. In the Short Stop convenience store, after lifting the bag of Huggies, he grabs an odd choice for a man—stockings. The visual payoff comes moments later when we see he uses his feminine purchase for his desperado getup, disguising his face with hosiery.

The driver whom Hi holds at gunpoint, instead of fearing him, teases Hi for his nylon headwear.

Hi's "dress code," which often consists of bright, flowered Hawaiian shirts, counterbalances Ed's austere uniformed appearance. He is flirtatious, speaks in poetic tropes, and talks of desert blooms. Before long, Hi decides to go straight, in the criminal sense, and trades in the male bastion of prison life for marriage, but, ironically, being a husband is not so different from his bachelorhood—gender-role reversals continue. Infertile, policewoman Ed hatches a criminal plan, which up to now has been a masculine activity, while Hi, who is unable to be either a biological or legally adoptive father, sires a monster (metaphorically gives birth to a being). In essence, this inversion leads them astray before putting them back on the right path. Her short stint at motherhood ultimately ends up becoming Ed, who gradually softens up and lets her feminine side shine through.

Despite Hi's feminization, he has a strong masculine side. After punching Glen, he refuses to tell Ed what provoked him. She is upset that he lost his job (as Hunter's hubby in the Coens' eighth film will also be) and asks him where that leaves the family. He responds, "With a man for a husband."[52] This thematic strand of what makes a man, which becomes a frequent Coen leitmotiv, tests their marriage. Ed questions Hi's character, but we see that he did the right thing by standing up for his wife and monogamy. He also proves his manhood by fighting the beast within—and without: Smalls. Ultimately, through spawning his double and literally facing his demons head-on, Hi shows his manhood through tests of wile and strength. Paradoxically, the criminal Hi is ethically superior to his "upright" fellow citizens such as obtuse parole officers, greedy Arizonas, and kinky Glen. In short, he is an Everyman who mends his ways and becomes a hero.

The personalities of the Snopes brothers are reflected in their names. Like Smalls, their Christian names beckon to literature, specifically the stories of William Faulkner whose Snopes clan is a perfidious bunch. The given names of the Coens' Snopeses also inform. *Evelle*, which sounds a lot like *evil* and contains the root *Eve*, suggests he's a tempter. *Gale* is an English word that means a storm-force wind. Gale and Evelle escape the prison during a storm and proceed to lure Hi back into crime. They take advantage of the fragility of Hi and Ed's domestic happiness, tempt him into a bank deal and then renege on it. When they steal Nathan Jr., they unleash a tempest, literally tearing apart the McDunnough family and destroying their "friend's" trailer. Hi, it would seem, keeps unwittingly experiencing the Bible's Golden Rule of having done unto him what he did to others—but in spades.

The Snopes brothers' threatening presence physically manifests itself when they destroy Hi's trailer. The violence climaxes when the boys exploit the fragility of Hi and Ed's domestic happiness and literally tear the family apart by stealing the baby. (Credit: 20th Century Fox/Photofest © 20th Century Fox)

The Arizonas, too, have appellations with significance. *Florence*, in addition to being the city home to the Arizona State Prison Complex, is a Latin word for flowering or prosperity.[53] This fits her role as the most fruitful mother and the wealthiest wife. The Arizonas represent the top rung of the social ladder. Next comes Glen, a loathsome guy but Hi's boss nonetheless—until he is fired. Thanks to Gale and Evelle, who denote some kind of alternative family, Hi and Ed are not quite at the bottom but they are a world apart from the Arizonas.

Nathan Arizona is introduced as an accomplished businessman through his TV spot, whose tagline calls attention to his sobriquet: "If you can find lower prices anywhere, my name isn't Nathan Arizona."[54] As one might guess, the surname and advertisement add up to "buyer beware" when the authorities investigating the kidnapping discover that the last name Nathan was born with is "Huffhines." "Huff," meaning a fit of resentment or anger, which he unleashes at the doughnut-eating detectives, and "hines," which means "servant" or "farm laborer" and conjures up an animal's rear, do not give the image he wants to project. Arizona makes for a better brand. For Nathan, whose ego is as big as the Sun State, names—and words—count. So does family—and wealth.

FAMILY VALUES

Arizona is an allegory that uses out-of-control parental urges to satirize class, economics, and the dogged pursuit of happiness. Amid the foreground ideas of dreams and visions is the McDunnoughs' American Dream gone haywire. It's not just that America has problems with lower-class rogues who move through a revolving prison door in an effort to survive in an inequitable economic system. An obsession with wealth is destroying family values.

The idea of family is everywhere in *Arizona*, where children are like manna from heaven or money in the bank. The rub is that all the couples have problems conceiving. Ed is barren, Hi tells us, using dated, King James vernacular. Nathan and Florence had to resort to fertility pills, which is why they ended up with "more than [they] could handle."[55] Glen confides to Hi that he and Dot are looking into adoption because "something went wrong with [his] semen."[56] The upshot is that the rich, like the Arizonas and Glen and Dot, can buy their way out of procreative difficulties, while the lower classes must, as with other issues of "wealth," resort to crime.

The McDunnough union merges Hi's remedy for joblessness with Ed's for childlessness, and it takes Hi's destructive alter ego to show them the error of their ways. Ed's fanaticism is emblematic of the picket-fence ideal that includes a couple of children in the yard. The decorated police officer rationalizes her hypocritical stance on stealing (babies are okay for the taking but not Huggies) with the Marxist notion that "it was unfair that some should have so many while others should have so few."[57] Ed is a bit of a social climber who wants "decent friends" like Glen and Dot as well as a similar lifestyle. Dot also wants a child, despite the fact that her hands are full with their current brood. In such a world where children are a status symbol, built into the struggle between the haves and have-nots is a rollicking indictment of capitalistic greed.

Arizona retools the "keeping up with the Joneses" storyline to one where trailer park yuppies aspire for a baby in the crib instead of a Lexus in a non-existent garage. Closely tied to having a child is the idea of *owning* one. And it's not just the McDunnoughs. When Glen figures out the baby is the stolen Arizona, he demands Hi hand him over, explaining that he'd prefer the reward money but Dot wants to keep him to cuddle. Back inside the trailer, the eavesdropping Snopes brothers change their plans and grab the baby. Excusing their traitorship as just business, the brothers violently wrestle Hi, destroying his family and home before absconding with Junior. They too originally want him for the ransom, but they find him so adorable that they pass up his financial value in favor of his cuteness. A baby's winning smile warming the hearts of folks who love cold cash is part of the big joke. But the notion of family trumping avarice does not work for Smalls.

The biker is the only one whose plans to get money from the baby are not thwarted by the tyke melting his ice cold heart. Once a black-market commodity himself, he does not feel the tugs of sympathy or fatherhood. The baby humanizes the others, replacing greed with love, but Smalls is immune to such baby magic. Thus, his brand of evil is both violent and mercenary in nature, and through him, Reagan's policies are skewered.

Hi's tongue-in-cheek claim is that he chooses robbery over earning an honest dollar because of Reagan and his advisors. Even after he has a legitimate job, "the gummint sure do take a bite" out of his pay.[58] The Arizona setting is a good fit for the film's assault on Reagan's conservative politics that are leaving Hi behind. The Sun State is the birthplace of America's modern conservatism, and its father, long-time Republican senator Barry Goldwater, appears in portraits in the parole and booking rooms. Goldwater's crushing 1964 defeat for the White House laid the groundwork for Ronald Reagan's successful presidential run as a conservative. Gale and Evelle learn the bank job particulars from one of "Dick Nixon's" men in jail for sex solicitation. Hi's evasion of Glen's question about how he was able to get Nathan so quickly alludes to the practice of cronyism: "Well, this whole thing is who knows who and favoritism," implying that white-collar, elite crime is more acceptable than his blue-collar variety.[59]

Nathan is one of the first characters in a long line of businessmen parodies.[60] Richer than just a successful "furniture king," he is a daddy five times over. Though not quite as fully developed as other Coen-created capitalist caricatures, he paves the way for *Miller's Crossing*'s mob boss Leo; *Barton Fink*'s studio executive Jack; company president Waring in *Hudsucker Proxy*; Wade, the father-in-law and car dealership owner in *Fargo*; the faux rich and powerful "Big Lebowski"; and department store tycoon "Big Dave" in *The Man Who Wasn't There*—wealthy, larger-than-life businessmen defined—and often doomed—by their success.[61] Workaholic Nathan, who barks orders to the staff over the phone while on a short paternity leave, comes to appreciate his family through the kidnapping ordeal.

Family and career are two main concerns at odds with each other in *Arizona*. Gale and Evelle are the exception to the rule. "Sometimes your career's gotta come before family," says Gale; Evelle concurs, "Work is what's kept us happy."[62] Their rationale is that whether they succeed as criminals or get caught, they are "set for life."[63] Crime and family don't mix as well in the McDunnough household, at least not after Ed satisfies her motherhood obsession by first quitting her job and then ordering a kidnapping. Her criminal diversion ends the moment she holds Nathan in her arms, or so she would like. After he loses his job, Hi, however, sees no choice but to take care of his family by robbing a bank. That plan backfires when the Snopeses steal Junior. So Hi and Ed come up with Plan B, to reclaim Nathan and put him back in his rightful home. But as usual with one of their ideas, that is easier said than done. Though the Snopeses run off with Nathan Jr., the "Lone Biker of the Apocalypse . . . with all the powers of hell at his command" is the one who grabs him off the road where the brothers inadvertently—and irresponsibly—leave him.[64] So Smalls becomes the new target of Hi's Plan B.

Viewed through the biggest threat facing America during *Arizona's* cold war setting, Smalls represents unbridled combat power. A walking arsenal, the biker is armed to the teeth with chains, guns, knives, and hand grenades, and he uses them all. Smalls symbolizes the anxiety of 1980s Americans, worried that all the stockpiling of weapons between the United States and Russia would lead to nuclear war. Birthed in the realm of nightmares that can come true, the biker walks out of Hi's dream into the film's "reality," set in the Arizona desert, close to the atomic bomb's New Mexican birthplace and Nevada's nuclear testing ground.

Smalls tells Nathan that he was sold on the black market in 1957, which is the era in which the U.S. government tested nukes in America's western deserts. In his wake Smalls leaves a "scorched earth." The damage from the 1950s testing was assessed in the 1980s.

> Many of [the downwinders in Nevada, Arizona, and Utah] began to use their Geiger counters . . . to measure the radiation released by an atomic explosion . . . [and] began to vent their fears openly. The tests "are not worth sacrificing our children and our children's children for," wrote a mother of six in a letter to *The Desert News* in 1957. "Let's stop them now."[65] (*New York Times*, 1986)

Smoke, fire, flames, and black exhaust surround Smalls. He enters Nathan's furniture store, striking a match. Cigar smoke marks his visit and even more so his departure. He perches by a campfire in one night scene and fires off his firearms at a desert bunny in another. In the culminating battle, when Hi pulls the grenade pin, Smalls's personal stockpile allows for his own destruction. In other words, one of the morals to Smalls's evisceration is a warning against too many weapons. Ultimately they can be used against their owners.

In its tango with violence and warfare, *Arizona* folds in a couple of homages to Stanley Kubrick. Scrawled across the bathroom door at the gas station where Gale and Evelle clean up after their escape are the large, red letters "P.O.E." and "O.P.E." The Coens "needed a visual cue, like graffiti," to help the audience recognize that Smalls is on their trail, and being "big *Strangelove* fans," they opted for a twofold homage to film director Stanley Kubrick.[66] First seen backward in the mirror, the jumbled red letters are reminiscent of *The Shining* (1983), in which the word "redrum" is mysterious until unscrambled into "murder" in a mirror. The second and bigger tribute goes to Kubrick's black comedy classic, *Dr. Strangelove or: How I Learned to Stop Worrying and Love the Bomb* (1964), in which one of the anagrams for the phrases "purity of essence," "peace on earth," and "our precious essence" is the all-important code needed to stop a fleet of planes on a wrong-headed mission to drop nuclear bombs on Russia.

Viewed in the context of its 1980s setting, the brutal battle between Hi and the treacherous biker can be seen as an allegory for the arms race between the United States and Russia. As in *Dr. Strangelove*, an apocalypse occurs, but unlike Kubrick's end-of-the-world climax, *Arizona*'s destruction is both disaster and rebirth. Eventually, Smalls is blown to bits, effectively becoming Hi's recall code for a life of crime. Hi and Ed return the child to the Arizonas.

While Smalls is the most violent persona, a swarm of minor characters are depicted as trigger-happy, suggesting Americans' love of violence is more rampant than Hi's unloaded gun play. When Hi tries to steal diapers after losing his job, the majority of people who cross his path during his escape are gun-toting Americans ready to blow his head off. Hi's attempts to steal Huggies from a convenience store are met with a teen cashier leveling a gigantic handgun at him. Emotionless, the robotic teenager sets his sights on Hi, who dodges the shot only to become a target for a policeman, and then a whole slew of everyday marksmen. Despite such a violent pursuit, Hi never loses sight of his Huggies goal. He runs into the supermarket, ducking bullets from a manager's shotgun that rip through food displays barely missing Hi and innocent shoppers. The violence is zany, slapstick fun, where fast-picking banjo music helps bolster the cartoon aspect of the frenzied fighting, but it also offers vivid commentary on the pervasiveness of weaponry.

An appetite for violence along with sardonic black humor comes across in Ed's lullaby choice for Nathan after he has had a bad dream. As Hi muses about how the world is hard on small things, Ed sings a folk song to soothe Nathan: "My race is run, beneath the sun/The scaffold now waits for me/For I did murder that dear little girl/Whose name was Rose Connelly."[67] "Down in the Willow Garden" is a murder ballad about a man about to be hanged for killing his lover. Her inadvertent gallows humor carries some hilarious hypocrisy. Ed wants the straight and narrow path for Nathan yet she chooses to sing to him about murder and hangings. It also highlights the potent ingredient of folklore—violence—that will also mark Hi's story. Though he chooses to use an unloaded gun, he seems to be the only one in Arizona making such a choice. And so evil creeps into the comedic satire in dribs and drabs through dreams, music, and references. In the end, Hi violently quashes his bad-boy alter ego, finally choosing, his vision suggests, a decent albeit twisted family life over a criminal one. At long last he grows up.

BRINGING UP BABY

Adults acting like children is a common strain in *Arizona*'s melodic fantasia whose banjo-plucking score helps vault the piece far from the land of naturalism. The film's Arizona is a land of symbols and similes, where small things represent larger ideas. Babies are a case in point. Part of the humor derives not only from the fact that the adults want more and more of them; the irony is that they *are* them. The so-called parents are large toddlers, crying and acting out and needing to mature.

Prison, Hi's symbolic safe harbor where he can hide from responsibilities (and women), is a womb. Gale and Evelle are birthed from its environs and return to it in the end, a couple of preemies not yet ready for the world. Portrayed by rather roly-poly, baby-faced actors John Goodman and William Forsythe, respectively, Gale and Evelle are the most maturity-challenged. Once they settle into Hi's trailer, they sit around their new home sweet hideout, looking and acting more like unwanted stepchildren than escaped cons. They crunch cereal, watch TV, and tease Hi for being married. They delight in things that appeal to children: Evelle sucks a lollipop en route to the bank heist. Separately, the brothers wonder if stolen balloons come in funny shapes. Their childishness is pure comic relief, which peaks with the botched robbery.

At the farmers' bank, the bumbling duo sweat through poorly rehearsed lines and shout out confusing orders to the customers. "All right, you hayseeds, it is a stick-up! Everybody freeze! Everybody down on the ground!"[68] When the addled farmers ask whether they should freeze or hit the floor, the brothers act like recalcitrant children. Later they blame the victims for the mistake: "That old timer threw off my concentration. Otherwise it would a gone smoother."[69] Without masks and forgetting to use fake names, they bungle on. In the getaway car, canisters of dye planted in the bank sacks explode. The Snopes boys, covered in blue and blinded by their mistake, shriek, as they did when they first emerged from prison.

More than anyone else, the Snopes boys love to make noises fit for a bantling or two, but all of the adults are babes adrift in *Arizona*'s fantastic wilderness, prone to outbursts, wailing, and temper tantrums. Ed bursts out crying when Hi hand-delivers the baby to her in the getaway car. "I love him so much," she sobs and then repeats and sobs.[70] Hi screeches uncontrollably after Gale and Evelle steal the baby and tie him up. Nathan Sr. goes into a tizzy when the authorities bulk up the stereotype of cops enjoying coffee and doughnuts to the detriment of their work. Angrily cleaning their mess in his living room, he snatches his cashmere jacket from an investigator despite warnings of the fingerprint ink still fresh on Nathan's hands. Seeing his mistake in the black smears on his coat sends him into a tantrum.

Glen is prone to childish outbursts, too. He is plum excited to get back at Hi after figuring out Nathan's origins. Wearing a neck brace from that broil amid the saguaros, Glen gives Hi an ultimatum: Hand over the child or he'll report him to the authorities. When Hi tries to calm and quiet him down so that the Snopeses do not overhear, Glen retorts with the classic child comeback: "Make me!"[71] He also laughs at his horribly behaved kids instead of disciplining them and, worse, he eggs them on by joining their game, throwing nuts at them. It's a violent gesture to which Hi reacts as if it's gunfire. Echoing her husband's violence is Dot's screaming at her children. No family in the film is happy

Barely able to control themselves, the adults need help when it comes to child rearing. An ongoing visual gag that carries this idea is *Dr. Spock's Baby and Child Care*. Florence is first seen reading it the night Nathan is stolen. Hi nabs it along with Nathan Jr. from the nursery, where Florence mistakenly leaves it behind. From then on, though no one else actually peruses it, the book goes where Nathan goes. When Hi delivers the baby booty to Ed, he tosses these "instructions" into the backseat.[72] The final payoff comes when Hi and Ed return the spotless, healthy Nathan and the tatty, burnt tome. Though both baby and book have been to hell and back, only the latter looks like it has. Nathan is as pristine and gleeful as ever.

Reading "instructions" could only help *Raising Arizona*'s adults, who all talk the parental talk but fail utterly when it comes time to walking the walk. Picnicking in the desert with Hi and Ed, mother Dot goes through a laundry list of musts: a "pediatrician," "bank accounts for his orthodonture and college," and "life insurance."[73] Interjected into this advice are stern commands to her out-of-control children ("Take the diaper off your head and put it back on your sister").[74] Such visuals act like a counterpoint to her litany. She also goes through the booster shots the young mother should arrange for her son. Later, Evelle also brings up the shots, leaving us to wonder if—horrors!—the Snopeses have more parenting sense than the McDunnoughs.

Many of the jokes surrounding parenting issues play off the pop psychology suggestion that parents are ultimately responsible for why people are the way they are—an idea introduced by the prison counselor. Such Freudian-inspired blame crops up several times for bad adult behavior. Evelle tells Ed, "Ma'am, if you don't breast feed 'im, he hates you for it later. That's why we wound up in prison."[75] Even Smalls, through another telling tattoo, traces his adult problems directly to his parents: "Mama didn't love me."[76] Hi, on the other hand, owns up to his actions and looks inside himself in his quest for responsibility. Hi asks Ed to accept him for who he is after he steals the diapers and insists that she view him nonjudgmentally: "I'm OK; you're OK," he says, quoting the title of psychologist Thomas Harris's 1973 bestseller that opens with a discussion of the duality of human nature. Hi, it turns out, is OK. In the end, his dream fixes his marriage problems, and once again he finds freedom through imagining the world how he wants it.

WRAP: DREAM ON

Raising Arizona focuses on baby desire. Hinging on creation, the movie subtly blasts the idea of keeping up with the Joneses (or Arizonas) while celebrating the power of stories. Imagining the world Hi wants, the film suggests, is his first step toward change. The movie and its dream motif hew closely to a storyline about babies and conception and related ideas of creativity and imagination. Hi's final vision makes a final case for the potency of mental conceptions. Thinking is, after all, how he and Ed become each other's in-laws (and outlaws) in the first place. Hi's daydreams of Ed set him free. And when her wild kidnapping plan catalyzes Hi's fears, which in turn breed Smalls, Hi's alter ego wakes him to the wrongness of his actions. He confronts the beast within and stands up as a man. His final vision of him and Ed as prosperous parents underscores a moral that suggests ripe imaginations can go a long way toward redemption.

On a broader level, *Raising Arizona* is an allegory. Parenting issues are systemic of a society in trouble. With explosive violence simmering below society's surface and an economy that elbows out the up-and-comers, H. I. McDunnough—whose monogram is H.I.M.—is an Everyman trying to work a system that doesn't work for him. Through his desert journey he kicks his illegal habits, wrestles with his soul, and finds himself—free of a stolen Arizona. Chances are, that newfound Hi sticks with Ed. "Me and Ed," he muses, at the end, "we can be good, too."[77] Whether in Arizona or Utah, with kids and cash or without, he and Ed can make it.

NOTES

1. David Edelstein, "Invasion of the Baby Snatchers," *American Film*, April 1987, 28.

2. Leonard Klady, "Wacky Movie's Sibling Producers Hit on Hot Formula," *Toronto Star*, April 1, 1987, D-1.

3. By 1990, the $4 million feature had netted $22 million. Betsy Sharkley, "Movies of Their Own," *New York Times*, July 8, 1990, 23.

4. The Coens wrote Ed's part for Holly Hunter, whose unavailability for *Blood Simple* led to her roommate, Frances McDormand, taking on the role. McDormand's playing of Abby launched her film career and a long-lasting romance with Joel Coen.

5. *Raising Arizona*, DVD, directed by Joel Coen (1987; Beverly Hills, Calif.: 20th Century Fox Home Entertainment, 1999).

6. *Raising Arizona*, DVD.

7. *Raising Arizona*, DVD.

8. *Raising Arizona*, DVD.

9. *Raising Arizona*, DVD.

10. *Raising Arizona*, DVD.

11. *Raising Arizona*, DVD.

12. *Raising Arizona*, DVD.

13. James Hillman, "Psychology and Alchemy," *Suicide and the Soul* (Dallas: Spring Publications, 1976), 126.

14. *Raising Arizona*, DVD.

15. Gothic Keywords, courses.nus.edu.sg/course/ellgohbh/gothickeywords.html (accessed January 27, 2006).

16. *Raising Arizona*, DVD.

17. *Raising Arizona*, DVD.

18. *Raising Arizona*, DVD.

19. *Raising Arizona*, DVD.

20. *Raising Arizona*, DVD.

21. *Raising Arizona*, DVD.

22. *Raising Arizona*, DVD.

23. *Raising Arizona*, DVD.

24. *Raising Arizona*, DVD.

25. *Raising Arizona*, DVD.

26. *Raising Arizona*, DVD.

27. In the screenplay, Lenny says he was traded on the black market in 1954, whereas in the movie the year is 1957—Joel's and Ethan's birth years, respectively.

28. *Raising Arizona*, DVD.

29. Carl G. Jung, *Man and His Symbols* (New York: Anchor Books, 1964), 112.

30. Jung, *Man and His Symbols*, 113.

31. *Raising Arizona*, DVD.

32. David Elliott, "Brothers in Fact and Film; Coens' Latest Movie Shows Comedic Bent," *San Diego Union-Tribune*, April 5, 1987, E-1.

33. *Raising Arizona*, DVD.

34. *Blood Simple*'s Visser screams when his hand gets knifed to a windowsill. In *Miller's Crossing*, the beefy wrestler "Drop" Johnson wails as Johnny bludgeons Eddie to death. In *Barton Fink*, Charlie hysterically hollers as he lets loose his madman persona. And in *Hudsucker Proxy*, Waring Hudsucker shrieks as he commits suicide.

35. *Raising Arizona*, DVD.

36. *Raising Arizona*, DVD.

37. Walter E. Bezanson, "*Moby-Dick*: Work of Art," *Moby-Dick* (New York: W.W. Norton & Company, 1967), 655.

38. Bezanson, "*Moby-Dick*," 656.

39. *Raising Arizona*, DVD.

40. *Raising Arizona*, DVD. Matthew George Easton, *Illustrated Bible Dictionary*, 3rd ed., (Thomas Nelson, 1897).
41. *Raising Arizona*, DVD.
42. *Raising Arizona*, DVD.
43. *Raising Arizona*, DVD.
44. *Raising Arizona*, DVD. They use this same passage in *O Brother, Where Art Thou?*, too.
45. *Raising Arizona*, DVD.
46. *Raising Arizona*, DVD.
47. "Jason," Behind the Name, www.behindthename.com/php/view.php?name=Jason (accessed September 9, 2006).
48. *Raising Arizona*, DVD.
49. *Raising Arizona*, DVD.
50. *Raising Arizona*, DVD.
51. *Raising Arizona*, DVD.
52. *Raising Arizona*, DVD.
53. "Florence," Behind the Name, www.behindthename.com/php/view.php?name=florence (accessed September 9, 2006).
54. *Raising Arizona*, DVD.
55. *Raising Arizona*, DVD.
56. *Raising Arizona*, DVD.
57. *Raising Arizona*, DVD.
58. *Raising Arizona*, DVD.
59. *Raising Arizona*, DVD.
60. *Blood Simple*'s Julian Marty (Dan Hedaya) could be considered the first. The bar owner hires a detective to kill his wife and her lover but is double-crossed by his own hit man.
61. Wilson was to play O'Bannon in *Miller's Crossing* but died unexpectedly before production began.
62. *Raising Arizona*, DVD.
63. *Raising Arizona*, DVD.
64. *Raising Arizona*, DVD.
65. Howard Ball, "Downwind from the Bomb," *New York Times*, February 9, 1986, 33.
66. Elliott, "Brothers in Fact and Film," E-1.
67. Charlie Munroe, "Down in the Willow Garden" (1957, 1972).
68. *Raising Arizona*, DVD.
69. *Raising Arizona*, DVD.
70. *Raising Arizona*, DVD.
71. *Raising Arizona*, DVD.
72. *Raising Arizona*, DVD.
73. *Raising Arizona*, DVD.
74. *Raising Arizona*, DVD.
75. *Raising Arizona*, DVD.
76. *Raising Arizona*, DVD.
77. *Raising Arizona*, DVD.

• 3 •

Miller's Crossing: A Hat

Gabriel Byrne keeps things tight to the vest and under his hat. (Credit: 20th Century Fox/Photofest © 20th Century Fox)

"You do things for a reason. It helps to have one."

—Tom Regan (Gabriel Byrne)

"Why are you so interested in the hat? Is it so important?"
"I'm only an amateur detective, but it looks like a thing that might have some meaning, one way or another."

—Dashiell Hammett, *The Glass Key* (1931)

69

PREVIEW

*W*hen *Miller's Crossing* kicked off the 1990 New York Film Festival, the Coens' gangster film left many critics nonplussed. "Is there a point?"—a line from the film—appeared in spirit, if not verbatim, in several reviews. *Newsday* grumbled, "Without a point, the film is all unique camera angles . . . sound and fury signifying little."[1] The *San Francisco Chronicle* wrote: "It's fine that Tom doesn't know what he should do. But it's not all right that Joel and Ethan Coen . . . don't seem to have a clue either."[2] "So what?" capped Vincent Canby's *New York Times* review.[3] Less perplexed, the *Washington Post's* Rita Kempley penned: "In its hard heart of hearts, it is a masterfully written and visually unsettling study in manly love."[4] The video's appearance on "gay" video shelves settled the mystery for some, intensified it for others.

What *were* the Coens thinking, to paraphrase another line? One item high on the brothers' minds when plotting the script was Dashiell Hammett's detective fiction, chunks of which are grafted into the Coens' revisionist gangster film. Sections of *Crossing's* story and lines of dialogue are lifted directly from *The Glass Key* (1931) and *Red Harvest* (1929), novels that pit hard-boiled types against forces of corruption. Hammett informs *Crossing's* milieu, relationships, and mysteries. Gabriel Byrne's astute wise-guy hero has a detective's deductive chops and unblinking toughness. He restores order to the underworld but never says why. The choice to burke the viewer's satisfying a-ha moment that often wraps up a crime story is another page out of Hammett. As literary scholar Robert Polito points out, "Never disclosing what [detective Sam] Spade is thinking, Hammett positions indeterminacy as an implicit moral stance. By screening the reader from his gumshoe's inner life, he pulls us into Spade's inner world."[5]

Indeterminacy, a hallmark of the Coens' cinema, in *Crossing* is a chief source of conflict. What sparks the action is a chiseling bookie who skims money off the top of a mobster's fixed fights, an otherwise "sure thing." Pushing the plot ahead are a mob boss, who overlooks these broken rules in the name of love, and his best friend and confidant—a thinking man who relishes the unknowns of gambling. The pull between knowns and unknowns lays the foundation for the film's dual world, which is set in two locales: the gritty city with its rackets, and the woods, where dreams, lies, and murders stay secret. Simply put, dualities and uncertainties—and double-crossing, as the title suggests—are the kernel of *Crossing's* meditation on knowledge.

REVIEW

The film begins with a mid-level, Italian gangster named Johnny Caspar (Jon Polito) making a case to Irish mob boss Leo O'Bannon (Albert Finney) for killing a crooked bookie.[6] The would-be dead man is Bernie Bernbaum (John Turturro), a Jew whom Caspar claims is cheating him. Leo refuses to give the hit a green light, citing lackluster reasons. This rejection sets off the Italian fire-cracker's short fuse, and Caspar threatens trouble. After he leaves with his flunky Eddie the Dane (J. E. Freeman), Leo's adviser Tom Regan (Byrne) challenges his boss on the issue. Despite Leo's obvious affection and respect for Tom, he won't budge because, as we learn later, he is in love with Bernie's sister Verna (Marcia Gay Harden).

The title sequence that follows opens up a view vastly different from the world of Leo's office. A moving camera shoots up into a tangle of trees and patch of sky, and immediately perspective and surrealism enter the picture. A pretty Irish-sounding melody accompanying this view gives way to a darker, minor theme, and the camera switches to a low angle. A hat blows through the woods during this ominous sonic change, and the sequence's dreamy quality edges toward nightmare.

Following the titles, Tom goes to retrieve his hat from Verna. Later, Leo visits Tom in the middle of the night distraught over his missing girlfriend and "Rug" Daniels (Salvatore H. Tornabene), the man he hired to tail her. Tom doesn't shed much light on Verna's whereabouts, but he presses Leo to change his mind about Bernie. Leo is unwavering. After he leaves, Tom returns to his bedroom and we see Verna is in his bed.

The next day Rug turns up dead. Leo believes the murder is Caspar's declaration of war. But Tom pins the hit on Verna or Bernie, and then on Verna or Mink LaRouie (Steve Buscemi). He suspects one of this gang since Rug was shot with a small pistol—a woman or gay man's gun. (Mink is the Dane's "amigo," the film's euphemism for gay lover.)

As the gang war builds to a boil, a power shift occurs. Leo used to rely on the local authorities for backup; now Police Chief O'Doole (Thomas Toner) and Mayor Dale Leander (Richard Woods) are in Caspar's pocket. As a result, Caspar's men almost kill Leo when his police protection never shows. Leo survives thanks to his fighting prowess, but it's now clear the conflict is escalating inexorably. In a last-ditch effort to avoid an all-out war, Tom confesses to Leo about his affair with Verna. But his attempt to show her unfaithfulness backfires, and Leo violently dispatches him. A rejected Tom offers his services along with information about Bernie to Caspar, who hires him conditionally. Tom must prove his new loyalty by killing Bernie. Tom takes Bernie into the Miller's Crossing woods, aims at the bookie, and then shoots into the air. He tells Bernie to get out of town and "play dead."

Tom moves effortlessly between the unnamed city's warring sides (much like the samurai in Akira Kurosawa's *Yojimbo*, 1961). He gathers information about Rug's murder and plants ideas in Caspar's head that it's not just Bernie cheating him—the Dane and his lover boy Mink are too. Caspar doesn't believe this at first, but Tom persists with the lies.

Eddie the Dane doubts that Tom killed Bernie, and insists on seeing the body. The thick-headed thugs Frankie (Mike Starr) and Tic-Tac (Al Mancini) hadn't thought to fact-check the hit. The hoodlums march Tom into the woods, where, much to the Dane's surprise and Tom's good fortune, they find a corpse. It turns out that Bernie, worried someone might look for a body, killed Mink (both the Dane's and his own sometime lover).

Verna thinks Tom killed Bernie and doesn't believe that Bernie is alive but in hiding—or rather *was* in hiding. Tom's gift of life couldn't cinch the deal with Bernie, who has reappeared with a new grift. He tries to blackmail Tom into killing Caspar, promising to show his face if he doesn't oblige. If Tom had no reason to kill Bernie before, he does now.

The Dane finally figures out that Mink not Bernie was killed. But by the time he starts to avenge Mink's death on Tom, Caspar shoots his right-hand man, having swallowed Tom's bait. Caspar proves a bigger sucker when he goes to take care of Mink, whom Tom says is at his apartment. In fact, Tom has lured Bernie there and bets the easy odds that the men will try to kill each other, Bernie thinking Caspar is Tom and Johnny thinking he'll teach the disloyal Mink a lesson. As it happens, Bernie ambushes Caspar. When Tom returns home, he takes money off the dead "Eye-tie" to settle his gambling debt, talks Bernie into relinquishing his gun, and then shoots the double-crossing bookie dead. With Bernie out of the way and Caspar out of the picture, Leo returns to power.

In the final scene, Tom, Verna, and Leo meet up in the woods at Bernie's funeral. After she storms off and leaves the two men alone, Leo tells Tom that he and Verna are getting married. Tom stiffens. Then Leo offers to give him his job back and says he forgives him for sleeping with Verna. Tom angrily refuses Leo's make-up attempts; then he softens and tells him goodbye. The film ends with Tom wistfully watching Leo walk away.

"A MAN CHASING HIS HAT"

The quizzical *Miller's Crossing* left more than just critics scratching their heads. While they were writing it, the story vexed the Coens so much that they had to put it aside for a while to see if fresh eyes could steer them out of their dead end. The break produced the critically acclaimed *Barton Fink,* a film about, among other things, a head, a "life of the mind," and artistic hell. Without relying too much on their fourth film to elucidate what's going on in their third, it is beneficial to note the kindred relationship between the two. Whereas *Fink* exposes the inner workings of a creative mind, making much use of heads, *Crossing* deals with a keen but hidden mind, playing with the hat's utility as a cover for the head. Put differently, the movie's iconic hat not only captures the gangster setting; it also symbolizes the story's—and arguably the crime fiction genre's—concern with keeping one's head—and its thoughts—under wraps.

The hat's introduction occurs in the woods, a place symbolic of hidden things. As Robert Pogue Harrison points out in his study of sylvan myths, throughout Western culture, woods represent "an outlying realm of opacity which has allowed that civilization to estrange itself, enchant itself, terrify itself . . . in short to project into the forest's shadows its secrets and innermost anxieties."[7] The ultra cool Tom has secrets directly tied to the woods. For instance, amid the trees, he chose not to kill Bernie. Eventually we learn that the title images relate to a stressful search for the body he never "planted." Hence, the impressionistic title sequence connects to Tom, who in the end chooses the forest over the city.

Before we have this connection to hang the opening visuals on, the forest provides an initial view of the film's "other" world, the place where mob hits occur (or don't, in Bernie and Tom's case), where a funeral for a gay Jew is held, and where Tom's secret about not killing Bernie is kept hidden. In other words, it is a place of decadence and deceit. It is also a mysterious realm where hats can be carried on the wind. Part two of the title sequence prefigures Eddie's toss of Tom's hat just before he plans to kill him. So it too gives us a window into Tom's mind, a place mostly off-limits. In short, the film's dual settings represent Tom's own internal split. He has a rational side, perfect for the unnamed urban gangland, and an ineffable side, where things are less clear cut. Like his head, which he prefers be covered with his hat, the woods are the movie's built-in "X" factor closely connected to dreams, fears, and other intangibilities.

"Big guys in overcoats in the woods—the incongruity of urban gangsters in a forest setting—" is the idea that prompted the film.[8] The forest is where *Crossing*'s mobsters kill their prey, and in the end, it's where the main guy in the overcoat remains. For him, the locale is not so incongruous, because he is both part of the gangster milieu and outside of it. But exactly why he stays there is never spelled out. The whys of Tom's actions are at the story's heart: There are things that are knowable and things that are not. Knowing what another person is thinking is impossible, but one can venture a good guess. After all, at various points Tom explains his modus operandi for figuring the angles: People's actions are motivated by reason. Leo's refusal to fix the Bernie problem is a case in point. He won't budge because taking out Bernie means losing Verna. Of course, he doesn't come out and say this. Tom figures it out by assessing the bad business decision. Like the opening impressions of fear found retrospectively in floating images of branches and a hat, Leo initially keeps his motives under wraps. In other words, both details concern secret emotions that offer solid clues to this meditation on knowledge.

The first inchoate reference to the credit sequence comes as Tom sits in bed, ruminating. When Verna asks what's on his mind, he responds, absently, that he was remembering a dream. In it, he says, he was walking in the woods when the wind blew off his hat. As his dream arouses our memory of the title sequence, Verna guesses that he chased the hat and when he finally caught up to it, it turned into "something wonderful."[9] Tom corrects her, explaining it stayed a hat, he didn't chase it, and nothing "is more foolish than a man chasing after his hat."[10]

Tom's pronouncement is funny. Foolish or not, Tom spends an awful lot of time chasing his errant hat. The pursuit starts early and lasts long. Following the titles, Tom wakes from a night of hard drinking and gambling to find his hat—and memory—missing. Thus, even before the hat is linked to his dreams, it connects to his taste for booze and betting, two escapes from the rational world. His friend Tad (Olek Krupa), the bartender at the Shenandoah (where Tom wakes up), tells Tom he lost his hat to Verna or Mink in a card game. Tom goes to Verna's to retrieve it, and the hat hunt is under way. At Verna's apartment (in room number three, as if to underscore the looming love triangle) Tom invites himself in for a "drink" (read sex) to get his hat back.

Often, beatings leave Tom sans chapeau. Like his prototype Ned Beaumont, Hammett's protagonist in *The Glass Key*, Tom is a punching bag. His hat is the Coens' quirky extension to the physical pain inflicted in hard-boiled novels that writer Jopi Nyman ascribes to a coping mechanism defining masculinity.[11] Tom's ability to take such abuse says something about his manhood while losing his hat—and getting it back—adds a footnote to it. His bookie's musclemen deck Tom outside his apartment, sending his fedora to the floor. Later, Terry (Lanny Flaherty), Tom's replacement, delivers him a message from Leo. Several hefty punches prompt Tom to get his hat. Along with isolated shots on it, Tom's focus on the hat instead of the pummeling emphasizes his toughness.

Tom's most lively hat-chasing scene is his break-up brawl with Leo, in which Tom accepts every punch doled out and refuses to fight back. In the choreography of their long, hard goodbye, each uppercut is followed by a reach for, grab, and clutch of his hat. The lopsided donnybrook begins outside Leo's office following Tom's confession about Verna. Walking past the army of men amassing for a gang war, Tom turns to meet Leo's fist with his jaw. The hit sends his hat flying, prompting a thug to pick it up and hand it back to him. Immediately, another gangster hurls Tom down a stairway. Again, he picks both himself and his hat up. Back on his feet Leo delivers a blow that propels him down the club's main staircase, sending his fedora on a slightly different course. At this point, Tad steps in to prevent any more humiliation of Tom. Leo doesn't object and caps the melee, so to speak, by pegging Tom's hat at his stomach.

Obviously, Tom chases his hat quite a lot. The question is what does the pursuit, the denial of it, and his dream about it mean? Taken in the context of the dual settings, the hat and its symbolism point to a dichotomy between the known, represented by the city, and the unknown, symbolized by the woods. Put differently, what we know is that Tom has chased his hat. What we don't, and can't, know is whether he also really chased it in a dream and why the dream needles him. We only know what he tells us, and that might or might not represent the truth. In other words, the hat indicates the indeterminate. We cannot know for sure what's going on in that furtive place underneath his hat. We can hazard guesses about Tom's head based on his decisions and actions, and follow his own lead of using logic and deductive reasoning. The only times when logic fails, Tom says several times, are when the "wild card love" is involved.[12]

In addition to presenting two opposing worlds (the sylvan and the urban), the movie pits physical actions against ethereal things like thoughts, dreams, emotions, and love. This duality is captured in Leo's and Tom's respective fortes. Leo is brawn; Tom is brains. But Tom has competing agendas: With great deductive skills and heady desire, he loves both the knowns and the unknowns and easily crisscrosses between them. Tom's hat pursuit, which is precipitated by dealings in the unknowns, helps map out the nondeductive side of his brain—the part tied to emotions, his female side. Consider the different circumstances under which Tom loses his hat: when his secret about Bernie is at risk of exposure, after disclosing his relationship with Verna to Leo, because of unpaid gambling debts, in the wake of drinking and gambling, and in a dream. What these all have in common is a move away from his rational world to his irrational side. Perhaps in addition to representing manhood and unknowns, the hat also limns the liminal. With its tendency to turn people and society inside out, like the woods, the hat seems to demarcate the boundary between real and surreal, truth and lies, order and disorder, masculinity and femininity—in other words, the threshold of "other."

Tom's anxiety over what the woods will disclose gives us the second clue to the title sequence. His fear-ridden death march through Miller's Crossing begins with an upward view of the heavens. As the Dane has pointed out, Tom cannot talk himself out of this one—either there is a body or there isn't. Tic-Tac and Frankie help comb the woods for the dead body they neglected to confirm. The viewer knows what Tom knows: He did not kill Bernie. The Dane, whose deductive skills rival Tom's, has a good hunch about this, too. Palpably terrified of what appears to be certain execution, Tom is so beyond his wits that he falls to his knees and retches. With Tom at his lowest point, the Dane yanks off his nemesis's hat and hurls it into the trees. But the degra-dation is cut short by a call for handkerchiefs and the faceless corpse that prompted the call. The life-saving body opens up new questions—whose it is and who planted it there. We can safely assume that the triggerman is neither Tom nor his three escorts.

We also now know a little more about the film. The title's first image is also the shot that begins the hunt for Bernie's body. That is, it's Tom's point of view at a time when he is most scared for his life, least in control, and dead afraid that his secret will be exposed. There are also opposites at play. Instead of the opening's instrumental, Irish lilt, the latter scene features Frankie singing an Italian air. At work are mirror-opposite forces, a principal organizing fea-ture of the movie. The Dane's hat-flicking recalls the second part of the title sequence and its blowing hat—an event Tom says occurred in his dream too. In short, each tandem detail—fear, dreams, and hat-chasing—points to the va-garies of the mind and add up to a bundle of emotions that distract from Tom's masculinity and point to a more feminine mystique.

Like Tom's motives, the hat is somewhat off-limits. While the movie makes much ado about it, there is no scene that directly explicates its impor-tance. During production, even actor Gabriel Byrne was kept in the dark about his fedora. "All the way through the movie, it was really weird that no one mentioned the hat. I said to Joel at one point: 'What's the significance of the hat?' And he said: 'Mmmm-hmm.' And that was it."[13]

Despite Joel's reluctance to elucidate, the hat and Tom's pursuit of it have a telling antecedent. A hat is crucial evidence in *The Glass Key*'s mur-der mystery (one of two main inspirations for the Coens' film). A good deal of Hammett's ink goes into Ned's own search of the hat's significance. "I'm only an amateur detective," Ned says, "but [the hat] looks like a thing that might have some meaning, one way or another."[14] Indeed, Ned's hunch is right. (Spoiler warning.) A father wears his son's hat back to their house to hide his hand in his son's inadvertent killing. Put simply, the hat becomes a cover up. The Coens' hat is a cover up, too, but a more cryptic one. Key comparisons are in order.

Crossing ends in similar but reversed circumstances from Hammett's novel. Instead of imitating the end of *The Glass Key*, which finds Ned getting the girl and breaking things off with his former boss and best friend, *Crossing* concludes with the boss getting the girl and his right-hand man choosing to stay alone. What's consistent across the two texts is the subtext of triangulated desire. Throughout, both male friends (Ned and the political boss Paul in Hammett, and the Coens' Tom and Leo) ostensibly want the female (June and Verna, respectively), but the woman also represents an indirect way for the men to be close to each other.[15]

Such triangulation stems from repressed desire between the detective types and their bosses. In both works, the younger (undisclosed homosexual) man exhibits divided loyalties between the woman and the older man (a Freudian father figure). But the younger man's affection for the woman is misdirected. In the film, this misdirection can be seen through the contrast between the men's good rapport and Verna and Tom's strained relations. In both the novel and the film when the young man gets the woman, the double bind leaves them unsatisfied—that is, they have what they think they want (the woman) but not what they truly want (the man).[16] Thus, when Verna suggests she and Tom go away together, he does not give the slightest indication that he is interested (before she mentions Bernie tagging along). Tom has a different agenda. He wants to please Leo. Modeled after Hammett's finale, the final scene caps the undertow of homosexuality. *The Glass Key* ends with the boss flustered by the news that his girlfriend and her new lover (his former best friend) are leaving town together. He awkwardly says goodbye and rushes out of the room, leaving Ned to stare "fixedly at the door."[17]

The Coen epilogue starts out as reconciliation between the two men, but their easy-going concord abruptly ends without a clear-cut reason. There are big hints, though. The first sign that things are strained comes when Leo announces he's going to marry Verna. Tom's reaction is as slight here as it is in the beginning when Leo refuses to help Caspar; in both instances Tom briefly registers disagreement or disappointment. But after Leo makes a case to have Tom work for him again, at the word *forgiveness* Tom closes the discussion. At this point, the whole tenor of the scene changes from rapprochement to stalemate. They face off intently for a moment—Tom chafed, Leo upset. Then Tom relaxes his stance, says goodbye, and stares at Leo's retreating form, recapitulating Ned's focus. But, unlike Ned, Tom stays truer to his feelings, not returning to society and its disappointing knowns. If he can't have his man, he'll stay in the woods. Along with fixing his gaze at Leo, he adjusts his hat.

The movie ends without full disclosure, the mysteries of the hat and Tom's actions never revealed. Tom simply stays in the woods with his secrets. Moments earlier, in response to Leo's question about his motives, Tom asks, "Do you always know why you do things?"[18] Leo insists that he does. Maybe Leo is right, but the ending and Tom's motivations bear a strong resemblance to the opening circumstances and Leo's actions and reasons for them. At the start, though he doesn't readily admit why he looks the other way when Bernie breaks the mob rules, it is clear he does so out of love for Verna. Now Tom won't return to Leo, knowing things cannot be the same with Verna in the picture. The rationale, whether he admits it out loud or to himself, is the same as Leo's at the start. All signs point to the implicit wild card of love as the unrevealed secret, the thing Tom keeps under his hat, the thing he denies chasing that never turns into something wonderful—and which he chases nonetheless until Verna snatches it away.

THE "SURE THING"

Before diving more deeply into the unknowns, a discussion of the movie's knowns is in order. A look at the opening is the best place to start, for from the get-go, a passel of visual codes defines the film's surface realm. Like Caspar's fixed bet, the narrative has a "sure thing": lush gangster chic. From the opening seconds, there can be little doubt about the circumscribed world. The colorful language of "fixed fights" and a frank conversation about killing a man "for starters" are dead giveaways, as are the garb and period set pieces.[19] Stylish suits and overcoats, the Prohibition-Era whiskey, and candlestick telephones all contribute to the familiar look and feel of the gangster genre. Soon, there are Tommy guns and their rat-a-tat violence, illegal alcohol ("paint"), corrupt officials, a dirty city, and lots of hats. And if all these clues are not enough, there is the opening's remarkable resemblance to Francis Ford Coppola's *The Godfather* (1972).

Where Caspar's "friendship," "character," and "ethics" monologue starts off the Coens' story, another balding Italian-American's ironic speech about values sets *The Godfather's* plot in motion.[20] Like Caspar, undertaker Amerigo Bonasera (Salvatore Corsitto) wants a man killed. He justifies his murderous request by explaining to mafia boss Don Vito Corleone (Marlon Brando) that the man he wants taken out has disrespected his family. Like *Crossing's* opening, the scene inducts us to the mob boss's extreme authority, institutes the film's underworld, and introduces key themes of power, family, and loyalty.

The similarities between the two scenes are solid—from the situations to the way they are shot. Coppola's lens frames Bonasera in close-up and slowly moves out to a larger view; as if a mirror image of that, the Coens' camera begins wide, incorporating an out-of-focus Tom in the far background and moving in to a tight shot on Caspar. There's another major divergence between these underworld introductions: the bosses' positions are inverted. In the 1972 classic, the Godfather initially refuses the request to punish the men who dishonored Bonasera's family because the undertaker has not played by mob rules. But the Don changes his mind and green-lights the hit in exchange for the promise of loyalty and repayment of the favor someday—nothing comes without a price in the gangster world. In *Crossing*, things are in such disarray that it's not the supplicant but the *leader* who flouts the underworld's implicit "honor among thieves" rules. Unlike the Don, Leo doesn't come around. This raises the ire of Caspar, who is sick of getting "the high hat"—a clever gag that verbalizes the main visual motif.[21] Tom diagnoses the problem: "Caspar hasn't broken the rules, Bernie has—and [Leo] too, by helping him."[22] Because of Leo's hand in the chaos, Tom, as much as he wants to help Leo, has reason to punish him. Unlike Ned who subverts Paul's power, Tom, living up to his mother-hen role, helps to reinstate Leo's power but then abandons him and leaves him suffering.

In effect, by following his heart instead of restoring order, Leo sanctions anarchy. Caspar warns against such a state of affairs, arguing that by infringing on his profit margin, the bookie is casting the "sure thing" of fixed bets back to "chance"—transforming what should be mob control into the "jungle" of unknowns.[23] Though the process of elimination clearly identifies Bernie as the culprit, Leo lamely argues that another inside man could be selling him out. It is doubtful that even Leo believes this possibility, but he throws it out there because he will not admit to the real reason behind his decision: his heart. Tom sees how his boss's foolishness could easily knock Leo's power out of its "sure thing" orbit and into the roiling turmoil of chance.

A clever inside tract to all this is worth a mention. The crisis that Caspar lays out does not only describe the problem facing Leo's underworld—it hints at what will shake the narrative domain itself. The self-conscious subtext of anarchy and sure things cleverly alludes to the upheaval produced by unresolved conclusions. And so Caspar's exposition subtly notifies the viewer of the movie's calculus. Replacing expected outcomes with unknowns can propel things back to the jungle, the Hobbesian natural state of all against all. This is what happens dramatically and narratively and is very much like *Blood Simple*'s warning about no guarantees.

But if the town is a mess and the finale counterfeits that disruption, the film's narrative structure is anything but chaotic. Using hats and the forest as piquant metaphors for the nonabsolute, the movie operates on a split plane, balancing between knowns and unknowns, male and female, truths and lies, and loyalties and betrayals. These dualities are excavated on various narrative and cinematic levels. Tom himself negotiates the competing Italian and Irish camps, a course advertised during the opening. In addition to delineating the underworld's primary problem, the introduction abstrusely maps out solutions through Tom's positioning. His bearings presciently indicate how he will play one side against the other while staying loyal to his true partner. This early scene indicates the importance of the film's framing and composition.

Whiskey splashing into a glass at once paints the gangster world with its essential contraband and indicates the stimulant that beckons inebriation's unknown realm. After the drink is poured, the camera cuts to Caspar, who is talking bets, bookies, and business. This physical arrangement of the pourer (Tom) visible but out of focus in the background will turn out to be indicative of Tom's take on the problem. Standing behind Caspar, Tom is figuratively behind his desire to take out Bernie, but like his fuzzy presence, that support only goes so far. At the mention of the name *Bernie*—the very issue that creates the story's sides—Tom crosses the room and sits behind Leo. Now the room's symmetry reflects the men's underlying dynamics. Opposite the Irish mob boss and his second are the Italian mobster and his consigliore. A slight rupture to this equilibrium occurs when Leo refuses Caspar's request. Tom's instantaneous flinch indicates his disagreement but he says nothing for now and remains physically backing his boss. After the Italians leave, Tom moves from behind Leo and sits on the couch opposite him. The conversation that follows clearly shows the men disagree on the Bernie issue and seals their relationship with sexual double-entendres.

No longer behind Leo physically or strategically, Tom tells him frankly he is making a mistake. Leo tries to laugh off the friendly critique with a phrase that speaks to the unfolding friction: "Woke up on the wrong side, huh."[24] Sides and moves certainly refer to their difference of opinion, but the words also forecast Tom's eventual move to Caspar's camp. In addition, the phrase adeptly slides in a sexual subtext through its implied ellipsis: One wakes up on the wrong side of *bed*. And beds, we will soon see, are a key factor in the men's changing dynamics. The opening shows how facilely the film moves between explicit and implicit communication.

At the close of the opening scene, Tom implores Leo to use reason: "Think about what protecting Bernie gets us. Think about what offending Caspar loses us."[25] Pitted against Tom's rational thought is Leo's irrational action. Leo, the brawn, warmly laughs that he doesn't like thinking. Tom, the brains, keeps up the pressure, lovingly advising that he should start. Tom sees how Leo's blind spot of love is blocking the right play. And so a clash between reason and emotional desire establishes the main tension—a conflict that also rages deep in Tom.

Leo's rationale at the start gives insight into Tom's at the end. Though they admit only to murky motivations, skirting the real issue, both men's choices are tangled up in desire. Their final rumpus provides both narrative and thematic symmetry pointing to their unstated reasons. Leo's argument that maybe someone other than Bernie is the chiseler is a flat-out cover up. Tom's half-formed rationale to Leo ("it'd only have queered things if it had—") similarly keeps his real rationale hidden.[26] In its place, though, we can substitute his own observation as to why act illogically: the wild card love. Add that idea to his use of the word *queer*—and its modern meaning—and the resulting equation suggests that the ending circumstances are a reversal of the beginning's. That is, where Leo scuttles reason for love of Verna, Tom hides his reasons because he's in love with Leo.

For some the suggestion that the introduction could figure so prominently in the conclusion and even go so far as to predict parts of the story might seem outside the realm of possibility. But prognosticating in their openings is a frequent feature in the Coen oeuvre. Visser slyly predicts his own demise in *Blood Simple*, for example. And in films that follow, *Barton Fink* begins with forecasting that prefigures his upcoming nightmare, and *O Brother, Where Art Thou?*'s pushcar driver is a Depression era Tiresias whose strange fortunetelling pans out. With *Miller's Crossing*, the ambiguous title itself holds clues: It suggests a hybrid, a thwarting, or passing from one place to another, as well as a double cross. Indefinites are a sure thing from the start. So are mirrors, prominent figures in the Coens' precision design.

A LOOKING GLASS KEY

From the start, physical space informs the shifting dynamics. In fact, there is a musical chairs aspect to the characters' movements and alliances but without the game's randomness. In an uncharacteristically illuminating comment to the *San Diego Union-Tribune*, the Coens hint at the design around which the film was shaped, all but admitting to the drama's thematic geometry. "There's a heterosexual triangle and a homosexual triangle," says Joel Coen. "It sort of seemed like it was an interesting mirror-image of each other, two triangles staring at each other."[27] This pair of love triangles and an iconography full of mirrors (actual and metaphorical) provide a cipher for understanding the underlying dynamic between Leo and Tom and thus the ending.

Symmetrical pairs pepper the film, suggesting that things have two sides, usually an apparent one and a hidden one. The opening's reference to *The Godfather*, for instance, counterbalances the closing allusion to *The Glass Key*. Often these corresponding pairs reveal opposite forces—an apparent one and its covert mirror opposite. Take the phrase "Verna and Mink . . . Mink and Verna," for instance. Immediately after Tad enunciates this pair of names in reference to Tom's missing hat, the two men switch places. As Tad tells Tom about the previous night's gambling losses, Tom takes his katzenjammers into the bathroom, from where Tad emerges to take up Tom's vacated spot on the couch. The remainder of their colloquy takes place in these reversed positions, and a mirror hanging behind the sofa captures half of their exchange.

Tad, we later find out, has a soft spot for Tom. When the seemingly turn-coat Irishman visits the bartender at the Shenandoah for information, Tad, mad that Tom has gone over to Caspar's side, indignantly asks why he should tell Tom anything. Tom laughs, citing, "No reason on earth."[28] The easy reading between the lines here is Tad's obvious feelings for him. Tad's capitulation of the betting information substantiates Tom's hunch. What's more, their friendship illustrates Tom's free mingling with homosexuals.

If Tom's motives are not clear from his longing look at the end, an examination of his relationship to Verna vis-à-vis his relationship to Leo shows a wild card for Leo alone. Tom risks everything for his boss whereas his feelings for Verna are at best lukewarm. Even when Tom seems to double-cross Leo by sleeping with Verna, he, in fact, treats Leo with respect and Verna with an array of feelings, ranging from mild indifference to rudeness and hostility with some sex thrown in.

Tom's price for getting his hat back the first time he loses it is sex. We learn this slowly. A close-up on the fedora is the first indication that he has his hat back. Behind it Tom's out-of-focus image is reflected in his dresser mirror. A reverse angle moves in on an in-focus Tom, sitting in bed, smoking and thinking. A knock at the door interrupts his thoughts. It's Leo, worried about the missing Rug and Verna. Tom invites Leo in for a drink and he bad mouths Verna so that he'll give up Bernie. The mob boss won't cave. He does, though, admit to his feelings for Verna here and pooh-poohs Tom's worries about losing power. After Leo leaves, Tom returns to his bedroom where we see what we couldn't before: Verna in his bed.

In addition to suggesting that initial views do not tell the whole story, we see some similarities between Tom's and Verna's approaches to getting what they want. Specifically, Verna uses sex to protect her brother while Tom uses sex to get his hat back. When Tom fails to get his hat back from Verna using the hard sell, he changes tactics and tries a soft approach. He invites himself in for a drink, a term he uses with Verna as though it's his personal euphemism for sex. Though vastly different on the surface in terms of importance—a loved one's life versus one's own hat—it is implied throughout that Tom's hat is more than just an ordinary accessory. Symbolically, Tom's hat is so close to his identity that it has a life-or-death aspect to it.

Verna's subsequent late-night call, under circumstances similar to Leo's, incorporates visual reversals of Leo's scene. He had shown up in a weak position, unsure of his girl and her tail's whereabouts. Now Verna is down and out because Leo dumped her along with Tom. She takes the chair Tom had occupied when talking to Leo. Tom takes the seat Leo had. The mirroring effect stresses the importance of opposites. After a brief exchange about Rug, Verna muses that Tom took the long way around to get her. Tom, in true detective fashion, never corroborates or denies his motives, but it does not seem that Tom has what he wants with her. He also does not agree with her that the two of them are double-crossers. Both are being dishonest with Leo, true, but one is feigning fidelity, the other infidelity.

Though there are no on-screen sex scenes, Tom and Verna's precoital and morning-after moments indicate their brutally honest—and plain brutal—relationship. When Tom returns to his bedroom following Leo's late-night visit, he shares part of his and Leo's conversation with her—including the detail of calling her a tramp. Obviously angry at his betrayal, Verna launches a shoe at him. He ducks and it misses him, bouncing against the door behind him. Such violent exchanges are par for the course between these two characters with cross-gender qualities. When Leo boasts that he can "trade body blows with any man in this town except" Tom, Tom adds Verna to the short list.[29] But Verna and Tom share more than just masculine traits; they both exhibit female characteristics. Just as Tom would "sooner join the Ladies League than gun a guy down" and in fact doesn't shoot Bernie out in Miller's Crossing, Verna cannot pull the trigger on Tom even when she thinks he has killed her brother.[30]

On an empty street under Chinese characters (a possible reference to *The Glass Key*'s China Street location of the central murder), Verna accosts Tom late at night after learning incorrectly that Tom killed Bernie. She explains her presence with a line of his: "I was in the neighborhood, feeling a bit daffy."[31] When she asks why he betrayed her, he looks warily at her gun and tells her a half-truth: Bernie is alive. This is technically true, but no thanks to Tom who tried to use her information to hand Bernie to Caspar. Here, he leaves out the detail that she is making him late for a date to murder Bernie or Caspar, whoever is still standing. Though she cannot kill him, she doesn't believe him, and Tom trots off to take care of the crooked bookie once and for all. Whatever fire burns between Tom and Verna, neither trusts the other much. This is the complete opposite of the two men.

It's understood that Leo and Tom trust each other explicitly. The party boss and his right-hand man, so obviously the focus of the film, have a tight bond, broken only at the end. This understanding is communicated through action and language. Often feminizing idioms surrounding the two men smack of homoeroticism and *cross* into homosexual territory. When the Dane doubts that Tom killed Bernie, he guesses that Tom was "straight with your frail and queer with Johnny Caspar."[32] His phrase adds a twist to his spot-on, topsy-turvy assessment of Tom, his loyalties, actions, and motivations while bolstering the notion that Tom acted for Leo's benefits. Further, the Dane's use of the word *frail*, a slang term for woman, so close to the words *straight* and *queer*, all but confirms a homosexual mainspring.

Leo himself remarks on Tom's gender-crossing. Trying to smooth over Tom's embarrassingly dramatic exit in front of the mayor and police chief, Leo jokes, "The goddam kid's just like a twist."[33] Like the word *crossing*, *twist* has several, applicable meanings here. In addition to being criminal slang for dishonesty, it is a pejorative term for a young woman. A feminine connotation also comes across when Leo calls him a "mother hen." Another applicable meaning for twist is "an eccentric or perverted inclination," which shores up an ongoing focus on homosexuality.[34] While one epithet stresses the familial and the other the familiar, sexual perversion touches them both. Though Leo himself is something of a father figure to Tom, his comparison of Tom as both mother and a "twist" brings up the idea of incest, a common subtheme in gangster films used to accentuate the criminals' debauched values. (Incest will crop up in relation to the Bernbaums, too, in a more overt fashion.) If there is any doubt about the deliberate play with gender and sexuality in *Crossing*, whose very title thrusts the first parry, a close look at the Shenandoah might provide some clarity. Leo kicks Tom out of the club to the strains of "Goodnight, Sweetheart" and then calls their goodbye the "kiss-off."[35] As with so much of the film, there is a straight way to read things and a "queer" way. When it comes to Leo and Tom, the latter holds more water.

"DOWN IS UP, BLACK IS WHITE"

Crossing's hall of mirrors gets full airing in the Shenandoah's ladies' room where "Running Wild" subtly amplifies ideas of jungle anarchy, unknowns, and gays. For one, it's a song that might help expose the scene's cross-dressers to film buffs, for it is Marilyn Monroe's first number in Billy Wilder's cross-dressing gangster comedy, *Some Like It Hot* (1959). This *Miller's Crossing* key scene, which exposes the gangland's sexual underbelly a little more, begins with scrambled norms. As Tom enters the ladies' room and strolls toward Verna, he inverts his words, saying, "Cover your eyes, ladies. I'm coming through."[36] The incongruities here ricochet off each other like the reflected images bouncing around the frame. Not only is a man crossing into a feminine realm, so if anyone's eyes should be shut, it should be Tom's, but also the people dispersing are not all female. Several "ladies" are men in drag, including Albert Finney wearing a maid outfit. Gender and sexuality, the scene implies, do not necessarily reflect surface images. Here, amid his doubled image, Tom reveals his motives, explicitly and symbolically.

Miller's Crossing's gender bending gets full airing in the ladies' room hall of mirrors where Gabriel Byrne reads Marcia Gay Harden the riot act. (Credit: 20th Century Fox/Photofest © 20th Century)

Tom parks himself behind Verna so that the first part of their exchange occurs between their reflected images. Like the mirrors' shape, Tom and Verna talk circles around each other, matching wits and vying to be Leo's number one. Their crackling one-liners speak not only to their literal love triangle but also to the metaphors that help define their world. The line about opposites attracting, for instance, is more than a put-down; it is a phrase calling attention to the main mirror metaphor and the "other" side it symbolizes. In fact, Verna and Tom are too much alike to attract—and the clearest way they resemble each other is in their romantic interest in Leo, but arguably one attraction is covert and true and the other obvious and false.

Verna tells Tom to butt out of her and Leo's affairs, but Tom has other ideas. He moves to her side so that Tom and his reflection appear and tells her Leo is his business. He doesn't come as clean as Verna who admits to sleeping with Leo to protect her brother. But he clearly indicates he wants Leo back— to himself. Then he warns Verna to stop "spinning Leo in circles and pointing him where to go."[37] Verna partially recognizes that she is taking over a role that Tom is used to playing, but she is too vain to see that Tom wants Leo not her. She does not get homosexuality, nor can she construe Tom's emotional loyalty. The fact is that she has trouble seeing much beyond herself in this man's world and doesn't read clues well. For instance, she pins people's dislike of Bernie on his homosexuality, but gay lifestyles are conspicuously okay in these environs as Caspar's easy acceptance of the Dane's relationship to Mink spells out. Verna is smart, for sure, but her vanity, visualized through her ongoing makeup application, is a major stumbling block. It prevents her from seeing that Bernie is loathed because he is the opposite of a good guy.

Her fixation on Bernie's sexuality, elaborated in the following scene, sheds light on her character, her relations with Leo, and her kinship with Tom. When Bernie seeks public-relations help from Tom, Tom asks what he will get in exchange (Leo got Verna; Tom already has her). Bernie denies involvement in Verna's decision to seduce Leo. He explains that she even tried to sleep with him to cure his homosexuality. This description of incest is an example of how far Verna—a twist—would go to protect the man she loves: Bernie. Her incestuous come-on is reflected or doubled in Tom's desire for Leo, a father figure who calls Tom his "mother hen."

Incest is not uncommon in the gangster genre. Gangsters' nearly insane desire for power is often epitomized in their libidos and especially sexual deviance and insidious lust. In *Scarface* (1932) Tony Camonte (Paul Muni) is extremely jealous of his sister's beaus, and his overprotective behavior betrays his incestuous attraction to her. James Cagney's Cody Jarrett in *White Heat* (1949) is more in love with his "ma" than his girlfriend. Homosexuality is no stranger to gangster films either. *Little Caesar*'s Rico (Edward G. Robinson) is too green-eyed over his friend Massara's (Douglas Fairbanks Jr.) girlfriends not to imply a repressed attraction to his criminal partner. Greed and perversion show the tough guys' downsides and map the crooked paths in the underworld, where women have little clout except through sexuality. Gay and incest subtexts take away what little power females in male-dominated worlds have.

As *Crossing*'s only major female character, Verna provides a sort of Smurfette role, badly masking the homosexuality of the other characters. Thus, in her attempts to get Tom, she may well be trying to "save" him and thus secure her power, just as she tried to cure Bernie. Homosexuality threatens her "order" just as much as Bernie threatens Caspar's order by messing with the rigged bets.

Tom's violent treatment of Verna derives from the gangster genre's pageant of male power and his repressed sexuality. In the bathroom when he aggressively pulls her to him, purportedly expressing his love, it's important to remember that he has just said he'll do anything to protect Leo. With Tom and Verna so much alike, the embrace begs the question whether his sexual offer is a strategic move toward Leo. He has just said that exposing their affair would ruin her pull with Leo and the chances of being discovered in Leo's club are short odds. Uninterested in a dance with Tom just then and there, she disentangles herself from his clutch and coldcocks him into a drink cart, proving she is indeed "man" enough to trade body blows with Tom. Though he never fights with his male friends, preferring to take and enjoy male-on-male beating, he strikes back at Verna with a vengeance. Matching her earlier missile launched in protest of his verbal "tramp" assault, now Tom fires a tumbler to retaliate her physical assault. The rhyme and its reversals exploit the Tom-and-Verna inversion of traditional gender roles. In the scene's final turnaround, complete with a reversed camera movement, Verna exits the bathroom and Tom stays in it. Instead of pulling Tom into the room, the camera first follows Verna's exit, and then pulls away from him, leaving him in the ladies' room talking about hell.

Mirrored scenes and dialogue pairs help to play up exposed and hidden meanings. Tom and Verna each use the phrase, "I was in the neighborhood, feeling a bit daffy," but in both cases the words are a smokescreen.[38] He visits her specifically to find out information and she visits him to try to kill him. In the first scene with his son, Caspar controverts a doctor's finding that his large son is overeating, arguing that a hot dog for lunch is hardly too big a meal. His affection here belies the tempest that rages within. The second time his son comes around, with good news about a prize, Caspar's temper explodes and he shows his displeasure at being interrupted by striking his son.

The vast differences between Leo's and Caspar's rule demonstrate the split plane of irrationality and rationality if not quite evil and good. Under Irish rule, when Tom walks into Leo's office as he holds counsel with the mayor and O'Doole, the two city puppets offer to leave, but Leo insists that they stay. When Tom walks into Caspar's office during a meeting with the mayor and O'Doole, Caspar orders them out. The starkest contrast is the mobsters' perceived betrayals by their right-hand men. When Tom admits to his affair with Verna, Leo gives him a beating but stops short of delivering too much abuse. When Caspar learns of the Dane's betrayal, he is not only ruthless; he is sadistic. He looses the Dane's stranglehold on Tom with a whack to the head. Showing none of Leo's mercy, Caspar clubs the Dane with a shovel and puts two bullets in his head.

Bernie and Tom are also contrasting counterparts with opposite value systems. Where one is solipsistic, the other is selfless. Bernie pays Tom two visits, breaking and entering both times. On the first occasion, he is in trouble and offers a friendly trade with Tom. He'll pay off Tom's gambling debts if Tom will say good things on his behalf to Leo. Tom won't accept anyone's offer to clear his IOUs, so though he says he'll think about it, we can be quite sure that his response is a euphemistic "no thank you." The next time Bernie

Jon Polito (right) plays a mobster concerned with "friendship," "character" and "ethics." He mistakes false appearances for reality and bludgeons his right-hand man before shooting him in the back as Gabriel Byrne, who has sold him a pack of lies, looks on. (Credit: 20th Century Fox/Photofest © 20th Century Fox)

breaks in, he believes he is in the catbird seat. On this visit, Bernie sits in the chair previously occupied by Tom, leaving Tom to plant himself in Bernie's previous seat—he even slumps like the bookie did. Their switched positions underscore this power shift. Instead of playing dead, Bernie looks Tom's gift horse in the mouth and goes for another graft.

Like a typical overreaching gangster driven by ambition, greed, and power, the small-time bookie makes a play to mend his wounded pride. Embarrassed by the raw emotion he unleashed in the woods in front of Tom, Bernie tries to leverage Tom's secret. Replacing his previous visit's bartering offer is a hostile threat: He'll show up around town if Caspar isn't dead in a few days. After Bernie leaves Tom grabs his hat and pistol to take care of him, but unlike Leo whose window jumping ends in complete triumph over his enemies, Tom's mad window dash is thwarted by a trip in the hallway downstairs. Bernie's glib, superior attitude toward Tom is nothing compared to the kick to the face of the man who spared him his life.

In fact, the film's key mirror scene involves Bernie begging Tom for his life. This converse of Tom's stoic death-walk-to-come finds Tom again plodding in deadly silence. Opposite his composure in this outing is the bookie's gushing with fear. Crying and screaming, Bernie pleads for his life and prattles on about how they are not killers. He compares himself to Tom and insists that the hoods can't make them different men—a comment that lends itself to sexual preference. Finally, Bernie uses the strange tactic of arguing against reality: "It's a dream, Tommy! I'm praying to you! I can't die out here in the woods . . . like a dumb animal! Look into your heart."[39] It is a dream, this nightmare situation in the woods, that no one else is privy to. Tom will walk this way again after he lets Bernie go, and that moment, as rendered in the opening, is dreamlike. Here with Bernie, perhaps Tom thinks of Verna—or Leo, more likely, if he examines his heart—and figures a way out of killing him. He shoots his gun into the air and dispatches Bernie into the woods, the place evocative of dreams, fears, and emotion. While he chooses life as a way out for Bernie, Bernie will chose Mink's death as a way out for himself. Then he will snub Tom's generosity. When his play fails and Tom points a gun at him a second time, begging fails. With means and motive, Tom shoots him dead and finally restores order.

WELCOME TO THE JUNGLE

Caspar warns at the outset that without rules, society reverts to an unruly, junglelike state. In addition to aptly describing the mobster mayhem that rocks the gangland, the Italian mobster invokes the philosophy of Thomas Hobbes, who maintained that people without laws and government were nasty, brutish, and anarchic. Such a state describes almost the entirety of the film and is called out in the title, *Miller's Crossing*, which refers to the forest, a naturally anarchic realm where animals run wild—as in gangster land.

Animals are well represented throughout the movie. Gangsters bet on them, liberally sprinkle them into their talk, and decorate with them. The decorative beasts reinforce notions of power. In a town whose economic structure is built in part on gambling rackets, for instance, a horse and chariot statue appropriately adorns the mayor's office and a horse ashtray and greyhound statue trim Leo's domains. His dog painting showing the upper-class, British sport of hunting imbues Leo with grace and a cut-above-the-rest style.

If Leo is thus represented as an urbane, august killer, Caspar is a dark hunter. The stuffed heads of wild deer and boars on his walls reflect his feral nature. Not just wilder than Leo, he is also more bloodthirsty. Like a grotesque perversion of Leo's peaceful domesticity, Caspar's home life is savage and sybaritic. He demonstrates his brutish nature first by blistering Drop Johnson's (Mario Todisco) face and then by barbarously killing the Dane.[40] When

Johnny is in charge, suddenly his claims that rules are the backbone of society go out the window, and anything goes. He'll have none of the mayor's insistence on doing things properly. He demands his cousins be installed as coheads of the assessor's office and then kicks the mayor out of his own office. Outside the sound of explosions and gunfire give an idea of Johnny's incipient anarchy.

Bestial comparisons, like the myriad ethnic slurs that are bandied about, are an easy way to boost one's own stature by cutting down one's enemies. Caspar lectures that moral codes separate humans from "beasts of prey," casting Bernie as a beast of burden because he's "a horse of a different color ethics-wise."[41] Though he can't see it, ethics-wise, Caspar's horsemanship is easily on par with Bernie's. Meanwhile, "Potato-eater" Leo, deaf to Caspar's Bernie problems, chuckles over the "Eye-tie's" fiery temper: "Twist a pig's ear. Watch him squeal."[42] Later, Tom not only watches; he makes Bernie squeal. As the story takes shape, scads of other animal references turn the gangland into Caspar's predicted Hobbesian jungle.

Animal names speak to character, gender, and even sexuality. Each of the three main homosexuals, for instance, has an animal associated with his name. Tom talks sarcastically of Bernie being a "saint" at one point, inchoately forming "saint Bernard." The great Dane, Eddie, was renamed from "Bluepoint" (a small oyster) in the script.[43] Mink LaRouie has the most apparent animal appellation. Their relationships are further expressed in animal terms, as when Bernie talks of him and Mink being "jungled up together" and Tom characterizing the same pair as "cozy as lice."[44] Tom expresses Bernie and Mink's power differential in both zoological and zoo metaphors when he remarks that Bernie "must have Mink jumping through hoops."[45] Caspar separates preying beasts from men but then later sics Tom on Bernie, the Italian's primary quarry. Like Caspar, Bernie doesn't recognize his own animalistic ways. At Miller's Crossing, he tries to distinguish himself and Tom from "animals" Frankie and Tic-Tac.[46] But as with everything he spouts about out there, he is hypocritical. He does cross his friends (Mink and Tom), and he is like Caspar's heavies. Bernie kills people (Mink and Caspar) as easily as flies.

It turns out the forest anarchy can be easily exported to the city when folks like Caspar and Bernie are let loose or when broken rules are not addressed. Such a climate can turn every man into an animal or hunter, even the usually cool-headed Tom, who corners Bernie in the end and shoots him dead. Like Hammett's *Red Harvest* narrator, known only as the "Continental Op," Tom indeed has some noble hunter in him, and the hunting angle and animal metaphors are carryovers from Hammett. As scholar Ralph Willett points out, Hammett describes "Poisonville's inhabitants as animals (monkeys, wolves, hogs) and the Op as their hunter."[47]

A DASH OF HAMMETT

"We weren't thinking so much of gangster pictures, just novels," explained Joel in the film's production notes. Ethan elaborated in the *Boston Phoenix*: "*Crossing* is pretty much just a shameless rip-off of Dashiell Hammett, mostly his novel *The Glass Key* (made into a movie twice, in 1935 and 1942), but to a lesser extent *Red Harvest*."[48] Tom's switch-hitting between the warring parties comes from Hammett's first novel, *Red Harvest*, in which the Continental Op plays each side against the other in order to solve a case. The murder mystery and love triangle are reformed from *The Glass Key*. In this story protagonist Ned Beaumont, while investigating the murder of a senator's son to clear his best friend, the political boss Paul Madvig, falls for Paul's fiancée Janet. Both the Coen movie and its blueprint, in their unsentimental, economic telling, leave open what their "heroes" were thinking—an intentional aspect of many a hard-boiled yarn.

Crossing owes a huge debt to Hammett. Here's a tiny fraction of just the borrowed language. "How far has this dizzy blond daughter of his got her hooks into you?" from *The Glass Key* in the Coen movie becomes "How far has she got her hooks into you?"[49] Ned's "Don't anything ever suit ya?" becomes Tom's grammatically correct line, "Doesn't anything ever suit you?"[50] Tom's "We're quits—as far as I'm concerned" was originally Ned's "As far as I'm concerned we're quits."[51] The Coens' use of "the original Miss Jesus" transplants its original context of a female character despairing over the selfish bum she left her loving parents for into Tom's snide comment about Leo's misplaced apotheosis of her.[52] With Hammett's patois as a base, the Coens' dialogue shows how language can be like a hat: It can hide or reveal.

The hard-boiled talk in *Crossing* and Hammett's influential novels bubbles up from their respective, squalid societies. A random but operative newspaper headline perhaps sums up *Crossing*'s milieu succinctly: "Municipal sewage."[53] Like its forerunner Poisonville, *Crossing*'s unnamed city is mired by corruption and greed, so much so that not only are social structures crumbling, but also language and other forms of communication are mixed up in the chaos. After Caspar presents a good case for rubbing out Bernie, Leo cavils, claiming his facts are muddy. This just isn't so. Leo understands Caspar's issues, but he cannot help out nor can he reveal why. Love and emotion are no-nos in this masculine world, and Leo is acting on them both. Such hiding and coloring start the language pendulum that swings between communication and miscommunication, truth and cover-ups.

Throughout, language is both weapon and shield and another substance for the gangsters to abuse. Leo hedges his romantic rationale with unlikely alternatives, showing how supple language—and how transparent true motivation—can be. Later Bernie verbally attacks Frankie and Tic-Tac and babbles on to deflect Tom's bullets. Ultimately his promises prove cheap.

Bernie might be the one who initially stirs up the hornet's nest, but in this Hobbesian realm no one is above poking it some more.[54] Tom dissembles to Caspar about the Dane and Mink, to chip away at the Italian's power structure. So adept is Tom with language that he keeps the dead man Mink alive in Caspar's mind through words alone. Tom carefully parses his sentences to Verna, trying to avoid outright lies where possible. When Verna questions why Tom wants to know Bernie's whereabouts, Tom first states a fact and then describes what appropriate behavior would be: "Leo can't protect him anymore. I ought to tell him to skip."[55] What he ought to do and what he wants to do (and does) are completely different things. Later, Verna is confused that Tom betrayed her to help Leo. When she reminds him that he "didn't care for Leo," Tom corrects her semantics: "I said we were through. It's not the same thing."[56]

Tom's meticulous use of language makes *Crossing*'s wordscape as instrumental to the film as language is to classic detective fiction, where words often offered in first-person narratives are the best clues to the thoughts of hard-boiled, close-to-the-vest private eyes. The trouble is, though, that their (read their authors') verbal skills match the bad guys' criminal skills. As writer Carl D. Malmgren explains, crime writers like Hammett often subvert "basic frames of intelligibility, including the frame that allows the art of fiction, language itself."[57] A good example of this can be found in *Red Harvest*, in which the Continental Op has a number of false aliases he uses depending on the situation. He hands a potential source a business card that identifies the Op as union worker "Henry F. Neill, A. B. seaman," upsetting the man with the added information that he is not the man on the card.[58] That is strange enough, but for the reader there is the additional double-entendre cleverly pointing to the Op's first-person narrator status. Perhaps he is not his card's Able Bodied seaman, but he is an "ABC man."[59]

As in Hammett, *Crossing*'s communicative subversions occur on all levels of language, not just the verbal plane. The offensive on the Sons of Erin, a scene re-created from *Red Harvest*, is a good example. Right away, the scenario of police attacking an Irish establishment tests viewer sensibilities—Irish being an ethnic group so closely identified with cops. But the real destruction occurs after the incursion when an officer orders survivors to come out. A man staggering through the door waves the white flag of surrender. A detective (played by Coen friend and fellow filmmaker Sam Raimi) laughs at the sight and then empties his gun on the unsuspecting man, violating the flag's meaning. The predeath twitch of the man's legs cracks up the entire police line. Then comes the Coens' karmic tag. An unexpected round of gunfire from the

Sam Raimi's snickering cop is sprayed with gunfire after he dispenses with the meaning of signs by glibly killing a man waving a white flag in surrender. (Credit: 20th Century Fox/Photofest © 20th Century Fox)

shelled-out club kills the detective who had been so callous with signs and meaning. Touché.

Jumbled symbols can mislead the unsavvy, as Rug Daniels's missing "rug" shows. Leo suspects Rug's death is Caspar's throwing down of the gauntlet. But he is mystified by the hairpiece. Tom's joke about Indian involvement shows he doubts the theft's significance. The viewer, who sees a random, inquisitive child steal the toupee, knows Tom is right. Looking beyond the unimportant "rug," Tom focuses on the .22-caliber murder weapon. He narrows his search down to people most likely to carry such a small gun and thus pokes around a shady gay character and the token female. His instinct to follow this lead and not the hairpiece pans out, and his hunch about the whys of the murder prove valid. Instead of Verna killing Rug to hide her affair with Tom, Mink killed him to hide his affair with Bernie. In other words, it was a mirror of the scenario Tom had imagined with Verna—not the heterosexual love triangle but the homosexual one. It's a narrative turnaround that rhymes with Tad's clue about the hat: "Mink or Verna . . . Verna or Mink."

Crossing's use of those natural signal-crossers called dreams fits neatly into the film's mirror design. In *The Glass Key* Janet's dream allows her boyfriend Ned to demonstrate his facility with reading clues. He doesn't interpret her dream per se, but he accurately reads her telling of it. Ned deduces she is lying because what "starts out as a nightmare . . . winds up something else."[60] Later she confesses that she had revised her nightmare set in woods to a more pleasant story.

The Coens' film reverses these details. Tom is the one who dreams about the woods, and his girlfriend Verna guesses the ending. Instead of giving us insight to Tom, as *The Glass Key* does with Ned, Tom's dream sheds light on Verna. Always quick to guess what Tom is thinking, she is rarely right about him. When she guesses that his hat turns into something wonderful, he defensively dismisses her speculation. Seconds later, he lies to her about wanting to know Bernie's whereabouts. Verna's attempt to manipulate Tom's dream into something good—her—reveals her play to control "the jungle," the dream-life beneath the hat. The trouble with her interpretations isn't just that they miss the mark—it's the *way* they miss the mark. A totally self-absorbed character, she cannot understand motives that don't involve her. Thus, she doesn't get Tom's loyalty to Leo. The jungle in part represents desire. It is a feminizing—or emasculating—place—where the wild card is often played—and it is the realm Verna is accustomed to manipulating rather than the "ordered" world men manipulate.

"TRADING BODY BLOWS"

Tom may cleverly manipulate language to "never let on more than [he has] to," in Verna's words, but the Coens are another story.[61] In orchestrating their meditation on knowledge, the Coens and their camera provide peeks into Tom's head. Take, for example, the curtain segue between Tom and Verna's lovemaking and the mob hit on Leo. Tom's investigation into Rug's death leads him to Verna. When she calls the cops on him, Tom takes the phone from her and requests protection for Leo. After another raucous discussion of what Verna did and didn't do regarding the dead Rug, Tom suggests they get "stinko."[62] As the two kiss, the camera moves away from their embrace to the violent attack just getting under way at Leo's, where no protection shows. The seamless transition from Verna's luffing curtains to Leo's is unexpected and suggests the possibility that while Tom is kissing Verna, perhaps Leo is on his mind.

Tom cannot see Leo's macho counteroffensive to Caspar's hit, but his stupendous fight serves as a substitute for the missing romantic spark in Tom and Verna's trysts. Moving from Leo's living room and the fresh corpse Caspar's men leave there, the action advances upstairs to the man of the house and the calm before the storm. Relaxing in bed, the mob boss enjoys a cigar and Frank

Patterson's clear tenor singing "Danny Boy." Smoke seeping through the floor-boards tells him something is awry and he nimbly slips into his slippers, grabs his guns, and dives under the bed just in time to shoot the goons at his door, first in their legs and then their heads.

The erupting gang war, seen so often on screen before, explodes with over-the-top carnage and makes the case for Leo's top-dog position. Leo grabs his would-be killer's gun and single-handedly takes out the army Caspar sent to retire him to an early RIP bed. He slips out the window with a gymnast's ease, takes up a position on the street, and empties his machine gun into the man framed in his bedroom window. The man performs a dance grotesque in-voluntarily choreographed by the bullets ripping into his body. The unflap-pable Leo goes on to stop the attack's final wave, shutting down the attempted Model-T drive-by. "Danny Boy" swells as Leo takes his cigar from his bathrobe pocket and sticks it back in his mouth, capping this chanson d'amour to mas-culine power.

Supporting the theory that Leo is on Tom's mind while he kisses Verna is another mirrored curtain transition, in which the scene changes from Verna's apartment to Tom's just before Bernie pays him a second visit. This second curtain segue begins when the Dane jumps Verna to squeeze information about Tom from her. Two of Leo's men interrupt her intimidation session, and while the Dane deals with them, Verna flees through the window. Vowing to "track down all a you whores," the Dane gazes out the window, and the scene cuts from Verna's curtains to Tom's.[63] Verna isn't the only whore the Dane would like to track down. If he knew that Mink was two-timing him with Bernie, Verna's bookie brother would be the primary hustler the Dane would want to get. And so, fittingly, Bernie shows up in the following scene at Tom's apartment. Akin to Tom's triangulated desire visualized by a transition that spurns Verna for Leo, the camerawork again brings clarity to the latent wishes of the scene's dominant male. While doing away with the bete noir Verna would be nice, the Dane really wants to get Bernie, the whore who is jungling up with Mink and who is bollixing his boss's fixed fights, the otherwise "sure thing."

INTO THE WOODS

When we think of gangster movies, mean streets come to mind, not groves. Yet, *Crossing*, as its name suggests, gives us a cross-pollination of both—a bit of sidewalks and speakeasies, and then some greenery and trees. The woods are the movie's darkly carnivalesque sphere, evocative of dreams, nightmares, and cinema past. Beyond working in dream references from *The Glass Key*, the

Gabriel Byrne turns down Albert Finney's request to go back to work for him, choosing to stay in the wild woods like a cowboy steering clear of the city that can't tame him. (Credit: 20th Century Fox/Photofest © 20th Century Fox)

woods push *Crossing*'s allusions and influences past Hammett toward films such as Bernardo Bertolucci's *The Conformist* (1971) and Carol Reed's *The Third Man* (1949). There's also a touch of Akira Kurosawa among the branches. The moving shot of the treetops is reminiscent of *Rashomon* (1950; a murder story carved from different characters' perspectives that never add up to a complete "sure thing"). Tom's cross-allegiances are akin to the samurai's in *Yojimbo* (1961; a movie thought to be based on Hammett's novel *Red Harvest*).

This latter reference to Kurosawa, who was heavily influenced by American Westerns, might shed light on Tom's cowboy ways. Sure, Tom has what it takes to thrive in the mobsters' rough-and-tumble world, but he's not your average gangster. Neither ambitious nor money-hungry, he refuses handouts that would cancel his debts (this is the opposite of Ned Beaumont) and does things to benefit Leo solely. Tom never loses control, even when he is least in control, and uses a gun only when necessary.

In terms of the genre, Tom is the opposite of Leo, the more typical gangster type—a tough, "pig-headed" "artist with a Thompson."[64] Experiencing the same difficulty Verna will have when she tries to shoot him, Tom is loath to kill Bernie. At Miller's Crossing Tom is silent as Bernie squirms for his life. A minor melody like the second part of the opening theme creeps in, but it's darker, and a sustained ringing interspersed with natural wind sounds gives it a haunting air. When the men stop walking and the shooting draws near, Bernie drops to his knees and looks into the barrel of Tom's gun. The moment is pregnant with tension; the positioning is homoerotic. After a cut to a long shot of the pair, alternating close-ups on each man capture Bernie's petition to Tom to look in his heart. Slowly, the eerie soundtrack adds a piercing insectlike noise (another *Barton Fink* sound), notching up the tension until Tom unloads the gun.

Pulling the trigger twice, he fires into the air, uncompelled to do Caspar's dirty work. Likely examining his heart and seeing Leo there, Tom keeps Bernie alive as Leo wants, granting him conditional freedom. Sparing and exiling Bernie can restore both order and Leo's position of power. Later, after Bernie double-crosses him, Tom has no reason *not* to kill him. Following the Westerner's code of shooting—not the gangster's—Tom shoots him when he has cause to. After all, as he says time and again, people do things for a reason. Tom's limpid cool makes him as much a cowboy as a gangster if not more so. Robert Warshow's critical essay explains:

> The gangster's pre-eminence lies in the suggestion that he may at any moment lose control; his strength is . . . in being more willing to shoot. . . . With the Westerner, it is a crucial point of honor not to "do it first." . . . He fights not for advantage and not for the right, but to state what he is, and he must live in a world which permits that statement.[65]

At the end Tom's return to the city would mean denying he is the guy used to "spinning Leo in circles."[66] Verna's procurement of that role means he must move on to stay true to himself.

Tom is a contemplative loner—an existential gangster with cowboy sensibilities. His large, roomy apartment, designed to resemble the inside of his head, is reminiscent of the flat, expansive spaces where the Western hero can escape societal confines. Tom's outsider status allows him to move freely between camps like *Yojimbo*'s samurai (Toshiro Mifune), a bodyguard who fixes a town's warring factions by helping each side kill the other off. Part-samurai, part-cowboy, part-detective, Tom reestablishes order. And like these character types, he leaves at the end when the job is done. The city can't tame him. He prefers the woods.

When Tom lets Bernie live, the bookie throws him a kiss and takes off into the woods. His crazed run is reminiscent of the climactic forest scene in *The Conformist*, a film about fascist Italy and a repressed homosexual who betrays a couple in a futile bid to be "normal." *Crossing*'s Bertolucci touches add up to more reversals. Tom is a nonconformist. Marcello Clerici (Jean-Louis Trintignant) is a conformist. Both lure adversaries into the forest to be murdered.

While it is arguable that Bernie deserves some punishment for his rule breaking, the couple Marcello helps take out—his former professor (Enzo Tarascio)
and his wife (Dominique Sanda)—does not. The fascists just want to suppress
the free-thinking gadfly, one of Marcello's favorite teachers.

The Conformist's climactic wooded murder scene is pure horror. The hit
men cut off the professor's car and knife him to death. Anna, Marcello's former girlfriend, watches the gruesome stabbing. She runs to Marcello and
pleads with him for help (a bit like Bernie tries to do with Tom after he is
dragged out of his apartment), but the weak-willed Marcello does nothing.
She sprints into the woods, followed by her attackers. Her flight is the opposite of Bernie's. Unlike Bernie who finds freedom in the forest, which he refuses, she is slaughtered.

Though Tom is for the most part Marcello's opposite, the two characters
share several telling traits. Tom's smoking and cogitating on his bed after getting his hat back from Verna is very similar to The Conformist's opening. In that
scene, a pondering Marcello sits on his bed smoking. After he takes a phone
call, he prepares to go out. His final gesture is to pick up his hat, which is sitting on the bare buttocks of a woman hitherto unseen. Verna is similarly revealed in Tom's bed after Tom talks with Leo. Like Tom, Marcello also engages
in some hat chasing, commenting at one point, "I lost my hat. Where's my
hat?"[67] Tom also echoes to Verna Marcello's lie to his fiancée: "I can't tell you
anything yet."[68] Through such small rhymes, Marcello offers insight into Tom's
suppressed or repressed homosexuality.

There is visual resonance, too. One of Bertolucci's most exquisite images
is a flurry of autumn leaves stirred up by the wind—the same force that carries Crossing's hat and helps evoke dreams and memory. Bertolucci's wind shot
operates on similar cinematic terms as the Coens' curtain transitions. What
starts out in the driveway of Marcello's mother's estate segues seamlessly to the
parking lot of his father's mental hospital—a transition that captures Marcello's
yearnings, psychological issues, and memory. The wind's inspiration, as a doctor puts it, has helped transform Marcello's thoughts about one parent to another.

If the forest, wind, and hats were among Bertolucci's influence on Crossing, a funeral, a symmetrical design, and a dead man walking comprise The
Third Man's influence on the Coens' film. Carol Reed's thriller starring Orson
Welles as Harry Lime and Joseph Cotten as Holly Martins sprang from a single Graham Greene sentence: "I saw a man walking down the Strand, whose
funeral I had only recently attended."[69] The first twist in The Third Man, which
shares with Crossing a breakdown in friendship, character and ethics, is that
Holly gets to Vienna to find that the friend who invited him there is dead. Or
so it seems. After attending Harry's funeral Holly decides to stay on a bit. He

snoops around his friend's past and falls in love with Harry's girlfriend, thus creating a strange love triangle between himself, the girl, and the dead man. But Harry is as dead as Bernie is after Tom takes him into the woods—in other words, Harry's alive. In much worse news, Holly learns his friend is a mercenary snake like Bernie.

Both films deal with moral, social, and economic corruption, and both end with funeral denouements. *The Third Man*'s funeral is symmetrical and karmic—Holly's adventure begins with Harry's false funeral and ends with his real one. It's fitting justice for his bare-faced inhumanity. Bernie only has one funeral, but his death scene plays out twice—in one ending he lives, in the other he dies. Harry's girlfriend Anna (Valli), despondent over his death, stays true to him to the end, just as Verna does with Bernie. The allusion plays up *Crossing*'s incest angle through several inverted details. In Reed's finale Holly jumps out of his car to talk with Anna. Holly's friend drives off, leaving him there on the road flanked by trees waiting for her to reach him. She finally does but passes him by without a word. Verna, the woman at *Crossing*'s funeral, is angry not about her corrupt beau's death but about her corrupt brother's. Just as Anna ignores Holly, Verna snubs Tom, and like Holly's friend, Verna drives off to leave the other parts of the triangle to walk. Like Holly watching Anna walk away, Tom watches Leo walk off with a wistful, yearning look in his eyes that can signify only one thing: love.

Certainly *Crossing* has the look and feel of a gangster film. It shares some themes with the genre and even references *Scarface* (when Tom strikes his match on the policeman's badge). But it is also a melodrama and a love story that exploits the very masculine arena of gangland cinema to, ironically, pursue a homosexual undertow. *Crossing*'s title suggests hybrids and swindles and the film appropriately pirates conventions from other genres, such as crime fiction, romantic thrillers, and even political satires (such as *The Conformist*) that deal with repressed homosexuality. In the end, Tom chooses to stay in the forest with his secrets. Flat and open, the woods become Tom's frontier, and like the samurai at the end of *Yojimbo*, the cowboy at the close of so many Westerns, and Holly in *The Third Man*, Tom chooses to linger there—in the land of animals—rather than return to the constraining, tame society.

WRAP: FOREST THROUGH THE TREES

Society versus anarchy—society versus freedom. *Crossing* contrasts the city's knowns with the wood's unknowns. Indeterminacy and subjectivity are keys to fill in the blanks of *Crossing*, where the power of belief can hold sway. As

Tom tells Leo: "You run [this town] because people think you run it. Once they stop thinking it, you stop running it."[70] Tom manipulates belief and knowledge to get what he wants: Leo back on top. Not that he ever spells this out. Tom likes to keep things under his hat. Using his own logic, when actions defy reason the wild card of love is usually at play. As in Hammett, triangulated desire puts amateur detective Tom in a double bind, unable to go back to Leo and not desirous of the girl. So he stays put in Miller's Crossing, the realm of freedom and secret desire.

NOTES

1. Mike McGrady, "Colorful Characters in Gangster Land," *Newsday*, September 21, 1990, 13.

2. Mick LaSalle, "Crossing Just Another Stylish Mob Film," *San Francisco Chronicle*, October 5, 1990, E-10.

3. Vincent Canby, "In Miller's Crossing, Silly Gangsters and a Tough Moll," *New York Times*, September 21, 1990, C-1.

4. Rita Kempley, "*Miller's Crossing*: Brutal Beauty," *Washington Post*, October 5, 1990, D1.

5. Robert Polito, "Introduction" to *The Maltese Falcon, The Thin Man, Red Harvest* (New York: Everyman's Library, 2000), xxiv.

6. Trey Wilson (*Raising Arizona*'s pitchman Nathan Arizona) was slated for the part, but died suddenly of a brain hemorrhage two days before production began. In casting Finney the Coens say the Irish-Italian war became more ethnically intense than originally conceived.

7. Robert Pogue Harrison, *Forests: The Shadow of Civilization* (Chicago: University of Chicago Press: 1993), xi.

8. From *Miller's Crossing* production notes.

9. *Miller's Crossing*, DVD, directed by Joel Coen (1990; Beverly Hills, Calif.: 20th Century Fox Home Entertainment, 2003).

10. *Miller's Crossing*, DVD.

11. Jopi Nyman, *Men Alone* (Netherlands: Rodopi B.V. Editions, 1997), 108–112.

12. *Miller's Crossing*, DVD.

13. Andrew Pulver, "Blood Ties," *Daily Mail and Guardian*, August 20, 1998, server .mg.co.za/mg/art/film/9808/980820-coen.html (accessed March 17, 2007)

14. Dashiell Hammett, *The Glass Key* (New York: Vintage Books, 1989), 176.

15. Eve Kosofsky Sedgwick, *Between Men* (New York: Columbia University Press, 1985), 50–51.

16. René Girard, *Deceit, Desire, and the Novel*, trans. Yvonne Freccero (Baltimore: Johns Hopkins University Press, 1965), 1–52.

17. Hammett, *The Glass Key*, 214.

18. *Miller's Crossing*, DVD.

19. *Miller's Crossing*, DVD.

20. *Miller's Crossing*, DVD.

21. *Miller's Crossing*, DVD.

22. *Miller's Crossing*, DVD.

23. *Miller's Crossing*, DVD.

24. *Miller's Crossing*, DVD.

25. *Miller's Crossing*, DVD.

26. *Miller's Crossing*, DVD.

27. Scott Eyman, "*Crossing* Straight but Not All That Serious," *San Diego Union-Tribune*, October 19, 1990, E-7.

28. *Miller's Crossing*, DVD.

29. *Miller's Crossing*, DVD.

30. *Miller's Crossing*, DVD.

31. *Miller's Crossing*, DVD.

32. *Miller's Crossing*, DVD.

33. *Miller's Crossing*, DVD.

34. "Twist, n1 and n3," Oxford English Dictionary, 2nd ed., 1989, OED Online, Oxford University Press, dictionary.oed.com/cgi/entry/50260698?querytype=word &queryword=twist&first= and dictionary.oed.com/cgi/entry/50260698?querytype =word&queryword=twist&third= (accessed August 28, 2006).

35. *Miller's Crossing*, DVD.

36. *Miller's Crossing*, DVD.

37. *Miller's Crossing*, DVD.

38. *Miller's Crossing*, DVD.

39. *Miller's Crossing*, DVD.

40. The scene at Drop Johnson's apartment provides insight into the Coens' play with perspective. On the wall is a poster advertising a fight with Lars Thorwald, a name from Alfred Hitchcock's point-of-view masterpiece *Rear Window* (1954).

41. *Miller's Crossing*, DVD.

42. *Miller's Crossing*, DVD.

43. *Miller's Crossing*, DVD.

44. *Miller's Crossing*, DVD.

45. *Miller's Crossing*, DVD.

46. *Miller's Crossing*, DVD.

47. Ralph Willett, "Hard-Boiled Detective Fiction," BAAS Pamphlets in American Studies 23 (first published 1992), www.baas.ac.uk/publications/pamphlets/pamphdets .asp?id=23#ch1 (2002).

48. Nicholas Patterson, "Gates of Ethan," *Boston Phoenix*, November 19–26, 1998, www.bostonphoenix.com/archive/books/98/11/19/ETHAN_COEN.html (accessed January 7, 2006).

49. Hammett, *The Glass Key*, 8; *Miller's Crossing*, DVD.

50. Hammett, *The Glass Key*, 70; *Miller's Crossing*, DVD.

51. Hammett, *The Glass Key*, 81.

52. Hammett, *The Glass Key*, 18.

53. *Miller's Crossing*, DVD.

54. *Miller's Crossing*, DVD.

55. *Miller's Crossing*, DVD.

56. *Miller's Crossing*, DVD.

57. Carl D. Malmgren, "The Crime of the Sign: Dashiell Hammett's Detective Fiction," *Twentieth Century Literature*, September 22, 1999, www.findarticles.com/p/articles/mi_m0403/is_3_45/ai_58926042 (accessed January 7, 2006).

58. Dashiell Hammett, *Complete Novels* (New York: Literary Classics of the United States, 1999), 8.

59. Carl D. Malmgren, "The Crime of the Sign: Dashiell Hammett's Detective Fiction."

60. *Miller's Crossing*, DVD.

61. *Miller's Crossing*, DVD.

62. *Miller's Crossing*, DVD.

63. *Miller's Crossing*, DVD.

64. *Miller's Crossing*, DVD.

65. Robert Warshow, "Movie Chronicle: The Westerner," in *Film Theory and Criticism*, eds. Gerald Mast, Marshall Cohen, and Leo Braudy (New York: Oxford University Press, 1992), 457.

66. *Miller's Crossing*, DVD.

67. *The Conformist*, DVD, directed by Bernardo Bertolucci (1970; Hollywood, Calif.: Paramount Home Video, 2006).

68. *The Conformist*, DVD.

69. "Shadowing the Third Man," Turner Classic Movies, www2.turnerclassicmovies.com/thismonth/article.jsp?cid=82840&mainArticleId=93530 (accessed September 25, 2006).

70. *Miller's Crossing*, DVD.

• *4* •

Barton Fink: A Head

In John Turturro's Hollywood nightmare, which is concerned with the creative process generally and heads specifically, the writer is unable to absorb anything useful. Here, his glasses reflect the wrestling movies he watches in an attempt at research. (Credit: 20th Century Fox/Photofest © 20th Century Fox)

"Daylight is a dream if you've lived with your eyes closed."

—from *Barton Fink*'s "Bare Ruined Choirs"

"On horror's head horrors accumulate."

—*Othello*, William Shakespeare (c. 1604)

PREVIEW

*Y*ou could call it a head game because if nothing else, *Barton Fink* gets you thinking. TV personality Larry King, who called the movie "one of the most unusual films I've ever seen," commented, "The ending is something I'm still thinking about and if they accomplished that, I guess it worked."[1] It also got the Coens thinking—which is why they wrote it. Dead-ended with the *Miller's Crossing* script, the filmmakers hoped turning to something new might release them from their writers' block. It worked. After an invigorating three-week "vacation"—Ethan's description for their writing diversion called *Fink*—they finished their gangster script.[2]

At its Cannes Film Festival premiere, the black comedy *Fink* was a block-buster, as in a hit. It slammed the competition with awards for Best Acting (John Turturro), Best Direction (Joel Coen), and the coveted top prize, the Palme d'Or.[3] Thanks to *Fink's* 1991 hat trick, films in Cannes can no longer win more than two major awards. Such a sweep had not occurred in over forty years, and the festival directors did not want another repeat performance. Back in the United States, the *Los Angeles Times* lionized the Coens as the country's "best-respected independent filmmakers," and the critical kudos kept pouring in, helping turn *Fink* into some vacation.

REVIEW

With the Coens' genre-bending flair, the eponymous *Barton Fink* recounts an outlandish, increasingly dark tale of a writer (Turturro in his second Coen role) in desperate search of a muse. Or so it seems. Following a hit Broadway debut, the promising dramaturge, based loosely on playwright Clifford Odets, accepts a screenwriting stint, despite the fact that he doesn't like movies and would rather peddle his socialist ideas to New Yorkers.[4] He checks into the spooky Hotel Earle on the outskirts of Los Angeles, and the film seems to teeter toward dementia.

His new boss, Capitol Studios head Jack Lipnik (Michael Lerner)—a fictional hybrid of real-life movie moguls Jack Warner, Harry Cohn, and Louis B. Mayer—assigns him a "wrestling picture." Lerner's brilliant take-off on the infamously bombastic studio heads, which earned him an Oscar nod, is one of many jabs at the studio system. Another is that while he is in charge, his mousy assistant and former company shareholder Lou Breeze (Jon Polito) does all the work.

At the hotel Barton tries to write but finds noises from next door too distracting. He gripes to bellhop Chet (Steve Buscemi), who phones the accused neighbor. Moments later, a disgruntled Charlie Meadows (John Goodman, in his second Coen role) appears at Barton's door. He cools off quickly, and the men seem to hit it off. Charlie's visits and a simple picture of a Bathing Beauty are the only perks in Barton's underwhelming digs where the wallpaper is peeling, disquieting noises leak through thin walls, and a dastardly mosquito torments him.

For writing help, he turns to fast-talking director Ben Geisler (Tony Shalhoub). Then, thanks to a serendipitous meeting with his favorite novelist, the Faulknerian William "Bill" P. Mayhew (John Mahoney) also agrees to mentor him when he's not busy drinking. But when Barton falls for Bill's secretary/girlfriend, Audrey Taylor (Judy Davis), things go from dismal to worse—and then really bizarre. He wakes up to find her dead in his bed, and still he has no script.

Despite such horrific events, and, disturbingly, in part due to them, things start to look up. Charlie disposes of the body, no questions asked. Then Barton bluffs his way through his meeting with Jack. Even bad news cannot stop his roll. When Charlie is out of town purportedly on business, detectives Matrionotti (Richard Portnow) and Deutsch (Christopher Murney) show up with questions about Barton's neighbor whom they call Karl "Madman" Mundt. They say Charlie is a psychopathic killer with a propensity for chopping up his victims. Barton reveals little about his neighbor. When he returns to writing, suddenly words flow. On his desk, as if for inspiration, is Charlie's box. It's about the size of a head. Barton finally finishes his script and then celebrates.

He goes out dancing and returns home to find the detectives snooping about. His blood-soaked mattress is the evidence they need to arrest him for the murders of Audrey and Bill, who is also now dead. As the detectives handcuff Barton to the bed, the temperature spikes: Charlie is back. With the hotel now inexplicably aflame, he kills the cops, enters Barton's room, and frees him. He explains that the killings were payback for the writer's complaints and his inability to listen. Charlie returns to his room. Barton takes the box and leaves the blazing hotel.

At the studio, Barton tries frantically and unsuccessfully to phone his parents in New York, whom he had told Charlie to look up while he was there. He is left to wonder if they too were part of Charlie's payback scheme. At his script meeting, Jack, who is dressed as a colonel, berates him for writing a bad screenplay. Rather than fire him, though, the studio will keep Barton onboard but with a Sisyphean caveat: The scripts Barton writes will not be produced.

In the epilogue Barton, curiously unfazed by all the weird events, strolls along a beach, toting Charlie's box. He plops onto the sand and spies a bikini-clad girl (Isabelle Townsend). They exchange hellos and she asks about the box, whose it is, and what's in it. Barton says he doesn't know and asks if she's in pictures. She tells him not to be silly and turns toward the ocean, uncannily assuming the Bathing Beauty's pose. The screen cuts to black.

OFF THE WALL

Fink opens on art imitating life (his play based on his family) and ends with "life" mimicking art (the Bathing Beauty). The opening salvo is more obvious: Barton's play is a product of his brain. The close is abstruse and coincidental if taken on face value. We think how odd that Barton would run into a woman—his muse—who has effectively drifted off his wall onto the beach. It is strange if we view California as reality; but if we see Hollywood as part of Barton's ongoing head game, then the ending is nothing more than what's conjured in his mind. His play and the beach scene are artful bookends exposing how singular the movie's design is to its subject: From A to Z, the movie focuses on Barton's head and the contents housed within, his personal box of wonder—his "life of the mind."[5]

The strange satire sandwiched between these cranial views turned inside-out churns comedy, film noir, and horror to plot a deeply sardonic tale of a writer enmeshed in thinking. His struggle to make sense of his vision of Hollywood as a dark, stifling, even cruel place becomes ours. The two settings of Broadway and Hollywood amplify the focus on art and become targets of an extensive lampoon. Barton's first love of live theatre may not get as full a critique as L.A., but it gets its share of digs. Producers like Derek (I. M. Hobson) want a big return on their money, patrons like Poppy (Meagen Fay) and Richard (Lance Davis) are shallow, and the critics fawn over the writer du jour. Yet, in spite of these drawbacks, Barton thinks he and his theatre group can make a difference via the Great White Way. Tinsel Town is another story.

Hollywood is an artistic hotbed of fantasy. Understanding that it traffics in unreality is key. A telling phrase of Garland's (David Warrilow) in the screenplay—but sadly not in the movie—spells this out: "if I can use that word [*realism*] and Hollywood in the same breath."[6] Perhaps the line too clearly points to the disjunction between reality and appearance that makes up so much of *Fink*'s California. Clear is simply not *Fink*'s objective; for, in its story of a writer becoming unmoored from reality, the focal point is the nebulous realms of art, dreams, and artifice. The movie deceptively charts a feast-tofamine trajectory, tracing a playwright's heady days to his head-y daze as a screenwriter. Distortions and magnifications create a picture showing that much, if not all, of the West Coast is mental, not physical.

Barton argues a screenwriting stint would strand him from his inspiration, the common man. In California his fears materialize. He isolates himself at the Earle—won't even consider moving when Jack suggests it—and though he befriends a seeming average Joe, he does not register Charlie's common manliness. Yet such ostensible irony is a joke on the viewer. It turns out Charlie is not common. The boy next door is a killer—a movie madman who can bend metal bedposts and enter blazing rooms. Ignoring dialogue clues—pointing to Barton's vanity, hopes, and fears—can put the viewer's befuddlement on par with Barton's. If we can't see his Hollywood sojourn-turned-nightmare as a sardonic trip through an off-the-wall fantasy, where things *seem*, we might lack the empathy that Audrey says is a requisite for comprehension.

"There are things in [the movie] that are intentionally ambiguous and certain things we think are fairly obvious but aren't stated," Joel Coen said.[7] Such deliberate ambiguity supports the idea stressed throughout that dreams, in which uncertainty reigns, are essential thought and plot drivers. Whether events at a given time constitute a daydream, brainstorm, or nightmare is not as important as understanding the West Coast is a product of Barton's vivid, twisted imagination. The Coens simply forgo the use of customary transparent markers that distinguish dreams from fictional reality. Such a choice draws us cryptically into the plot through Barton's mind's eye, a place that mixes reality with fantasy to create fiction.

The presentation of Barton's adventures suggests writer's block, but really his creative crankshaft may be in high gear, re-creating the movie-making capital as a madman's lair. *Fink*'s derelict Hollywood is akin to Nathanael West's description of "miraculous" events painted realistically, in his 1933 novel *The Day of the Locust*.

> . . . artists of the Middle Ages, when doing a subject like the raising of Lazarus from the dead or Christ walking on water, were careful to keep all the details intensely realistic. . . . [They] seemed to think that fantasy could be made plausible by a humdrum technique.[8]

Barton's work troubles are run-of-the mill to be sure, but extraordinary events chip away at plausibility. Surrealism is at play, and the bookend views of Barton's think tank offer a key to the subjectivity.

The opening scene offers a steady diet of dream talk that foretells what transpires in L.A. It also puts the viewer on notice of the upcoming dreamland by freely mixing objectivity and subjectivity. The first shot is a long meandering take exploring the backstage activity, stopping on Barton watching his play. The play's end prompts a new angle. Cutting from a shot on Barton to what he is looking at, an objective angle changes to a subjective angle that captures Barton's view from the wings. It holds that position as he walks into what is essentially his own POV shot, transferring his view to the viewer. Such blurring of objective and subjective shots is key to Barton's solipsism.

The opening shot of Barton intently soaking in his drama suggests the incestuous relationship between his life and art. His family has inspired his characters (Lil is based on his mother Lillian, the Kid on himself), and their dialogue conveys vital information about disputed consciousness. Lil claims that the Kid is "Dreamin' again"; he counters, "Not any more . . . I'm awake for the first time in years."[9] This conflict from the writer's head sets up a main tension that is carried throughout his California trip: dreaming versus wakefulness.

The Coens share a line of influence from Plato through Descartes and surrealist artists like Magritte, in which artists and philosophers explore the fertile disjunction between perception and reality. Here the filmmakers use surrealism, deliberately painting in broad strokes of the unknown for effect. After Audrey turns up dead, Barton worries that he has lost his mind. His question finally voices our own uncertainty about events, and we sigh with momentary relief at the bizarre turns of his experiences. But his self-reflection quickly evaporates. Longer lasting are arty, oneiric evocations. Lil's dreaming line, for example, is a passing note in *Bare Ruined Choirs* but a motif in the film: The Kid (aka Barton) has a propensity to dream.

The dream and its depot—the head—are vehicles for a strange journey through the creative process. Shown in bed as often as he is at the typewriter, Barton fuses dreaming and art. Like dreams, the movie stops short of delivering absolutes. But it drolly riffs on answers to the elusive question: What is dramatic art? In the end when the Bathing Beauty asks what's in the box, Barton answers confoundingly but rightly that he isn't sure. We can't be certain either, for our signifiers have been jumbled. Horror movie conventions suggest the gruesome answer of Audrey's head—which has become his perverse muse. Yet, if the movie turns his mind's life inside out, the box is simply a metaphor for *his* head, a vessel empty or overflowing with ideas.

The Coens shape the viewer's experience like Barton's so that we too are caught in a place with no discernible borders between fantasy and reality. Yet there are indications of the Coens' artful legerdemain. Perhaps Barton is dreaming; perhaps he is creating. *Perhaps* is the operative idea, for the mind is a difficult place to pin down. Ideas planted in New York strangely bear fruit in California. Complementing the dream references are embedded stories about interpretation, and in addition to the bookend inside views are verbal bookends focused on jokes.

The film's New York section closes on Garland clarifying that his remark about common men in Hollywood was said in jest. The California section closes on a similar note. The parting "don't be silly" line of dialogue may rank with I. A. L. Diamond's kicker to *Some Like It Hot* (1958)—the presumably heterosexual suitor Osgood Feeling (Joe E. Brown) shrugs with an enigmatic response, "nobody's perfect," when his date Daphne (Jack Lemmon) unmasks himself as a man.[10] Both clinchers thoroughly entertain and puzzle. The Bathing Beauty's line packs a funny, self-conscious if enigmatic punch to Barton's ironic question, "Are you in pictures?"[11] Yes, of course, she is. After he has stared at her artistic likeness, we now watch her celluloid image. The Coens' two finales to the New York and California sequences point to a joke underlying artifice.

Ultimately, the final scene is a parody of form, that thing with which the Coens often toy. Subverted conventions distract us into thinking things *are* when really they *seem to be*. A delphic mix of genre rules, strange camera angles and misleading audio cues leads us astray, making us search for meaning so that we, like Barton, foreground the quest for logic over the simple pleasure of enjoying a wild, nonsensical fantasy. Think of Bill's reason for writing (he "enjoy[s] making things up") versus Barton's (who says "writing comes from a great inner pain").[12] Whose theory holds, or do they both? Barton is our main guide, but Bill provides a tip-off.

Fink's unveiling of a creative mind depicts a place with few boundaries and where logic need not apply. In exploring how fiction is created, the movie makes fun of narrative rules, riffing on so-called writing formulas (morality plays, road maps), all the while following some, too. The result is a complex network of mixed signals that obscure our ability to make total sense of things. Audrey tells Barton several times that understanding results from empathy. Barton comprehends little despite an outsized ego that at times makes him seem monstrous. Using him as a poster child for an obtuse spectator—a nightmare existence for an artist—the Coens confect a fantastic story that calls into question how we intake and understand art.

In California, Barton becomes a nightmare version of an artist: a socially conscious writer blind to the common man's plight, a slave to Hollywood moguls, and a tattletale who outs his noisy neighbor. For us to empathize with him, we must escape his tunnel vision that traps him inside his mind. If we fall for believing his dream, we are doomed to incomprehension on par with his. But if we grasp that we are seeing an artist's inner machinations—a writer wrestling with his soul, as Jack later implies—understanding and empathy flow. Indications of the Coens' cinematic head game come early if

John Turturro struggles to write a screenplay under the portrait of a Bathing Beauty. (Credit: 20th Century Fox/Photofest © 20th Century Fox)

cryptically. Ultimately, the entire film is akin to watching a play from backstage, which is where things start.

INSIDE VIEW

Fink starts with a behind-the-scenes look at a play in progress, a creative world turned inside-out. This view is both oxymoronic and backward—important dualities that figure into the upcoming dreamworld. The movie's curtain-raiser is the play's ending, and though we listen to one scene, we watch another. As we hear dialogue from the play, the camera explores the backstage activity, finally homing in on Barton. The separation of sound and picture shows a crucial dichotomy between two "views" of artifice: the world created by the protagonist (his play) and the world outside it (what goes in to creating a performance).

We meet Barton through his creations, which eerily forecast his down-and-out-in-Beverly-Hills experience. From the start sound is of paramount importance. The Kid, Barton's stand-in, delivers lines describing Barton's departure from the Earle to a tee: "I'm kissin' it all goodbye, these four stinkin' walls, the six flights up."[13] In the end, Barton departs from his room on the sixth floor of the hotel, leaving behind its peeling wallpaper with its goopy paste, which Barton even smells at one point. "The el that roars by at three A.M. like a cast-iron wind. I'll miss 'em—like hell I will!"[14] The Earle's sixth floor hall sounds like an eerie wind tunnel. Barton leaves the place without looking back. Though at one point Barton says he'll miss Charlie, he seems of a different mind at the end. He is ready for another story. The prescient dialogue exposes the movie's meticulous symmetry. Such narrative design is a good indicator that just about all that we see is an artistic rendering of Barton's head.

The inherently loopy first-shall-be-last message showcases the Coens' authorial muscle with a big fat wink. The scenario winds so tightly around itself that careful scrutiny shows it could only exist as art or by artifice—or within the dream realm. From the pessimistic "bare ruined" preview to the postapocalypse punch line, the story's off-the-wall views of art as dream—or nightmare—are where opposites coexist. Not only does *Fink* open on a closing curtain, Barton's play closes on a philosophical twilight: Lil's "It is late" observation is countered with Maury's, "Not any more, Lil. It's early."[15] Both are correct. Subjectivity is the determining factor, and the play underscores interpretation and point of view—the alpha and omega of observation, the viewer's primary engagement.

Viewpoint is a perennial Coen subject. Perspective is critical to *Blood Simple*'s deadly game of knowledge. The end twist is that Abby's blindness beats out evil Visser's omniscient and Ray's enlightened POV. *Miller's Crossing* shows that while Tom can see the angles, he cannot truly know what someone else is thinking. *The Big Lebowski* avoids a conclusive ending to the mystery—Lebowski obviates the Dude's theory. *Fargo* plays with perspective by pretending to be true, an intriguing development that pits audience knowledge against its beliefs.

Point of view is critical to *Fink*, which shows the stuff between an artist's ears is both his gift to the world and his bane of existence—expressing John Milton's idea from *Paradise Lost* that "the mind is its own place, and in itself can make a Heaven of Hell, a Hell of Heaven." Jack's accusation that Barton "think[s] the whole world revolves around whatever rattles inside that little kike head" is uproarious and ironic.[16] What looks on the surface to be a comment on Barton's ego actually spells out what the movie is all about: Everything we see is an expression of Barton's mind, a locus where things *seem* rather than are and where anything goes.

The burrowing into Barton's mind begins with the credit sequence, during which the camera moves down and toward the wallpaper. This downward probing movement is repeated in the first scene with the camera following the stage ropes. Like the play's dialogue, these visuals predict the Hollywood tale: It will probe Barton's head and descend into the mayhem there. The opening long shot lands on a playwright engrossed in his play.

A similar effect occurs Barton's first night at the Earle when he is captivated by the Bathing Beauty. Time and again, the film shows how art is *the* thing, Barton's be-all end-all. His attraction to the picture, which grabs him like little else, is funny because though he aspires to high art, what he takes a shine to in California is this simple picture. Tellingly, it is the thing that releases him from the hotel's no-exit, "day or a lifetime" grind.[17] Closing in on the picture from an over-the-shoulder shot, the camera slowly crops him out. The following cuts between observer and observed emphasize that it is not so much what we're looking at but his take on it.

Point of view, says Coen cinematographer Roger Deakins, is the single quality a successful director of photography must possess.[18] Chockfull of inventive POV shots that disguise subjectivity as objectivity, *Fink* revels in Barton's point of view. The camera can be deceptive. Just as Barton falls prey to believing his reveries, the viewer can fall victim to seeing the dream as reality. Though the Coens have claimed "surprise" at the movie's "misconstruction," they've also admitted its portentous tone can make people think "something really important is . . . actually happening" when it is not.[19] Believing the ominous mood and oddness is tempting. The film language coaxes us into Barton's worldview by making us see through the dreamer's eyes, creating a fine line between knowledge and belief. By drawing us into his confusion, the movie sets up the equation: Art is to reality what dreams are to life; both are imaginary events beyond one's control and inescapable for a period of time. To understand the daedal dream, the viewer must unravel the finespun comedy of knowledge and belief.[20]

SEEING IS BELIEVING?

Fink represents the flip side of the imagination coin first tossed in *Raising Arizona*, a film about the mind's rich potential for creating solutions. Both movies incorporate gaggles of literary allusions, erupt into apocalypses, and end on dreamscapes. But where Hi constantly frees himself by envisioning release from prison, bachelorhood, his wicked alter ego, and his childless marriage, Barton's scenarios keep him trapped inside his head. In the end he extricates himself from Charlie, but the experience has no perceptible effect on him and he emerges from the ordeal disturbingly unchanged. So while the final scene suggests the dame on the beach might be his next story, the viewer stays stuck in his head to the very end.

Like the chimerical brainchild Hi conjures under extreme stress, Charlie is a product of Barton's dubious thoughts on screenwriting. Barton worries that a Hollywood move will make him an exile—a prediction that comes to pass on one level. Yet, Charlie seems the "working-class stiff" about whom Barton wants to write. The irony is that though he insults Charlie with such characterization, he can't see how his neighbor could be a good wrestler model. He can't, that is, until he finds out that Charlie is the uncommon Madman Mundt—a Hollywood wet dream. Charlie is the stuff of which horror movies—not social dramas—are made. Barton's mad alter ego Charlie finally reveals all: "Look upon me! I'll show you the life of the mind!"[21] And so *Fink* has it both ways: all the elements of a Hollywood blockbuster put together in an anything but Hollywood style. Thanks to its dream-logic structure, the film can at once exploit Tinsel Town fare, explore the artistic process, and razz the famed movie capital.

Fink's assault on the Hollywood dream has parallels to *Raising Arizona's* critique of the American Dream. Both satires rely on superstretched sureality for their attack. Leonard Smalls, for instance, appears first as a dream figure then turns "real." Things are similar but much more adumbrative in Fink-land. After the New York setup, it looks like Barton goes to California, but an actual trip is debatable. The viewer takes the crashing wave and hotel check-in as a setting change, but there are no new setting markers to match the opening's "New York City . . . 1941" title cards. Though plausible events at first outweigh such subtle omissions, the weirder his Hollywood stay becomes, the more we reconsider the fictional "reality." Swallowing things at face value lands us in trouble. But if we see the signposts pointing toward dreams, heads, and creativity, we can distinguish between knowledge and belief and see things as a creative think box ticking away.

The many shoes ready for a shoeshine in Barton's hall illustrate the disconnection between assumption and evidence. They indicate a busy hotel; yet, except for one man glimpsed grabbing his shoes, Charlie and Barton are the only guests seen. So where are the shoe owners, and why so much ado about footwear? If we infer California and the Earle are Barton's creations, perhaps the shoes, like the Bathing Beauty, represent characters yet to be. After all, we do *hear* other guests, and Barton's characters such as those in the play and Charlie are introduced by sound.

When Barton checks in to the Earle, Charlie asks him if he is a transient or resident guest. Coupled with the choice, Barton's inexact response suggests his stay at the hotel is tied to his imagination, a transient place where we're all exiles and somewhere a writer can get lost. Charlie connects the dots when he gripes that while he is a resident Barton is a lucky tourist. The viewer, like Barton, may believe the writer's inner workings are real in large part because they are possible and realistic up to a point. But such reasoning is tantamount to a dreamer believing he's awake. Ample then overwhelming evidence reveals the hotel's strange world is filtered through Barton's vivid, artistic mind—his nightmare story turned inside out.

Like magicians who direct attention away from the trick to avoid revealing how it's done, the Coens use visual and acoustic ploys to make us believe what we see is reality and not, up to a point, question it. The resulting conflict between knowledge and belief lets us slip comfortably into the dreamer's shoes. And yet alongside these feints is a road map, the first "page" of which is Barton's self-reflexive play, orchestrated as the first key to understanding events as a projection of Barton's mind. From the start sound, rife with omens, helps to reveal the view.

The title of Barton's play, *Bare Ruined Choirs*, suggests ill tidings for the writer since the Kid—who represents Barton—counts himself among the desperate group: "We're part of that choir, both of us—yeah, and you, Maury, and Uncle Dave too!"[22] Translated, the lines set up the working-class paradigm of which he and his family are part. It's a clever, twisted duality. We think this writer of social dramas will pen uplifting, hope-filled stories of the struggle against brute forces. But we are informed off the bat that in his world, the brutal forces are victorious.

The opening, backstage tour peruses the mechanics that animate dramatic artifice and includes a good look at an author. These early moments clue us in to Barton's closeness to his creations. The Kid dressed in hat and overcoat and carrying a suitcase looks like Barton upon his arrival in California; he also resembles Charlie, suggesting a kinship between Barton, the Kid, and the traveling salesman—in other words between Barton and his creations.

Well before the all-out California dreaming, the soundscape invites us to question what is presented to us. In this world neither hearing nor seeing should be believing. At the play's end, the proud playwright mouths its closing line, visually accentuating his creator role. Caven's review amplifies the stress on sound through choice language describing Barton: "A tough new voice in the American theater has arrived."[23] In California, the play on sound continues with the hotel's aural canals and wind tunnels and the word *audible* that graces all of Barton's screenplay drafts. To open the film on Barton's play establishes his head as a focal point, and the postplay scene carries the focus on his head forward, emphasizing both point of view and ego. First off, he enters the restaurant through a subjective camera, which again gives import to his line of vision. At the table, he exhibits smugness even though he feigns humility. Ego becomes a hallmark of the writer and pushes the head conceit into satire—and close to farce.

HEAD GAMES

In the end, everything—Barton's play and screenplay and the entire film—is about himself, as all the titles suggest. *The Burly Man*, his Hollywood Bogey Man, is more of the same. In a telling shot with the shoes, Barton and Charlie swap mixed-up footwear, their symmetrical alignment on the bed suggesting Charlie is Barton's mirror opposite—or alter ego. The whole story is a figurative head swelling of ideas that all lead back to the artist. Barton's dilemma isn't so much that he cannot write; it's that everything reflects back on himself.

Charlie is what Barton is not—a big, strong, sexually active extrovert to Barton's introverted, repressed, bookish self. The writer is cut off from things; Charlie is tuned into the world around him. He hears and feels everything. Though he is chummy with Barton, he winces at Barton's snobbery when the writer refuses to shake hands when they meet. This is not the first indication of Barton's superior attitude. He looks down his nose at the fishmonger; he complains about the theatre people; he reacts strangely to the genial Chet. But with Charlie, Barton's condescension buys tit for tat, propels a gilded friendship, and sparks a dangerous head game. Charlie claims he can't keep up with the writer's "mental gymnastics," but he proves a brilliant opponent—a match for his maker.[24]

Like the Kid, Charlie's dialogue gives a foretaste of events. "You might say I sell peace of mind. Insurance is my game—door-to-door, human contact. . . . Hell yes. Because I believe in it. Fire, theft, and casualty are not things that only happen to other people."[25] After their first, strained meeting, Charlie's visits ("human contact") brighten Barton's day. The "fire, theft, and casualty" bit refers to the sixth floor's inferno, the shoe swap, and murders. And his point that unfortunate events don't just befall other people—complete with the ironic "that's what I tell 'em," pointing to the conversation at hand—is a clear-cut warning to the writer. On a more positive note, Charlie also gives his creator insurance for finishing the screenplay. As Barton's hero ("Make me your wrestler"), he will eventually help bring the screenwriter literal peace of mind—and possibly *piece* of mind, considering Audrey's head is part of his payback scheme.[26]

John Turturro as Barton and John Goodman as Charlie become seeming buddies, but Charlie's got a secret and a secret identity. (Credit: 20th Century Fox/Photofest © 20th Century Fox)

Charlie is both Barton's invention and his insidious foil who would expose the havoc of the street poet's mind. Barton's initial worry about distancing himself from the common man pans out, and Charlie embodies the kind of man Barton *expects* to meet there: a monster. Barton's fantastic "what if" scenario becomes a head trip—not a California trip—a pipe dream bursting under the pressure of phantasmagoric fears. The Hotel Earle is a conceit for the creative process, a strange corpus which Barton inhabits while diving into his writerly mind and turning its inside mayhem out. If we listen and watch closely, we can't miss the fixation on heads, the powerful metaphor the film exploits with deep, dark, devious mischief.

The word *head* appears some sixty times in the *Fink* screenplay. Characters cock them, hold them, and arrange their hats on them. Charlie and Barton complain of headaches. Keeping and losing heads are ideas infused throughout. Lou and Jack talk about owning heads, and the detectives talk about missing ones. A grisly scene in the script that didn't make it into the movie prefaces Charlie's return with Pete's decapitated head rolling into the hall.

Charlie speaks the word *head* first and uses it more than anyone else. He boosts Barton's ego with the adage "You've got a head on your shoulders" and then misquotes an axiom, "Where there's a head, there's hope." After grousing about his ear goop, Charlie jokes about being unable to trade in his head. When Barton lobs another insult at him, Charlie mutters, "Well ain't that a kick in the head!"[27] In short, Charlie bangs around Barton's head like the Kid walking on and off stage. Charlie is an idea sprung from a dark recess. Every time Barton sits in front of his typewriter, Charlie walks through Barton's door like an idea entering the writer's head. Charlie's New York trip, taken because things are "all balled up at the Head Office," helps Barton unravel what must come next: a couple of detectives.[28] When Audrey loses her head, ironically, her loss is Barton's gain as Charlie's box (presumably her head) becomes the writer's macabre muse, and we get to see what kind of horror translates as inspiration for him.

Audrey's writing-coach visit throws the horror genre into high gear. Prior to her arrival Barton sleeps on his bed, his glasses perched atop the pillow on his head. He looks like he is blocking out the external world—a bad situation for a writer. Help arrives with the sound of a bell, one of the film's key sonic elements. The elevator ding puts him on his feet. He scrambles for his glasses and greets Audrey, a model of calm amid his raging sea of deadline stress. She tries to pacify him by getting down to work, but in laying out some writing tips, she lets slip that she is Bill's ghostwriter. Barton is incensed to learn his hero is a phony, but fails to see the hypocrisy of his situation.

Audrey again mentions that empathy is a prerequisite for understanding. Her remark to the writer is good advice for the viewer. Then, the two have sex as it might be portrayed in a 1940s film. The camera angles down their bodies and lingers on them just long enough to catch shoes coming off while one foot stays planted on the floor. Such details mock the puritanical Hays' Production Code which would have been in effect in *Fink*'s 1941 setting.[29]

Typically shy of intimate scenes, the Coens' camera strays from the budding romance on the bed and aims for the bathroom sink. There, it "frames up its drain, a perfect black circle in the porcelain white . . . [and is] enveloped by it," the screenplay reads.[30] The shot dives into the plumbing system, Charlie's purported acoustic connection to all the Earle's happenings. The overt sexual symbolism spoofs and perverts an oft-used metaphor inspired by the Hays Code that encouraged emblematic intercourse to the real thing. Among countless examples is Hitchcock's *North by Northwest* ending shot of a train roaring into a tunnel after Roger Thornhill (Cary Grant) embraces the spy who loves him, Eve Kendall (Eva Marie Saint).

The Coens' postmodern update of the metaphor plunges the sexual conceit into a nightmarish gag that coalesces many of the Earle's sounds. Snaking through the pipes in another down-and-in movement, the visuals plumb the plumbing metaphor of Barton's creative channels as we hear a disturbing, familiar soundscape. Barton's and Audrey's moans blend into a woman's painful cries; a man who sounds like Charlie screams; dragging, scraping, and swoosh sounds mix in; water running then dripping echoes in the dank, hollow space—all noises (read ideas) we have heard before. Going beyond mere sexual imagery, the strange odyssey gives us a quick aural tour of Barton's thought passages. Like Charlie who hears the hotel's noises through the pipes, the viewer gets another inside tour of Barton's creative process, a slither through the hotel story creature that Barton inhabits.

The drain's "perfect black circle" has a rhyming image: the trumpet. At the end of the USO sequence, the camera swishes toward the bandstand, disappearing into the horn. The rhyme shores up the connection between on-screen events, the Earle, Barton's head, and his fears. After Barton acts like a lunatic at the jamboree, a dissolve transports us back to his hallway where we hear familiar dialogue. The detectives are reading a passage from *The Burlyman* that is almost a word-for-word match with lines from *Bare Ruined Choirs*: "We'll be hearing from that crazy wrestler, and I don't mean a postcard."[31] The film has produced a black comedic circle. We're back where we started: with Barton's creations.

Circular symbolism abounds. Repeatedly, the camera twists around the sleeping writer. In New York, he dines with the theatre crowd at a semicircular booth. (The studio's similarly shaped lunch booth called for in the screenplay never made it to the film.) Globes decorate Jack's office. Chet spins the registration book almost a full 360 degrees when Barton signs in, and the camera continues the twist. At the end when Charlie/Karl releases Barton from the bed, a metal ball rolls conspicuously across the floor. The circle is a cipher that helps decrypt the self-referential plot. The pipe sequence symbolizes not just sexual intercourse but a deep probe into the pitch-black pathways of the writer's most personal space: his thoughts.

"DAYLIGHT IS A DREAM"

"Daylight is a dream if you've lived with your eyes closed," the Kid remarks.[32] Technically, Barton's eyes are open in California; but practically he is blind to his world, stuck in a daylight dream, full of art, turmoil, and fear. The satire holds a mirror up to image-saturated L.A. and makes grimaces in it, tarnishing Hollywood's Golden Era through a heady exposé of its sadistic system. Like the Earle's peeling wallpaper that reveals a sticky, stinking wall behind it, the movie pulls back an artificial skin covering ugly, naked truths. The big man helming Capitol Studios is Barton's best fair-weather friend. Cross him and become a Sisyphus, doomed to script rewrites that never get produced. In many respects, Jack's draconian payback system parallels Charlie's.

Embodying Barton's biggest anxieties are Charlie and Jack, phantoms who tumble into the film's complex dreamscape. Early on, Barton states that he wants to "make a difference" and realize what "we've been dreaming about—the creation of a new, living theatre of, about and for the common man."[33] He explains that moving to California, right when he is on the brink of success, would shatter his career dreams. As with so much of the film, his words are prescient, and his misgivings take the form of large, overpowering men. His California is a frightening, at times gripping, gory, sardonic look at a writer selling out his dream for a Hollywood nightmare.

While much of the movie suggests that Barton is hardly thinking—he stares blankly at the page punching scant words into his typewriter—in "truth" he is thinking hard. He pictures not the Hollywood highlife but the screenwriter's low life. In this vision, he is not just a pawn in the studio's cynical chess game. He is also a party to murder. In befriending a killer posing as a common-man type, Barton wrestles with his soul vicariously through his putative soul mate. Part of Barton's personal hell is an acute focus on minutiae that crowd out the larger picture. Take the mosquito, for instance, which commands significant screen time. Barton battles the bloodthirsty bugger three times, and its bite marks spark two conversations. When Jack meets his new writer, Barton looks like an acne-ridden adolescent—a role he embodies. Jack asks Barton and Lou about the splotches. Later, Ben notes the red spots and gives a short entomology lesson about mosquitoes being unable to live in a desert climate like Los Angeles's. A logical follow-up question is that if there are no mosquitoes here, what is flying around and biting him?

For starters, Ben is technically correct: In the 1940s, L.A. was too dry for mosquitoes. So why include this fact? On the one hand, facts don't matter—because the film is fiction, it needn't subscribe to any "reality" but its own self-made one, which is largely the movie's point. But something else is happening, too, for the turning point that pushes the comedy into horror is the shocking coda to the mundane mosquito finale. Once Barton discovers there are two dead bodies in his bed, his victory over the bug curdles, just like his entire Hollywood experience, except that, strangely, things start going well. So why is the mosquito so important? It fits into the philosophical debate between knowledge and belief and gives the latter the upper hand.

The Coens' artful dodge with the bloodsucker appears in the screenplay with a giveaway suggesting the indefinite: "The hum—a mosquito, perhaps—stops."[34] This ambiguity is conveyed onscreen via a disjuncture between sight and sound: We hear but do not see the mosquito at first, and being familiar with the sound, we assume its presence. Next time we see its shadow, and when it finally appears, it is larger than life, taking up the entire screen in a monstrous close-up. But is it there or is it a decoy?

At the end of Barton's first insect hunt, its hum resumes after Barton gets in bed. The telltale pitch accompanies a camera twist over Barton. Perhaps the odd angle is a joke: the mosquito's POV. Or maybe it is just a detail of Barton's crazy dream—as if he is both author and star of a dream spiraling out of control. Bizarre camera movements help distract us from questioning the bug (and other things), just as the mosquito distracts Barton from writing and observing the world beyond room 621. Part of the joke is that Barton picks up on nuisances like loud neighbors and insect hums but fails to listen to his neighbor's hard-luck stories or consider America's entrance into World War II. His morality tale is one of isolation and blindness.

Though Barton's final round with the mosquito climaxes with the viewer's first sighting, such payoff occurs when Barton's eyes are at their weakest—yet the bug is humungous. It is the only scene in which the writer appears for any length of time without his glasses, a telling detail. Without his glasses, previous actions indicate, his eyes might as well be shut. This scene begins like the others except that he scans the room sans spectacles. A reverse angle shows his POV as usual, but unlike the other scenes, there is full marriage of sight and sound. Alternating cuts between Barton's eyes and the insect's trail culminate with the insect landing and supping on Audrey's back. An extreme close-up (ECU) of Barton's bugged-out eyes is followed by an ECU on the mosquito, full screen. He slaps the monster bug dead-on, but when he nudges Audrey to see why she has not stirred, the dead insect's red spot floods into a pool of Audrey's blood.

The montage coaches us that we see the mosquito as we see everything else: *through Barton's eyes*. Reality and clarity are not a big part of his vision—especially with naked eyes. Why would we trust him and his poor eyesight as our viewing guide? We believe a lot of what is happening based on situational knowledge—the hum, the bites, the mosquito in close-up, and Barton himself—while we brush aside the one extenuating zoological fact about mosquitoes not living in deserts. In effect, our eyes are closed to knowledge but open to the belief. If Barton has fallen so headlong into his head that such realistic details are lost on him, the audience suffers from a similar affliction.

The mosquito scenes collectively reveal the soundtrack and camera as unreliable narrators that draw us into Barton's twisted inner world. The bug reinforces that perspective and dreams are key to the film. Can we easily believe that a hum wakes him up while a brutal murder next to him does not? Other illogical details help point to Barton's improbable experiences. These include, in increasing order of implausibility, Barton's not throwing out his blood-stained mattress, the Earle erupting into an inexplicable fire, and Charlie returning to his inferno of a room. Again, close scrutiny shows we're in the realm of daylight dreams.

Dreams are integral to the Coens' cinemascape. Oneiric sequences that confuse story "reality" with altered states of consciousness occur in *Blood Simple* and *Raising Arizona*, as well as *The Big Lebowski*, *O Brother, Where Art Thou?*, *The Man Who Wasn't There*, and *Miller's Crossing*. An exchange in *Crossing* resonates with important *Fink* ideas. When a man rebuffs his friend's gentle prodding to wake up, explaining he's already awake, the friend observes that his eyes were shut, to which he responds, "Who're you going to believe?"[35] The conversation is similar to Lil's observation about the Kid's dreaming and his denials.

The mosquito exploits our gullibility to believe and hammers home the potential horror of paying attention to the wrong thing. Regarding the former, the mosquito scenes share some common ground with the fly in *Raising Arizona*. When Smalls, making the move to the film's "real" world, tells a furniture tycoon he's got flies, the businessman scoffs at such a possibility in his airtight office. Moments later, the biker plucks said fly out of thin, climate-controlled air. The catch is improbable, but is the whole scene unbelievable? Odds are we suspend our disbelief, even as we try to figure out just where Smalls fits in the fiction. His conversion to a "real" character compels the viewer, consciously or not, to reconsider belief, knowledge, and understanding vis-à-vis perception and story comprehension. Situational "knowledge" can prove false. We change our view about Smalls and conclude he is as "real" as the other characters. Similarly, the *Fink* mosquito, though more cryptic, helps convey the congenital iffyness of "reality" in fiction, especially the Coens' variety. Furthermore, there's mordant humor in Barton's predicament: he ignores "real" problems while making a mountain of the mosquito molehill.

The mosquito hum, set to the same pitch as the main theme's strings, ties together Barton's inner and outer worlds, suggesting they are one. It is the hum that awakens Barton symbolically if not literally. Into his empty room (his mind) fly ideas: a Bathing Beauty (a dame) and a mosquito (a noisy, bloody nuisance). These parallel another set of ideas: dame Audrey and noisy, bloody pest Charlie, who also enter his workspace (his head). The token "dames" visualize beauty and are exploited by the plot. Charlie and to an extent the mosquito are antagonists first heard, then "seen." They all support some standard movie conventions while also forming narrative twists. The mosquito is to the dream what Charlie is to his fiction—elaborate "rationalizations" of Barton's world. With so much focus on dreams and art, the movie amounts to an exercise in hermeneutics and so a look at the hotel's goings-on is in order.

WELCOME TO HOTEL CALIFORNIA

Barton's story takes off from his play about working-class folk and dreaming, then settles in Hollywood, a place synonymous with artifice. Dreams are so potently conjured in the movie-making capital that they shroud the Earle in an enigma. Though we understand the hotel to be generally located somewhere on the outskirts of a city renowned as a wholesale dream factory, more important, it is located in the back of Barton's noggin. Otherwise how else could he have described the place so accurately in his play "before" he "arrived" there?

Echoes of New York reverberate in California. Low rumblings like those underneath his walk on stage accompany the evocative West Coast wave. The ominous sound seems to announce the horror elements in waiting. From a not-so-peaceful Pacific Ocean we cut to the hotel's enormous, stagnant, gothic-infused interior characterized by hot-house plants and not a living soul.[36] Dwarfed by the lobby's capaciousness, the playwright pauses at the door so that the seclusion and gloom can sink in. Ironically, this writer, who wants to live with, and speak for and to the masses, has chosen an empty, insular new home.

Familiar genre conventions kick in and lead us toward known cinema worlds. The Hotel Earle's creature comforts and atmosphere stem in part from the film noir tradition. The hotel's sense of alienation echoes the mood of John Huston's noirish *Key Largo* (1949). *Largo's* hotel setting provides shelter from a ferocious storm outside while internal tempests stir among the hostages and kidnappers. The Earle's metaphors are more personal and body-oriented, but it too houses inner turbulence: the creative mind at work. In size and atmosphere, the Earle also resembles Nora Desmond's mansion in *Sunset Boulevard* (1950), another locale through which a stumbling sleepwalking wanders. Both movies examine the predicament of a writer struggling to exist in Hollywood's dreamworld where reality and dreams mesh with fantasy.

The Earle is also a revenant horror-film setting—the type of place you might expect voices to whisper "Get out!" and the characters to ignore them. In particular, the mood is that of psychological horror, found in such classics as Stanley Kubrick's *The Shining* (1980) and Roman Polanski's *The Tenant* (1976).[37] Ethan Coen acknowledges the latter's influence, explaining, "If you had to describe [*Fink*] generically, you couldn't do better—not that this is a genre—but it is kind of a Polanski movie. It is closer to that than anything else."[38] The film itself acknowledges Kubrick's influence. The sixth floor hallway and its old, green carpet are reminiscent of the haunted corridors in *The Shining's* Overlook Hotel, where Stephen King's Jack Torrance (Jack Nicholson) suffers a psychotic writer's block against the stunning visuals of Kubrick and production designer Roy Walker. Barton also suffers a kind of writer's block, but the horror derives from his inability to recognize that he is caught in his mind.

Like the Earle, the hotel and apartment-house settings of Kubrick's and Polanski's films, respectively, play an integral part in the main characters' mental decline—or perceived lapse in *Fink*'s case. In all three films, regardless of their actual spaciousness, the locations become a claustrophobic prison for the protagonists. Ambiguously real or imagined supernatural elements cloud the characters' psyches, eyesight, and thought processes, crippling them to a point of no return. Only in *Fink* does the antihero remain alive at the end, and though he literally walks out of the hotel, it is unclear that he has escaped its hell. We certainly haven't. At the end when he sees the Bathing Beauty, we are obviously still locked inside his head as he explores possibilities for his next script.

The abundant identifiable film references and genre conventions work on the same level as the mosquito. They dupe us into a comfort zone of recognition—a diversionary tactic that does an excellent job of luring us away from more important information. We become so engrossed with the act of recognition—perhaps to the point of self-congratulation—that we can easily become like Barton, blind to the reality, which is fantasy.

California has a decidedly different feel from the New York scenes. Time, for instance, is stretched, and the result is a sense that we're in a kind of twilight zone. A tap of the service bell sets off an unnaturally sustained ring that only stops when Chet mutes it. Barton seems unfazed, but the viewer can't miss such oddities. The place is empty, but the reservation box is full. Shoes sit outside every room, but with one minor exception, Charlie is the only other guest seen. What we believe and what we know about the Earle amount to a shell game. Suggestive but misleading audio and visual touches are easily mistranslated into conclusions better suited to objective fictions. Instead of seeing *Fink* as a meta first-person narrative, we think something is in the air, and our first guess is likely not a joke.

Religious touches bait the viewer into seeing the movie as a Faustian morality play, which, in part, it is. But all the bells and religious references are also miscues suggestive of the supernatural. We can easily draw an association between Chet's subterranean entrance and hell—especially when the connection seems forged with three intonations of the word "six" in the elevator ("six please," "next stop six," "this stop six"), which conjure up the Bible's sign for the devil: "666."[39] Pete (Harry Bugin), the elevator's cadaverous gatekeeper, even seems like a kind of evil twin of St. Peter. Such religious "clues" pique the viewer's curiosity while Barton, oblivious to any signs, seems as clueless as countless horror-film characters before him. Barton is not strictly this character type, but his ignorance adds to a sense of foreboding like the religious details.

While the rings carry a Christian flavor, they also echo New York. The first in-story ding occurs in the restaurant after Barton's play. A pageboy's bell summons Barton to the bar where Garland proposes a screenwriting gig. Touches of a Faustian bargain lace the scene when Barton argues a Hollywood stint might earn him money but lose him integrity. As if to highlight the impact of money on the proposed screenwriting venture, their conversation takes place in front of a cash register. Subsequent bells seem to fit into the writer's acknowledged fear that taking a screenwriting job would be like making a deal with the devil.

The Gothic is at work, too. Barton enters his "House of Usher" room and stares at it. Like the "vacant eye-like windows" in the short story by Edgar Allan Poe, Barton's room features two viewless windows that return his empty gaze with equally dull gloss. The metaphor of the hotel as an ailing creature soon lumbers to life. The wallpaper peels like drooping skin on a decrepit body, leaving behind a smelly goop that resembles Charlie's ear pus. The hotel and Charlie's symbiosis, as exemplified by the gunk and his knowledge of all goings-on, shows them to be part of the story body. And both derive from Barton's head.

In effect, Barton sets up shop in his mind. After unpacking his typewriter, he spies the Earle's motto, which stops him short. A possible description of hell, the idea of a "day or a lifetime" also describes the creative process. Stories are self-contained structures with no exits for their characters (like Charlie). Writers, by contrast, can leave whenever. *Fink* explores a realm of appearance and reality, where the writer walks among his creations. During his first night at the tenebrous hotel, his rest is disturbed by a flying pest . . . or not. Flights of fancy are just as plausible as reality in a film that's all about art—creating it (or trying to), "reading" it, understanding it, and most important laughing at it, and, if possible, escaping through it.

THE GREAT ESCAPE

Fink bursts with stories that illuminate different aspects of Barton's sojourn through his mind, yet he repels their influence. Charlie is half right about Barton's main flaw—true, he won't listen, but he also doesn't see. In his existential hell, he hears only pesky things like insects and neighbors while instructive stories and news of the war elude his attention. If only he could awake and sing, but unfortunately his lot is with the *Bare Ruined Choirs*. For the viewer, though, the many allusions leaven his dream and ultimately help us navigate his heady terrain.

Odets and Awake and Sing!

Barton is loosely based on leftist playwright Odets, whose *Awake and Sing!* is an inspiration for *Bare Ruined Choirs*. Both titles evoke music, and both works focus on dreams and champion the poor. Caven's descriptions of Barton's characters sharing a "brute struggle for existence" could have been lifted from Gerald Weales's biography on Odets whose characters "struggle for life amidst petty conditions."[40] Barton's bloated ego finds a model in Odets who purportedly proclaimed to the *New York Times* that he was the most talented dramatist.

Shakespeare's "Bare Ruined Choirs"

Bare Ruined Choirs is a phrase in Shakespeare's Sonnet 73, a meditation on old age and death: "That time of year thou may'st in me behold/When yellow leaves, or none, or few, do hang/Upon those boughs which shake against the cold,/Bare Ruined choirs where late the sweet birds sang." Fittingly, Barton's play instigates a meditation on artistic death. Echoing the point made by the poem's speaker that because life and thus careers are short, one must "love [them] well" and pursue one's passions before time runs out, Barton tells Garland that he should stay in New York and pursue his thespian dreams. In California, he suffers artistic death at Jack's hands.

The Book of Daniel, King Nebuchadnezzar, and "Solomon's Mammy"

When Bill signs a copy of his novel *Nebuchadnezzar* for Barton, a small, clever clue about Barton's dreamscape appears. The imprint "Swain and Pappas," while not based on an actual publishing house, has a real existence beyond the movie that ties into the movie's capriccio. Marshall W. Swain and George S. Pappas are philosophers whose writings on epistemology and metaphysics include *Essays on Knowledge and Justification*, a collection that scrutinizes the nature, bases, and limitations of knowledge and being—the same sort of ideas *Fink* probes.

Nebuchadnezzar, whose reign is chronicled in the Book of Daniel, also relates to Barton's journey. The title of Bill's novel recalls the Babylonian king who was plagued by troubling, inexplicable dreams—hint, hint. Instead of perusing Bill's book, Barton goes to the source. The biblical passage he reads touches on three of *Fink's* main subjects—dreams, interpretations, and heads—and is yet another interior text with seemingly predictive qualities: "And the king, Nebuchadnezzar, answered and said to the Chaldeans, I recall not my dream; if ye will not make known unto me my dream, and its interpretation, ye shall be cut in pieces, and of your tents shall be made a dunghill" (Dan. 2:5, King James). When Barton cannot make sense of his daylight dream, his friends are cut into pieces.

Besides his book's foreshadowing, Bill cryptically projects the future by referencing Solomon's "mammy," Bathsheba. Sensing that Barton will backstab him by wooing Audrey, Bill starts to talk about a biblical love triangle that ended badly for the cuckold. Through his "sojourn among the Philistines" phrase, Bill indirectly likens Barton, a Hollywood exile, to King David, the poet-shepherd turned military man who, before he became the Jewish ruler, was exiled in the land of Philista.[41] When King David takes a liking to the beautiful Bathsheba, who was married to the warrior Uriah, David has Uriah killed so he can have her for himself.[42] Their subsequent marriage produces Solomon. As with the biblical triangle, so with the movie's: Shortly after Barton falls for Audrey, Bill is killed.

Genesis

Barton feigns humility, propping himself up whenever he can. Though unattractive, his oversized ego is essential to the satire. In his mind's eye everything he encounters relates to him, his dreams, and his head. The epitome of his solipsism occurs when his words appear in the Bible. Its famous opening "In the beginning, God created the heaven and earth" is revised to "Fade in on a tenement building on Manhattan's Lower East Side."[43] His hubris here is on par with Goethe's Faust, who is so full of himself that he thinks his ideas should replace the scriptures. And yet a more playful, less blasphemous reading puts the appearance of Barton's screenplay within the satirical framework of creating art. Barton, though not the Supreme Creator, is *the* creator of his universes. Like all writers, he plays god to the kingdoms he creates. So what seems like sacrilege is really just a joke on the writing life.

Slave Ship and "Old Black Joe"

In Barton's Hollywood vision, the screenwriter is a slave. This metaphor's most prominent embodiment is Bill but Barton too is shackled by the end. Bill's sinking writing career finds him chained to the bottle and a screenplay titled *Slave Ship*, as his apartment door indicates. The title harks back to the 1937 movie of the same name, written by Bill's model, William Faulkner, and starring Wallace Beery, the actor slated for Barton's wrestling movie. Parts of the studio lot give form to the slave ship metaphor. The walkway to Bill's apartment is several feet above the ground and features side rails running along it, resembling a ship's deck. Further out on the lot by Ben's secretary's desk is a porthole-shaped window. Eventually, Lou and Jack spell out Barton's servitude in no uncertain terms: "The contents of your head are the property of Capitol Pictures" and "Anything you write will be the property of Capitol Pictures."[44]

The far-flung slave theme reflects the puny stature that movie moguls afforded screenwriters. As Lester Cole, a founding member of the Screen Writers Guild, put it, writers were "the niggers of the studio system."[45] Ben espouses this low opinion of writers while playing up casting prejudices prevalent in 1940s Hollywood when he asks Barton if he would play an Indian, arguing: "Writers come and go; we always need Indians."[46] His job offer to non–Native American Barton is another Hollywood dig.

Furthering the portrayal of an autocratic studio system is Bill's identification with the fictitious slave hero from "Old Black Joe," a folk song that syncs up to the film's themes. Bill is whistling the 1860 ditty when he and Barton meet. At the picnic, he adds words to the melody, prefiguring his eventual membership into Barton's bare-ruined chorus: "Gone are the days when my heart was young and gay/Gone are my friends from the cotton fields away/Gone from the

John Mahoney as Barton's fellow "slave" on the Hollywood ship, and Judy Davis as the film's token "dame." (Credit: 20th Century Fox/Photofest © 20th Century Fox)

earth to a better land I know/I hear their gentle voices calling Old Black Joe."[47] Bill finds solace in Stephen C. Foster's plantation song that empowers its slave protagonist with a dignity not usually given by the era's white songwriters.

In addition to finding a kindred spirit with the song's hero, who seeks escape in death, Bill represents the great authors whose Hollywood stints ended in despondency and alcoholism. (A similar tragedy befell balladeer Foster himself who penned such classics as "Oh! Susannah" and "Camptown Races" and died in poverty in New York City at the age of thirty-seven.) Bill's slow artistic death nods to Dashiell Hammett, Ernest Hemingway, F. Scott Fitzgerald, and Faulkner, who all floundered in California after becoming great men of letters.

John Keats's "Silent upon a Peak in Darien"

Though on decline in Hollywood, Bill provides glimpses of his former passion for creating. One example is his cry, "Silent upon a peak in Darien," on his drunken stumble toward the Pacific, the body of water central to the line's original context. In "On First Looking into Chapman's Homer" John Keats likens the excitement of reading new material to discovering a new land. "Then felt I like some watcher of the skies/When a new planet swims into his ken;/Or like stout Cortez when with eagle eyes/He stared at the Pacific—and all his men/Look'd at each other with a wild surmise—/Silent, upon a peak in Darien." This prelude to his Pacific stroll is ironic. The place that once incited thrills in its discoverer—who was actually Balboa, not Cortez as Keats's poem mistakenly indicates—now borders the giant slave ship called Hollywood. Art being reflected in art is largely what *Fink* is about—even if the sight of it is breathtaking and breathtakingly frightening.

The Burlyman: Barton "Wrestling with His Soul" Mate

Part film noir, part horror movie, *Fink* uses the obscure wrestling "genre" to spin a frightening male adventure. "Ethan likes to call it a buddy movie for the '90s," said Joel Coen.[48] Charlie, Barton's only friend in California, is at the center of the writer's universe.

> Once the backbone of genre films, the male friendship has become . . . the overt and exclusive love interest, as well. . . . The point is love—love in which men understand and support each other, speak the same language, and risk their lives to gain each other's respect.[49]

The twist to *Fink*'s buddies is that the friendship is a sham. Charlie is not who he purports to be.

A homoerotic subtext can be gleaned from the men's first exchange. The more aggressive Charlie barges into Barton's room with the familiar pickup line, "I'd feel better if you'd let me buy you a drink," which Barton accepts with a sexual double-entendre: "Okay, a quick one."[50] Later, Charlie shows undue interest in Barton's sex life, first asking if he has a girlfriend, then embarrassing the writer with a girlie picture, then bringing up the noisy lovebird neighbors. After Audrey is discovered dead, Charlie asks Barton the oddly worded question, "Between you and me, did you have sexual intercourse?"[51] The cap comes when the detectives ask if he and Charlie had a "sick sex thing," to which Barton replies indignantly, "We're men! We wrestled!"[52]

The homoeroticism is not all talk. When Charlie assumes the wrestling position, Barton joins him on all fours. Here, unlike its distance from Barton and Audrey's embrace, the camera gets up close and personal. Barton leans his head on his big friend's shoulder—a move he repeats when Charlie leaves for New York. Charlie swiftly and violently pins him, finishing off with more sexualized lines: "Usually there's more grunting and squirming" and "I'm pretty well endowed physically."[53] And so man-on-man love is added to the latent fears in Barton's vivid imagination. Yet, the movie's take on the buddy film is revisionist. Instead of a typically superior male-male relationship, Barton and Charlie's friendship devolves into a deadly double cross.

"Devil on a Canvas"

With no knowledge of wrestling, of course Barton has a hell of a time painting a devil. For help, he is told to look at art rather than life—terrible advice for a writer who yearns to sing the common man's song. Footage from "Devil on a Canvas" means nothing to Barton, despite the similarities between the movie wrestler and Charlie. For example, there are "scene 12-Charlie" shots and a beefy wrestler (Darwyn Swalve) built like Goodman who throws and pins his opponent similar to Charlie's demonstrated move on Barton. Staring blankly at the screen, Barton absorbs nothing. Successive close-ups alternating between spectator and spectacle show Barton visually repelling the ring's morality play. In a shot reminiscent of Hitchcock's *Notorious* (1946), when the viewer sees the racetrack only through the reflection in Ingrid Bergman's binoculars, the dailies sequence climaxes with a wrestling image reflected in Barton's glasses. The composition symbolically points to the twisted effect that this instrument designed to clarify and correct one's eyesight has on Barton. As if defying their purpose and the laws of physics governing them, his glasses reflect light (ignorance) rather than let it in (understanding).

"The Choir's All Set"

"Down South Camp Meetin" is another internal text exploiting religion. Played at the dance where Barton mixes without mingling among the military crowd, the bouncy swing tune offers mordant commentary on events, at least to those familiar with the lyrics. The song celebrates a sinner's sudden enlightenment—and subtly amplifies Barton's bare-ruined choir status: "Git ready (Sing)/Here they come! The choir's all set."[54] The problem is that Barton's choir is tattered and his solipsistic celebration negates the "real" world around him. He does not acknowledge that the dance is the last hurrah for American soldiers about to enter the war. The Pearl Harbor attack (the date on the dailies slate is "December 9") has not even registered on the writer's radar.

The scene's other jape is its transformation from big band swing dancing into a wrestling ballet. As befits a buddy pic, Barton ignores his dance partner—that is, until a sailor tries to cut in. Suddenly Barton takes interest in the "dame," the walking narrative device who graduates from a prop to spin to the impetus for a fight. The punch-drunk, one-track-mind writer starts rambling about his head, as more and more soldiers take issue with him. A fight ensues. At this point, the camera begins gently tilting from side to side, giving the effect of being on a boat, like the Hollywood slave ship, of course. Jostled to the ground as quickly as he was pinned by Charlie, the screenwriter looks up at the bodies tumbling over and around him in a slow-motion brawl—finally, a wrestling scene! Events keep reflecting or paralleling the movie he is writing.

New York Café

Like the movie itself, Hollywood is portrayed as a great mirror reflecting art. When Ben and Barton do lunch, they sit in front of a "New York Café" sign displayed backward. It looks like a window, but close examination shows that it's pretend. It's part of a mural depicting a street scene—an artistic rendering of Barton's "Lower East Side" setting. Once again, the film deceptively depicts an artistic view. Barton's attention is most rapt when looking at art. The Bathing Beauty on the wall, for instance, the girl "in pictures," serves as both muse and amusement. Hollywood is a place where nothing is real, and reality is virtually indistinguishable from fantasy.

HOLLYWOOD SHUFFLE

Fink trains hard uppercuts on the controlling movie-making capital (which the Coens have adeptly kept at bay). One jab is the slave ship metaphor. Another blow is its casting of its writer as a "bad wrestler type." The artist, who gives up his dreams for a bit of Hollywood cash, "finks" on his neighbor in a World War II setting where such informing can mean life or death. And then there's Jack.

At first glance, the studio looks like the Earle's opposite. Where the Earle has hellish window dressings—Chet's subterranean entrance, the triple sixes in the elevator, and the climactic conflagration—Capitol Studios has a heavenly patina. Contrasting with the lugubriously paced hotel sequences are the bright, sunny, fast, and funny studio scenes. The hotel's big spaces are dark, decaying, and suffocating. Sunlight pours into Jack's airy office and shines brightly at his pool.

On the surface, the studio looks swell. Dressed in white and surrounded by light colorings, Jack appears to be a benevolent boss, eager to show Barton the Hollywood ropes, but in truth he is a beast of a boss who rules Capitol with an iron fist. Loud, commanding, and funny as hell, Jack is a "stock" Coen character. The studio exec follows Visser (*Blood Simple*), Nathan Arizona (*Raising Arizona*), and paves the way for Wade Gustafson (*Fargo*), Jeffrey Lebowski (*The Big Lebowski*), and Big Dave (*The Man Who Wasn't There*)—hulking, cut-throat businessmen with endomorphic builds. The studio is just as hellish as the hotel, it turns out.

Statues flanking the office door are figures of Atlas shouldering the world—talk about hubris. Atlas, a golden-age Titan in Greek mythology banished to the underworld for attacking Olympic gods, is an apt effigy for the studio boss. Jack is a titan of a boss who runs a studio during Hollywood's Golden Age (1920s–1940s), a big hell for a lot of little folks.

Slave master Jack represents an oppressive business system: "Few industries resorted to the intimate, familial forms of economic and psychological manipulation," author Nancy Lynn Schwartz wrote, "used to retain absolute control in Hollywood."[55] Thus, the caricatures of Odets and Faulkner, who both did stints in Hollywood, represent victims of the ruthless Hollywood taskmasters. In this light, the movie can be seen as a tribute to the American writers who made the move to Hollywood only to become choir boys in a bare, ruined choir—men whose literary gifts withered away in the stifling hot Hollywood desert. The movie refracts their experience in Hollywood into Barton's nightmare.

Jack is a superbly drawn caricature of a ruthless studio boss who knows nothing about storytelling. First and foremost a businessman, he has the authority but not the understanding to pull the artistic strings. Why is he in charge? As he himself explains, because he's big, bad, and mean. In other words, he's a wrestler, like Charlie. Also as much the hatchet man in the business sense as Charlie is in the killer sense, Jack gives the axe to Lou and Ben, both on account of Barton. Charlie takes a literal axe to Bill and Audrey.

Fink is so much about itself that even its subplots reflect each other. The hotel and the studio, for instance, have more in common than an initial look might suggest. Unholy trinities with a supreme power in charge characterize both. Charlie is the de facto head of the hotel with Chet and Pete as helpers; Jack runs the studio with Lou and Ben at his mercy. Both top men rule autocratically and viciously while pretending to be a best friend. Both oversized personalities strong-arm their underling Barton and pin him (figuratively or literally) underneath. Jack's eventual artistic stranglehold on Barton is analogous to Charlie's murderous power squeeze on the writer's friends and possibly his family.

The hell of both places is literal, figurative, and ironic. For example, when the Earle becomes engulfed in flames, it takes on the main characteristic of hell—fire—becoming a literal interpretation of the concept. The studio's promise to retain Barton but not produce any of his work shows a figurative view of hell. And the World War II theme about informing coupled with the good wrestler-bad wrestler motif gives us the ironic view.

With World War II as a backdrop, *Fink* exploits the dreamworld to effect a kind of fog of war scenario, Carl von Clausewitz's term to describe the intrinsic difficulties in ascertaining truth and reality in wartime. He wrote in his 1832 magnum opus *On War:*

> The great uncertainty of all data in War is a peculiar difficulty, because all action must, to a certain extent, be planned in a mere twilight, which in addition not infrequently—like the effect of a fog or moonshine—gives to things exaggerated dimensions and an unnatural appearance.

In effect, the Coens create a narrative fog not to obfuscate reality (as in warfare) but to confuse what we understand to be the fiction's "reality." And yet a fog of war creeps in too, especially in the form of anti-Semitism, moral compromises, and isolationist tendencies.

Set during World War II, the movie employs a Jew from Minsk, a center of workers' rights that was occupied by the Nazis around the time of *Fink's* setting. Lipnik (a place name in Eastern Europe) fascistically runs *Capitol* Pictures, a name implicative of state power. Coupled with the studio's harsh

Michael Lerner received an Oscar nomination for his portrayal of Barton's bumptious boss, studio head Jack Lipnik. (Credit: 20th Century Fox/Photofest © 20th Century Fox)

working conditions, these names add a subtle Red Scare to the plot. Allegorical flourishes continue after Jack's self-dubbed "kike" epithet unleashes some anti-Semitism, which the bigoted detectives push to extremes. They can be taken to symbolize the two main Axis forces. Mastrionotti, whose Italian-sounding name includes the Italian word for *night*, is a stand-in for fascist Italy while Deutsch, which means German, represents Nazi Germany. Before blasting the detective's head off, Charlie gives him a "Heil, Hitler!"

In Barton's nightmare, a war is on but he is so far removed from it that he is effectively blind—or asleep—to the horror next door. Herein lies a grim portrait of America's complicity in the war. Like Barton, the United States kept its nose out despite the top-level news that was leaked to high levels of government about the atrocities being leveled against the Jewish people. Dressed in a colonel costume, Jack casually mentions he has enlisted in the reserves thanks to the help of Henry Morgenthau. The only Jewish member of Roosevelt's cabinet, Morgenthau was one of the lone voices demanding intervention to help rescue the Jews. Snatches of World War II add up to an indictment of the country's isolationist stance.

Charlie's "hill of beans" quote from *Casablanca* (1942), for instance, references a line that puts into perspective personal problems when it comes to gigantic issues like war. Just as Barton is disinterested in Charlie's woes, he also ignores the global conflict. The dailies that Barton watches were shot on December 9, 1941, two days after the Japanese attacked Pearl Harbor.[56] In the 12-Apple and 12-Baker shots, the large (fat) wrestler dressed in black performs Sumolike movements with his opponent (they raise their arms to the side and stamp their feet) before announcing that he will destroy him. And so the third Axis power creeps in.

On the detective's second visit, Deutsch calls *Fink* a Jewish name and complains that the Earle isn't restricted. *Fink* is not a Jewish name, but a word that literally means "informant." In WWII, European informers who ratted out Jews aided the Nazis in the Holocaust. All the hell that visits Barton stems from his initial snitching action—when he complains about his noisy neighbor Charlie, aka Karl Mundt, the same name as the South Dakota congressman who cosponsored legislation (with Richard Nixon) to register all Communists. In 1948 Representative Mundt (whose middle name was Earl) chaired the House Un-American Activities Committee (HUAAC), which investigated Americans and encouraged finking. In short, the entire movie is a projection of hell unleashed from informing on the wrong person.

In *Fink*'s allegory about "finking"—an activity that chafes his socialist agenda—Barton is both snitch and snoop, personae non grata, especially in wartime. At one point, he eavesdrops on his neighbors, pressing his ear against the wall to hear them better. In the men's room on the studio lot, when he hears a man retching in a stall, he actually kneels down on the floor to see who is sick.[57] As soon as the toilet flushes, he scrambles to the sink to cover up his spying. Perhaps worst of all, he names his parents' names, Sam and Lillian, to a madman.

This story thread spills into Hollywood blacklisting, a systematic attempt to create a bare, ruined choir out of idealist, left-wing artists who were promoting workers' rights and labor unions. The seeds of the government's attempts to gag when it deemed subversive, anti-American mouthpieces were planted in the 1930s and 1940s and bloomed just after WWII. Barton is fashioned after one such artist. Odets named names after film director Elia Kazan implicated him as a Communist before the HUAAC. Barton's parents' names, Sam and Lillian, on the other hand, belong to a pair of writers who refused to implicate fellow artists. When Samuel Dashiell Hammett (one of the Coens' literary heroes) and his long-time romantic partner, playwright Lillian Hellman, went before the HUAAC, both refused to name names. Odets was never blacklisted, but some have blamed his eventual writer's block that followed his move to Hollywood, on his name-naming. Barton's block incorporates unwitting snitching and deliberate stonewalling.

In Barton's nightmare vision, he tattles on a noisy neighbor but refuses to give out information on a psycho killer. Part of Barton's backward logic ignites Charlie's murder spree. All the horror, death, and destruction are simply payback for Barton's initial "fink." Barton thus helps create a bare, ruined choir. His association with Audrey and Bill leads to their murder. Lou and Ben are fired for Barton's own lack of output, though, not surprisingly, Lou is hired back since he does all of Jack's work for him.

Where Barton goes out of his way to know other people's business, Charlie can't help but be tuned in; he hears their revelry and acknowledges their pain though he wished he didn't. His eyes and ears give him the empathy and understanding of which Audrey speaks, and his response is to release them from their pain. And so in *Fink*'s twisted logic, Charlie can be viewed as the good wrestler. As in Audrey's explanation of the wrestling morality play, the convict Charlie protects Barton, who is both the love interest and the "idiot man-child." Charlie confronts bad wrestler Barton at the end. And since orphan is the other choice for the good wrestler's buddy, things do not look good for Barton's parents.

In the end, *Fink* takes on a journey through the creative mind at work and shows us both personally and politically the hazards along the way. If it is the writer's job to observe the world and incorporate those observations into a work of art that makes sense of them, *Fink* spins this idea on its head. It substitutes surveillance for observance and packages the resultant mayhem in a dream structure. The artist's life can be hell, it suggests, especially when one compromises artistic goals for money—or sells out friends and family for some peace of mind.

WRAP: THINKING INSIDE THE BOX

Cutting through the Coens' fog of artful craft lets us see that Barton's misadventures add up to a cosmic joke on creating art. Drama, the film suggests, can empower the common man or keep him down. It can be as puzzling as a dream or as frightful as a nightmare. Much ado about dreams and heads provides a porthole into Barton's creative process, and the trope of the Hollywood slave ship helps us navigate Hollywood history and Barton's fears of Tinsel Town.

The journey into his mind begins after his conversation with Garland about screenwriting and playwriting. The two-shot of Barton and his agent in front of a cash register dissolves into an iconic wave signifying California's coast. The segue links screenwriting to selling out, and soon Barton's fears start to materialize. Instead of working-class heroes, he finds only cinematic bogeymen and artifice. Nothing is real. California is a mix of allusions and illusion. Sojourning among fictitious characters, Barton loses his way and becomes a fink in dreamland.

The crashing wave visual resurfaces at the end right before Barton meets the Bathing Beauty. She wants to know what's in his box. He's not sure. Are we? We know that Barton has checked out of the Earle and thus Charlie's narrative and is looking for a new one. Perhaps his next invention will feature a dame like herself. Here, with Barton in search of a new idea, is where the Coens cut off our peek inside his "box," as surf sounds gently drift into the credits.

NOTES

1. Larry King, *USA Today*, "The Barton Fink Anomaly," September 17, 1991, D-2.
2. Jim Emerson, "That Barton Fink Feeling," 1991, www.cinepad.com/coens.htm (accessed January 1, 2006).
3. Other films at Cannes included Spike Lee's *Jungle Fever*, David Mamet's *Homicide*, and Lars von Trier's *Europa*.
4. Odets also wrote *The Sweet Smell of Success* (1957), a *Hudsucker Proxy* inspiration.
5. *Barton Fink*, DVD, directed by Joel Coen (1991; Beverly Hills, Calif.: 20th Century Fox Home Entertainment, 2003).
6. Joel Coen and Ethan Coen, *Barton Fink & Miller's Crossing* (London: Faber & Faber, 1991), 12.
7. The Coen Brothers, an IFC interview with Elvis Mitchell, from "Independent Focus: The Coen Brothers."
8. Nathanael West, *Miss Lonelyhearts & the Day of the Locust* (New York: New Directions, 1962), 107.
9. *Barton Fink*, DVD.
10. *Barton Fink*, DVD; *Some Like It Hot*, DVD, directed by Billy Wilder (1958; Santa Monica, Calif.: MGM, 2001).
11. *Barton Fink*, DVD.
12. *Barton Fink*, DVD.
13. *Barton Fink*, DVD.
14. *Barton Fink*, DVD.
15. *Barton Fink*, DVD.
16. *Barton Fink*, DVD.
17. *Barton Fink*, DVD.
18. David Geffner, *MovieMaker*, no. 29, www.moviemaker.com/issues/29/shooting/29_shooting.html (accessed January 1, 2006).
19. Joel and Ethan Coen, speaking together with Elvis Mitchell in IFC's "Independent Focus: The Coen Brothers," 1998. Ethan began the sentence, and Joel finished it.
20. John Unsworth, "Tom Jones, The Comedy of Knowledge," *Modern Language Quarterly*, 48, no. 3 (September 1987), www.iath.virginia.edu/~jmu2m/modern.language.quarterly.48:3.html (accessed January 1, 2006).
21. *Barton Fink*, DVD.
22. *Barton Fink*, DVD.
23. *Barton Fink*, DVD.
24. *Barton Fink*, DVD.
25. *Barton Fink*, DVD.
26. *Barton Fink*, DVD.

27. *Barton Fink*, DVD.

28. *Barton Fink*, DVD.

29. In 1934, Hollywood instituted a set of guidelines that governed what was appropriate to show on film. From the code: "Excessive and lustful kissing, lustful embraces, suggestive postures and gestures, are not to be shown." www.artsreformation.com/a001/hays-code.html (accessed January 12, 2007).

30. Coen and Coen, *Barton Fink & Miller's Crossing*, 81.

31. *Barton Fink*, DVD.

32. *Barton Fink*, DVD.

33. *Barton Fink*, DVD.

34. *Barton Fink*, DVD.

35. *Barton Fink*, DVD.

36. In addition to Lerner, Dennis Gassner and Nancy Haigh received Oscar nominations for Best Art Direction-Set Decoration, and Richard Hornung got a nod for Best Costume Design.

37. Polanski was head judge at Cannes in 1991 when *Barton Fink* scored three awards.

38. Emerson, "That Barton Fink Feeling."

39. *Barton Fink*, DVD.

40. Coen and Coen, *Barton Fink & Miller's Crossing*, 9; Gerald Weales, *Clifford Odets, Playwright* (New York: Pegasus, 1971), 62.

41. *Barton Fink*, DVD.

42. Ellen Cheshire and John Ashbrook, *Joel Coen and Ethan Coen* (Great Britain: Pocket Essentials, 2000), 54–55.

43. *Barton Fink*, DVD.

44. *Barton Fink*, DVD.

45. William Triplett, "Busting Heads and Blaming Reds," Salon.com, January 11, 2000, www.salon.com/ent/movies/feature/2000/01/11/blacklist (accessed January 1, 2006).

46. *Barton Fink*, DVD.

47. Stephen Foster, "Old Black Joe" (circa 1860).

48. Emerson, "That Barton Fink Feeling."

49. Molly Haskell, *From Reverence to Rape* (New York: Holt, Rinehart & Winston, 1973), 23–24.

50. *Barton Fink*, DVD.

51. *Barton Fink*, DVD.

52. *Barton Fink*, DVD.

53. *Barton Fink*, DVD.

54. John Hendricks, Irving Mills, and Fletcher Henderson, "Down South Camp Meetin'" (Hendricks Music and EMI Mills Music: 1997).

55. Triplett, "Busting Heads and Blaming Reds."

56. Dailies, or rushes, refer to footage developed quickly so that the filmmakers can screen them at the end of a day's shoot to ensure they got what they needed.

57. Regurgitation is a recurring motif in the Coens' work. Here in *Barton Fink*, Bill throws up not quite in private as Barton listens, and Charlie, a bit like *Blood Simple*'s Marty and Norville in *The Hudsucker Proxy*, vomits (or pretends to) off-screen. Other retchers include Tom (*Miller's Crossing*) and Marge (*Fargo*).

• 5 •

The Hudsucker Proxy: A Circle

Tim Robbins (Norville Barnes) gives his hula hoop a spin. (Credit: Warner Bros. Pictures Inc./Photofest © Warner Bros. Pictures Inc.)

"Finally there'd be a thingamajig that would bring everyone together . . . you know, for kids?"

—Amy Archer (Jennifer Jason Leigh)

"The man and the hour have met."

—William Yancey (1861)

139

PREVIEW

$\mathcal{A}$lthough *The Hudsucker Proxy* was not produced until the early 1990s, the Coens and their friend and cowriter Sam Raimi put corporate America in their sights during the corporate friendly, deregulation days of the Reagan era.[1] In the 1980s the trio wrote a Big Business satire about an inventive, have-not naïf freeing a business universe from rapacious haves. The Coens and Raimi primed their satire with movie riffs and philosophical tidbits but put off making it until they could get more funding. Until then, the Hudsucker Industries label on *Raising Arizona*'s Hi's overalls would remain an in-joke awaiting a payoff.[2]

Proxy's ship came in after the Coens' three-picture contract with Ben Barenholtz and Circle Releasing was fulfilled. Warner Brothers saw potential crossover material, pitched in money, and suggested that Joel Silver join the project. Thus began an odd marriage of Silver, the multibillionaire producer of such high-octane movies as *Die Hard*, *Lethal Weapon*, and *The Matrix*; the independent Coen brothers; and Eric Fellner and Tim Bevan, the co-chairs of Working Title Films, an up-and-coming, British indie powerhouse.[3]

Despite strong track records all round, the talent mix didn't translate into ticket sales. Like Waring Hudsucker's opening splat, the $25-million movie made just $2.8 million domestically. "We were responsible for [the Coens'] almost-demise," said Fellner, who has continued to work with the brothers.[4] "It was their next movie, *Fargo*, which broke them," said Silver. "Who knows why?"[5] Ultimately only the movie gods can answer that, but countering *Proxy*'s initial flop has been a slow, steady rise to cult status from strong video and DVD rentals and the stage adaptation by the University of Pittsburgh's repertory theatre.[6] In a strange reenactment of its theme, *The Hudsucker Proxy* play, combined with the rentals, has given the movie a new birth, proving it, like its hero, a winner over time.

REVIEW

Proxy opens on the verge of two events: the year 1959 and a possible suicide. During the final seconds of 1958, a narrator named Moses (Bill Cobb), who moonlights as a clock keeper, introduces us to a man edging along the top ledge of a skyscraper. Norville Barnes (Tim Robbins), president of Hudsucker Industries, has just stepped out of the window of his lofty office. Dressed in mailroom duds, he looks like he is contemplating a New Year plunge.

Keeping us—and him—hanging, the story warps back to Norville's arrival in New York when the Muncie Business School grad, fresh off the bus, sets out to seek his fortune. He can't find work until an ad mysteriously attracts him to the Hudsucker Industries mailroom. Just as he arrives, company president Waring Hudsucker (Charles Durning) exits via a swan-song dive from the forty-fifth-floor boardroom despite the fact that business is great. VP Sid Mussberger (Paul Newman) and his board of directors cobble together a scheme to shanghai his company stock: They'll install a callow, no-name proxy as president who will run the company into the ground. Once the share prices fall, they can snatch up the devalued stock, oust the proxy, and return the company to a booming business.

Norville's first big assignment at "the Hud" is to deliver a Blue Letter, the most important type of internal communication. But instead, when he gets to Sid's sky-high office, he flies an idea by the exec: a circle drawing and a pitch line hinting it's a toy. At first Sid thinks Norville is the perfect proxy; then, reconsidering, Sid fires him. But when Sid's lit cigar sets fire to a contract and it flies out an open window, he nearly follows Waring's path out of this world. The tyro clerk's quick executive save lands him the puppet presidency.

This change of the Hudsucker guard catches the eye of Al (John Mahoney), chief editor of the *Manhattan Argus*. He wants to run a profile of Hudsucker's new "genius," but his Pulitzer Prize–winning reporter Amy Archer (Jennifer Jason Leigh) smells a rat. She goes undercover as Norville's secretary to get the real scoop and is convinced the new president is a simpleton. Her muckraking articles expose his naiveté and addle her faux boss but miss the Sidney-proxy connection and fail to recognize Norville's inspired ability, yet to be unveiled. She eventually falls for him romantically, but when he gets caught up in the VIP high life, she loses interest.

When Norville's hula hoop idea becomes a hit, Sid's new plan is to spread a rumor that Norville stole the idea from the truly dim-witted elevator boy Buzz (Jim True). Meanwhile, Sid's henchman Aloysius (Henry Bugin)—the silent, sinister janitor—discovers "Miss Smith's" true identity. This dirt gives Sid more ammo to fire Norville. Although Amy discovers Sid's latest ploy, she is now powerless to report on it because the chief and her pal Smitty (Bruce Campbell) think she's "gone soft" on Norville; in fact, she has but that is beside the point. The *Argus* publishes Sid's planted story.

Here is where Norville takes to the ledge. Now we see that no sooner does he step outside than he changes his mind. But he cannot get back in because Aloysius locks him out. Then the sinister janitor exhales, the window fogs, and Norville falls. After rushing past several stories of the building, he stops suddenly in midair, and an angelic Waring reminds him of the undelivered Blue Letter, still in his pocket. It is Waring's will. After briefly explaining his suicide—though rich, he was distraught over losing the love of his life to Sid—it goes on to bequeath his shares of Hud stock to his successor instead of the public. Waring had assumed that Sid would get the stock, but thanks to his greed and Norville's nondelivery, the shares go to Norville.

While Norville receives news of his new fortune, Aloysius investigates why time has stopped. It turns out that Moses has jammed the clock's gears to give Norville a helping hand. His clock block suspends the actions of everyone but himself, Waring, Norville, and Aloysius.[7] Irate over this intervention, Aloysius and Moses fight over control of time. Moses wins, the clock starts up again, and Norville falls gently to the earth. He runs to Amy at a beatnik bar. Moses's epilogue finds Sidney on the ledge, about to be carted off to the psychiatric hospital, and Norville back in business as president. Ruling with "wisdom and compassion," he lets loose his next big idea, "you know, for kids!"[8] A frisbee sails out the boardroom window.

TIME OUT NEW YORK

With hula hoops front and center, *Proxy* traffics in nostalgia. It looks backward to progress through its story about the little guy taking on the fat cats, before finally coming full circle—the movie's all-round, hard-to-miss main emblem. Central to the story is the past and its pivotal role in informing the future. The raft of related art that the movie recycles reflects the point. Built from used parts, *Proxy* is a satiric allegory promoting workers' and creators' rights. To both symbolize and overcome tyranny, it exploits concepts of time.

For one, the Coens' time-honored tale of a talented, naïve nobody making it to the top integrates a number of old-time stories about battling oppression. It plucks ideas from ancient Hindu and Judeo-Christian traditions to stress the value of enlightened existences where people are connected to their fellow man rather than wealth. It intersperses classical music, beatnik poetry, mime, dance, literature, and opera to further ideas about eschewing materialism and to have fun with concepts of low- and highbrow art. Ultimately, it pays tribute to those who enrich society through entertainment (hula hoops, frisbees, movies, and so on) throughout the ages.

Proxy starts as many Coen plots do, taking off in worlds beset by chaos. *Blood Simple*'s establishing images show disorienting angles—an extreme low angle on a road followed by a two-minute view of characters' backsides. *Raising Arizona* begins with characters acting on unbridled obsessions that summon a broker from hell. *Miller's Crossing* takes off from a bad decision that sparks a gang war. Here in *Proxy*, time and space are out of whack.

Space is where things begin, in an extreme long shot of a new world, familiar to the one we know but distinct. As the opening strains of Aram Khachaturian's "Spartacus and Phrygia" evoke a sense of nostalgia, the cluster of skyscrapers immediately conjures up New York. But even as the narrator confirms the locale, the visual exposition of the snow-globe city suggests an allegorical realm. For example, the artfully crafted location, a miniature model of mid-twentieth-century Manhattan shot to look life-size, shows lighted windows but no people behind them. Despite talk of rejoicing at the Waldorf and in Times Square, there is no movement in the hushed metropolis except for the camera itself. Hardly literal, the setting looks less like an international city and more like Storyville USA—the New York of movies, myth, and memories.

"It's very hard for us to imagine a story absent a very specific locale," said Joel Coen. "You can say that about all the settings of our movies: They're certainly very specific, but not real."[9] *Proxy's* locale is like *Raising Arizona's* Roadrunner desert, *Blood Simple's* Lone Star hell, *Miller's Crossing's* city and woods, and *Barton Fink's* dreamy L.A. Even *Fargo*, the Coens' most realistic film on the surface, depicts a caricatured Midwest strewn with as many tall tales as bodies. Locations inform atmosphere, themes, and characters but not literal places. In *Hudsucker's* reenvisioning of New York, the corporate entity has a 9-to-5 focus that helps describe it as a cosmos unto itself: Hudsucker—the Hud—is Corporate America.

Right away, equations emerge in this representative world: Size counts, and big means oppressive. After snaking around snow-tipped spires, the camera finds the mammoth Hudsucker tower. It eclipses everything, including Norville, our rather dwarfed hero who walks along the ledge just outside a hulking window. Built into the building's verticality, we soon learn, is its power structure. The haves lounge in sprawling offices high above the have-nots, who rush about cramped, crowded spaces below. But both groups move to the beat of the clock, which by no small coincidence is kept in working order by the narrator, a cosmic story force more powerful than any top-floor exec. After the plot progresses by way of a regression, stressing the idea of the past's influence on the future, strictures such as beginnings and endings give way to more fluid views of time. Soon natural cycles—symbolized by a circle, the geometric figure with no ending or beginning—win out over the initial dominant power of oppressive Hudsucker Time.

At the start, there are two main wrinkles—one narrow, the other wide. Norville's future, the micro problem, is in jeopardy: He is "out of hope, out of rope, out of time."[10] The macro trouble has to do with business as usual.

The so-called rat race has "a way of chewing folks up so that they don't want no celebrating. Don't want no cheering up. Don't care nothing bout no New Year's."[11] For Norville to make things right, two things must occur: Norville must gain back hope and get time on his side to end its tyranny.

Though introduced in terms with which we are familiar (December 31 turning to January 1 at the stroke of midnight), concepts related to time quickly become unique to the setting. The blaring announcement from the anonymous PA system spells this out clearly when it puts Waring's death at 12:01 Hudsucker Time (HT). The corporation's autocracy is epitomized by the minute of silence ordered to be taken for the late president—time, the workers are told, that will be deducted from their pay. The abusive HT is an emblem of the satire's targets: namely, industrialized exploitation, over-stretched power, and greed.

With a setting so integrally tied to a clock, the phrase "time is money" is not just a bromide—it's a mantra. The place is autocratically ruled by time, and worker exploitation is dramatized through relentless temporal control—ideas with cinematic forebears. The clock as mechanized tyranny is reminiscent of Charlie Chaplin's *Modern Times* (1936), which opens on a clock face and goes on to chastise industry's dehumanizing effect on the working classes. *Proxy* incorporates snatches of Fritz Lang's *Metropolis* (1927), whose mechanized Under World makes the executive lifestyle a cakewalk at the expense of over-worked, low-level employees.

The clock's domination even taps the cruelty surrounding penal labor explored in Stuart Rosenberg's *Cool Hand Luke* (1967). The Mailroom Orienter's (Christopher Darga) broken-record instructions to Norville ("Get it wrong, and they dock ya!") in nature, rhythm, and substance echo Luke's orientation by the prison guard Carr (Clifton James) who stresses that infractions buy a guy "a night in the box."[12] Like *Luke's* convicts who suffer their boss's draconian treatment, Hudsucker staffers are enslaved to the dictatorial chronometer.

Everything Hudsucker revolves around the clock, revealing a corporate universe not heliocentric or geocentric but *chrono*centric. Time is of utmost importance, and yet all signs point to a time out of joint. Filmed through a 1990s lens trained on history, *Proxy* wends through a clever temporal jumble. Blending the here and now with the there and then, the filmmakers create a world at once predicated on, chained to, and flummoxed by time.

From the get-go, time runs amuck, not sure if it is coming or going. "Time flees" is the newsreel logo translated from the Latin phrase, "Tempus Fugit."[13] As Moses introduces the past, the clock's giant second hand sweeps into the future. Though the year is 1958, things onscreen look different, older. Skyscraper tips piercing the boardroom's horizon are art deco clones of the

Chrysler building. The lamps and sofas dressing the set have a pre-1950s look too. Amy is a retro rainbow of mostly black-and-white personalities from yesteryear. "Amy is very reminiscent of all those 1930s and '40s heroines in the screwball [Frank] Capra and Preston Sturges movies, Howard Hawks, [George] Cukor," Leigh told the Los Angeles Times. "It's not just Hepburn though. I'm doing everybody."[14] The film branches into different eras, making it look and feel, as the Baltimore Sun noted, "unstuck in time."[15] Patching together tidbits of time, the filmmakers establish an instantly recognizable setting, a business hub in 1958 America, only to shake it up into a metaphor with social, political, and philosophical implications.[16]

Norville and Amy's balcony scene touches on some of these areas by zooming in on an Eastern view of time. The night before his hula hoop pitch, Norville flirts with Amy in a love scene patterned after one in Preston Sturges's The Lady Eve (1941). He says their connection transcends time: "Perhaps we met once, a chance encounter in a forest glade."[17] He also foreshadows the power his hula hoops will unleash with talk about animal reincarnation and "'karma'—the great circle of life, death and rebirth."[18] Tapping into the Hindu concept from about 1500 B.C. of "what goes around comes around," he forecasts that his hoop will cause a rebirth of the Hud. His Eastern borrowings wrap the story in the fundamental Hindu concept of the unity of being in which one sees one self in all being and all being in oneself—a progressive idea that is light years away from Sid's greed. So Norville with his circles and Eastern philosophy sets out to right time, with some help from the clock keep Moses.

When Norville tumbles off the ledge with a gusty push from Aloysius, Moses halts time to make sure he doesn't fall and hurt himself—or his chances of aiding Hudsucker. The narrator is no disinterested party. He sees that Norville has the power to bring people together even while separating them spatially, as Amy jokes. In his dual role as narrator and clock keeper, Moses can see that Norville's hoop applies to the cyclical nature of time and the ups and downs of the business cycle as well as the recrudescence of similarly themed stories across cultures.

Moses describes himself to Amy as an omniscient power broker: "Ah speck ole Moses knows jes about everything, leastways if it concerns Hudsuckah."[19] This omniscience applies to both his clock keeping and narrating roles. Moses exists within the story and above it, somewhat like Blood Simple's narrator. Visser is a malevolent force ultimately done in by his own scheming. Here, it's the opposite. Moses is a positive force whose life-saving, time-stopping actions allow Norville to beat the system. He elaborates on his two roles with double-entendres about keeping "the ol' circle turning."[20] Understanding that he is referring to storytelling as well as commerce helps give shape to the allegory's self-conscious fulcrum of art with a social bent.

Jennifer Jason Leigh gets an inside view of the Hudsucker clock—and an inside view of some story mechanics. (Credit: Warner Bros. Pictures Inc./Photofest © Warner Bros. Pictures Inc.)

In other words, the film is as much about storytelling as it is about Big Business. The story is *the* thing, and all its internal stories reflecting a David-versus-corporate-Goliath struggle magnify the idea that knowledge of the past can help build a better future. Remembering, the movie demonstrates, is key to breaking patterns of tyranny. Thus, the allegory turns metaphors inside out, and time, that critical narrative force, must be tamed to make things better.

RECYCLING, HUD STYLE:
"THE HUD IS DEAD—LONG LIVE THE HUD"

Overblown materialism is a primary source of Hud's discord. Business is booming at the start, but all is not well. Things take off in the sky-high boardroom where the all-white, all-male, geriatric chorus of execs is all ears except for the president. Not only are the staggeringly positive earnings numbers unemotionally crunched, but also there is no mention whatsoever of what the company actually does to reap such strong results. The bottom line is the bottom line, period. Like time, such monetary focus is out of whack. Waring's disinterest is the first sign of the dissonance of such imbalanced priorities. His twelve o'clock sprint through the plate-glass window makes his discord more explicit. But like his jump, change is in the air, and the synchronicity of his leap and Norville's entrance is a sign suggesting positive change.

Signs are key and fate looms large in this Big Business fable. For instance, Norville's position at Hudsucker occurs amid supernatural events in which circles figure prominently. After striking out at the job board, he scours the want ads at the Epicure Diner but fares no better. He leaves a tip and starts to go but tightens the belt first—and takes back a lucky penny. As he leaves, circular objects start to work their magic. The camera, instead of following him, holds on the counter and pans from the round ashtray and saucer to his mug, under which a coffee stain rings a job listing. Underneath the mug, it had escaped his eye. But now a strong, inexplicable breeze, like a divine breath, carries the broadsheet outside to where it literally attracts Norville's attention and wraps around his leg. Struck by the ad copy—emblazoned with the phrase "The Future Is Now"—he heads to the company and enters through doors that, naturally, revolve.

Doors revolve, toys spin, time cycles from noon to midnight, from December 31 to January 1. It's practically impossible to miss the potency of circles in these environs. Whether mystical or natural, circles make Hudsucker tick. Sid's inability to see any significance in Norville's circle idea—in a world where Moses "keeps the old circle turning" (except when he stops it)—spells trouble.[21] Though everyone is skeptical of Norville's crude drawing, Sid is the most dubious. He eggs on Norville to produce his preposterous-seeming ring toy, and Sid's eagerness for Norville's demise makes his own that much karmically sweeter—just desserts, as it were. Norville rightly predicts that his hula hoop is his ticket to the top. And though it looks like he may return to the ground floor via the ledge, Moses saves him with a quick clock block, stopping the turn of the wheel just long enough to right things.

Norville's "great wheel that gives us each what we deserve" squashes Sid, who just doesn't get the idea of karma or understand the power of cycles.[22] Sid is surrounded by circles, but he is too "square" to benefit from them. He doesn't recognize the potential power lurking in his office globe or the painting of partial circles outside his door. Tellingly, when he looks through the elliptical hole left by Waring's dive, he does not see the opportunity Waring affords him: to change the status quo that sent his friend and boss searching for something better. No, Sid continues on the path that led to Waring's destruction and schemes to coerce market forces rather than let them rise and fall naturally. Though his language at times uses circular phrases ("Sure, sure, the wheel turns, the music plays, and our spin ain't over yet"), because he can't read the signs, ultimately his spin is short lived.[23] Not surprisingly, Sid is also out of sorts with time.

Sid's bad-guy status is mostly evidenced by his power-grabbing and money-grubbing. He wants to send the stock into single-digit territory and snatch it up low to keep the public's hands off any profits. It's a great premise for both the 1980s and the 1990s when, as we now understand much better, some of America's CEOs were pulling—and getting away with—illegal shenanigans. Though *Proxy* focuses on the power play between the execs and the proxy, there is also metaphoric exploitation of low workers by the managers. Some of this is linguistic.

Sid's office abounds in disorder. Backward signs point to Sid's injurious rule. For example, his use of pig latin ("Ear-clay? Ood-gay!") jumbles language.[24] Complementing his confused speech are backward numbers and disordered time. Behind his desk, numbers appear as if in a mirror, and the clock's second hand moves counterclockwise. Such chaos suggests discord in a world so structured around time; the inverted symbols are code for Sid's baleful tyranny.

Sid's office also features a timepiece representative of unnatural time and energy—a signal to a potential problem in a place where time reigns supreme. During Norville's first meeting with Sid, the motion balls halt abruptly the moment the thought strikes Sid that here might be the perfect pawn. He cries, "Wait a minute!" and the balls do just that, as if on command.[25] Sid might be trying to pull the corporate strings behind the scenes, but there is nothing to suggest he can control time in this world. Only the story's two gods, Aloysius (the evil power) and Moses (the good power), can do this. While foreshadowing the more powerful stoppage of time, Sid's timepiece and its linear, flawed time hint that his time in power will be false and nonlasting. After all, the balls' putative nonstop energy—a violation of the laws of dynamics—symbolizes how the Hud's own attempt to keeps workers in ceaseless motion is flawed. In short, Sid and Hudsucker's systems of time are tyrannical. To right things and restore better working conditions, time must be realigned and Sid must get his comeuppance.

POWER, PEOPLE, AND PEOPLE POWER

Riddled with symbols, Hudsucker is an archetypal world where tyranny and justice duke it out. In other words, the conflict is dramatic and symbolic. Air, for instance, is associated with power. Wind, after all, brings Norville to Hudsucker and air helps keep his flying toys aloft. Things that can soar represent forces of good. Very tall things suggest gross power. The fat-cat execs are so far removed from the workers that they are oblivious to their important contributions. Cycles and circles hint at the import of regeneration. Numbers and letters, including the special Blue Letter, point to the power of the written word—symbols. Thus, rather than personalize the lowly Hud worker, the film personifies him, and Norville's struggle for control is the difference between heaven and hell for the working class.

Hudsucker's top-level communication attests to executive power running amuck. The communiqué sends the already frenetic mailroom into a backwash of commotion. Sirens spin, alarms ring, people run for cover, all because one VIP had something to tell another. Never mind the inefficiency of sending the missive down forty-five flights only for a clerk to take it back up and deliver it to the office next door. The letter's ability to inflict fear in mail workers is indicative of the executives' domination. Norville, not attuned to such insider ways, does not hide and thus draws the proverbial short straw, unwittingly launching his upward mobility.

Even the happy-go-lucky Buzz bows down to the Blue Letter. At first it's business as usual, and he greets his regular riders with rhyming couplets, for example, "Ladies and gentlemen, please step to the rear, for the gargantuan Mr. Greer."[26] When the letter suddenly catches his eyes, the verbal frivolities stop, and he puts this correspondence ahead of all the workers by expressing the lift to the top. The episode continues the portrait of Hudsucker's skewed power system when Sid's secretary (Mary Lou Rosato) insists Norville needs an appointment. The sight of the letter provokes a blood-curdling scream and cancels the need for an appointment. In sum, everyone but one kowtows to the Blue Letter. In fact, Norville's first (unwitting) steps toward seizing control of the Hud are to first take on and then ignore the top-level letter. His follow-up move involves circles.

Sid, in beatnik speak, is square, so much so that he doesn't get the idea of rebirths—a tragic flaw in these parts. Contrary to Sid's belief that "When you're dead, you stay dead," there's such a thing as the afterlife, as the angelic Waring demonstrates when he returns singing "She'll be Coming Round the Mountain" (an in-joke referencing the Snopeses' song in *Raising Arizona*).[27] His Blue Letter suicide note talks of "join[ing] the organization upstairs—an exciting new beginning."[28] Rather than a terminal plunge, Waring's leap jumpstarts a new journey that is part Christian heaven, part Hindu reincarnation. The letter discusses cycles: "'Our next president must have the liberty . . . to experiment and even fall' ['fail'] . . . 'And learn. To fail' ['fall'] 'And rise again by applying what he has learned. Such is business. Such is life.'"[29] Now we understand the serendipity of Waring's departure and Norville's arrival—it's karma. The men's actions are complementary. Sid cannot be part of the cycle because he's too sleazy.

While the circle is the movie's main figure, up-and-down cycles are its main pattern. Characters experience rises and falls often charted in montages that advance the plot visually while harking back to old movie techniques. The first of these—the "Laughing Montage"—is an "up" supposedly shared by the execs and Norville when he becomes president. Really, the executives think they are pulling one over on the naïf. The board members chortle at Norville pantomiming the life-saving clutch that puts him in power, deceptively laughing at, not with, him. Words fill the screen through headlines tracking his progress and decline: "Untried Youth to Helm Hudsucker, Stockholders Wary" and "Hud Stock Dropping, When Will Fresh Ideas Bear Fruit?"[30] Norville's suit fitting at Sid's tailor foreshadows his downfall. Like the avaricious Sid scorning the generous tailor, Norville will eventually turn on his laborers. But for now, things look up for the scheming board.

The hula hoop montage changes the who's-on-top score. Norville's spinning toy produces the turnaround. Where the Blue Letter sequence demonstrated inefficiency and the tyranny of power, the hoop production montage celebrates enterprise—not simple busyness. Organizational teamwork and the power of creativity win out.

From a pair of legs running down the corridor to a sheet of paper placed in a tube en route to the design department, a network of workers brings Norville's idea to life. The invention moves off the page into three-dimensional form amid a flurry of narrative nods that ridicule bureaucracy and spotlight artisans. Outside the promethean bullpen, for example, the secretary reads *War and Peace* and *Anna Karenina,* Leo Tolstoy novels that champion the worker. Such tribute is echoed in the music.

Like the opening theme, the melodies that help tell the hula hoop story are lively themes originally written by Khachaturian to celebrate the Soviet laborer. At the start of *Proxy,* the adagio from Khachaturian's ballet *Spartacus and Phrygia,* which is about a slave uprising in ancient Rome, subtly prefigures a story about overcoming abusive power. Like Spartacus, Norville goes up against powerful forces in the name of freedom and nobility. Such power struggles at the heart of Hudsucker are reflected in its internal artwork and its subtle homage to the worker. For example, the creation of Norville's toy reflects the ideology that Khachaturian tried to express in his music: the importance of making "art relevant to the people. Not art for the sake of art," as pianist Sahan Arzruni said on NPR.[31]

Proxy celebrates the working man allegorically. The sets approach characterization. The proving facility, where explosives' testings conjure up cold war readiness drills, acknowledges the risks workers routinely take on the job. The system of tubes connecting all the departments is reminiscent of Terry Gilliam's *Brazil* (1985), a movie that blasts bureaucracy. The accounting department's long, neat rows of seemingly endless desks highlight the orderly, systematic world of number crunchers. They also resemble the accounting floor of Billy Wilder's Oscar-winning *The Apartment* (1960).

The focus on numbers and price once the toy hits the marketplace also maps out a fall-and-rise pattern. The $1.79 price tag that the greedy, corporate "suits" stick on the hoop seems too high for the new product when it just won't sell. The expectant shopkeeper adjusts the cost, successively marking it all the way down to "2 for 25¢" before bottoming it out with "free with any purchase."[32] Unable to give it away, the disappointed shopkeeper throws the hoops onto the trash heap. One lone hoop trundles past the garbage pile and down the street, a bit like the paper mysteriously blowing out of the diner toward Norville. Again a circle works some magic.

Like the paper finding its mark, the hoop rolls toward a little boy, circles him, and then drops directly in front of him. The scene recalls the magic of Albert Lamorisse's *Le Ballon Rouge* (*The Red Balloon*) from 1956 in which a balloon inexplicably and delightfully follows a little boy around. Here in *Proxy,* the intrigued child steps into the circle and starts to play and sway. Soon his enjoyment turns to enchantment. When a swarm of children just out of school see the boy swinging the hoop around his hips, his leg, and his neck, they scream for joy and rush to the shop. Now the price goes in the reverse direction, soaring past its original sticker price to a whopping $3.99. The production sequence ends on this high note.

Khachaturian's music, again, speaks to the scene's dynamics and thematics. As the boy demonstrates that the toy's ability to produce joy makes it a worthwhile buy, Khachaturian's most recognized theme, the "Sabre Dance," kicks in. His music provides a subtext that impassions the Hud workers' need to overcome their oppressors: "Soviet songs are a fighting weapon," Khachaturian said, "and it is our duty to forge this weapon with all the passion, responsibility, knowledge, and talent at our disposal. We shall give the front songs throbbing with wrath and fury, songs of revenge, songs of victory, and songs of glory worthy of our Soviet soldiers."[33] In *Proxy*'s case, it is class warfare being waged, but the stakes are still high and the boots on the ground need well-honed artistic weapons to overcome their fat-cat foe.

REPACKAGED GOODS AND EVILS

At its most basic level *Proxy* is an allegory of good and evil, right and wrong, beneficent corporate stewardship and public-be-damned greed. Though the movie includes snatches of dramatized worker exploitation, its universe works on the level of symbolism and pastiche. It is shaped in large part from movies and other art that tackle similar subject matter. Where a character sits on the good-evil spectrum is determined in large part by whether he is for or against the have-nots. Those treating workers well and upholding their rights are good guys; those stomping on workers' rights are not. To this end, *Proxy* pays homage to Frank Capra, a maverick director who often worked outside the studio system to produce classic screwball comedies steeped in populist themes. Norville's reach toward the greater public good over Sid's care for individual gain has roots in Capra's *Mr. Deeds Goes to Town* (1936), *You Can't Take It with You* (1938), and *Meet John Doe* (1941).

The satirical *Mr. Deeds Goes to Town* is an example of Capra's comedy-meets-social drama. When the allegorically named country bumpkin Longfellow Deeds (Gary Cooper) inherits a fortune, he moves to New York City where he decides to give the money to people hit hardest by the Depression. The greedy lawyers take such altruism as a sign of craziness. Plus, they care less about victims of an economic downfall than about their own potential windfall if they can legally prove that he is mentally unfit. Deeds's relationship with Babe Bennett (Jean Arthur), a young reporter who wants the inside scoop and poses as a fellow yokel to get close to him, is an inspiration for Amy. To snag his attention, Babe feints a faint and lures the bumpkin to come to her aid, providing a model for Amy's whisker-trimmed gag.

Amy's hoodwink is not just an allusion to Capra. It is a time-honored tactic, as the blue-collar Greek chorus explains. Benny (John Seitz) and Lou (Joe Grifasi) deliver an inventive blow-by-blow of Amy's entrapment technique as she pantomimes recognizable ploys. The inventive narration itself is reminiscent of another screwball comedy. In Preston Sturges's *The Lady Eve* (1941), Barbara Stanwyck's character watches a swarm of single women try to pick up the bookish man (Henry Fonda) she plans to swindle. Commenting on their gestures, she calls the events as she surmises, just as Benny and Lou do. Both scenes get across the idea that romance and swindles are oft-used plot devices. Stanwyck's line "Holy smoke, the dropped kerchief! That hasn't been used since Lily Langtry" is a precursor to Smitty's comment regarding Amy's lumbago ploy: "That gag's got whiskers on it."[34]

Later, Norville riffs on such a narrative device when he is peeved about Amy's newspaper profile of him. He dictates to her an angry letter more ridiculous than scathing, but then drops the idea. Just before she leaves, though, he stops her with his imagined view of the girl reporter. The picture he paints of an imagined Amy makes her squirm. He guesses that she acts like one of the boys, dresses in "men's clothing" and hangs out "with some smooth-talking heel in the newsroom named Biff or Smoocher."[35] Her "Smitty" correction adds more irony. Just about everywhere in *Proxy*, the story's the thing, whether it's a news article, a headline, a newsreel, a joke, or an allusion.

Proxy's cinematic medley revives a slew of old movies while riffing on tried and true methods of good storytelling. The newspaper chief, who decries that "facts, figures, charts!" never sold a paper in one breath only to insist later that "Facts, figures, charts . . . are the tools of the trade!," takes after the story coaching of *Deeds*'s chief editor Mac (George Bancroft).[36] "It's got to be personal," Mac instructs, adding, "What does he think about? How does it feel to be a millionaire! Is he going to get married! What does he think of New York! Is he smart? Is he dumb?"[37] Al too emphasizes "the Human Angle": "Where is he from? Where is he going? Has he got a girl? . . . What are his hopes and dreams, his desires and aspirations? Does he think all the time or does he set aside a certain portion of the day?"[38]

From women reporters who become double agents to a perfectly sane rube labeled a crazy man, Capra plot points are liberally peppered throughout *Proxy*. Like Norville after him, Longfellow is declared to be a manic-depressive, a disorder that fits snugly into the overarching fall-rise/fail-succeed pattern. The chart that *Proxy*'s Dr. Bronfenbrenner presents to the executives to support Norville's madness looks just like the loop-de-loop graph that plots Longfellow's emotional highs and lows.[39] In the end of *Deeds*, the allegedly "insane public benefactor" helps expose the corrupt establishment's real insanity and consequently revitalizes the power of the people to change the system. With less emphasis on people and more focus on symbolism, Norville does the same.

The other primary Capra influence on *Proxy* comes by way of *Meet John Doe*, whose plot turns on a letter (though not blue) and features a scheme to improve a company's earnings by pulling the wool over the public's eyes. When journalist Ann Mitchell (Barbara Stanwyck) is about to lose her job, she pitches a win-win idea to her boss: She can boost newspaper sales and save her career by publishing a fake letter. Its author will be a fictitious man hit so hard by the Depression that he threatens suicide if he cannot pull himself out of his dire straits. Her editor (James Gleason) tells her to run with the plan. After writing the letter she must find a proxy who can play the part of its Average Joe author. While the letter boosts newspaper sales, as expected, the John Doe proxy (Gary Cooper) sparks a populist movement. But soon the compromised ethics of all involved start to spring leaks in the plan. The movie climaxes with Cooper contemplating a real suicide, an unforeseen product of their manipulations. Considering a jump on Christmas Eve instead of Norville's New Year's Eve, John Doe, like Norville, though with a more somber conclusion, decides against the jump.

To be sure, *Proxy* works on its own, regardless of whether one picks up on its innumerable allusions. But the movie experience enters another level when the references shine through. So much of the infused art underscores the relevance of art to societal struggles. It can critique institutions, expose far-flung corruption, and give voice to "the unempowered." Taken together, *Proxy*'s movie tributes form a sweeping indictment of power and greed.

The corporate goliath's name hints at such aims. Not only does Waring's surname rhyme with bloodsucker; it is also a caricatured amalgamation of J. J. Hunsecker (Burt Lancaster's ruthless newspaper man) in Alexander Mackendrick's *Sweet Smell of Success* (1957) and Hud, an unscrupulous cowboy played by Paul Newman in Martin Ritt's *Hud* (1963).[40] One of the silver screen's most despicable antiheroes, the selfish, unscrupulous Hud values and respects nothing, as his father tells him. Hud shrugs off such criticism, castigating the entire country as a bastion of corruption: "Where you been? Big business, price-fixing, crooked TV shows, income tax finagling, souped-up expense accounts. How many honest men do you know?"[41]

As a bad guy in a comedy, Sid is base but not nearly as lowdown as either Hud or Hunsecker. Hunsecker and Hudsucker might have similar-sounding names, but it is Sid, not Waring, who speaks J. J.'s tough language: J. J.'s message to his crony (Tony Curtis) ("You're dead, son. Get yourself buried") is

Paul Newman fires up Tim Robbins's cigar to see if he'd make a good proxy for his shady business plan. (Credit: Warner Bros. Pictures Inc./Photofest © Warner Bros. Pictures Inc.)

similar to Sid's fallacious note to Norville ("When you're dead, you stay dead").[42] The *Sweet Smell of Success* tribute goes further than this. The noir, which was co-scripted by Ernest Lehman and the playwright Clifford Odets, on whom Barton Fink was modeled, climaxes with a contemplated suicide through a skyscraper window.

The dishonest men jockeying for power in the Hud boardroom have a host of cinematic forebears. The setup of Sid's power play, for example, parallels the predicament in the uneven satire *Putney Swope* (1969), in which an ad agency's sole black executive becomes the unlikely boss when the president keels over at the start. An even closer setup can be found in Robert Wise's *Executive Suite* (1954). This drama, which was Lehman's first screenplay, begins with the company's clock tower ringing ominously over the power struggle that ensues when the corporate head drops dead in the opening scene. As in *Proxy*, the vice presidents must figure out who will take over and what will become of the dead president's stock shares.

On the lighter end of the tone scale comes *Proxy*'s affinity with Jerry Lewis's *The Patsy* (1964), in which an unlikely naïf topples the smarmy and powerful. Lewis's acid comedy about Hollywood superpowers takes off from the idea hatched by a creative team to hire a patsy. They need to replace their recently deceased star comedian and bet that they themselves are so talented that they can turn any nobody into a success. Bellboy Stanley Belt (Jerry Lewis) walks into their plan and becomes the patsy. They mold him into a brilliant success, or so they think. In the end, they find out he is talented in his own right. Lewis, of course, gets the last laugh through the movie's own falling motif. The final shot bookends *The Patsy*'s animated title sequence. In the opening a cartoon Lewis plummets past a series of hotel balconies, intermittently suspended in a freeze frame every few seconds. (Freeze frames punctuating Norville's fall appear in an early draft of the *Proxy* screenplay.) At the end, Lewis goes sailing over the railing much to his girlfriend's horror, but he pops up immediately on the other side, safe and unhurt.

As with most Coen films, *Proxy* blends light and dark tones. Norville, for instance, briefly visits Corporate America's dark side when as CEO, he basks in luxury at the expense of poor, mistreated workers. His short fall from grace wispily references Alfred Hitchcock, who loved the idea of conflicting passions in a single person. The reference occurs at Norville's lowest point, when the mob chases him, and Buzz, who is much like Norville himself was not too long before, punches him to the ground. The altercation occurs outside a nightclub called the Til 2 Club, the name of the bar in *Shadow of a Doubt* (1943). With help from Waring and Moses, Norville quickly restores his upright standing.

Norville's inclination is toward the light. Just as he pulls himself up in the end, his inventions give to the community rather than take away from it. Such action is the opposite of Sid's. He wants to prevent the public from buying Waring's shares. Norville and his toys revive the workforce and spread happiness throughout the land, wresting Hudsucker from the grips of evil executives and an oppressive clock, turning around the depersonalized, tyrannical nature of Hud with airborne circles, "you know, for kids!"

MYTHMAKING 101: WHEEL OF FORTUNE

With all its cinematic allusions *Proxy* is no doubt the Coens' billet-doux to film, but it is also a story of enlightenment and an American myth. Appropriately seeded with mythical elements and tidbits of Eastern philosophies, the story revolves around Norville's "great circle of life." The character arcs of Amy, Norville, and Sidney all map out the Hindu idea of rebirth with each getting his just, karmic desserts, depending on the person's level of enlightenment. Amy, the first to become enlightened, realizes her folly in thinking Norville a fool and works for the remainder of the story to reform herself. She goes from being a fast-talking career girl and suspicious know-it-all to a dreamer in a beatnik bar. She quits her job in favor of a less materialistic quest. In the end, she bonds with her lover through a ritual dance after he returns, having found himself, too.

Protagonist Norville follows a more convoluted road to enlightenment. He starts on the right path, makes a 180-degree turn in the wrong direction, and is then guided back to righteousness by the hand of Providence. When he transitions from an innocent with big hopes and dreams to a cynic after he tastes success, he trades places with the jaded Amy. While she begins to see the world through fresh eyes wide with idealism and optimism, he transforms into the self-obsessed, egotistical braggart that the "I'll stake my Pulitzer on it" Amy once was—but even worse.[43] He becomes like Sid and the board: He is unproductive (he rehashes the hula hoop concept for different-sized people), uncompassionate (he rudely scoffs Buzz's "buzz" straw idea), and unwise (he initiates huge layoffs while a host of minions pamper him). Soon he gets a taste of his newfound medicine when Sid treats him as unjustly as Norville began to treat his workers. Only after wandering this desert of corporate dystopia does Norville return to his creative roots and produce his next big hit for the company—the frisbee.

Like his hoop, the frisbee captures the Hindu concepts of rebirth, karma, and transcendence, which symbolize Norville's, Amy's, and Sid's plots. Unlike Norville who transcends both death and time when he falls off the ledge, Sid hangs himself by being completely unenlightened, knotted up in his own vicious selfishness and deceit. When Norville's hoop becomes a runaway success, Sid tries to reassure the board that all is not lost, but since he never appreciates the power of circles or inclusiveness, his spin falters and sputters. In fact, because he doesn't learn that self-interest does not pay, he dooms himself to a Santayanan cycle in which those unable to learn from history repeat it. His second idea to power grab the company stock spins so completely out of control that he gravitates to Norville's ledge, and his fabricated story about Norville's manic-depression is visited on himself. In Christian terms, Sid reaps what he tried to sow. In Hindu terms, his fate shows "what goes around comes around."

Eastern thought imbues the movie with the power of circles, figures that symbolize time and rebirth. Norville's finesse at surviving his fall, thanks to the stoppage of time, demonstrates the key Hindu belief of transcendence, which involves liberation from the cycle of life and death. The suspended time, so critical to Norville's second chance, alludes to the sacred Hindu text, the *Bhagavad Gita*, an allegory about enlightenment, which opens with the freezing of time. The time freeze in the long Hindu poem allows its hero to reassess his values before entering war. During *Proxy*'s suspension of time, Norville also reexamines his morals. In the process, he learns that his action of not delivering the Blue Letter puts him in charge of the company again.

The Hindu text stresses individual selflessness and action—two qualities that Norville needs to rule wisely and compassionately. The poem also explicates the basics of rebirth, reincarnation, and time as a cyclical continuum—the same themes that *Proxy* explores ad infinitum: the narration over the film's final shot of a frisbee spinning through space teases another tale. Norville's hoop loops into the important Hindu concept of the unity of being. Amy emblematically speaks to this idea: "Finally there'd be a thingamajig that would bring everyone together—even if it kept them apart, spatially—you know, for kids?"[44] Though she is referring to the hoop, the implication of her words goes far beyond the toy into the realm of symbols. The hoop is a subset of a much bigger connector, for what truly connects everyone is the story itself, the myth of how the yokel named Norville Barnes makes a name for himself in The Big City and in the annals of Hudsucker through his popular toy. The film demonstrates that unifying things, such as toys and movies, are regenerative forces.

The concept of Norville's "great wheel of life" is woven throughout. The story begins on New Year's Eve, that seasonal time of renewal when the earth is about to start a new revolution around the sun. It's an occasion for folks to ring out the old and in the new and wait for the Times Square ball. That's the macrocosmic view. The microcosmic view presents a picture of corporate renewal. Norville is moments away from his own possible "merger with the infinite" and about to meet the man whose departure from Hud gives him opportunity instead.[45] This company karma is expressed unwittingly in the board's strangely regal mantra, "The Hud is dead—long live the Hud."[46] At every turn, cyclical forces are at play. In short, *Proxy*'s circle symbolism—best indicated by, but in no way limited to, the pivotal hula hoop—is effectively the Coens' mandala, the Hindu graphic representation of the universe. From the Sanskrit word for *circle*, mandala refers to something "symbolically designed so that it has the meaning of a cosmic order," in the words of Joseph Campbell.[47] The circle, then, helps designate Hudsucker as a universe with its own culture, to which the hula hoop and frisbee bring order and harmony.

Hudsucker's representative cosmos draws from art through the ages. Along with film quotes, art in the form of sculpture, dance, music, and poetry enhances Norville's myth. Prominent traces of religious traditions round out its landscape, enabling Norville to become an archetypal hero who succeeds only after failing (and falling), as if rising from the ashes of defeat like the phoenix. Ancient Greeks and Romans, whose vast imaginations gave us captivating stories to explain the world, appear throughout the film as well, underscoring their continuing influence in the modern world.

From the Latin word for *nest* or originating place comes the name of Norville's employment agency where his journey begins: Nidus. Norville then takes his job search to the Epicure Diner, named after the Greek philosopher Epicurus who gloried in life's simple pleasures. The movie's main rag, the *Manhattan Argus*, is a fitting moniker that delivers a clever dig to boring storytellers. The *Argus*, the supposed journalistic watchdog that can't get the Hudsucker story right, takes its name from the many-eyed monster of Greek mythology whom the jealous goddess-queen Hera tasks with keeping an eye (or two or one hundred) on her husband's lover, Io. But when Zeus learns of this, he sends the messenger god Hermes to kill his wife's spy. To avoid the monster's many eyes, Hermes tells Argus a story so boring it puts him to sleep, and once his guard is down, Hermes chops off his head. As if commenting on this potential pitfall all storytellers face, the most prominent sign in the newsroom asks, "Is it interesting?" *Proxy's* inventive recycling tries to make sure that the answer regarding its own inventions is yes.

In addition to such borrowings, the film fashions its own myth-making ingredients, such as ritual dances, art, and animal totems. It also creates its own small-town hero myth, similar to Capra's but distinct. For example, to successfully work her way into Norville's life, Amy must prove herself a Muncie insider, and for a few moments, it looks like she might fail. After trapping him with her hard-working-but-unemployed-and-broke story and then falling faint (all major characters fall), he carries her up to his office. He pours her a drink to help her spell but cannot handle a shot himself and rushes out of the room to regurgitate (that oh-so Coenesque activity). When he returns, his strange noises and movements cut Amy off mid-spiel. She eyes him warily but then she catches on. He is performing the well-known American ritual of the fight song. She tries to join him, but her performance is poor at best. "Fight on, fight on, dear old Muncie," Amy struggles to keep up. "Hoist the gold and blue. You'll be tattered, torn and hurtin' once the Munce is done with you. Go Eagles!"[48] Norville quite hilariously bonds with his "fellow Muncian" who barely knows the words or hand gestures and should be outed as an imposter. Yet, his naiveté time and again proves a strong suit, and eventually their fake connection grows into a genuine bond, and the song helps forge the legitimacy.

The scene is a variation of the "Swanee River" bonding duet in *Deeds*. Like Amy, Babe falls for the naïf whose humility, eccentricity, and creativity far outweigh those of the establishment men. The first inkling of their camaraderie comes when they sing together. But where Babe and Longfellow bond over real small-town roots and harmonize to the well-known "Swanee River," *Proxy's* Norville and Amy sing a song that works on a more universal level. Norville's grunts, kicks, and arm flaps initially shock, but the moment he adds the words, the song is instantly recognizable as a school ritual. This chord of kinship underscores the power of connections such rites hold. Like the hula hoop, the ritual unites.

With a nod to Frank Capra's *Mr. Deeds Goes to Town*, Jennifer Jason Leigh pretends she's a small-town girl by singing the Muncie fight song with true Muncian Tim Robbins. (Credit: Warner Bros. Pictures Inc./Photofest © Warner Bros. Pictures Inc.)

The Muncie eagle, alluded to in the fight song, helps chart Norville's power struggle. The finger flaps denoting the bird's wings go from being a test of Amy's sleuthing abilities to a means of ridicule and ultimately to a gesture of love. After faking her way through the Muncie song, back in the newsroom she flaps her fingers for Smitty to mock Norville. Later, after Sid takes Norville down a notch, Amy tries to pull him out of his slump by singing the song and performing the hand movements, but, alas, he is far too low—and drunk—to be inspired. Eventually, though, the Muncie story works its magic and connects. In the final scene, having survived his precipitous fall, Norville rushes to Amy. They reconnect at the beatnik bar, flapping the eagle hand symbol, and then clinching their communion with an embrace and a kiss.

The fight song also fits into the Coens' cross-film mythology. That is, fans might recognize the song's coded language pointing to *Barton Fink*. When the hula hoop becomes popular, it is covered in the newsreel *Tidbits of Time*, voiced by actor John Goodman, whose character name in the credits is Karl Mundt. In *Fink*, Charlie Meadows, alias Karl "Madman" Mundt (also Goodman), is a psycho killer. Relating the song's "Munce" to Goodman's earlier "Mundt" gives whole new meaning to the otherwise figurative line, "You'll be tired, torn and tattered once the Munce is done with you."[49] The lyrics also foreshadow Sid's downfall.

In the Hud cosmos, flying denotes power, and in a realm where everyone important freefalls in some way, the eagle mascot becomes a kind of hieroglyphic for Norville's power. Its first sighting as the business school logo on Norville's suitcase foreshadows his ascension. In scoffing Norville's small-hometown roots and his alma mater, Sid and others fail to recognize the potential power of *his* nidus, represented by a powerful bird of flight: the Muncie eagle. Signs are important in the Hud, and so the emblematic raptor augurs Norville's rise. Those who fly—or who can at least defy gravity through toys or helpful story gods like Moses—are successful. Waring flies out the window and lands, we later learn, in heaven. He floats back into the picture with huge eaglelike wings suggesting he sure can fly.

In effect, Norville's gift is flight. He can't fly per se, but winds usually work in his favor and his creations glide through air. Sid, in contrast, is earthbound. Though he assumes the position at the window twice, he never quite becomes aloft. First, despite his cheap, sartorial choice, the good-hearted tailor gives him a double-stitch, which helps Norville save him. Later, the men from the asylum snatch Sid from the ledge before he can jump. Norville, on the other hand, as the signs point out, is of this earth but not bound by it. He is free to fly, fall and fail and take wing again, as Waring's letter indicates. This hero has the mojo necessary to keep soaring to new heights.

APOCALYPSE NOW

Despite an overall light tone and an uplifting ending, *Proxy* flirts with darkness and disaster. At its core is a universal face-off between good and evil, and embedded codes offer solid evidence that it is more than just a comedy. A staggering amount of words, letters, and numbers fill *Proxy*'s frames and soundtrack, symbols all suggesting its deep allegory. Here are a few of note. Moses talks of an annual change, from 1958 to 1959 as the clock moves from 11:58 to 11:59. Midnight and noon figure prominently in setting up Norville's and Waring's karmic moves. The company report reveals earnings are up 18 percent; when Amy spies on Sid, he mentions a 15 percent downward move. What emerges in Hud land is an unnatural disturbance in natural ebbs and flows of things like time and the free market. Such meddling creates havoc. The executive's manipulation of numbers for their own profit at the public's expense means trouble. By contrast, workers who engage with numbers, letters, and other symbols for the good of production and creation provide benefit.

Amy, for example, is a wordsmith. Her impressive multitasking shows three simultaneous levels of communicating: As she types up her story, she tells Smitty all about Norville, and breaks the crossword code by yelling out answers to a coworker. She does this all against the deadline clock inching from 4:59 toward 5:00. She may be a bit off on her understanding of the doings at Hudsucker—she's only half right—but her intentions are, for the most part, noble. She wants to spread the truth through printed communication.

Words, letters, and numbers appear all over the screen. At the employment agency and in the paper *really* odd jobs (such as corner man, bombardier, minstrel, pearl diver, and carny) jump out at him, along with the word *experience* connected to them.[50] Later at the news conference, words and letters create visual chaos and excitement. Standing by a huge board of names, Norville is bombarded by flashes and questions. In front of him are the mics with their respective stations' call letters—ABC, NBC, etc. The sound of flash bulbs popping is sonically reminiscent of the job board scene, which is similar to the background sound in the newsroom.

A sign hanging in the newsroom wonders, "Is it interesting?" while signage in the accounting area asks, "How much does it cost?"[51] The interplay of words and numbers and creativity is important to Hud in their added layers of communication. The hoop makes the rounds through production stages trackable by departmental signs such as "Proving Facility" and "Creative Bullpen." A secretary reading a Tolstoy novel outside pantomiming brainstormers reminds us it's the word guys without even having to read the department sign the second time around. Newspaper headlines updating Norville's presidential feats and defeats add to the screen's nonstop alphabet soup. The list goes on, and such an extensive display of onscreen symbols coupled with animal imagery and otherworldly journeys makes the case that *Proxy*'s Big Business satire is in part an apocalypse narrative.

Apocalypse, from the Greek word *apokalypsis*, means revelation. It derives from Jewish and Christian traditions and refers to a deity's unveiling of hidden things usually tucked inside a dream or vision. It was traditionally a first-person narrative told by a narrator using an earlier prophet's name to give credence to his story, such as Moses in *Proxy*. The works usually detailed violent clashes between good and evil, often in eschatological scenarios, and were written in times of crisis as a means of hope for the distressed. All of these conditions fit *Proxy*. Norville fulfills the messianic role built into apocalyptic narratives. He and his toy enter a world weighted down by dismal working conditions and crooked managers, and he leavens it with good will and joy. What's more, apocalyptic stories generally involved clock stoppages. As historian Ernest Lee Tuveson notes, "The measure of time, the sun's revolutions, for example, must be interrupted or discontinued when the Day of the Lord shall arrive."[52] The main message of such stories was to demonstrate that good forces eventually conquer wickedness—which is precisely what transpires in *Proxy*.

The three main ingredients of an apocalyptic narrative are animal imagery, number symbolism, and otherworldly journeys, all three of which find form in the Coens' film. Norville's New York is riddled with animals. He arrives on a Wolverine bus, suggesting a dog-eat-dog world, though Moses prefers the "the rat race" idiom. The narrator refers to the execs as "little pigglies" trying to get all the stock for themselves.[53] The advertised job listings include "card shark," "cat's meats man," and "goat herd." After a stockholder punches Norville at the banquet, his wife reprimands him for being a grizzly bear. The chief disparages the quality of the newspaper by saying it's fit for wrapping fish in or training his poodle on. Then, he says (quoting a line from Robert Altman's *McCabe and Mrs. Miller*), "If a frog had wings, it wouldn't bump its ass a hoppin'."[54] As Amy composes her first story about Hud's new idiot-in-charge, she tosses out crossword answers "gnu" and "emu" for the "flightless bird" clue. Little does the faux Muncian reporter know that she's missing the boat on Norville, who is symbolized by not a flightless bird but one that soars. We know that, of course, not just from the fight song. His suitcase sports his power source: the eagle.

On the balcony, Amy muses that people look like ants. Her simile prompts Norville's philosophical waxing about reincarnation. He explains that Hindus believe that people return in other lives as butterflies, elephants, or creatures of the sea. He goes on about an encounter the two of them might have had in previous lives. He guesses she was a gazelle and he an antelope or an ibex. He follows all this serious talk up with a "Can I call you deer?" joke.[55]

Number symbolism is just as prevalent. Norville begins his adventure deep in the bowels of Hudsucker where random letter-number combinations such as K-15, B-13, and K-D5 plaster the mailroom walls, signaling pandemic chaos. His orientation is cacophonic mumbo jumbo: "Letter 'Size A'—green voucher! Folder 'Size A'—yellow voucher!"[56] The docking refrain is the only comprehendible detail: Get something wrong and you will pay, literally. And really that's the Hud's bottom line. The room and the oppression it encompasses are modeled in part after Lang's nightmarish underworld in *Metropolis*, where subterranean workers toil long hours enslaved by a clock. The Hud's cavernous mailroom, also tyrannically run by a clock, is a similar hell. As with Lang's laborers, the mailroom work is an exercise in existentialism. The Ancient Sorter (Patrick Cranshaw), for example, has spent forty-eight years on the corporate ladder's bottom rung. A mailroom lifer (who *might* finally get a promotion to parcels!), he's also a human automaton, who can fling envelopes with the rapid fire motion of a machine. Worker exploitation is so accepted here, that its long hours and low pay are promoted in the company's job ads.

Norville is not just destined to escape this world, he is also fated to end the horrible conditions. His facility with symbols comes early with his resolution of the Kloppitt dilemma. Whereas the Old Timer just throws out problematic deliveries, Norville solves it by writing a note. It's a simple solution, to be sure, but his solution compiling words, writing, and a letter exemplifies creative problem-solving with symbols. Later, his circle on paper idea will yield bigger benefits all-round. Time and again, Norville shows an affinity for creating with signs, numbers, and letters to get him out of tight spots.

We don't spend much time in the mailroom because Norville escapes his first day, but the few scenes there are so visually stunning they easily convey the deep chasm between the bosses in their lofty offices and the slaving have-nots far below. The picture is clear: The executive suites are huge and anemic; the crowded mailroom is frenetically though not productively busy. The only time work stops for the laborers below—and then just momentarily—is for official business from above. This occurs twice: when Waring's death is announced and when the Blue Letter needs delivery. Both work interruptions are as absurd as the busywork itself. Obviously, this world's dark forces wind tightly around power, money, and bureaucracy.

Combining the onscreen symbols with heavenly journeys and religious trimmings, the movie seems to encase coded references to the system of ancient Hebrew mysticism known as the Cabala—a term actually uttered in the film. As ace reporter Amy writes her first inside story, she animatedly describes Hudsucker's happenings: "This guy's the real patsy and I'm gonna find out what for. There's a real story here, Smitty, some kind of plot, a set-up, a cabal, a—oh."[57] Certainly Sid has hatched a cabal, but written in the screenplay and spoken by Amy as such, the end of the phrase phonetically forms the word "Cabala," which translates literally as "tradition" and is a mysticism based on symbolic representation. With so many metaphysical layers and the more obvious "Munce" phonetic code, a solid case can be made that the veiled reference exists. The film's cross-fertilization of Moses and Hinduism bolsters such a theory.

Cabala is a complex system of mysticism and philosophy marked by the belief that divine answers lie in coded religious texts. The system is thought to have been handed down orally for centuries until 80 A.D. That's when followers began writing it down. Its original messenger was none other than Moses.[58] How far-fetched is it that the Coens have taken a page from this mystical tradition? Theirs is an apocalyptic story narrated by a prophetic Moses who tells of a hero who saves a world from evil forces. It's heavy on codes and built around Hindu ideas, circles, and clocks and incorporates a key clock stoppage.

Part of the Cabala closely resembles sections of *The Bhagavad Gita*—the main Hindu scripture that explains creation and karma, about which the film makes much ado. Cabalistic belief holds that letters and numbers in the Torah contain the key to discovering the way to return to divinity. Norville is the only one who instinctively knows enough to shun the Blue Letter. Had he delivered it, Sid would have taken over the company, and the place would have been sunk. Instead, a series of symbolic circles lead Norville to Hud's corporate universe where he pitches an idea that benefits all of Hud. After Aloysius blows onto the window and seemingly causes Norville to tumble off the ledge, Moses suspends time to save him by way of Waring's counsel. *The Bhagavad Gita* opens on the Supreme Being Krishna freezing time so that he can counsel a young warrior.

The Cabala teaches that people who understand its mysteries can break free of the "enchanted circle" of life that ensnares unenlightened humans. Norville breaks through the Hud's unjust snares through his circle. After losing his way on the path to greed, he is saved by an angel, a Blue Letter, and Moses, who stops time to help him out. Throughout, Norville's focus is on the universal symbol for unity (circles can embrace all regular polygons), infinity (it has neither an end nor a beginning), and democracy (it allows for an assembly of equals). Through this geometric figure, Norville brings harmony to a discordant Hudsucker.

ART SHOW

The movie basks in looking at the past, not just to load up on self-conscious references for the astute viewer to recognize. It also looks backward to acknowledge the importance of the past in creating the future. Peter Gallagher's Dean Martin–inspired performance of "Memories Are Made of This" might augur the budding romance between Amy and Norville, but, more important, it underscores the movie's main idea of remembering. Much of the internal artwork expands on the idea of recollection, and both the allusive and original art often reflects the struggle of the worker against a corrupt system.

One example is the boardroom's mural of laborers. Prominently featured during Norville's induction as Hud president, the wall art highlights the working-class values he is destined to enshrine at Hudsucker. Depicted in the piece are boots, wrenches, and helmeted men engaged in a struggle with their tools. One prominent worker grabs a circle. Thus, the mural foretells Norville's representative battle against Big Business and notes circle power.

The internal art often juxtaposes high- and lowbrow art to reveal the class struggle. A prime example of this occurs when Amy struts into Norville's office to tell him about the layoffs, which, she is about to learn, *he* has requested. Her discovery and dismay broaden as she gazes around the room and takes in Norville's transformation. His office is a bastion of excess and outright disregard of his workers. A string quartet fittingly plays "Eine Kleine Nachtmusik," a Mozart composition written expressly for the entertainment of Viennese nobility. Also played at the black-tie ball, Mozart, in counterpoint to Khachaturian's working-class odes, comes to represent the elite executive class. With people about to lose their jobs to save the company money, a sculptor taps away at a huge bust of Norville, which, when placed in the lobby, provides a reference to Terry Gilliam's *Brazil* (1985), a film about the futility of class struggle in a bureaucratized world. The massage machines used on Norville ironically bear a close resemblance to the torture devices used in *Brazil*. Disgusted by what she sees, Amy dismisses everyone. She goes on to read Norville the riot act and then resigns on the spot. By the scene's end, all that remains are the bodyguard's comics, the art of the working class. She adds a final touch of lowbrow art in the form of slapstick comedy and kicks the bodyguard on her way out.

High- and lowbrow art mix again in Norville's tangential dream sequence. After Amy quits, Norville falls asleep at his desk. His dream of dancing with an elusive woman spoofs the divergent ballet number from the elaborate dance sequence in *Singin' in the Rain* (1952), a satire of Hollywood's move from silent films to talkies. The scene that *Proxy* references is the dramatization of a brainstorm belonging to hero and Hollywood heartthrob Don Lockwood (Gene Kelly). The fantastic sequence encapsulates a rags-to-riches story similar to Norville's: A small-time dancer goes to Broadway to make it big, meets a sexy girl who is a ganster's moll (Cyd Charisse), loses her and then by chance dances with her again later. Charisse's long, billowing scarf is like the dancer's (Pamela Everett) outfit in the Coen sequence. Set to Georges Bizet's *Carmen*, *Proxy*'s bull-and-toreador dance between Norville and the dream woman spoofs the graceful, lyrical dancers in *Singin' in the Rain*, the lovers in Bizet's opera, and moves from *The Karate Kid* (1984).

Norville's dance fantasy also alludes to Amy's role as a harmonizer in Hud's universe. This function comes across symbolically, through the letter *A*, as emphasized in her name, *Amy Archer*. Not just the alphabet's first character, *A* also represents the musical note for a string vibrating at 440 cycles per second. The name of the beatnik bar is Ann's 440. (Her undercover pseudonym in the script not used in the movie is *Ann,* the same name as her model from Capra.) In Hudsucker's highly representative, allegorical realm, Amy represents an ideal, a perfect note in a disordered world. The beatnik poetry covering the walls of the juice bar fuses words and music to advocate a simple life free of materialism. Like the Hindu universal truth, Amy, music, and poetry represent those cultural necessities that connect us to each other and all living things.

In the end, the ritualistic Muncie song is what brings Norville around. Before this, with Norville at his lowest point, drunk at her nonalcoholic hangout, Amy tries to talk sense into him, but he is unreachable. She tries to appeal to his Muncie strength, earnestly stressing each line in the song and its gestures, but it doesn't work. After Waring's angelic form visits, an enlightened Norville becomes president again. He returns to the beatnik bar, and communicates with Amy through first the fight song's wacky gestures and then kissing. In the end, they connect through words, music, and signs—universal symbols that like the circle have unifying powers.

WRAP: THE CIRCLE GAME

The Coens' follow-up to the elliptical *Barton Fink* is a satirical fable about square—as in corrupt—business practices that are reformed into "hip," honest ones. The maverick who transforms the company specializes in circular designs that reinforce cyclical, regenerative themes. In its familiar corporate ladder–climber story *Proxy* suggests that system-bucking innovators, creative "you know, for kids!" ideas, and well-told stories make the world go round. The movie showcases the idea of rebirth through its superstructure: The hero's meteoric rise to the top spoiled by a precipitate fall is turned around by a decisive ascent. Such an up-and-down cadence also relates to the business cycle, which ebbs and flows over time.

Opening on the edge of the world, then moving to Norville on a ledge at the edge of midnight, the story starts poised on the verge of change. It's not only the cusp of a new year; this is a pretipping point moment for Big Business. The current power structure based on Western capitalism is about to come tumbling down, replaced by Eastern philosophies of all-for-one-and-one-for-all. From the get-go, a wealth of symbols and related art point to the forces currently at work. From Capra's working-class heroes to Soviet music and literature celebrating the industrious worker, *Proxy* winks at the power of the little guy who can topple tyrannical forces and replace them with a unifying vision through art, entertainment, and circles, "you know, for kids."

NOTES

1. Well-known for his *Spider-Man* blockbusters (2002, 2004), Raimi is something of a cult figure in the horror genre, thanks to his *Evil Dead* horror movies (1981, 1987). Joel Coen's first professional film gig was as a film editor on Raimi's first *Evil Dead* movie.

2. Another sneak peek of "Hudsucker" can be spied in Sam Raimi's *The XYZ Murders* (1983), also called *Crimewave*, which was co-written by the Coen brothers and features a Hudsucker State Penitentiary.

3. Working Title scored big with its maiden film, *My Beautiful Laundrette* (Stephen Frears), which burned up the box office and earned screenwriter Hanif Kureishi an Academy Award nomination in 1987. In 1994, the production house topped that success with the runaway comedy, *Four Weddings and a Funeral* (Mike Newell), which garnered two Oscar nods in 1995.

4. Andrew Pulver, "Profile: The Coen Brothers: Blood Ties," *The Guardian*, August 20, 1998, Features-6.

5. Danny Leigh, "The Silver Age," *The Guardian*, December 8, 1999, Features-12.

6. When the Pitt Theatre Department asked director Robert C. T. Stelle about compelling plays dealing with American enterprise, *Proxy* sprang to his mind: "It's one of my favorite movies because of the theme." John Hayes, "Coen Heads: Pitt Attempts a Live Adaptation of the Cult Hit *The Hudsucker Proxy*," *Pittsburgh Post-Gazette*, November 5, 1999, 16.

7. Aloysius was a Catholic monk who solved two key time-related problems: the calendar and Easter. Though as early as 325 A.D. the Christian church had a day to celebrate Easter, because it was based on the variable moon cycle, scholars knew for centuries the holiday drifted. In the late 1500s, Aloysius Lilius figured out how to correctly determine Easter Day. He also lobbied Pope Gregory to adopt a good calendrical system that would accurately reflect the time it takes Earth to make one revolution around the sun. That calendar is still in use today. The Coens' possible reference to this much less sinister Aloysius subtly nods to the premium the film puts on time.

8. *The Hudsucker Proxy*, DVD, directed by Joel Coen (1994; Burbank, Calif.: Warner Home Video, 1999).

9. The Coen Brothers, interview by Elvis Mitchell, "Independent Focus: The Coen Brothers." Independent Film Channel.

10. *The Hudsucker Proxy*, DVD.

11. *The Hudsucker Proxy*, DVD.

12. *The Hudsucker Proxy*, DVD; *Cool Hand Luke*, DVD, directed by Stuart Rosenberg (1967; Burbank, Calif.: Warner Home Video, 1997).

13. The phrase tempus fugit, commonly inscribed on clocks, comes from the verse "Georgica" by the Roman poet Virgil. The full quotation reads: "Sed fugit interea fugit irreparabile tempus," which translates as, "But it flees in the meantime: irretrievable time flees." The often misquoted "time flies" translation misses its original meaning of time's irretrievability.

14. John Anderson, "Screen's Mercurial Girl Is at It Again," *Los Angeles Times*, March 11, 1994, F-13.

15. Stephen Hunter, "Dazzling *Hudsucker Proxy* is a Delightful Echo of Old-Time Flicks," *Baltimore Sun*, April 8, 1994, 14.

16. *The Hudsucker Proxy*, DVD.

17. *The Hudsucker Proxy*, DVD.

18. *The Hudsucker Proxy*, DVD.

19. *The Hudsucker Proxy*, DVD.

20. *The Hudsucker Proxy*, DVD.

21. *The Hudsucker Proxy*, DVD.

22. *The Hudsucker Proxy*, DVD.

23. *The Hudsucker Proxy*, DVD.
24. *The Hudsucker Proxy*, DVD.
25. *The Hudsucker Proxy*, DVD.
26. *The Hudsucker Proxy*, DVD.
27. *The Hudsucker Proxy*, DVD.
28. *The Hudsucker Proxy*, DVD.
29. *The Hudsucker Proxy*, DVD.
30. *The Hudsucker Proxy*, DVD.
31. "The Sabre Dance Man," NPR's *Morning Edition*, June 5, 2003, www.npr.org/templates/story/story.php?storyId=1287262 (accessed January 15, 2006).
32. *The Hudsucker Proxy*, DVD.
33. Probably Khachaturian's most famous and recognized composition, "Sabre Dance" is the Armenian composer's tribute to the Soviet people, who had just entered World War II. Culminating the ballet for which it was written, the song celebrates the marriage of the two main characters, thus saluting the Russian people and their lives. Quote taken from http://faculty.weber.edu/tpriest/FacetsMdl_files/Sabre%20Dance.html. Facets Model Assignment: "Sabre Dance," Music 3824: Music for Elementary Teachers, Allegra Helper, by Juanita Wasatch, April 16, 2002.
34. *The Lady Eve*, DVD, directed by Preston Sturges (1941; New York, N.Y.: Criterion, 2001); *The Hudsucker Proxy*, DVD.
35. *The Hudsucker Proxy*, DVD.
36. *Mr. Deeds Goes to Town*, DVD, directed by Frank Capra (1936; Culver City, Calif.: Sony Pictures, 2000).
37. *Mr. Deeds Goes to Town*, DVD.
38. *The Hudsucker Proxy*, DVD.
39. In a film focused on circles, the psychiatrist's name—Bronfenbrenner—is an unlikely coincidence. Urie Bronfenbrenner is a Cornell University professor whose work on childhood development puts a premium on culture. In diagram form, his idea of nested influences is a series of concentric circles. In both form and substance his theory fits the film's design.
40. The Coens often write parts with an actor in mind. They wrote Visser's part in *Blood Simple*, hoping to snag well-known character actor M. Emmet Walsh for it, and Abby's part for Holly Hunter. They had Billy Bob Thornton in mind for Ed in *The Man Who Wasn't There*.
41. *Hud*, VHS, directed by Martin Ritt (1963; Hollywood, Calif.: Paramount, 1991).
42. *Sweet Smell of Success*, DVD, directed by Alexander Mackendrick (1957; Santa Monica, Calif.: MGM, 2001); *The Hudsucker Proxy*, DVD.
43. *The Hudsucker Proxy*, DVD.
44. *The Hudsucker Proxy*, DVD.
45. *The Hudsucker Proxy*, DVD.
46. *The Hudsucker Proxy*, DVD.
47. Joseph Campbell, *The Power of Myth* (New York: Doubleday, 1988), 216.
48. *The Hudsucker Proxy*, DVD.
49. *The Hudsucker Proxy*, DVD.

50. *The Hudsucker Proxy*, DVD.

51. *The Hudsucker Proxy*, DVD.

52. Ernest Lee Tuveson, *Redeemer Nation* (University of Chicago Press: 1968), 5.

53. *The Hudsucker Proxy*, DVD.

54. This line from Altman's 1971 feature is also quoted in *Raising Arizona*.

55. *The Hudsucker Proxy*, DVD.

56. *The Hudsucker Proxy*, DVD.

57. *The Hudsucker Proxy*, DVD.

58. Though Moses is likely modeled after his famous biblical namesake, the character could also allude to the twelfth century Jewish philosopher known as Maimonides or the "Second Moses" who was well versed in Cabalistic teaches and regarded as a leading Judaic philosopher. He wrote extensively about both religion and Aristotelian philosophy and wedded mystical and religious ideas with interpreting signs—all things the film deals with.

· 6 ·

Fargo: Snow

Academy Award winner Frances McDormand investigates a crime scene to uncover a snow job. (Credit: Gramercy Pictures/Photofest © Gramercy Pictures)

"You lied to me, Mr. Lundegaard. You're a bald-faced liar! A fucking liar."

—Irate Customer (Gary Houston)

"Hide, oh hide those hills of snow
Which thy frozen bosom bears,

171

On whose tops the pinks that grow
Are of those that April wears!
But first set my poor heart free,
Bound in those icy chains by thee."

—John Fletcher, *The Bloody Brother*, Act 5, Scene 2 (c. 1617)

PREVIEW

*T*hough the quirky noir *Blood Simple* triggered Ethan and Joel Coen's maverick moviemaking career and opened doors to a loyal art-house following, it wasn't until their chiller *Fargo* some twelve years later that the brothers caught the eyes—and raised the eyebrows—of a mainstream audience. In its opening week during March 1996, the film netted $730,265 on a scant thirty-six screens.[1] Within the year the $7 million feature had earned $24 million. By the end of its theatrical run, *Fargo* would hit 716 theatres—the largest showing of a Coen movie up until that time.[2] The Motion Picture Academy also took notice, nominating *Fargo* for seven awards and bestowing it with Oscars for Best Actress (Frances McDormand) and Best Screenplay.[3] The combination of critical praise and box office success meant the fiercely idiosyncratic Coen brothers were a whisper away from being a household name.

Without detracting from its devious creativity, timing also likely had a hand in *Fargo*'s broad appeal. Edward Burns's 1995 runaway success *The Brothers McMullen* had opened up the distribution playing field for small films. A year later, Hollywood movies had some real competition from their low-budget cousins, so much so that 1996 was dubbed the "Year of the Indies." Independent features made a good showing at the sixty-ninth Academy Awards. *Trainspotting* (director, Danny Boyle; writer, John Hodge) and *Lone Star* (John Sayles) were up for Best Screenplay, Lars Von Trier's *Breaking the Waves* for Best Actress, and Mike Leigh's *Secrets & Lies* for Best Picture, Best Actress, Best Director, and Best Screenplay. Billy Bob Thornton's *Sling Blade* won Best Screenplay, and *Shine*'s Geoffrey Rush took home the Best Actor award. Four of the five Best Picture nominees were low-budget indies, including the winner, Anthony Minghella's *The English Patient,* which swept the Oscar ceremony with nine statuettes. With a sliver of the marketing money and distribution opportunities of studio films, *The English Patient*, *Shine*, and *Fargo* went on to make the top one hundred box office hits for 1996. In the long run, *Fargo* would unleash more surprises than just wide success.

REVIEW

Fargo tells the story of Jerry Lundegaard (William H. Macy), a stereotypically two-faced car salesman who kidnaps his own wife (Kristin Rudrüd) to solve some money problems. The idea is that his wealthy father-in-law and boss, Wade Gustafson (Harve Presnell), will pay the large ransom. The tale begins in Fargo, North Dakota, where Jerry hires two men to commit the crime. Really only one of them comes recommended by Shep Proudfoot (Steven Reevis), a paroled mechanic at Jerry's dealership, and it appears from the action that it is probably Carl Showalter (Steve Buscemi). But appearances continue to deceive, as the sleepy town of Fargo retreats into the background and Minnesota becomes the main setting.

With a new Cutlass Ciera as a down payment, Carl and his partner Gaear Grimsrud (Peter Stormare) nab Jerry's wife, Jean, but an oversight leads to deadly consequences. When a state trooper stops them for driving a vehicle without license plates, in moves that dramatically describe each man's motivation, Carl tries to pay the officer off and Gaear shoots him dead. When rubbernecking passersby see the limp, bloody body being dragged off the road (a nod to *Blood Simple*), Gaear chases them down and mercilessly kills them too.[4] As bloody events continue, Jerry's moneymaking cozening suffers a snowball-from-hell effect, and his arrangement with the lowlifes becomes tantamount to a deal with the devil and company.

As the "staged" kidnapping story segues into a "real" murder mystery, the unlikely but unforgettable character of Marge Gunderson (Frances McDormand), Brainerd's police chief, enters the picture. Here the film begins to pursue two main story lines that are inextricably linked but only tangentially connected: Jerry's attempts to control the crime scheme and Marge's investigation of the murders. Marge is awoken in the wee hours of the morning with news of the multiple homicides. Husband Norm (John Carroll Lynch) jumpstarts first her workday with breakfast and then her battery-dead prowler, and the pregnant cop heads to the crime scene.

Meanwhile, both Wade and the kidnappers start calling the shots, thus upstaging Jerry, and the death toll climbs. Having reneged on the "no-rough-stuff" deal in spades, Carl—who is growing more erratic with each kill—demands more money to compensate for the accumulating liability.[5] Jerry, barely awakening to the real danger to which he has subjected his wife, is upset by the request, but the point becomes moot when Wade overrides Jerry's need to deliver the money himself. The controlling father-in-law's insistence on confronting the kidnapper gets him killed, and unwittingly cuts Jerry once and forever out of this most important deal.

Carl, on the other hand, is in the money. When the kidnapper, bleeding profusely from a facial gunshot wound, discovers $1 million in the ransom bag, instead of the expected $80,000, he decides to keep the extra for himself, hiding it in a nondescript snow bank by a fence. He returns to the hideout to find that Gaear has killed Jean. The kidnappers argue over money, and Carl meets his own gruesome demise at the end of an ax. The story concludes when Marge, patrolling the lake near the hideout, spies the tan Ciera and apprehends Gaear in the act of stuffing Carl into a wood chipper. In a denouement, police stake out a motel and capture an unstrung Jerry.

TALL TALE

Set in an area famous for its larger-than-life character Paul Bunyan, *Fargo* is a modern tall tale—it pretends to be true. "The events depicted in this film took place in Minnesota in 1987," an opening title card reads. "The names have been changed. Out of respect for the dead, the rest has been told exactly as it occurred."[6] The words say one thing, but their intent and meaning are another. And even though dressing fiction as fact is as old as ancient myths, that doesn't mean the Coens' play is easily spotted. Yet, a close look at *Fargo* shows deceptions steamrolling across the film from the start, blanketing it like a layer of hard-packed snow on turf.

The title is a starting point for the duplicity. It suggests a setting of Fargo, North Dakota, but the movie takes place mostly in Minnesota's Twin Cities and the nearby suburb of Brainerd, home of the legendary giant Paul Bunyan and his gigantic blue ox, Babe—and Marge. These mascots pop up on screen like signposts pointing to the movie's main technique of the tall tale. During Jerry's opening jaunt to Fargo to meet with a couple of thugs, a mix-up occurs: Jerry is late. Worse, we find out later, only one of the two men comes with a recommendation. Jerry doesn't think twice about two showing up for the job. The viewer probably should, for *Fargo* has particular if not quite peculiar setting markers: "twins"—the film's many pairs point to the duality of fact and fiction—and size—Gaear is "big," Carl "little." Such markers matter— big-time—in a place where blood-red tall tales and mushrooming white lies are the primary colors for a whitewash.

Following a disclaimer about events being true, the movie opens on a whiteout. The textured background against which the credits appear suggests a sky thick with snow and clouds. But shortly after a bird flies into view, a pair of headlights emerges, and it becomes clear that we're looking at a road—a treacherous swath of land smothered by the blizzard. What we thought was one thing—sky—is really another: sky and land. With no distinguishing horizon line between them, the true image is hidden until the car comes into view. Also obscured is the driver, a main character of this sketchy tableau, whose moral compass, we soon learn, also has no dividing line between truth and lie, perception and ignorance, need and greed. In this universe, such an opening implies all is not what it appears to be. Lines are blurred.

Jerry's introduction provides a foretaste of his personality. His initial predicament of being trapped inside a car, unseen, battling brute conditions will be sustained. Small and insignificant against the forces of nature, he is en route to a meeting he hopes will catalyze a change in status. That is, he wants to be big, he yearns to disengage himself from thumping money problems, and he has a plan to make this happen. He is driving to the aptly named King of Clubs bar where his gamble with his wife's life is to begin.

The more his persona is revealed, at work and at home, the more metaphorical the opening situation appears. Jerry feels trapped by his life and overshadowed by his commanding father-in-law. This is clear from the moment Jerry gets home to find Wade there. Wade is everything Jerry is not: virile, strong, successful, and rich. Jerry is visibly displeased that Wade is staying for dinner, but he does not object. When Scotty (Tony Denman) excuses himself from the table to go to McDonald's, Wade criticizes Jerry's permissive parenting. The exchange is more evidence of how Jerry feels less the man of the house with Wade around, as if his subordination on the job is paralleled on the home front. Though Jerry's money problems are the stated impetus for the kidnapping, his family standing is also at issue, and his big plan could fix both difficulties. Having Jean kidnapped, he thinks, will help him get dough and run the show—allowing him to bamboozle and upstage Wade. Put differently, though Jerry's up-front motives are pecuniary in nature, his abundantly apparent hidden motives are of the vindictive kind.

Marge is Jerry's opposite. She is what she appears to be. She is large instead of diminutive and in control from the start, not late for a meeting. Her pregnancy and close partnership with Norm palpably illustrate her good marriage while Jean's abduction shows Jerry's dissatisfaction with his. In addition to being domestically satisfied, Marge the cop is a pro. She sleuths through a string of murders as well as any celluloid gumshoe before her—a fact all the more interesting because we likely believe the story and thus her character are reality based.

We meet Marge when work encroaches on her domestic life. Despite the hour and inconvenience of the late-night call, she is a model of professionalism. "Oh my," she says, in characteristic understatement, continuing, "Where? Ya. Oh geez. OK. There in a jif."[7] Her calm, laconic response coupled with her gender does not prepare us for her police chief role until we see her in uniform at the breakfast table. Norm has gotten up to cook her eggs. Though they don't say much, their first family meal is a far cry from Jean and Jerry's. The Gundersons have what the Lundegaards don't: a true and honest partnership, a satisfying marriage, and a happy home life mirrored on the job. In the crime scene's frigid air, Marge sips her hot coffee and reads the clues like an ace detective, describing exactly what happened. In control and after the truth, she is what Jerry is not.

Jerry's first scene on the job starts on an establishing shot of the dealership showroom, where Wade's last name ("Gustafson") along with the slogan "Satisfaction, Sales, Service" help spell out Jerry's problem: It's not his shop, and his salesmanship is light-years away from those three *s*'s. We're about to learn that there's only one "s" in the tagline about which Jerry cares, but unfortunately for him, sales are not his forte. The next shot shows a picture of Jerry grinning widely with his arms crossed in front of him. A cut to a wall of salesmen's pictures shows him to be the only one with folded arms, as if gesturing as children do when they lie (arms crossed instead of fingers). We hear the argument-in-progress before we see it. Later on, hearing before seeing helps to unravel the theme of knowledge versus belief. Here, an argument in process indicates Jerry's prevaricating personality. The Irate Customer (Gary Houston) is complaining, with good reason, about the charge for the ironically named TruCoat on his bill. The buyer hadn't wanted it, but the paltering seller is bent on letting him have it.

Where Marge's police job is built around gathering facts and discovering the truth, Jerry is the car salesman stereotype: a liar. He dissembles to this customer over the sealant the man did not want, and then pretends to do something about it. Really, he ducks out of the rough sales meeting and into a colleague's office where he asks about hockey tickets. He returns with a bogus better offer, delivering the "deal" with a weasel smile as wide as the gulf between what he is saying and the truth. He chalks up a small, monetary victory. It is doubtful that the extra money goes toward any sealant, which was likely never put on the car. Jerry needs cash and will go about getting it any way he can. This white lie pales next to the trail of blood his kidnapping scheme will yield.

Jerry has undisclosed money problems, and though he doesn't want to ask Wade for a handout, he has no qualms about taking one or laying out a dangerous plan to secretly power-grab one. Ironically, just as Jerry's day job is connected to his wife and her powerful father, his kidnapping idea banks on them, too. He may feel emasculated and obscured by his familial ties, but even his attempts to make good supposedly on his own require their aid, unwitting or not. His presumably legal moneymaking idea relies on his family ties, too. The parking lot deal is his one chance at getting money legitimately and his only shot at redemption. It's also an opportunity to prove himself as the man of the house. He tries to inveigle Wade with the prospect of financial security for his family. Wade dismisses the bait and leaves Jerry out of the picture. "Jean and Scotty never have to worry," he harrumphs, eviscerating Jerry with a single phrase.[8]

Jerry's backup plan to the parking lot deal is his crime scheme, an opportunity to kill two birds with one stone. Either way, he thinks he'll get his money and power by finally getting the upper hand of Wade. The problem is, more than the proverbial birds wind up dead, and his little, no-rough-stuff plan snowballs into a gargantuan crime with a body count of seven. It's up to the matter-of-fact Marge to uncover the truth. As police chief, it's Marge's job to see behind the TruCoat lies, find the sales exec with crossed arms, and ultimately locate the dividing lines between truth and lies and good and evil in a world of mix-ups with few clear markers.

The movie starts on Jerry traveling to Fargo for an illicit business meeting and closes on Marge and Norm happily awaiting their first child. Well before this conclusion, the film racks its focus from Jerry, the de facto criminal, to Marge, the gravid hero. Both unlikely representations of "evil" and "good," respectively, the two characters give shape to a morality tale that makes "good" (Marge's deadpan, even naïve, brand) victorious over "evil" (Jerry's greed-inspired variety). On a broader dramatic plane, these two main characters also push the boundaries of narrative expectations. The good cop taking on an underachiever who plots the supposedly perfect crime is a familiar tale, but the movie doesn't entirely look like the classic story of good against evil. Plus, with its veneer of truth, the tall tale is more easily swallowed whole.

"The most important thing about using a fact-based drama, rather than a fictional one," said the Coens, "is that the audience gives you permission to do certain things, if they feel the story is real."[9] Part of the novelty comes through plot, part through tone. Though Jerry's harebrained scheme becomes a serious crime that spirals out of control, between the characters' understated reactions and their regional dialect, there is a lot to laugh at. It's the banality of evil meets the banality of good with priceless expressions and deadpan deliveries. "The Jerry character . . . is ordinary in a very evil way, and Marge . . . is ordinary in a very good way," explains Joel Coen. "To Marge, nothing is a big drama, even though it actually is a big drama."[10]

Marge and Jerry are opposing forces that never quite clash. The one time they almost do, he dodges a figurative bullet and skips out on her interview. For the most part, each of them follows an intimately related but separate story line. This innovative use of dual protagonists—used to a similar effect through the characters of Vito and Michael Corleone in *The Godfather* (1972), a movie concerned with power, family, and morality—does more than provide balance to *Fargo*'s ethically skewed world. The two characters provide the poles for truth and fabrication. Marge, the seeker of truth, presents a model for the viewer who has a similar de facto goal. But the viewer has some hurdles: The supposedly fact-based drama gives the filmmakers their own "TruCoat" cover for exploring viewer perception and perspicacity by effectively telling their audience one thing and showing it another. All hinging on the ruse of being true, *Fargo* mixes farce and probably the Coens' deepest tongue-in-cheek morality play yet to explore filmmaking by challenging its audience to scrutinize the art of lying—and fiction.

UNNATURAL DISASTER

Marge's and Jerry's story lines cross directly only twice. But they indirectly crisscross throughout the cold, stark Midwestern setting, where nature is an unruly, vicious power. This world is essential to the movie's thematic concerns. "We knew fairly early on what we wanted the movie to look like and how we wanted to shoot it," said Joel Coen. "We wanted to move the camera less. We wanted it to be sort of more observational in terms of the shooting style. And we wanted . . . the sort of landscape where you couldn't really tell where the horizon line was in terms of the sky and the snow."[11] In a locale where dividing lines are deliberately blurred, lies are freely propagated and crimes are glacially committed, images can constitute perceptual deceptions that can only be overcome by persistence of vision, the very foundation and physics behind cinema—and police work.[12] Put differently, both Marge and the audience benefit from a close look at what is presented as "truth," and the region's elements are a good place to start such an examination. The natural snowstorm sets up Jerry's unmitigated snow job of his attempted extrication from a life of dissatisfaction.

Jerry's hazardous drive to Fargo conjures up the universal struggle of man against nature, where the latter has the advantage. The vast Minnesota tundra swallows him up, as he appears and disappears with the road's contours. Even when his car is in view, he is hidden, unidentified and anonymous. He moves through perilous conditions burdened by inclement weather and a heavy load. And yet this car ride is one of Jerry's rare high points, for he is putting in motion his plan to get control of his life. The minute he steps into the bar for his meeting, his power starts to wane. He has made it through the blizzard, but that is pretty much the last thing that goes right for him. More important, as tough as the battle between him and the frosty wilderness is, more formidable is a raging internal struggle. He's a nobody who wants to be a somebody.

Jerry has ownership issues, as evidenced by his favorite pronoun form: the possessive. It's his personal problems, his deal, his wife. His real conflict is with himself and his feelings of inadequacy, underachievement, and emasculation. Following the initial mix-up over the appointment time, mix-ups become Jerry's unfortunate specialty. He blames his lack of power and success on a lack of opportunity rather than nepotism, his engulfing ineptitude, or his hideously unethical choices. If Wade can only spot him money for the parking lot deal, Jerry thinks, he can prove his business prowess, collect the large sums of money he desperately needs, and get the opportunity he thinks he deserves. He wants a loan for his lot deal, not a finder's fee, and we can see from his naïve outlook, regardless of Wade's gruff manners, that Jerry's logic and business ken are faulty. As Wade and Stan (Larry Brandenburg) rightly explain, they are not a bank and cannot simply give over a chunk of money without a guaranteed return.

Jerry's priorities as the family breadwinner are also muddled. He is not only greedy, staging a kidnapping to attain money he cannot earn, but also his excessive ego and selfishness allow him to put his own needs above his wife's and son's. First off, he treats Jean like a fungible commodity and puts her in grave danger. No matter how pretend or nonviolent he thinks the crime can be, he plans to have her seized. So though Carl and Gaear carry out his dirty work, the fear, violence, and ultimate death they inflict on Jean come courtesy of her husband. Lacking the foresight to consider a bad outcome, Jerry also forgets about how this all might affect his son. Following the kidnapping, Jerry has a semisuccessful meeting with Wade and Stan over how best to respond to the kidnappers. Stan sides with Jerry for a change, but outside the diner, Jerry's high from this validation is deflated when Stan expresses concern over Scott's welfare. Jerry's vexed look makes it plain that he neglected to factor his child into his plan. Having fallen down as businessman and spouse, now he fails in the role of father.

At home the distressed teenager is worried sick over his mother's safety. As Scotty sits on his bed distraught and crying, his father looks at him from a distance much further than the few feet between them. Standing in the doorway, where he so often finds himself, as if in limbo, neither in nor out of a room, Jerry offers his son no comfort except idle words. Ironically, the son exhibits more worldliness about the situation than his father when he worries something awful could happen. Such wise questioning echoes the reason his grandfather balked at loaning Jerry money for the lot deal. A return—on Wade's money *or* Scott's mother—cannot be guaranteed. But Jerry, blinded by his need for money and power, lacks such critical thinking. He is sure no one will get hurt regardless that two unknown men are carrying out the job. He assures Scotty that all will be fine and backs his logic up by trotting out Wade and Stan's imprimatur on Jerry's plan to take care of things. It's a bald attempt to puff himself up and show his son he's worthy of Wade's esteem. The scene ends with perverse fatherly instruction. Jerry tells Scott to fib about his mother's disappearance if asked. Lying is Jerry's way of wriggling out of tight spots. The problem is, the more he lies, the tighter his jam.

Though he cannot see it himself, Jerry's lack of control is staggering and his desire for it crippling. As his deceptions snowball into murder, Jerry keeps attempting power grabs that leave him more empty-handed than before. Throughout, he has difficulty getting ideas off the ground, and when he does there are few high moments of success and many long stretches of vain lows. The zenith comes when Wade expresses interest in the parking lot deal, his backup plan. This, however, is followed in quick succession by two washouts: First, he can't contact Carl and Gaear to cancel the kidnappers' deal; then he learns his role is only good for a finder's fee. And so the kidnapping scheme is back on.

The staged crime scheme follows a similar up-and-down pattern. When Jerry meets with Stan about the ransom, Jerry nixes Wade's idea to involve the police. He insists that it's *his* deal and *his* wife, reinforcing his craving for ownership and entitlement as well as cash. His language countenances his treatment of Jean as property with which he wheels and deals. Stan's siding with Jerry gives him a momentary boost, and he argues the husband's case using a suitable gambling metaphor: "We're not holdin' any cards here, Wade. They got all of them, so they call the shots."[13] This is twice the valorization Jerry craves because in his view the "they" Stan mentions actually refers to himself. He has yet to comprehend that he has relinquished that power to the real "they": Carl and Gaear. He gets a glimpse of this, though, when Carl demands more money after three deaths.

When the trio meets for the second time about the ransom, Wade and Stan are back on the same page: Wade will do the drop-off. Now Jerry has lost control over the pair of thugs on the one hand and his own role on the other. Worst of all, this means that Jerry will never get hold of the ransom money, the main reason behind the entire kidnapping plot. Just as his father-in-law edged Jerry out of the lot deal with a finder's fee, now Wade's insistence on handing $1 million to Jerry's hired hands completely cuts Jerry out of his share. Such power problems might be the least of his worries. As the "brains" of the whole scheme, he is behind a string of murders, which will soon include his wife's.

Every step Jerry takes to wield power loses him more ground, a fact underscored by a set of tantrums. He first loses his grip following his second phone call with Reilly Deifenbach (Warren Keith) who needs real vehicle numbers not those that Jerry smudged and fudged.[14] Jerry uses the old "in the mail" routine, promising to send them. After he hangs up, the camera moves outside his office to shoot him through the picture window, a framing that elaborates his sense of constriction. Through vertical blinds that slice through the glass like cell bars, Jerry madly slams down his paperwork and flails his arms about. His "Minnesota nice," the locals' term for their polite interpersonal dealings, is wearing thin.

He throws his second tizzy after his unsuccessful meeting with Wade and Stan about his investment find. Again, the framing elaborates his character, this time emphasizing his inconsequential size and import. An aerial view captures Jerry as a speck plodding across the parking lot toward his lone car. With scraper in hand, a now familiar scene plays out: A man of small stature battles humungous Mother Nature and his own petty nature. As he works the windshield, the stubborn ice clinging to the glass enrages him. He jumps up and down beside the car, batting his arms at the air, angry at his bad luck.

Jerry transforms from pathological liar to depraved individual when he gets home to find the unnatural disaster he has turned loose on his wife. After his greeting meets no response, he enters, and without removing his jacket or setting the groceries down, he traces the kidnappers' path upstairs. He examines the evidence of chase and struggle with barely a vague look of concern. Back downstairs, he sounds distraught. As the camera explores the evidence of violence—a crowbar, rumpled shower curtain, shattered glass, and the odd snowy TV set—Jerry's broken-up voice indicates possible worry or regret. A cut to the kitchen shows him with head in hands crying over his wife. But then he stops and starts in again, switches to a straighter posture, changes expressions, and tries a more controlled tone. He is alone and has no phone in hand. The scene is a marvelous bait and switch. As he had done with his customer, Jerry is playacting. With his dress rehearsal over, he calls Wade for the actual performance.

FARCE OF NATURE

Performing, deception, and role-playing are integral parts of *Fargo*'s landscape, and it doesn't take long for the menacing, snow-swept vistas to transform from a crime-story setting to a backdrop for farce. The moment Jerry steps into the bar, the gravity of his stormy trip, inflated by the theme's minor chords and the drag of the car he is towing, lifts and shifts. As the story takes shape, the dual tones of dark comedy are refracted through Jerry's comically quizzical expressions and tragicomic persona. After stomping the snow off his boots just inside the bar, he scans the place with a dumbfounded gaze that never quite goes away. Seconds later, the film enters the world of "mix-up," giving us license to laugh.

At every step, Macy's wonderful, Oscar-nominated portrayal of Jerry shows a little man pursuing his need to be big, a pursuit marked by unwitting buffoonery. Part and parcel of farce and *Fargo* are heavy doses of theatricality in the form of costumes (uniforms), disguise and identity issues, humor and puns, extravagant situations and hidden agendas. These farcical elements are established in the opening scene. First comes ironic humor. When Jerry enters the bar, the somber theme music that beds his trek to Fargo gives way to Merle Haggard's artful forecast of Jerry's economic jam and his need to extricate himself from them: "Keep your retirement and your so-called social security. Big city, turn me loose and set me free."[15] Moments later, the salesman tells Carl and Gaear he has money problems that the staged kidnapping will help fix.

From the start, Jerry speaks in halting, self-correcting phrases, unsure of himself in one way but overly confident in another. After all, it takes chutzpah to plan and run a kidnapping. When he meets Carl and Gaear, who have been waiting for him for an hour, he stumbles through his own introduction, betraying his identity crisis. "I'm, ah, Jerry Lundegaard," he says, not quite convincingly.[16] Carl responds skeptically, "You're Jerry Lundegaard?"[17] Jerry nods vigorously, then shakes his head and starts to mention Shep to remind them of their mutual acquaintance and deflect any mistake he might have made. Carl cuts him off, reproving him about the time mix-up. We don't yet know that another mix-up has occurred: Shep vouched only for Gaear.

Questions surrounding identity percolate around Marge and Jerry's meeting too. She introduces herself to him as a Brainerd officer on an investigation. Then she asks if he is the owner. Not letting on that she has touched a nerve with his lowly status, he explains his title and his father-in-law's owner position. Then he avoids the inevitable inquiry by commenting on Brainerd's "Babe the Blue Ox" mascot.[18] It's a wonderful moment in which Jerry, the fictional liar, calls attention to *Fargo*'s tall-tale framework via the locale's homegrown, mythical figures.

The Minnesota legend crops up here and there as if to wink at a model for *Fargo*'s own extravagant exaggerations disguised as fact. The hulking lumberjack hero and his huge ox, whose girth was measured in ax handles, are comedic, even absurd inspirations for Gaear's exaggerated size and violence. Sporting a plaid shirt implicative of lumberjack garb, Gaear eventually strikes down his partner with an ax and stuffs him into a wood chipper. The lore is present, but its application in the film completely twists the cyclopean folk tale almost beyond recognition. Jerry also represents a forgery of the tall tale legend by inadvertently perverting its light-hearted lore of hyperbole into a murder-filled canard.

Identity issues crop up around both Marge and Jerry in the form of aliases that reinforce their character's essence. Marge's is her maiden name, "Olmstead," which Mike Yanagita (Steve Park) uses when he calls. This former name honestly acknowledges her life pre-Norm and underlines her closeness to the man whose name (and bed) she now shares. Conversely, Jerry's other name highlights his inability to accept who he is and sustains his pattern of lying and hiding. At the end, in a futile attempt to disown the scheme he put in motion, he tells two policemen outside his motel door looking for a Mr. Anderson to wait a moment. He lies once again. The officers break into the room just in time to stop Jerry as "Mr. Anderson" from wriggling through the bathroom window to freedom, the same outlet Jean considered. This is his ultimate low point. Dressed in boxers and a T-shirt, he is so undone that he has gone from stumbling introductions and halting sentences to mere blubbering. When the police pin and handcuff him, he has lost complete verbal control. His screaming befits a babe (if not a blue ox), and his clothing is the lightest it has been in the movie.

Prior to his capture, Jerry wears two basic outfits: winter outerwear that hides and constricts him and his inside garb, the clothes he lies around the office and house in. Initially dwarfed by a vast, blustery landscape, the bungling

William H. Macy plays Jerry Lundegaard, a schlub whose harebrained scheme to kidnap his wife "with no rough stuff" leads to a spate of murders. (Credit: Gramercy Pictures/Photofest © Gramercy Pictures)

Jerry never escapes his small stature. Just as he never frees himself from the drag of financial woes, his wardrobe and other types of characterization box him in and weigh him down. He tows a car through the snowstorm at the start, and when we first see him, his puffy down parka and large, goofy hat corset him. At home, his grocery bags stay in his arms for longer than seems necessary. All these props and wardrobe symbolically add weight to a man who already seems overly burdened with problems.

His bulky cold-weather gear stays on too long, too, as if suggesting that, as with his life, he has trouble getting out of burdensome things. When he does take them off, removing his clothes can be flustering. We witness this after he returns home from the bungled drop-off that resulted in both the parking lot attendant and Wade's death. Jerry slumps on the bench in the foyer with his jacket still on. He tells Scott who yells down for an update that everything is okay, but his difficulty removing his boots illustrates how not okay things are. Like his boots that won't come off, Jerry is quite stuck.

And yet, the fix he is in is not without dark humor, and the comic part of his tragicomic character comes through the little man whose head peers out from his big hood, looking at the disasters he has caused and seeming unfazed by them. "My theory with the Coens always is that the costume is approved if they laugh," said costume designer Richard Hornung who worked with the Coens on four films.[19] Coupled with Macy's priceless expressions, Jerry's garb helps him look the buffoon. The comedy ends when he is caught in his skivvies, stripped of his clothes and with them his dumbfounded inscrutability.

In addition to Jerry's informal get-ups are assortments of uniforms that provide commentary on the performance aspects of everyday life. Hockey players, car mechanics, hotel workers, parking lot attendants, and, of course, police officers populate the screen. Like Jerry's outfits reinforcing his constriction, the costumes help convey characters' scope of vision. Carl alludes to this idea in his tirade to the parking attendant, an outburst that humorously captures pessimistic philosopher Arthur Schopenhauer's idea that "every man takes the limits of his own field of vision for the limits of the world":

> I guess you think, ya know, you're an authority figure. With that stupid fucking uniform. Huh, buddy? King Clip-on Tie here. Big fucking man. You know, these are the limits of *your* life, man. Ruler of your little fucking gate here. There's your four dollars. You pathetic piece of shit.[20]

Carl fails to see the limits of his own life are circumscribed by anger and greed. Perhaps after subsequently killing the next lot attendant he encounters, whether sparked by the earlier disagreement over money or by Carl's unexpected meet-up with Wade, Carl catches a flash of his own foibles in the glint of the ax wielded by Gaear coming at him in lumberjack ensemble.

Opposite Gaear's big, ferocious ax man is a big, nonviolent character whose two main uniforms acknowledge the main focuses of her life. Marge's police uniform signifies her job and her nightgown indicates her family life. Again, she is Jerry's antithesis. She is comfortable in her maternity-sized clothing skin, and it fits her well—actually and metaphorically, for she is a good cop and a happy wife. Still, she, too, emphasizes the performance aspect of everyday life. Before she interviews Jerry about the missing cars, for instance, he watches the detective through a picture window in the body shop. The scene begins outside the room from Jerry's vantage point before moving inside to where she questions Shep about a late-night call. Jerry cannot hear the conversation, but he witnesses a pantomime that causes him worry enough.

Characters viewed through windows and doors are a prevalent part of *Fargo*'s geography and one that underscores the routine activities of performance and viewing. Put differently, shots framing internal frames help elaborate the farce and help limit even further characters' and viewers' scopes. More than anyone else, Jerry is framed in this way. At home, he stands in the threshold of the front door and Scotty's bedroom door. He is also frequently shot in his car, where every angle offers a limiting window view.

In *Fargo*'s inescapable world where natural frames routinely trap characters, even windows that indicate a world beyond its borders offer no escape. When the kidnappers try to nab Jean, they discover she has not climbed out the window, as Carl suspects. In this respect she is like her husband Jerry, who cannot flee his circumstances even by trying to use his wife to do so. The screen compositions consistently show him cornered by his situation.

Jerry's feelings of imprisonment on the job are reinforced through the vertical blinds slicing through his office window. Behind these celllike bars he makes futile attempts to break free. When he finds temporary freedom by cutting out of his interview with Marge, she watches him drive off through a window that looks out onto the dealership lot. In other words, the framing, like his choices, will continue to lock him in.

Emphasizing his nonstop performance is his consistent pretence. After standing just in the door frame of the King of Clubs, Jerry conducts his crime planning as if it were a business meeting. He feigns being Jean's loyal husband after he plots her abduction. At work, he doodles on his memo pad before trying to play the above-board salesman for Marge. He tries to convince Wade and Stan he is an investment whiz. The frames highlight his role-playing and help reveal the farce at play, which from its very definition "[aims] at raising laughter by the outrageous absurdity of the situations or characters exhibited." Bit by bit, this is what occurs in *Fargo*.[21]

MINNESOTA TWINS

Fargo takes place primarily in twin locales—specifically, Marge's town of Brainerd and Minneapolis where Jerry lives. The preferred term for the Minneapolis area is the "Twin Cities," a phrase repeated throughout. While the urban pair is emphasized, it is not the movie's only "twin." Jerry's kidnapping hire was conceived as a solo act, but he finds out in the first scene that a pair of emissaries will carry out his plan.

The theme of duality looms large in *Fargo*. The first sign of it appears in the fine line drawn in the film's opening: between fact and fiction, appearance and reality, lies and truths, belief and knowledge. The devious claim that the movie is based on actual events that took place in Minnesota in 1987 is just one jape from the movie's outstretched con. After all, the story actually starts in Fargo, North Dakota. Is the setup not true, then? And, if so, wouldn't it follow that everything else would be false despite the hyperbolic claim of an exact re-creation of the incidents? By leaving Fargo out of its true-story claims, the film reveals a trickster spirit at work from the start through a mixed message regarding its factual basis.

The Coens wanted to do a true-crime movie based in their home state of Minnesota. "Not being acquainted with any true crimes that seemed sufficiently compelling," said Ethan Coen, "we made up our own 'true crime' story."[22] The Coens' true-story ruse dovetails with Jerry's flimflam modus operandi. The time-tested narrative device, author Karl Miller points out, is creative subversion.

> The literature of duality runs to comedy and to chicanery, to a fascination with tricks and hoaxes, and to a principled or accidental subversion of the author—a kind of author who is deemed to create and control plot and character, to be separate from his characters, to be himself something of a character, and to hold, rather than administer or orchestrate the opinions that go with a given work.[23]

Put differently, authorial duplicity or cons are a common fit for the drama of duality.

Fargo's free play with the duality of fact and fiction can be spotted in an undercurrent of performing—Jerry hires thugs to "perform a mission," he insists that he call the shots in his "show"—and key pairs. Jerry's gaffe of hiring the kidnapping duo—thus hiring someone without a reference—provides insight into Jerry's poor business sense along with a dab of black humor: Shep's recommended man, we later learn, is the bloodthirsty Gaear. Jerry's gamble is that he can control these hires and finally get his hands on a pile of cash. But he is stealing by proxy, and his two thugs only amplify his personal problems. With speech peppered with lies, "ah's," and half-thoughts, communicating is not one of Jerry's strong points. The same is true for the kidnapping duo.

Duplicity and communication breakdowns mark the relationship between the kidnappers whose verbal exchanges are more than simple comic relief. Their nugatory discourse augurs their undoing. In the end, the nonstop chatterbox little guy, who is motivated by greed, won't listen to his large, mute partner when Gaear articulates that he wants his fair share: half of what the car is worth. The prolix Carl insists that he needs more money because of his bloody facial injury. But he has already scored an enormous extra payment that he has hidden from his partner. Unaware of Carl's duplicity, Gaear cuts down his partner's stupid cupidity with an ax.

The men's failed communications echo Jean and Jerry's, and Gaear's shocking violence is a reflection of Jerry's inner demons. Gaear, after all, is one of his proxies, the one who was recommended and the one who does the bulk of the killing. Like Gaear with Carl, Jerry is incommunicative with the effusive Jean. Her first words are an invitation to her husband to share how his trip to Fargo went. He brushes the conversation off with a quick, disinterested answer. He is more concerned, and upset, that his father-in-law is there.

"Odd couple" kidnappers Peter Stormare (left) and Steve Buscemi watch Kristin Rudrüd make her second blind-folded run for her life. (Credit: Gramercy Pictures/Photofest © Gramercy Pictures)

Though Jean and Jerry communicate superficially about dinner and groceries, Jerry hides his true wants from his wife. By having her kidnapped he furthers this distance between them, cutting himself off from her completely and silencing her in the process. The moment the men take her, her voice is cut off. She whimpers a bit in the car. During her last-ditch effort to escape her captors when she gets out of the car in front of the lake house, she screams futilely. From that point on, Jean makes no sound. With a sack over her head, she is ordered to keep quiet. Apparently, her need to be heard incites Gaear's violence, and he silences her once and for all.

Opposite the incommunicative pairs of Jean and Jerry and Carl and Gaear are the communicative partners, Wade and Stan, on the business side, and Marge and Norm on the familial front. Unlike the antagonistic odd couple that is Carl and Gaear, Wade and Stan finish each other's sentences or reinforce what the other is saying. This is most profoundly witnessed in the finder's fee scene at Wade's office. Jerry is characteristically speechless as the men back up each other, agreeing to give Jerry a fee for his services. Marge and Norm operate similarly, their conversations reflecting their good rapport. Where Norm makes Marge eggs in the wee hours of the morning, Marge makes sure to surprise him with night crawlers for his fishing trip. In the final scene, when

Frances McDormand's enduring character Marge, shown here with John Carroll Lynch as husband Norm, is a cinematic oddity in her equally balanced career and married life. (Credit: Gramercy Pictures/Photofest © Gramercy Pictures)

Norm disparages that his mallard drawing got only the three-cent stamp, Marge cheers him up with the fact that the little stamp is of prime importance when postal rates go up. With this boost, the movie closes on an expression of love and previews the fulfillment of their partnership that will take place in just two months.

FRAME-UPS

Ever since Abby armed with her mirror "weapon" survived Visser's plotting in *Blood Simple*, the Coens have made use of duality and narrative bombshells to uncover and probe ugly American failings. In *Raising Arizona*'s strange coming-of-age story, late-bloomer Hi confronts his inner demons through his battle with Lenny Smalls. Barton Fink creates an alter ego who at once brightens and darkens his dramatic creations in his Hollywood vagaries. In the film that follows *Fargo*, two Lebowskis will go head-to-head over antipodal views on war and economics. In *Fargo*'s critique of an image-laden landscape where lies are freely posed as truth, Jerry struggles with himself, and his inner conflict finds outer form through the duo of Carl and Gaear. Unable to do for himself, he hires others to perform for him and winds up with two for the price of one. In thematic terms, the scheming, duplicitous Jerry is an unwitting trickster who helps project the fear and failed ideals of the surrounding American culture.[24]

A pair of mirror scenes highlights Jerry's trickster role through his proxy, Gaear. In the first of them, Gaear takes a break from hunting down Jean to search for unguent. He must nurse the hand that she has bitten. Rummaging through the medicine cabinet, he pauses and locks his gaze in the mirror. Suddenly, the shower curtain lunges toward him. Here, the pursuer Gaear catches his prey, Jean. The next time he appears in a mirror, the tables are turned.

At the end, Gaear's reflection appears a second time, but his—and soon Jerry's—fortunes are reversed. This time, Jerry's nemesis, Marge, is the pursuer and the catcher, and Gaear, Marge's prey and Jerry's dark proxy, is captured in her rear-view mirror as he sits in her cruiser's backseat cage. The scene itself is like a mirror image of Jerry's initial drive. Instead of a schemer towing a stolen vehicle en route to the start of a crime, a righteous police officer tows a criminal whom she found through the stolen car to resolve the crime. Gaear's arrest, like Jerry's Fargo trip, strikes a somber note. Yet, throughout, a lighter tone marks the action, one that accentuates the Coens' trickster spirit at play. Beneath the smothering drama of Jerry's kidnapping plot and Gaear's violence is a more light-hearted performance piece that offers commentary on our image-saturated culture, where lies are par for the course.

Despite the camera's deliberate, documentary approach—a departure for filmmakers who pride themselves on madcap shots—self-conscious and observational elements help reveal the Coens' true-crime charade. TVs, for example, offer a window into the movie's snow job. From the opening bar scene to the final shot in Marge's bedroom, television sets dominate the screen, revealing the infusion of watching as an everyday activity. The many TVs provide social commentary on the daily barrage of images and help pursue thematic ideas about *rec*eption and *per*ception. Whether actively being watched or sitting unobserved in the background, the little screens flicker away. How folks interact with them show the viewer a world often tuned into the tube at the expense of realizing what is happening in "reality."

Though the ice-skating athletes on the King of Clubs' TV screen may embellish the snowy Minnesota setting, *Fargo's* TVs often do more than just sit unnoticed in the frame. With characters frequently engaged in the activity of watching, we film viewers watch watchers. Jerry returns from Fargo to find Wade watching hockey. The men's interaction vis-à-vis Wade's viewing tells us a lot about the game, the men, and their relationship. By never moving his eyes from the set to his son-in-law, Wade bestows more import on the game than on Jerry.

We also sense Jerry's lack of clout and the importance of hockey at the dealership when Jerry walks into a coworker's office under the pretence of asking his boss for a favor. His colleague is taking in a game over lunch, and like Wade, he keeps his focus on the game as Jerry makes small talk. Only after Jerry asks a ridiculous question about available tickets does the hockey fan divert his attention from the game to Jerry. The fact that Jerry is the only man who doesn't care about hockey enough to watch it or even know who is playing on a given night shows us how outside of his own community he is. It also shows him missing a masculine edge.

Where characters choose to direct their attention helps us discern relative importance, as when Jean encourages Scotty to get better grades. We watch them look and watch. Scott sits at the table facing the camera, idly listening to his mother but more engaged in eating cereal and watching TV. Behind him, Jean, also facing camera, splits her attention unevenly between her son, who is her focus, and the food she's making. Scotty only really perks up to his mother when she tells him he can't go out for hockey, at which point he whips around to protest her straight on. Finally, she has said something more important than his TV show.

Characters more engaged with the tube than with other characters or events reveal if not quite a societal epidemic, then certainly a problem. What we take in visually—and in the case of the hookers physically—is too often lackadaisical. After Gaear and Carl argue over hookers or pancakes, the two have unremarkable sex with a pair of prostitutes in a shared room at the Blue Ox motel. A cut to the postcoital scene shows the two couples propped up in bed watching *The Tonight Show*. Their languid postures cinematically editorialize on the banality of crime, criminals, and evil. Later, the prostitutes' recollection of their johns demonstrates the hazards of inattentive, careless viewing. All the girls remember is that one looked funny and the other resembled the Marlboro Man, possibly because he was a smoker.

The other talk-show scene furthers these ideas of banality and passive viewing. Barging into Jean's morning viewing is a shocking dose of her husband's temerity. A man in a ski mask on her back porch causes Jean to split her attention between the insipid talk-show chatter and the crowbar-toting man at the window. Jean's two views shed light on the cruelty of Jerry's scheme that he himself in some sort of Panglossian view could or would not consider: Sheer, unexpected terror disrupts her morning routine. Her delayed reaction to the hood's appearance is both puzzling and riotous.

In one respect, a strange masked man on her porch might not be so out of the ordinary in such cold climes. But a man with a crowbar is another story. Her delayed fright and flight could be a product of passive watching to which daytime TV has inured her. We giggle at the juxtaposition of the mundane talk show and the horror in waiting, as we cringe at the break-in. Her frantic scramble following the window smash is more powerful because of her initially passive reaction. The ensuing chase and catch are not just a wake-up call to the real, ugly world beyond the TV. It's a horrible peephole into her husband's true nature. The crime is Jerry's way of getting her father's dough. We never know if she realizes this, but it is clear that prior to this, she had no idea that Jerry is not what he appears to be. His duplicity is a lesson for how to take things in *Fargo* and its Twin Cities setting. Face value can be worthless.

LIAR LIAR

With snow as a main motif, performance and observation as primary activities, and televisions dotting the frame, a pair of snowy TV sets stands out as a possible breadcrumb leading to the Coens' snow job. The first of these, showing up between the evidence of Jean's abduction and Jerry's rehearsal, suggests a culture suffused with the white noise of images. As the camera canvasses the remnants of the violence and violation that occurred, flashes of *Psycho*'s famous shower scene come into view. First we see an empty shower stall, reminiscent of the one in *Psycho*, and then downstairs a rumpled shower curtain on the floor. The thugs didn't wrap Jean in it as Norman did with Marion, but there's a definite connection here to Hitchcock's movie and what Hitchcock biographer Donald Spoto terms its "running concern for the truth that physical vision is always only partial and that our perceptions tend to play us false."[25]

Beyond the crowbar and the shards of glass in Jerry's living room sits a television set. While it reminds us of Jean's presence, it is puzzling that it has no reception. No struggle occurred near it. Perhaps it's due to the weather. Or perhaps it is pointing to the Coens' whiteout. With snow symbolizing the effusive lying and hidden agendas at work in *Fargo*, the snowy set points to the multiple levels of deception at play. It winks at the truth of the situation: Jerry's—and the Coens'—subterfuge. The second snowy set also buoys the Coens' craft.

After Jean's mad run in the snow outside the lake hideout, her second of two blind dashes, we visit the house again at night. The scene begins with an establishing exterior shot of the cabin from which loud, angry yelling is erupting. Hitting sounds make us wonder if Jean is getting abused, but a cut into the house shows an angry Carl merely striking a TV set with poor reception. The montage builds around the object, with the camera alternately closing in on the prattling Carl banging the tube for a picture, Gaear silently watching the entertainment that is his partner, and Jean with a bag over her head cut off from all visual stimuli. Suddenly a decisive hit is followed by a close-up on a TV image and the sound of a program coming in clearly.

The segue is a signature Coen transition that initially misleads but then makes perfect sense. Similar trick shots occur in *Blood Simple* with the fans and *Miller's Crossing* with the curtains. Here in *Fargo*, the cut from the kidnappers' snowy set to a nature documentary likely dupes the viewer into thinking that Carl's pounding on the TV finally produced a signal. But a cut to the TV viewer reveals Marge, barely tuned in. Only at this point do we realize we're at a new setting. Sight and sound produce a false impression that only persistent watching can correct. Such cinematic legerdemain and logic hint at the Coens' role as professional prevaricators. And just as Marge is tasked with seeing the clear picture of the crime, the viewer is tasked with seeing through the Coens' tricks and lies.

Like flipping from one channel to another, the switch to the new location snaps the viewer out of a lazy eye syndrome that can lull one into comfort, complacency, and a mode of not questioning. Dreary-eyed Marge who's nodding off to the show demonstrates that TV can be a sedative. The segue is a wake-up call for the viewer. Visual knowledge benefits from being suspect of what we see and actively tuning in. *Fargo*'s many televisions warn that images barrage everyday life. Such Coen curve (snow?) balls as the deceptive segue suggest that one's eyes—and beliefs—can easily be snowed. In the dead of a harsh winter, *Fargo*'s conceit of snow—in nature or in media—shows that things aren't always apparent. The power of snow to impede visibility and block acute perception is sustained throughout—in the many ways the camera distorts what we take in. From snowy TV sets to everyday role-playing, *Fargo* is strewn with things that look to be one thing but are actually another.

At the center of Marge's investigative journey is the Twin Cities trip. It is here on Jerry's turf that she finally gets a handle on the case and eventually finds the culprits. But before she catches Gaear literally red-handed, stuffing his accomplice into a wood chipper, Marge has a mysterious interlude with a former schoolmate, Mike Yanagita. After he calls her out of the blue, she meets him for lunch. Aside from the bedroom scenes with Norm, this is the only time Marge appears in civilian clothes, suggesting perhaps that when not in her police uniform she is outside her police persona and its questioning mindset—and her guard is down.

Things are awkward from the start when Mike hugs the gravid Marge a little too hard and long. This is one of the few times she alludes to her pregnancy. After they sit down, he tries to slide in next to her, intruding again on her personal space. She fends off his advances and shoos him back to the bench opposite her, so that she doesn't have to crane her neck, she tells him, hoping to smooth over any embarrassment with her Minnesota nice. He launches into his life's ups and downs: He has a good job, he reports cheerfully, but sadly, he lost his wife to leukemia. In another clumsy move, he confesses that he always liked Marge, explaining that he remembered her after seeing her on TV investigating the murders. This is the first clue that Mike has difficulty separating what's on TV from reality. The bizarre, awkward scene seems as out of place in the film as his oddly upbeat toast given after speaking of his wife's death. After their meeting, a friend of Marge's sets her straight. Mike, who never married their friend (who is still alive) lives with his parents and is dealing with psychological issues.

With regard to *Fargo*'s overall scheme, Mike's vacillation between his imagination and the real world ultimately parallels the movie's own fiction and fact pull. He is to Marge what the Coens are to the viewer: liars. Simply put the Yanagita scene shows how hard it is to see through liars to the truth, especially when the audience is caught unaware. Mike, thus, offers a big "viewer beware" hint to the Coens' own whitewash. When the truth about Mike is uncovered, another dimension is added to the Coens' commentary on perception. There's fact and fiction . . . and source. Mike, after all, is a virtual unknown, an acquaintance from years before who reconnects with her after he watches her on TV, a very detail that suggests he might have difficulty separating fact from fiction. Perhaps most abstrusely telling, Mike is a tall-tale teller with a name in common with cultural anthropologist Yanagita Kunio, considered the father of Japanese folklore studies, whose work focused on folk tales, dialects, and other grassroots customs.[26]

Marge, the internal audience, doesn't get Mike or his kind: liars. Though she can solve cases and catch bad guys, when it comes to believing someone who lies to her face, she can be as gullible as the next person. She is perhaps as susceptible to liars as a film viewer. The odd narrative detour pointedly shows how facilely folks—like Mike and Jerry—can lie and how easily audiences— like Marge—can be duped if they take things at face value. Look again, the episode suggests. Be skeptical. Lying can be pervasive—and where you might least expect it.

The Coens pulled the wool over most viewers' eyes, including many critics who watch movies for a living.

"*Fargo* [is] their derisive new true-crime comedy. . . ."—Richard Corliss, *Time*

"Based on a true-life crime, *Fargo* is something of a comic noir."—Georgia Brown, *Village Voice*

"*Fargo* is based on a true story. . . ."—David Denby, *New York*

"Don't let excess keep you from the Coen brothers' earthy, brilliant crime saga based on the true story of a Minneapolis car dealer. . . ."—Bruce Williamson, *Playboy*

"I am, however, willing to grant the likelihood of this being based on a true story: it is far too good for the brothers (Ethan writes, Joel directs, both produce) to have invented it."—John Simon, *National Review*

"Purportedly based on real events, it brings them as close as they may ever come—not very—to everyday life and ordinary people."—Janet Maslin, *New York Times*[27]

There were skeptical critics like Maslin and *Rolling Stone*'s Peter Travers, who sniffed something foul with the "true crime" assertion. Still, it's somewhat surprising more critics didn't question whether the Coens might have simply stuck a disclaimer of truth on a fictional crime story. After all, the Coens are predominantly fictional filmmakers with a penchant for delivering content with no guarantees, as advertised in *Blood Simple*. *Fargo*'s exact reconstruction claim is overly bold. Consider the details of Wade's and Carl's deaths, witnessed by no one. How could a dead-on re-creation occur if the only witnesses to the scene are two dead men? The same holds true for Carl's burial of the ransom money, a solo act. Easiest spotted is the twenty-nine-cent stamp, which went into effect in 1991, some three years after the movie's events were said to have occurred.[28]

Fiction presented as fact stretches back to ancient myths whose very creations were ways of answering life's unanswered questions. Where do we come from? Why does it rain? What controls night and day and the seasons? Imaginative stories resolved these mysteries and became a cultural backbone. Centuries later, books capitalized on the narrative device. For example, Daniel Defoe's *Moll Flanders* (1722), considered to be the first novel, has an extended title that reads, in part: "The Fortunes and Misfortunes of the Famous Moll Flanders, Etc. Who was born in Newgate, liv'd honest and died a Penitent. Written from her own Memorandums."[29] About a century later, Edgar Allan Poe's fabricated story about a balloon crossing over the Atlantic appeared as a news item in the *New York Sun*. The faux reportage of the imaginary event caused a stir and sold many a paper.[30] Perhaps most famous is Orson Welles's radio broadcast of "War of the Worlds," which fooled many a listener into thinking aliens were invading the planet. The Coens follow a tradition of telling fictional tales cloaked in the guise of truth. Despite countless examples, why is it that audiences can trust explicitly purveyors of fiction? This is a question at the heart of *Fargo* and its false true-crime heart.

Though visually calmer than most Coen fare, *Fargo* is not an example of realism. Looming large in a bleak whiteout are the Coens' proxies for Paul Bunyan and his sidekick Babe: liars Jerry and Mike, thugs little Carl and big Gaear and the singular hero Marge. Though Joel and Ethan hail from Minnesota and are thus intimately acquainted with the real place, *Fargo*'s Midwesterners approximate and exaggerate for extended comic relief. Place is important for providing a tableau and setting a mood but not reconstructing the literal area. In this way *Fargo* resembles *Rashomon* (1950), a film where alternate observational theories coincide.

Based on two Japanese folk tales by Ryunosuke Akutagawa ("Rashomon" and "In a Grove"), Akira Kurosawa's Oscar-winning movie is about lying. Five witnesses to the same events tell differing accounts of a crime. "The film's engine," says film critic Roger Ebert, "is our faith that we'll get to the bottom of things—even though the woodcutter tells us at the outset he doesn't understand, and if an eyewitness who has heard the [other] testimony . . . doesn't understand, why should we expect to?"[31] Set in a place torn apart by civil war and natural disasters, *Rashomon* posits that there might not be a way to get to objective truth.

Fargo, set in a region where snow blurs dividing lines, similarly suggests truth can be hard to find, and warns against easily taking things at face value and believing everything seen and heard. Belief and knowledge and other epistemological concerns are recurrent Coen themes. (*Barton Fink* deals with such issues in spades.) *Fargo* operates under the assumption that the viewer will believe the disclaimer that the story is true. Working from that "knowledge," we interpret and perceive within a faulty belief system and so perhaps don't examine details that fly in the face of an exact reconstruction, such as the stamp, Wade's and Carl's deaths, and Carl's loot burying. Thus, our own view is colored. So if hindsight often lends even the most myopic view a clearer vision, then another look at the movie and its brilliant farce is in order to show the Coens' show.

NORTHERN EXPOSURE

The fact-based claim purporting that the movie represents *exactly* what took place is a tough buy considering how humorous, bordering on absurd, *Fargo's* characters are—even the lovable hero. Though drawn from Midwestern models, the characters are caricatures whose collective understatement and exaggerated mannerisms comprise a morality tale of gigantic proportions. "Caveat spectator" is the movie's message hiding next to the more overt moral about greed being at the root of the unnecessary mayhem and murder.

The story is a leg pulling that aims for Bunyan heights, and a tragic news story suggests it came close to reaching such stature. In 2002 the Associated Press and other news outlets reported that a Japanese tourist had perished in the Fargo area supposedly after searching for Carl's unclaimed cache of cash. Local police and residents interviewed about the Japanese woman's appearance in town expressed dismay over unfortunate miscommunications (there was a language barrier) and the tragedy surrounding her trip. This intersection of fact and fiction—real life and the movies—suddenly became a disturbing nexus. The *Guardian Unlimited* some time later tried to clear up the mistaken assumptions about the death of the woman, Takako Konishi, reporting that she had actually traveled to Fargo to commit suicide over a difficult breakup with someone from the area.[32] The readiness of the press and media consumers to believe Konishi might have taken the movie as fact underlines *Fargo's* narrative might and potentially destructive power. It was not Konishi who had been fooled, after all; it was the public's belief that the Coens' "legend" could hold such sway.

The Bunyan statue and Blue Ox motel are visual reminders of the movie's tall-tale heart. (The real Bunyan statue in Brainerd stood in an amusement park in 1987, not by the highway.) Allusions to the legend are scattered throughout. For instance, Gaear is described as a large fellow. Marge notes the perpetrator's big footprints. Carl, by contrast, is described as the little guy. At the end when Marge is taking Gaear into custody, they drive by the Bunyan statue. Gaear, still dressed in his lumberjack flannel, turns to look at it as they pass. His deliberate gesture suggests a connection between him and the legend. Is it their ax brandishing that links them? Or is it the similar silence of the inanimate statue and the ominously taciturn Gaear for whom garrulous Carl is a foil? Of all the nods to the legend, this final statue shot looks to be a self-conscious visual joke showing the Coens' tall-tale hand.

The statue marks Bunyan territory, not the actual place to which you can book a flight. Like the Bunyan wink, other regionalisms point to *Fargo*'s fictional heart. "You betcha" and "Yahhhh" are two of the most commonly quoted lines from the movie, much to the chagrin of some Minnesotans who openly complained about their treatment. To take the characters as representative of the actual state rather than the hyperreal fictitious land from which they have been carved is to miss the point. It is on par with taking the story at face value.

The language fits the tall-tale schema. The "you betchas" have more to do with flavor than verisimilitude. The setting is a representative Midwest where Scandinavians with names like Gunderson, Grimsrud, and Lundegaard live. It's a grim folk tale with a language scheme that stretches colloquialisms familiar to the Minnesota native brothers into its thematic framework of truth and lies. There is understatement and politeness that is above board, and then there is understatement that creates communication gaps and politeness that is a veneer hiding rage.

The characters' general geniality is a counterpoint for Jerry and his building frustration. His internal tension between what he wants and what he has, what he thinks he can achieve, and the mix-ups that keep embroiling him comes across in his struggle to remain cool and polite. He needs to stay anchored to "Minnesota nice," but really he is closer to "Minnesota ice," especially in his ill-conceived, cold-hearted scheme for money.

He distractedly pays the bill at the diner after learning of Wade's decision to handle the ransom. The chipper cashier who asks Jerry how the meal was provides stark contrast to a seething Jerry whose insincere, half "nice" response indicates the fissures between him and his peers. Up until then, he has been adept at hemming and hawing his way through snowballing lies that he believes will help him financially. With Wade slated as deliveryman, Jerry's chances of getting his money grow ever slim. As his plan falters, his verbal faculties diminish, and he approaches a reticence on par with Gaear's. In the end, his characteristic stuttering is reduced to nonverbal screams.

Words, sounds, and even songs work on different levels to illuminate themes and situations. Jose Feliciano's "Let's Find Each Other Tonight," for instance, heard in the Celebrity Room scene, goes beyond showing 1980s Minnesota stuck in the 1970s as "Do You Know the Way to San Jose," "Tie a Yellow Ribbon Around the Old Oak Tree," and "Up, Up, and Away" do. Like the Haggard lyrics marking Jerry's entrance, the blind Feliciano's song points to the story's concern with finding the truth behind appearances and looking beyond what we see to what really is. In a movie where sighted characters (and viewers) can miss essential details revealing the true picture, the song suggests the blind can be perceptive if they are tuned in.

The prostitute pair—who is neither observant nor perceptive—shows the flipside of this proposition. Unable to recall much about the men with whom they had sex, the girls represent a complete breakdown in perception and communication. They are also comic relief. For example, Hooker One's (Larissa Kokernot) recollection of the uncircumcised little guy indirectly hooks into the motif of size. Hooker Two's (Melissa Peterman) realization that her john looked like the Marlboro Man comments on a societal saturation of image. Here brand recognition edges out specific details of someone with whom she is intimate. At the end of the dysfunctional interview the patient-as-a-saint Marge perks up at the one piece of helpful information: The little guy and big man were headed for the Twin Cities.

In sharp contrast to the exchange with the prostitutes, Mr. Mohra's (Bain Boehlke) story about Carl shows how colloquial language and simple constructions can still get across a lot of meaning.

> So I'm tendin' bar . . . and this little guy's drinkin' and he says, "So where can a guy find some action—I'm goin' crazy out there at the lake." And I says, "What kinda action?" and he says, "Woman action, what do I look like," and I says, "Well, what do *I* look like. . . . This ain't that kinda place." So he says, "So you think I'm some kinda jerk for askin'," only he doesn't use the word jerk.[33]

Mohra's detail about the lake leads Marge to the tan Ciera while overall his compact story and euphemisms support Marge's theory that the perpetrators are not locals. His colloquy was obviously with an outsider since swearing is taboo in these parts, as Mohra's censoring shows. Rare exceptions occur when characters are pushed to the edge as when the Irate Customer calls Jerry a "fucking liar" and when Scott swears when told he cannot go out for hockey. And finally, Mohra and the officer's parting exchange caps the story with more local humor. These men who are bundled up to their necks with hat and hood talk about a cold front coming in the next day.

LARGE MARGE

Like the nonchalant attitude toward the cold, Marge's character is remarkable in part because her gender and pregnancy are so unremarked upon. Except for Norm's occasional pampering, they never become a factor, a point of discussion, or an impediment to her excellent detective work. Part of Marge's enduring character, then, stems from the fact that perhaps viewers buy this untraditional treatment of pregnant women because she is most likely thought to be real. There is less of a chance for her sui generis personality to be questioned under such circumstances. The detective brilliantly solves the case like her celluloid brethren of so many crime thrillers, but she is hardly a stereotype. As she marches to the beat of a happily married, incredibly comical, uniformed officer, she blazes new paths of female power that, surprisingly and refreshingly, do not readily call attention to gender uniqueness. She just *is*.

No one remarks on her sex; no one treats her differently; and she doesn't act like anything but a police officer . . . who happens to be seven months pregnant. Even this detail, however, doesn't so much coerce audience identification toward some feminist agenda as much as it rounds out a very specific character trait that often dictates her activities—as when she nearly regurgitates from morning sickness, not because of the crime scene.[34] The name *Marge* comes from Margaret, the patron saint of expectant mothers. Most important, being pregnant is not a hindrance to her profession—in fact, it is quite the opposite. The pregnancy points to a good balance between work and home. "Reversing the film noir convention," writer Linda Holt points out, "Marge's home life is creative, happy and nurturing: the condition, rather than the price, of being a successful cop."[35] Her dual satisfaction is the positive to Jerry's negative. Her Everywoman, who sees life as more than a bit of money and who consistently does the right thing, triumphs over Jerry's greedy persona who makes all the wrong choices.

Ultimately, Marge, a mother-to-be, is a creator, that vaunted character type in the Coen oeuvre that has power over destructive types like Jerry. Marge's role as expectant mother rounds out her character as both nurturer and protector. Often, when not climbing over snowbanks to examine a crime scene or hunting down criminals in her protector role, Marge is eating for two, and her nurturing side is reflected in her relationship to Norm. For instance, when she gets back to the office to find Norm is treating her to a Hardee's lunch, she has a surprise for him: night crawlers. The juxtaposition between the burgers and worms is like a fleeting cutout from a horror movie, but the focus on food and worms here cleverly ties into the familial responsibility of caring for the life developing inside her. In this way, the scene also connects to the nature documentary she watches in bed. Like Marge getting Norm worms for his fishing trip and eating for two, the expectant beetle on TV brings food, in the form of worms, to her nest for her babies.

Dining is a frequent activity in *Fargo* and one that delineates family dynamics. Each Lundegaard food scene expounds on the tension and dysfunction of the family's interactions. There is argument over Scotty's McDonald's outing at dinner. At breakfast, Jean and Scotty quarrel over grades and hockey. Over coffee, Stan sides with Jerry over Wade; later over dessert, Stan sides with Wade over Jerry. Marge and Jerry's meals show just the opposite.

Fargo's treatment of food contains cultural commentary. From Jerry's colleague noshing on a burger to Gaear enrapt in his soap eating a TV dinner, characters are shown gobbling up food almost as much as they consume TV. Amid all the paper bags of burgers and fries strewn across the screen seems to be a critique of America's fast-food culture. We are what we eat, both literally and metaphorically, seems to be *Fargo's* food for thought. The images we consume, like the food we ingest, can lead to better understanding and healthier bodies or can just fill us for the moment but leave us empty in the long run. This comes across most palpably when Marge eats her burger while chewing on the strange Mike Yanagita.

Like Mike Yanagita and Jerry, Gaear is Marge's opposite: a liar who goes up against an upholder of truth. But by dint of her pregnancy, Marge does share with Gaear one common trait. They are both large. The connection is not purely descriptive or visual, it is also figurative. While Gaear is linked visually to Paul Bunyan, it is actually Marge who owns Bunyan's traditional protector role. It's just that *Fargo* twists the Minnesota mascot on its ear. When Marge outlines a lesson on greed to Gaear, who sits impassively silent behind the cruiser's cage, he turns to look at the looming Bunyan statue marking Brainerd's city line. If one misses the totem of Tall Tale country, one might link the mythical character's penchant for ax wielding with Gaear's attraction to violence. In this somewhat perverted, ironic reading, the legend whose gigantism was marked by a mostly pacific, even protective nature becomes symbolic of Gaear, an ad hoc lumberjack who hacks his partner and then stuffs his body in a chipper as if it's another log. With no small bit of irony, he is the one for whom Shep vouched! At a most basic (base?) reading, Gaear represents evil without a conscience. While money is a factor in his crimes, an unrelenting savagery is more at the root of his motivation.

Like the story-pointed references to the Bunyan legend, the wood-chipper scene might well be the biggest and most clever indicator of this next generation of "pulp" fiction, which the Coens try to pass off as true. As if obscurely acknowledging the process by which the low-grade, "pulp" paper on which detective fiction was typically printed, the Coens have their lumberjack-like villain stuff his partner into a wood chipper, the first stage of a log's metamorphosis into paper. Considering the great lengths to which the Coens went to pretend their *film blanc* was true, it is not much of a stretch to imagine a conceit as well hidden as its fictional heart.

Marge gives her speech about life being more than money to Gaear, but its lessons also pertain to Carl who has died because of it and Jerry who was

Peter Stormare as Gaear Grimsrud in the Coen brothers' tall tale set in Paul Bunyan country. (Credit: Gramercy Pictures/Photofest © Gramercy Pictures)

motivated by it. Marge sees no point or benefit to avarice. Though she can fall prey to the occasional liar, she can solve the crime without a hitch. She successfully tracks down the tan Ciera and helps quash the bad elements that have infested her small town. Endowed with the gift of sight, Marge, the surrogate audience, triumphs. But does the Coens' audience?

As *Fargo* escalates to a portrait of untamed brutality and its effects on a surrounding community, the Coen brothers' parlay into the American Gothic stays grounded in the context of a morally ambiguous, comically saturated, and self-consciously steeped crossroads where the banality of evil meets the banality of good. Just as the iconic image of a powerful and gargantuan but benevolent Paul Bunyan can inchoately and incorrectly be reduced to a symbol of pure savagery—or be a nod to Marge and her role as protector of the Brainerd community—so this archetypal story of good and evil is deceptively attenuated with a mundane and humorous simplicity. *Fargo* whets the American appetite for violence with a disturbingly bland attitude toward it. By blurring an already thin line with unabashed bravura, the Coen brothers expound on fictional truths dormant under visual deceptions, and, in so doing, implicate their characters, their audience, and even themselves.

Ultimately, the Coens' initial "lie" is at once disturbing and ingenious—disturbing because no one really likes to be fooled that badly, and ingenious because, although this type of fictional "disclaimer" has prefaced so many dramas before it, rarely is it done in cinema so baldly and boldly. By directly imitating the main character's action of concocting a plot and pretending that it's true, the Coens make a film where the onus is on the individual viewer at every level of reading—whether real-life (the audience) or fictional (Marge Gunderson)—to see through their snow job to the truth.

WRAP: ARTISTIC LICENSE (TO KILL)

Jerry is an avaricious, overambitious, and feckless weasel. He is the type of middle-class loser, minus the femme fatale, about whom James M. Cain wrote, but Jerry's counterfeit kidnapping and the Coens' true-story claim make the Cainian roots tough to spot. And yet, the plot parallels *Blood Simple*'s. In both films, scheming husbands plot against their wives, and money is the main motive of the spouses' hired hands. But while greed is part of *Fargo*'s morality tale, so is perspicacity. To the dialectic of good and evil, the Coen brothers ingeniously add a supposition about perception vis-à-vis fiction: The knowledge that a story is real can profoundly affect the way one experiences it.

Symbolizing the hidden, *Fargo*'s snow illuminates the underlying imperative of uncovering what's below the surface. The initial image that appears to be sky but in fact is earth and sky sans horizon line illustrates the fallacy of the black-and-white disclaimer that the ensuing movie is factually based. In other words, the opening whiteout is a shrouded caveat to the perspicacious viewer. By directly imitating their main character's action of lying, the filmmakers add another level to their narrative. The movie prods viewers to take after its fictional hero Marge and try to see through a snow job to the truth. Such an intake requires more than viewer reception, it calls for acute perception. In this way the morality tale is not just about how greed can turn a regular Joe into a vicious killer-by-proxy, it's also about the imperative of scrutinizing what is presented rather than taking what is offered without a hint of skepticism, that attribute of all good cops, readers, and viewers.

NOTES

1. "*Fargo*," Box Office Mojo, www.boxofficemojo.com/movies/?id=fargo.htm (accessed December 4, 2005). *The Big Lebowski* (1998) and *O Brother, Where Art Thou?* (2000) will blow *Fargo*'s numbers away, with $5.5 million and $1.9 million tallies, respectively, in their first ten days.

2. Robin Derosa, "Box Office," *USA Today*, March 18, 1996, D-1.

3. It was nominated for Best Picture, Best Director (Joel Coen), Best Supporting Actor (William H. Macy), Best Cinematography (Roger Deakins), and Best Film Editing (Ethan and Joel Coen under the pseudonym Roderick Jaynes).

4. The scene rhymes with one from *Blood Simple* that has a different outcome. The setup is the same: A vehicle approaches a man holding a dead body. In the earlier film, Ray escapes detection just in time. Here, Carl is not so lucky nor are the witnesses whom Gaear kills. The Coens' frequent storyboard artist, J. Todd Anderson, plays the passerby, who is mischievously listed in the credits by the symbol for The Artist Formerly Known as Prince, a Minnesota native.

5. *Fargo*, DVD, directed by Joel Coen (1996; Santa Monica, Calif.: MGM, 2003).

6. *Fargo*, DVD.

7. *Fargo*, DVD.

8. *Fargo*, DVD.

9. Chris Peachment, "Brothers With One Eye," *Sunday Telegraph*, May 26, 1996, 8.

10. Amy Dawes, "Chaos and the Coens," *Los Angeles Daily News*, March 15, 1996, 4.

11. From an interview with Elvis Mitchell on "Independent Focus," Independent Film Channel, 2000.

12. The phi effect is based on the fact that the human eye can only focus on images that are at least 1/13th of a second apart. This optical phenomenon is how a series of still images shown in rapid motion gives the illusion of movement.

13. *Fargo*, DVD.

14. Warren Keith, the voice of the loan officer, is a member of the punk rock band the Adicts, who dress like the Droogs from Stanley Kubrick's *A Clockwork Orange* (1971). Kubrick films pop up in many of the Coens' films. Here, *A Clockwork Orange* gets a wink in the Celebrity Room scene when Carl says he's in town for "the old in and out." This alludes to the *Clockwork* line: "Sorry gal, no time for the old in-out, just came to check the meter."

15. Merle Haggard and Dean Holloway, "Big City" (Shade Tree Music, Inc., and BMI: 1981, 1982).

16. *Fargo*, DVD.

17. *Fargo*, DVD.

18. The exchange is vaguely reminiscent of Ernst Lubitsch's *To Be or Not To Be* (1942), a black satire about a troupe of actors who give the performance of their lives in order to dupe the encroaching Nazis. The buffoonish protagonist, Joseph Tura (Jack Benny), impersonates a spy when meeting Colonel Ehrhardt. Tension builds from the beginning of the scene with awkward laughs around the repeated phrase, "Concentration Camp Ehrhardt."

19. From *Miller's Crossing* production notes. Hornung designed costumes for *Raising Arizona*, *Miller's Crossing*, *Barton Fink*, and *The Hudsucker Proxy*.

20. *Fargo*, DVD.

21. H. W. Fowler, *A Dictionary of Modern English Usage* (Oxford: Oxford University Press, 1985), 96.

22. From an interview with Elvis Mitchell on "Independent Focus," Independent Film Channel, 2000.

23. Karl Miller, *Doubles: Studies in Literary History* (New York: Oxford University Press, 1985), 99.

24. "Trickster Tale," Encyclopedia Britannica, www.britannica.com/eb/article-9073359 (accessed June 20, 2006).

25. Donald Spoto, *The Art of Alfred Hitchcock* (New York: Doubleday, 1992), 314.

26. John W. Hall, Delmer M. Brown, Marius B. Jansen, eds., *The Cambridge History of Japan* (New York: Cambridge University Press, 1988), 750–51.

27. Richard Corliss, "Swede 'n' Sour," *Time*, March 1996, 91. Georgia Brown, "Only the Lonely," *Village Voice*, March 1996, 46. David Denby, "Swede 'n' Sour," *New York*, March 18, 1996, 50. Bruce Williamson, "Movies—*Fargo* directed by Joel Coen and written by Joel Coen and Ethan Coen," *Playboy*, April 1996, 26. John Simon, "*Fargo*: Movie Review," *National Review*, April 22, 1996, 60. Janet Maslin, "Deadly Plot by a Milquetoast Villain," *New York Times*, March 8, 1996, 1.

28. Bent on keeping their trickster m.o. under wraps, prior to the Oscar ceremony, the Coens asked the Academy's permission to allow an actor to accept the award if *Fargo* won for editing. Why? Roderick Jaynes, the frequent Coen editor, is a pseudonym for Joel and Ethan.

29. Daniel Defoe, *Moll Flanders* (New York: Signet Classic, 1981), iii.

30. Kathleen Squires, "Magic Markers," *Time Out New York*, April 1–8, 1999, 18.

31. Roger Ebert, "*Rashomon*," *Chicago Sun-Times*, May 26, 2002, rogerebert.suntimes .com/apps/pbcs.dll/article?AID=/20020526/REVIEWS08/205260301/1023 (accessed June 24, 2006).

32. Paul Berczeller, "Death in the Snow," *Guardian*, June 6, 2003, film.guardian.co .uk/features/featurepages/0,4120,970908,00.html (accessed November 11, 2005).

33. *Fargo*, DVD.

34. Regurgitation is a running Coen in-joke. Marge would have been the first—and so far only—female character to do the honors except that her morning sickness is a false alarm.

35. Linda Holt, "I'm So Prouda You," *Times Literary Supplement*, June 14, 1996, 20.

• 7 •

The Big Lebowski: A Bowling Ball

John Turturro's sexually transgressive character Jesus licks a bowling ball, a modern-day, urethene tumbleweed. (Credit: Gramercy Pictures/Photofest © Gramercy Pictures)

"What the fuck does Vietnam have to do with anything!"
—The Dude (Jeff Bridges)

"Roll on, thou ball, roll on!/Through pathless realms of Space."
—Sir William Schwenck Gilbert, *To the Terrestrial Globe* (1865)

PREVIEW

$\mathcal{T}he$ *Big Lebowski* is one of those rare films that become an event—since 2002 fans have pilgrimaged to Lebowski fests around the country to honor the film's misfits. It is not without irony that the inspiration for such pageantry delivers something the Coens' previous, supposedly true film lacks: some basis in fact. Despite its claims, *Fargo* is a canard.[1] Though *Lebowski* claims no authenticity, it features, strangely, a fact-based hero. The Dude (Jeff Bridges) is based on Jeff Dowd, an L.A.-based producer's rep and former member of the Seattle Seven. "Dowd is much more successful than Lebowski (he has played an important role in the Coens' careers as indie filmmakers), but no less a creature of the moment," explains film critic Roger Ebert.[2] Walter (John Goodman) has real-life models, too: Coen friend and Vietnam vet Pete Exline, who had a rug that "tied the room together," and filmmaker John Milius, who wrote the screenplay for *Apocalypse Now*, directed *Conan the Barbarian*, and is fond of firearms.[3]

While *Lebowski* bolsters the maxim that "fact is stranger than fiction," the cult film also suggests that history repeats itself. Frequent cowboy actor Sam Elliot, the narrator dubbed "the Stranger," spurs this notion as the film gets rolling in cowboy country where a tumbling tumbleweed connects the frontier to a modern, dark City of Angels. Meeting our unlikely hero, a Vietnam-era throwback and pacifist, as a U.S. president makes tough war talk, subtly links the 1960s and the 1990s. When a case of mistaken identity embroils the peacenik in a mystery, the film shifts to a shaggy dog tale that wags to the rhythm of a revisionist film noir. After the James M. Cain–influenced *Blood Simple* and the reworked Dashiell Hammett of *Miller's Crossing*, the Coens try on Raymond Chandler's episodic drama. *Lebowski's* baroque noir trundles through excursions and incursions as seemingly random as a channel surf through digital cable. But if the prankster Coens have delivered any message in their work, it is viewer beware. A bit like *Fargo*, their Day-Glo noir is a snow job: It's not haphazard despite its rambling nature and it's very much about wars and peace despite comments to the contrary. It's an antiwar polemic disguised as a hilarious hippie boondoggle—a cinematic memorial to Vietnam War–era leftists that lampoons art, crime dramas, Hollywood, stoners, conservatives, nihilists, and warmongers.

REVIEW

The story's opening tumbleweed and concluding bowling ball, along with the narrator's wrap-up about "westward the wagons," suggest recurrence, cycles, and a Zen outlook. After the quick tour of a grass-splotched prairie followed by a look at urban decay, the film introduces the Dude at the grocery store on the eve of the 1991 Persian Gulf War. He watches George H. W. Bush talk of international conflict and makes out a check for sixty-nine cents, coyly playing on the film's primary concerns: war and sex. After the titles play over a slow-mo bowling dance, the Dude returns home and gets jumped by two hoods (Phillip Moon and Mark Pellegrino). They demand money that a "Jeffrey Lebowski's" nympho wife Bunny (Tara Reid) owes a porn king named Jackie Treehorn (Ben Gazzara). They rough the Dude up and commit further indignity by urinating on his rug, and only then grasp they have tagged the wrong guy.

Taking the advice of his best friend Walter (John Goodman, in his third acting role for the Coens) the Dude, born Jeffrey Lebowski, finds his rich namesake (David Huddleston) to get a substitute rug. The two Lebowskis are from different generations and have polar opposite values. The older man won't give him a thing, but the Dude uses some social engineering to score one of his rugs.

Days later, Lebowski hires the Dude to deliver the ransom of his recently kidnapped wife. With designs on the cash, Walter helps with the mission and drops off a fake satchel of money instead of the real one. The ringer fails to get Bunny back. Fearing she may now be dead but not knowing what to do, the Dude goes bowling with Walter and their other teammate Donny (Steve Buscemi). Afterwards they find that the Dude's car, along with the money, has been stolen.

Maude (Julianne Moore), the Big Lebowski's artist daughter, calls on the Dude, asking for help reclaiming money her father stole. She thinks Bunny kidnapped herself, but when her father shows the Dude a cut-off toe with green nail polish, which is Bunny's shade, the Dude doesn't buy her theory. He goes to Treehorn's sex pad for answers but has a Mickey Finn–induced sex dream about Maude—with a strange Saddam Hussein cameo in it—instead. Treehorn throws him out and sics the cops on him. The Malibu police chief (Leon Russom) picks up the Dude, assaults him, and then lets him go.

Meanwhile, the police find his car, but Lebowski's money is gone. A piece of paper wedged between the seats leads the Dude to Larry Sellers (Jesse Flanagan), the dimwit son of a TV writer (Harry Bugin, in his third Coen role). Larry is mum about the cash, so Walter destroys the sports car in front of the house, assuming it is the found money's spoils. Alas, it's a neighbor's car. (Walter's hunches are often wrong.) Back at the lanes, the boys bowl against two main rivals, the pacifist Smokey (Jimmie Dale Gilmore) and Jesus, a Latino pederast (John Turturro in his third Coen role).

Maude seduces the Dude, desiring a child not a lover, when their post-sex talk uncovers the fact that her father has no money. The Dude suddenly gets it and goes to confront Lebowski with his theory: The old man faked the kidnapping so that he could steal money from Maude's charity and then blame the crime on the drop-off guy. Lebowski admits nada. Walter thinks Lebowski's paralysis is also faux, but his theory—again—is wrong.

Back at the lanes, ace bowler Donny suddenly rolls an imperfect, premonitory nine. After the game, German nihilists jump them in the parking lot. They have set fire to the Dude's car and now demand the bowlers' money. Walter's refusal provokes a brawl. The bowlers win, but Donny has a fatal heart attack. After they disperse his ashes—or try to in a scene that apes Mel Brooks's *Life Stinks* (1991)—the Stranger visits the Dude at the bowling alley before the credits roll.

LIFE DURING WARTIME

"Your revolution is over, Mr. Lebowski," Jeffrey Lebowski tells the Dude.[4] This line is a perfect springboard for discussion since the movie makes much ado about tumbling orbs. Beyond its surface meaning pointing to the 1960s counterculture, the buzzword *revolution* relates to tumbleweed, the Dude's favorite pastime, and probably the Coens' favorite shape—since most of their movies involve some kind of circular design. It also reflects the wheelchair of the assumed affluent scion of society. In short, the senior Lebowski's line keys in on several main themes and his fait accompli assertion is wrong on all fronts. The Dude's bowling team is rolling toward the finals. The struggle between the establishment and counterculture is ongoing, at least as an undertow. And it's the old man's spin that will soon be over, thanks to the Dude.

Lebowski presents a world where little but the Dude himself is as it appears on the surface. The Dude's relationship with his namesake is the linchpin to seeing beyond appearances to reality. The old man who rails against the hippie seeking rug compensation only looks the part of a respectable millionaire with a disciplined work ethic and a business pedigree. The key to the crime story is that the ersatz rich man is broke. In the final act the Dude deduces Lebowski was the real handout-seeker, stealing $1 million from a charity and making it look like the Dude's crime. Pitting appearances against hidden agendas, the movie presents another round of the culture wars that rankled Vietnam-era politics and never died out. *Lebowski* is more political than its rambling nature suggests. It is a subversive political piece disguised as a stoner's stream-of-consciousness mystery ride showing that the "bums," in fact, rock.

With several key pairs front and center, the motif of the double is in play. The most important duo is the Dude and Big Lebowski. Their opposition exposes the ongoing left-right antagonism between falsehoods and truths. Clashes between the baggy-clothed peacenik and the business-suit wearing war vet doppelgänger telescope the lefty-conservative battle of ideas. Symbolically, two main time periods, two wars—Vietnam and the impending Gulf War—and a pair of balls—more sexual subtext—further this idea, suggesting that while time has transformed California's landscape, yesterday's political strife is still around. It's just buried under the rug. It will take the Dude to respark, however briefly, the revolution. And though it won't be televised, the Coens put it on film to revive a California once alive in political upheaval now dead in a commodified, culturally starved, artistically dull, yet oh-so-droll modernity.

"I don't see any connection to Vietnam," the Dude complains when his buddy rants about the war.[5] "Well, there isn't a literal connection," Walter counters.[6] But there is many a figurative link, and, as is usual with a Coen film, perception is key. *Lebowski* exposes two worlds: the one shown and its mirror opposite. The former is a California not only run by authority figures but also concocted by them—it's a facade hiding ugly truths. The other world is where the Dude and his ilk hang: the bowling alley, where the sport of the proletariat meets the counterculture through its Googie architecture dappled in Day-Glo. When Dude figures out Lebowski's scheme, the old man's response is typical of a white-collar bad guy who is caught red-handed: "You've got your story; I've got mine."[7] Such subjective "truth" by a member of the establishment is a legacy of a nation still roiled by Vietnam. Drawing links between that war's rationale and the impending war's, the movie is a scathing unveiling of Lenin's cui bono: Who benefits? The answer for Vietnam, Desert Storm, or the kidnapping mystery is the power elite. The movie illuminates this deep, dark American secret.

As with the deceptively meandering script, Walter's Vietnam tie-ins are anything but random even if his rationale for them sounds absurd. His charges rekindle fundamental battles at the heart of the culture wars as when his explosive temper in a diner prompts a polite request to tone it down. His "prior restraint" comeback has little to do with the situation but a lot to do with the movie's war themes. The line recalls the tipping point for antiwar sentiment: The Pentagon Papers, the secret history of America's involvement in Vietnam brought to light by the *New York Times*, became a lightning rod for troop removal. The unmasking of the government's real motives parallels the ultimate exposure of Lebowski as a sham, even if the linkage between the two is absurd. The secret truth behind the lies also applies to the Dude's mistaken belief that the amputated toe is Bunny's. When it comes to war rationale, at least, Walter the vet can get it right.

The Dude's ultimate discovery of the Big Lebowski's crime reveals how today's power elite are replaying yesterday's scandals. The *New York*

Times' description of the Pentagon Papers and what they uncovered could apply to the Coens' fictional yet historically grounded noir.

> To read the Pentagon Papers in their vast detail is to step through the looking glass into a new and different world. This world has a set of values, a dynamic, a language, and a perspective quite distinct from the public world of the ordinary citizen and of the two other branches of the Republic—Congress and the judiciary. . . . The Papers also make clear the deep-felt need of the government insider for secrecy in order to keep the machinery of state functioning smoothly and to maintain maximum ability to affect the public world.[8]

The movie presents its own fictitious looking glass—a funhouse mirror, if you will—whose look at the 1960s vis-à-vis the 1990s shows little has changed when it comes to the powerful and the little guy. President George H. W. Bush's fighting words in the opening about "unchecked aggression" set the tone for a film that looks askance at war. The Big Lebowski's exploitation of the Dude as his fall-guy parallels the societal problem of the rich and powerful sacrificing the have-nots. If only conflict were limited to the bowling lane, the film wryly suggests.

Just as there was more going on than the government acknowledged during Vietnam, there is more to the 1990s desert conflict than the official line. In muffled tones Walter points out as Donny rolls his ill-fated nine: "This whole fucking thing is nothing but nothing about oil."[9] His muted opinion is a far cry from Bush's opening war talk, but between the two, they provide fictional unofficial and official reasons. They also point to the fog of war—secrets supposedly necessary during wartime. The *Washington Post* reported a decade after Desert Storm:

> When Iraqi troops marched into Kuwait in August 1990, the oil-for-security bargain at the center of the Saudi-American relationship was fulfilled. Saddam Hussein threatened the world's greatest oil basin in and around the Persian Gulf, with Saudi Arabia at its center. Within months, half a million American soldiers had arrived in Saudi Arabia preparing for Desert Storm, a massive military campaign to expel the Iraqis from Kuwait.[10]

Walter becomes easier to hear as the camera moves from Donny to the bench. At full volume, Walter contrasts technological fighting to man-to-man combat, foreshadowing their imminent fight with men in "black pajamas"—the black-clad nihilists awaiting them outside by a torched oil machine. And so one idea easily leads to the next and warfare is heavily in the air.

Shades of war stalk Walter's thoughts and the Coens' L.A., where connections to Vietnam keep cropping up. In this buddy film, the Dude and his sidekick Walter are more than teammates; they are "soldiers," combating hostility and their foes' hidden agendas. Each piece of the Dude's rug-chasing mystery is a minor skirmish, and the affair culminates with a blackly comic brawl between the three bowlers and the nihilists. The narrating Stranger mentions the conflict with Saddam and the Iraqis upfront. Following Bush's war talk two marauders in the pay of Treehorn invade the Dude's sovereign territory. Later, the nihilists (Peter Stormare, Flea, and Torsten Voges) molest the Dude on his home turf. Dude and Walter go on a night-time mission to outwit an enemy. Jesus threatens the Dude's team before they are assaulted amid Desert Storm imagery. The fighting terminates with a fatality—part collateral damage, part war casualty.

The Dude's current enemies are tied to the past. We see this in the way the secrets and lies behind Walter's jungle exploits continue to haunt him. While he grabs at thin air trying to connect the then to the now, his scabrous jabs at a broken system carry a serious message: Wars not only produce shell-shocked, explosive types like Walter; wars for nothing or with hidden agendas breed discontent and anarchy—the state of Los Angeles in the early 1990s. The climactic link is Donny's death amid tepid justifications for the desert's brewing storm. Thus, Walter eulogizes the young, ace bowler Donny as if he were a fellow soldier downed in battle. Analogously, and yes, quite outrageously, his needless death is like that of many young Americans killed in Vietnam—surfer dudes like Donny about whom little is known because their lives were taken before they really got to live them.

Well before Donny's demise, bowling emerges as a striking combat metaphor full of aggression and justifications. It all starts when Walter goes ballistic over a line foul and pulls his gun on Smokey (a conscientious objector played by real-life pacifist Gilmore, one of many musician-actors). Walter's "Over the line!" objection recalls Bush's famous speech to justify the Gulf War: "I will draw a line in the sand." Both of Bush's prewar lines become amusing memes—cultural ideas that naturally spread through society via things like songs ("Tumbling Tumbleweeds") and catchwords ("I'm talking about drawing a line in the sand").[11]

Walter's brand of bellicosity is a product of his Vietnam years, which fomented his craving for rules. The explosive vet is a study in contrasts. He'll threaten a bowling rival with a gun but won't bowl or drive on the Sabbath. He'll question the legality of the nihilists' "marmot" (actually a ferret that the Dude identifies incorrectly) but lets his ex-wife's Pomeranian run about the bowling lanes. Walter is a lovable combustion of contradictions, but he has an excuse: the war. The power elite do not, for their class somehow exempted them from it, and anyway their violence has far more bite. Punches from Treehorn's heavies or Maude's squad come with the detective territory, but it's the ruling class that does the most harm, and they justify their violence with vacuous excuses. The Dude is a bum, they say. But regardless of his employment status, he doesn't deserve their battery.

Jimmie Dale Gilmore (far left) as the pacifist Smokey faces off with John Goodman's short-fused vet Walter (far right), who brandishes a gun over an alleged line foul as teammates (Steve Buscemi, second from left, and Jeff Bridges) look on. (Credit: Gramercy Pictures/Photofest © Gramercy Pictures)

Justifications run amok through the plot, often through memes. "We're talking about unchecked aggression here. I'm talking about drawing a line in the sand," Walter tells the Dude.[12] And so they hilariously apply Bush's warmongering words about Iraq's invasion of Kuwait to the Dude's rug problem, which, after all, also results from an invasion of his turf. Such rationales edge toward Maude's porn-film comment about the story being ludicrous. Seeking redress for his rug sets the Dude on a wild chase that ultimately underlines the absurdity of such justifications. In other words, the movie brilliantly turns around and exposes the hokum of the official case for war by making it the primary reason for the liberal Dude's silly but hardly frivolous story. Soon "cui bono" becomes a touchstone for bellicosity and false rationales.

Walter's "over the line" comment also links to the movie's Western fringes. In 1836, the legend goes, Colonel William Travis drew a line in the sand, inviting the outnumbered men trapped in the Alamo to cross over it and stay to defend Texas against the much bigger Mexican army surrounding them. One story has it that all but one man stayed to fight to their deaths. The movie makes a distinction between such honorable fighting—the Dude defends himself against the nihilists as a last resort—and the elite's ruthless aggression. A raft of cowboy references couches some conflicts as honorable—such as self-defense. The West may have been wild, the allusions suggest, but differences in fighting styles separate the good guys from the bad.

BRANDED

The Dude, of course, is *Lebowski's* good guy, a throwback to the 1960s and 1970s whose models include the cowboy, as well as Chandler's ace detective. Author Megan Abbott locates a kinship between Marlowe, cowboys, and knights: "Chandler's honorable detective Phillip Marlowe shares with the cowboy a deep connection to a possibly imagined past in that he conceives of himself as a knight trapped in a world where knightly values no longer seem to belong."[13] Telling cowboy characteristics, as outlined by film historian Robert Warshow, illustrate how close in disposition and attitude the Dude is to the Westerner.

> "The Westerner is *par excellence* a man of leisure." (The Stranger says upfront that the Dude is mighty lazy.)
> "What he defends, at bottom, is the purity of his own image—in fact his honor." ("I'm not trying to scam anyone here, man."[14])
> "Employment of some kind—usually unproductive—is always open to the Westerner, but when he accepts it, it is not because he needs to make a living, much less from any idea of 'getting ahead.'" ("Music business briefly. Roadie for Metallica. Speed of Sound tour. The guys are a bunch of assholes. And then, you know, a little of this, little of that. My career's uh slowed down a bit lately."[15])
> "We know that he is on the side of justice and order, and of course it can be said he fights for these things. But such broad aims never correspond exactly to his real motives; they only offer him his opportunity. . . . he does what he 'has to do.'"[16] (As his "Man in Me" theme song puts it, he will do nearly any job without asking for anything in return.)

The close correspondence between the Dude's nonviolent ethos and the cowboy honor code ties the Dude to Jason McCord from *Branded*, a TV Western starring Chuck Connors.

Cowboys and *Branded* are ideas planted in the Dude's head while hunting down the lost ransom money. The search for Lebowski's briefcase, stolen with the Dude's car, leads to the son of Arthur Digby Sellers, a fictional writer of the real TV show that aired from 1965–1966. Weaving fact and fiction, the movie uses the program to show how commonplace it is for the authorities to get it wrong. The show's opening tells how though the captain does the right thing, he is wrongly punished and forced into a nomadic lifestyle trying to escape his false reputation. At odds with the establishment, McCord is a typical Western hero. The Dude wears the same boots.

The cowboy undercurrent resurfaces as the Dude runs away from Treehorn's mansion, singing the *Branded* theme song. The filthy rich man has destroyed the Dude's rug, through his cohorts, drugged him, and made false statements to the cops about him. Like the TV show's Colonel McCord who is ostracized after he is wrongfully labeled a coward, the Dude is branded a bum instead of a coward. A policeman hurls first invectives and then a coffee mug at him. The cop's "jerk-off" ad hominem sexualizes the insult and semantically reflects that the police are in bed with the rich smut purveyor. Fighting only with sarcasm, the cool-headed Dude applies pacifism and offers no physical resistance. The powerfully rich (Jeffrey Lebowski, Jackie Treehorn) and the officially powerful (the Malibu police chief) reject ethical choices for down and dirty ones. Just as Lebowski repeatedly calls the Dude a "bum" although the older man is the real slacker, at every turn, the elite run roughshod over the Dude.

When the Dude finally sees Lebowski's smoke-and-mirrors power play, the have-not spells out this cycle of branding by a have: "You thought, hey, a deadbeat, a loser, someone the square community won't give a shit about."[17] Yet, though he is consistently treated like an outlaw or criminal because of his look, in fact, he is the real deal, true to his ethics, one who rises to the occasion. The authorities are the exact opposite. The Dude might not conform to society's idea of what makes a man, but he plays by its rules. Lebowski and his crowd do not.

WONDER WALL

In *Lebowski*, a civil war brews among philosophically disparate characters. Put differently, the film represents the Coens' latest spin on anarchy in the United States, specifically L.A., where things are not as they seem. As in *Miller's Crossing*, which also cribs heavily from the detective genre, the conflict boils down to questions of friendship, character, and ethics. Not since *Miller's Crossing* and *Barton Fink* has a Coen film gaily gallivanted through buddy-picture material like *Lebowski*. To the two-man gang of Leo and Tom and the tag team of Barton and Charlie/Karl (an earlier Goodman role), the Coens add a lovable pair of misfits: the Zen-like Dude and his captious sidekick, Walter. After Walter's outrage produces the mystery's germinating seed—he suggests the Dude be recompensed for his rug—their tiffs keep the story heading in wild, mind-boggling directions.

But despite their odd-couple friendship, they are on the same side when it comes to the war of ideals—pacifism being the exception. They and their formative 1960s–1970s ideals take on the establishment and its rapacious appetite for power.

"Condolences!" Lebowski yells to the Dude. "The bums lost. The bums will always lose."[18] These debatable lines beg the question, Who exactly are the bums? They also cryptically spell out the crux of the film: Who lost the culture wars, and who is losing now? Answers come in the form of a satire that portrays a depraved California full of pop art and commercialism but low on inspiration or meaning. Technically, the Dude's side might have lost, but what is portrayed is a mixed-up world where the so-called winners are phonies and raunch is king—as in *Crossing*, "black is white, up is down."[19] This backward view is illustrated in the wall-of-achievements scene. Here the Dude meets his doppelgänger through awards that make crystal clear Lebowski and he are at opposite ends of the political spectrum. Bookend mirror shots visualize an inverted bum-hero view and give a preview of the real achiever.

Long before we learn the man in the manse has no money of his own— as with *Fargo*'s Jerry Lundegaard and Ed Crane in *The Man Who Wasn't There*, Jeffrey married into it—the Dude's frosted image appears in the first wall plaque that reads "Achiever of the Year." He speaks his name as he examines the award up close, underscoring the idea that the Dude is the real Jeffrey Lebowski achiever. At the end of the sequence, his face appears in a "Man of the Year" award. For Coen aficionados, this particular accolade hints at Lebowski's true nature, for it is the same honor bestowed on *Blood Simple*'s murderous Visser. It turns out that Lebowski, like the venal PI, is not qualified for such an honor. The Dude, on the other hand, is.

As if to drive this point home, the scene's closing bookend on *Time* magazine's vaunted "Man of the Year" award frames the Dude's face in the award's mirror. Again, he mutters his name as he appears in the award, and the suggestion is that this appearance is more correct than what his namesake passes off for reality. Just then the Big Lebowski wheels into the room and announces the double motif directly: "OK! You're a Lebowski! I'm a Lebowski!"[20] True, the Dude does not go by these names, but the fact is that the Dude is the story's achiever, the man who discovers his namesake is a fraud, thus calling into question everything the old man stands for—namely, the establishment. In other words, things are the opposite of what they appear.

Beyond supplying clues as to this backward world, Lebowski's wall hangings give a good idea of who he is and what he represents. It also presents the Dude's antagonists: Republicans. The photo of Lebowski and Nancy Reagan, for instance, paints him in conservative tones a world apart from Dude's Day-Glo liberalism. Brandt's (Phillip Seymour Hoffman) explanation that the picture was taken when Mrs. Reagan was the first lady of the nation, not of California, puffs up his boss, but it also points to the diametrically opposed viewpoints these men offer. This becomes apparent when the Dude tells Brandt what he did in college while Reagan was governor: "occupying various, um, administration buildings . . . smoking thai-stick, breaking into the ROTC . . . and bowling."[21] In another connection between conservatives and the ramifications of war, the Dude learns of Lebowski's handicap through the Reagan picture. Later, claiming in one breath that he didn't blame anyone for his injuries, Lebowski accuses a Chinaman in the next before going on to brag about how he achieved anyway. As it turns out, the Big Lebowski didn't achieve—he married into his money. Words and images often lie in the movie to create a veil over truth, veracity, and reality—creating a kind of fog of war.

Reinforcing Lebowski's conservative creds is a picture of him and Charlton "Chuck" Heston, who campaigned for both Ronald Reagan and George H. W. Bush, the two presidents who appear in "Lebowski" introductions. These Republican leaders reflect a continuum between the California governor's turbulent, famously antiwar state and Bush's eve-of-war nation. The huge photo of Nixon in the Dude's living room is ironic since it portrays the bowling-enamored president in a less harsh light playing the working man's game. Or, perhaps, because the shot is seen most prominently during the phone call about Walter's outburst, it's yet another reminder of over-reaching power. These public figures and their pro-war stances help lay the groundwork for the ongoing culture wars as played out between the Dude and his calculating double.

The wide gulf between the two Lebowskis' attitudes and values is riotously exposed through the Dude's misinterpretations of the supposed citations and Brandt's swift corrections. For example, when he refers to the "Little Lebowski Achievers" as his boss's children, the Dude takes him literally and approves of the many mothers and racial openness. Brandt corrects him, explaining they are not offspring but rather "inner-city children of promise without the means for higher education."[22] Ultimately, we learn how low Lebowski will go when he steals from these underprivileged, inner-city children—a description that also reflects the minority groups who were sent by the thousands to Vietnam. The country that treated its citizens unequally had few qualms about sending young men of color off to fight, and many of the "lucky" ones who returned home came back, regardless of their race, with missing limbs and nonfunctioning parts.

The specter of war injuries keeps cropping up through body parts. There are the amputated toe of the nihilist girlfriend (played by musician Aimee Mann) and the nihilist's ear that Walter bites off. Maude's art studio, strewn with bodies—standalone torsos and busts—is a visual expression of nihilism in a society beleaguered by shadows of war. The first plaque on Lebowski's wall is for "Variety Clubs International," a charity founded in 1928 to aid disabled children—which might make one wonder whether Lebowski lost his legs in a war or was crippled since he was young.

Two deserts provide the backdrop for the movie's philosophical and ethical battles: the physical L.A. and the much discussed Middle East desert where a war brews. These dual settings prime the film for a cultural and political showdown. The Dude is introduced writing out a sixty-nine-cent check for milk as President Bush threatens the invading Iraqis. Opposite Bush's hostility is the Dude's "Aw fuck it—let's go bowling!" mentality.[23] But complementing this Zen, gutters-and-strikes mindset is his former activist self, which gives us hope regarding the ongoing struggle on the home front between the haves and have-nots. The Dude might be lazy, if the Stranger is right, but he represents the ideals of progressive politics and ethics. He survives.

"Say what you like about the tenets of National Socialism," Walter tells the Dude, adding, "At least it's an ethos."[24] This early 1990s Los Angeles is a moral vacuum—decadent and decayed to the point that the word *hero* need not apply. Avoiding such a label, the Stranger talks about the right man for the right time, and he identifies that person as the Dude. A product of the turbulent 1960s and 1970s, the Dude proves he still at least has values in the 1990s.

A supposed writer of the leftist manifesto the Port Huron Statement, the Dude is thus against racial inequality, and so Lebowski's gouging of a group of underprivileged minority children goes against the Dude's progressive grain. Like his model, Jeff Dowd, the Dude was one of the Seattle Seven antiwar activists.[25] Branded conspirators and indicted for conspiracy to damage federal property, the group found itself in 1970 the target of a right-wing conspiracy. In the words of Roger Lippman, another member, "It was a continuation of Nixon's Chicago strategy, which was to blame protest leaders for the national chaos caused by the war in Vietnam, as well as to tie up leading organizers and get us off the streets."[26] The coffee mug the police chief hurls at the Dude seems poetic payback for the rock Lippman was accused of lobbing at an officer. Such interweaving of past and present shows the Dude's revolution is not over—abuses by the power elite continue. Fortunately, the Dude is still around to tell his story of power abuse.

CHANDLER REDUX

After opening on a slice of nostalgia, the landscape gives way to the smoggy, asphalt jungle of L.A.—Philip Marlowe country. The tumbleweed tour of the urban ghost town brings into view a highway, a taco stand, an empty street, and a deserted beach. This bridging of past and present introduces the main genres from which the film draws: the Western and Chandler's crime fiction. Along with the Vietnam era, these are the focal points of the Dude's moral compass.

When we meet the Dude in the dairy aisle, it's late night and he's decked in boxers, a bathrobe, and slippers. Reminiscent of Robert Altman's 1973 *The Long Goodbye*, in which Elliott Gould's Marlowe goes to the store at an odd hour to find food for his finicky cat, the scene foreshadows the Dude's date with mystery. On returning home, a pair of thugs mistakes him for a different Lebowski and roughs him up. The mix-up sets the Dude on a rug-reparation course that leads to his gumshoe role and a slew of references to *The Big Sleep*, the Marlowe novel from which the Coens' movie takes part of its name.

The Big Lebowski tie-ins to *The Big Sleep* (also a 1946 movie directed by Howard Hawks, scripted by William Faulkner, and starring Humphrey Bogart) are many and droll: The Dude's employment by a wheelchair-bound man who has two rascally female relatives is like Marlowe's hiring by infirm patriarch "General" Sternwood (Charles Waldron) who has two coltish daughters. The Dude's interactions with Treehorn and Bunny are similar to Marlowe's discovery that a pornographer is blackmailing Sterwnood's daughter Carmen (Martha Vickers).

Central to both films is the idea of death—the "big sleep." Not only does the Chandler story incorporate seven murders, some of whose killers stumped the very author, but also Sternwood is on a steady march toward his own end: "My sleep is so near waking that it's hardly worth the name."[27] Then there's the figurative death of being asleep to one's world and its enveloping sleaze. This idea looms large in *Lebowski*, where the wheelchair-bound man is not merely seeking help with family problems. He is a Reagan-supporting fraud who authors the very blackmail scam by which he pretends to be victimized. In other words, it's the powers that be that comprise and create much of the problem.

If a cornerstone of the Chandler's Marlowe mysteries is a troubled society, an integral part of the detective's antiheroism is his knightly values. He desires to right, as best he can, a crooked social order. Yet, as Marlowe scholar Peter J. Rabinowitz points out, "while few readers miss the promises held out by the imagery of Marlowe's knighthood, a curious number have failed to realize that they are never fulfilled."[28] Thus, the detective has a world-weary persona. He knows he cannot fix the frayed societal fabric; he can only mend tiny patches. The Dude suffers a similar affliction and self-medicates with booze and marijuana. He sees modernity is in trouble. Larry's school paper indicates kids don't know basic history. Money and nihilism threaten cultural values. A corrupt police force is in the pockets of a rich porn king who thinks he's an artist. Alas, sex itself is in trouble.

A loose thread in Chandler's novels, sex becomes practically a societal unraveling in the Coens' film. *The Big Sleep* was such a racy novel for its time that when it was made into a movie, Warner Brothers had to avoid details that wouldn't pass muster of the strict Hays Production Code, the film industry's method of self-censorship enacted from 1934 to 1967 to avoid government restrictions. Chandler's taboo subjects include the pornographer's bisexuality—or homosexuality—and overt references to Carmen's nude photos. In spite of the code, Hawks did what he could to keep the sizzle between Marlowe and the sexy Vivian Sternwood—especially since they were being played by Bogart and Lauren Bacall, real-life lovers with great, on-screen chemistry. And yet, while Bogart and Bacall's scenes pushed the envelope in their day, comparing their repartee to the Dude and Maude's conversations shows a gigantic shift in cultural tectonics. Bogart and Bacall's metaphor and innuendo are electric; the Dude's pillow talk with Maude is burned out.

In the Coens' reconstruction, Chandler's risqué bits are so much the norm that sex is no longer exciting or titillating. It is verging on being aseptic. "He treats objects like women," the Dude says of Treehorn, and he doesn't necessarily mean it the other way around.[29] With gadgets and porn films supplanting this natural, essential human interaction, *Lebowski* depicts sex as commodified (Treehorn), perverted (Jesus), or intellectualized (Maude, who also makes it strictly biological with no strings attached). And so rather than sizzle with libidinous excitement, the movie offers up sex as one of the many big sleeps—or little deaths—in its 1990s' Los Angeles.

To understand the female Lebowskis a bit better, a look at their models is in order. Sternwood says about his daughters, himself, and the rich in general, "Vivian is spoiled, exacting, smart and quite ruthless. Carmen is still a little child who likes to pull the wings off flies. Neither of them has any more moral sense than a cat. Neither have I. No Sternwood ever has."[30] Vickers and Bacall animate the screen with portrayals of feisty, sexualized beings, not quite femmes fatales but not innocents either. Bunny's model Carmen is in trouble with an underground pornographic ring because of (implied) nude pictures of her taken when she was drugged. Vivian will do anything to protect her family's reputation and her sister, who also has murdered a man. Such strong women are not limited to these main characters. Hawks's women in *The Big Sleep* are what it is all about:

Lauren Bacall's sleek feline lead, Martha Vickers' spoiled, strung-out younger sister, Dorothy Malone's deceptively dignified bookstore clerk, Peggy Knudsen's petulant gangster's moll, and an unbilled woman taxi driver. Their lechery is as playful as the plot, and they are not stock figures of good and evil but surprisingly mixed and vivid.[31]

Women as a whole do not command such strength in the Coens' buddy picture, but as send-ups of Sternwood's daughters, Bunny and Maude help show what's wrong with L.A.

Carmen, the young spendthrift nymphomaniac, is revamped into Lebowski's young, sex-crazed wife Bunny, who associates with pornographers and nihilists. If Carmen was racy for her days, Bunny is simply a whore. Carmen's initial "You're cute" come-on is nothing compared to Bunny's offer of a sexual favor for money when she meets the Dude.[32] A twist in Bunny's reconstruction is that she's not a wayward daughter—she's the patriarch's trophy wife. The other strange turn for the "Viva Las Vegas" vamp is that Bunny is neither a femme fatale nor a Bunny. In another *Big Sleep* nod through the actor Peggy Knudsen who played Mona Mars, Bunny is actually a Fawn, Fawn Knudsen, a runaway daughter. This revelation further challenges Lebowski's contemptible character, begging the question just how old she is.

On the other end of the scale is Maude, who says she likes the "zesty enterprise" of sex, but she is less a sex kitten than a tame house cat.[33] First off, she seduces the Dude for purely practical reasons. In a twist on type, she isn't out for cheap thrills ("What did you think this [sex] was all about? Fun and games?"); she wants a child.[34] While Bunny sees sex as a business opportunity offering oral sex for cash, Maude uses it for procreation or artistic creation (she conceives her "vaginal" art while painting nude).

The Dude is too laid-back to exude Marlowe's macho cool that effortlessly attracts women. In fact, his perpetual drug-induced stupor precludes a fired-up reaction to Maude's proposition. When she drops her robe and says simply, "Love me, Jeffrey," he responds, "That's my robe."[35] But he does go to bed with her, and there a lot happens. He elaborates on his odd jobs and student activist days. They conceive a child, and the Dude realizes her broke father must have stolen the money. In other words, the sex scene is about the mystery and conception but very little about the act itself. It's hilarious—the film's one sex scene is not primarily about sex.

His dreams are a different matter entirely.

"GUTTERBALLS"

In the Dude's fantasy world, he's a sexual dynamo like the original Marlowe—and perhaps porn star Karl Hungus (Peter Stormare, also a nihilist). At least, that's how things start, but what begins as a lubricous, wish-fulfillment feast turns into a nightmare of castration fears. What's consistent is the dream's medley of found art—a patchwork of memes that have drifted into the Dude's mind on his mystery ride. The dream compresses the hippie's unlikely gumshoe tour of L.A. into a spoof of a Busby Berkeley sequence. The dream uses Berkeley's oft-used device of a story within a story to cryptically and imaginatively explore a society in collapse.[36]

Treehorn catapults the Dude into dreamland by way of a spiked white Russian. The screen goes black, and the Stranger introduces the Dude's tumble into sleep through a send-up of Chandleresque prose: "Darkness warshed over the Dude—darker'n a black steer's tookus on a moonless prairie night. There was no bottom."[37] (Compare this with *The Big Sleep*'s his "dry white hair clung to his scalp, like wild flowers fighting for life on a bare rock."[38]) Over a black screen, Mickey Newbury's psychedelic "Just Dropped In (To See What Condition My Condition Was In)" kicks in, with lyrics that play to both drug and sexual experiences. Appropriate to the Dude's circumstances and recent encounters—he's in Hollywood, has just chatted with a porn king, and has the sexy Maude on his mind—his subconscious creates his own porno flick.

The dream has a title sequence that recalls *Lebowski*'s opening and the subject matter of Bunny's porn video *Logjammin'*: A bowling pin phallus injects itself between two bowling balls, simulating sex. From there, the dream moves into a full-fledged tribute to Berkeley, the musical choreographer famous for his slyly symbolic representations of sex. In *Footlight Parade*, as movie critic J. Hoberman explains, "The girls are in a formation that suggests a zipper unzipping; their legs are meshed together and they part. Then he cuts to some incredible phallic arrangement where the girls come out of the water, and the water ejaculates."[39] The first and tamest nod to Berkeley comes via the Dude's entrance as a speck casting a giant wall shadow, a visual lifted from *Gold Diggers of 1935*. Things get more titillating from there.

Dressed and holstered with a tool belt like Karl Hungus in *Logjammin'*, the Dude takes a pair of rental shoes from Saddam Hussein and dances his way on a black-and-white checkered floor, like Lebowski's. There, he meets up with Maude who is dressed as a Valkyrie of the lanes. Her breastplate is made of bowling balls, and her horned helmet and trident are objets d'art from Lebowski's manse. Such found art, the ribald takeoff on porn, and its assortment of memes and homages work together to create a flavor of Fluxus, the antiestablishment art movement of the 1960s and 1970s that stemmed from the earlier Dada movement, itself an innovative response to a perceived breakdown in civilization. Coined from the Greek verb "to flow," the Fluxus art spoofed here celebrates political confrontation and social rebellion through a mix of media including performance art. *Lebowski*'s dalliance in Fluxus adds to

Jeff Bridges dreams of Julianne Moore as a Valkyrie, a mythic female who selects which warriors are to be slain in battle and whisks them off to Valhalla, the war god Odin's splendid home of heroes. (Credit: Gramercy Pictures/Photofest © Gramercy Pictures)

the deep-felt nostalgia for better times as the Dude plunges into sexual fantasy a la Berkeley.

The Dude is surrounded by chorines sporting bowling-pin headdresses fanned out like showy peacock feathers when he thrusts his arm straight up into the air. The gesture mimics Jesus's in the bowling alley, a nod to perverse power. Both pay tribute to Stanley Kubrick's antiwar satire, *Dr. Strangelove*, a Coen favorite, to which *Raising Arizona* also alludes. After a Berkeley-styled overhead shot of the chorines, the Dude suggestively inserts Maude's fingers into a bowling ball's holes and, holding her tight, sways back and forth, preparing for a throw. The dancers move to the lane and straddle it. And when the Dude and Maude let go of the ball, the Dude—as in his earlier dream—becomes the ball again and glides down the lane through the girl's legs. This nods to Berkeley's *42nd Street* in which the camera also moves through a set of legs. After moving toward the pins face down, he twirls around to look under their skirts and smiles a lascivious smile. (This technically challenging shot, due to the size of the Dude's body being unable to physically go between the legs, was resolved by using a computerized, slightly shrunk version of the Dude.) When he collides with the pins, the music changes to a darker, avant-garde instrumental, and a nightmare overtakes the sex fantasy.

John Turturro's strange Jesus character borrows from Peter Sellers's Dr. Strangelove. Both have one black-gloved hand, which each man thrusts into the air in defiance. (Credit: Columbia Pictures/Photofest © Columbia Pictures)

A topless Treehorn girl marks the transition, suggesting perhaps that yesterday's Berkeley fantasies were more fun than today's porn. Next, a red-suited nihilist chases the Dude snipping huge scissors. Morphing castration threats with Jesus's sexual threats via the body suit, the nightmare grafts art with cinema. The giant scissors are wall art in Maude's studio, as well as a flash homage to Alfred Hitchcock's *Spellbound,* which features a gigantic set of scissors in a dream sequence choreographed by Surrealist painter Salvador Dali. The Dude's dream furthers the motif of a society in trouble. The nihilists' immorality and violence (they do cut off a girl's toe) make them pugnacious sadists who would cut off the Dude's pleasure for their own benefit. In the end, though, when they fight the bowlers, their ineptitude paints them comical—a conclusion foreshadowed in the dream by the red body suit and silly run. So while nihilism lurks in *Lebowski's* Los Angeles, the movie's tone captures a blackly comic vision of nihilism—in other words, it gives us a lot of "nothing" to laugh at.

"WHERE'S THE MONEY, LEBOWSKI?"

Part of this nothingness involves an oft-visited Coen theme: an obsession with money. The question "Where's the money, Lebowski?"—with two different meanings aimed at two different people—bookends the plot.[40] Initially posed by thugs to the wrong man, the question sparks the ensuing chaos and gets to the heart of today's crisis. Posed by the Dude to the right man at the end, it resolves the crisis to the extent the Dude's power allows. That is, he solves the mystery but in his everyday role as a lazy, lovable loafer, he is powerless to do much about it. Like Chandler's Marlowe, he is a knight who can't change the status quo. He can only offer up a model of pretty good behavior and expose the societal rot. (In the following film, the hate-not hero will find political solutions, albeit in an earlier time period.)

Stolen money is key to the corruption and nihilism draining the town dry and short-changing the little guy. The initial mix-up over his name shakes up the Dude's lackadaisical existence and recharges the protest ways of his youth. His nonmaterialistic, Zen-like gutters-or-strikes persona goes up against the fat-cat Lebowski, not even suspecting the old man has a reason to manipulate and lie. The Dude shows us that reality is the mirror-opposite of what it appears. The old man who called the money-grubbers, "Cowards! Weaklings! Bums!" actually stole it, showing his words would work better if self-applied.[41] Money is the primary corrupting force. It not only drives men to steal from needy children—like oil greasing the military-industrial complex—it can lead to nihilistic forms of art and entertainment.

"The story is ludicrous," Maude scoffs when she shows Dude *Logjammin'* (which features a cameo by real porn star Asia Carrera).[42] Porn is one way the movie shows that artistic nihilism is polluting Los Angeles. Things are in such bad shape that deluded purveyors of smut try to pass off their wares as "publishing, entertainment, political advocacy."[43] When porn is pervasive and porn kings are among society's elites, the movie suggests, culture is in trouble. Narrative art is one of many art forms on display—and often in decline—in *Lebowski*.

The mainstreaming of pornography is a prime example of the slow death of an art form, namely the narrative. Maude implies as much when she dismisses *Logjammin'* as absurd, made all the more so through its in-jokes. Dude's exclamation that he knows the porn actor triggers a multilayered response in loyal Coen fans. Like the Dude, the viewer has seen Karl Hungus in Lebowski's pool. But viewers familiar with *Fargo* have also seen the actor Stormare stuffing his accomplice from that movie into a log shredder, a gesture intimated in the very title, *Logjammin'*. Then there's the broken TV. A stale setup for a porno movie, a television set on the blink is also a plot point in *Fargo*. Ulee's nihilism, through actor Stormare, extends beyond *Lebowski* to his roles in *Fargo* and *Logjammin'*. All these characters he plays care nothing about art or human life. They care just about sex, violence, and finances.

Again, Donny's demise, that seemingly random event, provides insight to *Lebowski*'s multitextured satire. He dies because even the nihilists who are supposed to care about nothing love cash. When the Dude tells them there never was a million dollars, their response is get whatever money they can—quite a commentary on the import placed on cash in this corrupt L.A. Beyond this, Donny's death can be seen as a dark, self-conscious joke. Sure, he is the victim of savage lust, but he also perishes from poor story comprehension. Because he is always bowling while the Dude and Walter discuss the Dude's strange mystery, Donny lacks knowledge of what is really going on ("You're like a child who wanders in in the middle of the movie").[44] Donny's frame of reference is bowling, as Walter tells him, not the story. When the nihilists attack, Donny mistakes the men for Nazis and has a fear-induced heart attack. In effect, he dies needlessly in a senseless battle, having become part of a fight about which he knows nothing.

Such associations are ridiculous, but the interrelation between *Lebowski* and *Fargo*, especially where viewership is concerned, goes deeper—and gets more satirical. Claiming to be true, *Fargo* strews its cinematic landscape with television screens to highlight the pitfalls of passive viewing. Where *Fargo*'s image-saturated world shows how viewers can be lulled into a little sleep or at least a little misunderstanding, *Lebowski*'s concentration on porn suggests narrative death—an artistic sleep. After all, as writer Umberto Eco observes, with porn "no one has the least intention of spending time and money thinking up a worthwhile story, and the spectators aren't interested in the story either, because all they're waiting for is the sexy bits."[45]

The slow death of narrative art collides with Treehorn's monied power. Pornography, used to characterize the amoral, venal bad guys in *The Big Sleep*, is no longer an underworld enterprise in *Lebowski*'s 1990s. Porn kings are now social pillars. Put differently, the modern bad guys are in bed with the authorities, and money greases the relationship. But one look at Treehorn's treatment of the Dude and his young nihilist employees shows how rotten he is.

Introduced at night with bonfires behind him, Treehorn is an incubus with a hard-on. (The Coens routinely denote malefic characters with fire, including *Blood Simple*'s Marty, *Raising Arizona*'s Lenny, *Barton Fink*'s Charlie, Sid in *The Hudsucker Proxy*, and the sheriff in *O Brother, Where Art Thou?*) Treehorn's pleasure dome is an uneasy mix of pleasure and pain. Yma Sumac's vocal acrobatics help set the erotica-meets-exotica scene in which lascivious men toss up and down a topless woman. Less arousing than disturbing, the scene's strange brew of sex, power, and money exposes the seedy underbelly of what on the surface could otherwise look like fun. Treehorn greets the Dude amicably, but then he drugs his guest and kicks him out.

Like Lebowski, Treehorn is not as he appears or who he fancies himself to be. Both pass themselves off as legitimate businessmen when neither is. Treehorn considers himself an artiste, to boot. When the Dude calls his line of work what it is, smut, the porn king recharacterizes it in euphemistic terms, "publishing, entertainment, (and) political advocacy."[46] His wealth might buy him influence with the Malibu police, but as *Logjammin'* shows, his porn is hardly political. It's exploitative fluff. Before double-crossing the Dude, Treehorn laments declining aesthetics and faults video for falling standards in "story, production value, feeling." Such sentiments echo real-life pornographer Ed Deroo's take on the subject: "Film had soul; video had nothing. Video's just a way of making money. It flows like water, but film had a texture, a feeling, something you could grab onto and feel."[47] But more important is the overall decline in art, so overcommodified, oversexualized, and hilarious in *Lebowski*'s Los Angeles.

Pornography and other types of artistic nihilism, the movie suggests, are dangerous, for art is our collective cultural watering hole. *Lebowski* showcases art that is at once riotous and ludicrous. The odd Panlike dance of the Dude's landlord (Jack Kehler)—which includes knee bends and arm flapping reminiscent of Norville's fight song in *The Hudsucker Proxy*—is what Walter can only describe as "the what have you."[48] Maude, on the other hand, knows just what to call her avant-garde art, which she creates while flying over them in the nude: vaginal. When she presses the Dude to find out his comfort level with the female form, grateful for the help in interpreting her painting, he comments, "Is that what that's a picture of?"[49] When art becomes so abstract that it is ridiculous, indescribable, or unrecognizable, it can border on meaningless and nothingness. But it can also point to weighty issues underneath the surface, as *Lebowski*'s satire does.

Studded with art forms from painting and other visual art to interpretative dance, statuary, and all kinds of music, the film seems to jokingly question whether art is still a tenable medium in a place like Los Angeles where money and corrupt forces rule. What artistic existentialism is to *Barton Fink*, artistic nihilism is to *Lebowski*. Art that says nothing, the movie suggests, is as close to hell on earth as nihilist thought. While pretending to ramble through a druggie's magic carpet ride, *Lebowski* offers an incisive critique of the politics of art and war in America. Along with the idea that art and culture are in danger comes the Stranger's suggestion that the term "hee-ro" is passé in these sad, modern times. And so we are back in Chandler's world, where the antihero Marlowe wants to do what's right even if he cannot fix the whole corrupt system.

LOST ANGELES

The dirty character of Los Angeles, so central to *The Long Goodbye*, is also pivotal to *Lebowski*. Introduced alongside the Dude, the city is his main antagonist, representative of all that ails its crooked denizens. While the Dude clashes with a passel of perverted people throughout, a la Marlowe, it's the metropolis and by extension its governing forces at the root of the trouble the Dude encounters—hence, the president's appearance in the opening.

L.A.'s twinkling metropolis comes into view as the Stranger calls the "City of Angels" a misnomer. The nighttime cityscape is a stark contrast to the natural prairie that precedes it. The following traffic scene adds wisps of modern pollution. In Chandler's smog-filled L.A., smog is a metaphor for the stink and reach of corruption. The Coens' L.A. character sketch taps key ideas from Chandler for its expansive homage to *The Long Goodbye*.

The tumbleweed's trundle along an overpass creates visual tension with the stream of traffic that crosses underneath. The orb rolling along modern city streets sets up a continuity between the old days and modernity as well as a possible clash between eras. In the next shot, a taco stand and its four patrons recall the alienation in Edward Hopper's late-night diner tableau, *Nighthawks*. This sense of isolation is carried into the next two shots of an empty street and a deserted beach, a setting evocative of so many movies including *The Long*

Goodbye. Like the tumbleweed's bridge between past and present, the Coens' film connects Chandler's original stories, the movies that were faithful to them, and Altman's 1973 revision.

The Long Goodbye tribute revives Chandler's themes about money and corruption and ties them into *Lebowski's* ideas of revolution. L.A.'s literally and figuratively foul air is a setting rife for a social change. Yet, instead of a public up in arms about entrenched malfeasance, there is just a single individual struggling against an immoral machine, when he's not bowling. In the novel, Marlowe fights the dirty city and barely comes out on top. In Altman's revision, he loses. In the Coens' film, the Dude's Day-Glo dick borrows from both. A testament to the positive aspects of the counterculture—a movement lambasted and devalued in Altman's film—the Dude like the original Marlowe cannot change the world, but he survives and offers a glimmer of hope even as he exhibits touches of Gould's torpor.

One highpoint of *Lebowski's* inventiveness is its ability to draw from both an original and a dramatic revision. To parse this feat, a quick look at both *Long Goodbyes* is in order. Chandler's story follows Marlowe's journey to clear his friend Terry Lennox's name, but, like most of the detective's relationships, the friendship will prove hollow and empty. At Terry's request, Marlowe drives him to Tijuana in the dead of night, no questions asked. On his return, the police tell Marlowe Terry is suspected of killing his wife, Sylvia. The private eye doesn't believe his friend capable of this and goes to jail for protecting him. He is let go when Terry is reported dead of a suicide. Marlowe opens his own investigation into Sylvia's death, still believing Terry innocent. He also takes on a missing-persons case, which turns out to be closely tied to the first. As in *Lebowski,* little is as it initially seems.

The missing man is Roger Wade, an alcoholic novelist married to Terry's friend and neighbor, Eileen. As Marlowe slogs through the writer's world, he finds a man so disappointed in life that he drinks to oblivion. Roger fears that during one such blackout he might have killed Sylvia. Though a host of characters tries to manipulate, seduce, or threaten Marlowe to keep their secrets hidden, the detective digs in his heels to find the truth. In the end he learns that Terry and Eileen's past history led to both Sylvia's and Wade's deaths at the hands of Eileen. Though Marlowe is right that Terry is not the killer, he was wrong about his so-called friend's character, for Terry was complicit in the crimes. Crushed by the betrayal, Marlowe closes the book with, "So long, amigo. I won't say goodbye. I said it to you when it meant something."[50]

The corruption Marlowe uncovers in every pocket of society is inspiration for the Dude's similar findings. L.A.'s pollution figuratively seeps into everything from relationships to institutions. Wealth, greed, power, and lust befoul the city's denizens. Pernicious minor characters are menacing L.A. fixtures. Wade's houseboy Candy, for example, a seeming model for the Coens' Jesus character, attacks Marlowe with a knife. His warning, "Nobody fools with me," is echoed by the intimidating pedophilic bowler who warns "Nobody fucks with the Jesus" and threatens the Dude with sodomy.[51] Violence and fraud contaminate institutions from journalism to big business, the law, medicine, Hollywood, advertising, family, and friendship.

Money is a potent, corrupting force and a graven image. Chandler's vile gangster Marty Augustine (Mark Rydell) considers murder a minor crime but stealing money deserving of "capital punishment." Sylvia's rich, powerful father Harlan Potter, one of many who try to stymie Marlowe's work, is a newspaper magnate who anthropomorphizes money suggesting it has "life" and "conscience." Marlowe later describes the smoke and mirrors behind people like Potter, who create themselves, godlike, in their own preferred image—much like Lebowski:

> Guys with a hundred million dollars live a peculiar life, behind a screen of servants, bodyguards, secretaries, lawyers, and tan executives. Presumably they eat, sleep, get their hair cuts, and wear clothes. But you never know for sure. Everything you read or hear about them has been processed by a public relations gang who are paid big money to create and maintain a usable personality, something simple and clean and sharp, like a sterilized needle. It doesn't have to be true.[52]

Framing the Dude is the once-rich Lebowski's strategy for cash. Though money is a pollutant, fortunately, the Dude is around to at least expose the corruption. The Dude shares with the good cowboy and Marlowe a moral backbone. Armed mainly with wisecracks, these types are ethical and rarely combative, the opposite of their foes. When the Malibu police chief verbally and physically assaults him, the Dude fights back with sarcasm: "I'm sorry, I wasn't listening."[53] In response to his initial attackers' question about the money he applies his own special brand of toilet humor, wisecracking that it's in the bowl into which they plunge his head again.

Altman's deconstructed Marlowe is a bit different. A man obviously distressed by the times, Gould's Marlowe is not as pure as the legendary PI. California in the 1970s with its hippies, drugs, and war protests is so unpleasant that the antihero does not just indict society, he shrugs off his steely moral code and joins the slime. Hardly Bogart's debonair detective, Gould's Marlowe is a laid-back misfit whose characteristic "It's OK by me" mantra belies his contempt for a society in decline.[54] Altman and screenwriter Leigh Brackett's drastically altered ending makes Terry the killer. When Marlowe finds this out, it is so not OK with him that after hunting down this truth, he guns down Terry.[55] Brackett, also *The Big Sleep* screenwriter, explained, "I know [Chandler] wanted

Marlowe to be depicted as an honest man, and somebody who was his own man. I wanted to get that in the screenplay. But I also had to show Marlowe the way he looks to us now in the '70s."[56]

A key point of departure between Altman's film and *Lebowski* is their views on the 1970s and drugs. While Marlowe and the Dude have similarly mellow attitudes, one is a natural melancholy, the other a drug-induced survival tactic. Marlowe is so turned off by drugs that even the sight of topless neighbors disinterests him because they are drugged-out deadbeats. "They're not there," he mutters, reiterating a comment made earlier to his cellmate about the mind's ability to detach from the body.[57] The first iteration is a positive—the mind can escape bad situations—while the latter is a negative—his drugged neighbors are oblivious. For the Dude, drugs are a primary way to escape his troubled world; dreams, music, and bowling are other means of escape. Despite the fact that *The Long Goodbye* condemns the decade the Coens' movie glorifies, *Lebowski* takes many a cue from the Altman film. A couple of these details have to do with character and attitude. Both Marlowe and the Dude are throwbacks adrift in their modernity. Beyond this are the iconoclastic protagonists' introductions.

Altman's *Long Goodbye* opens on a long, hard eccentric look at Marlowe's main character flaw: loyalty. It's a quirky forecast of Terry's ultimate betrayal. When Marlowe is woken by his hungry cat, he goes out to buy cat food. He scours the shelves for his cat's preferred brand, but he is out of luck and has to buy a substitute. At home, he goes to great lengths to hide the wrong brand from the cat. His grand efforts have disastrous results: First, the cat won't eat; worse, it runs away. Marlowe spends much of the rest of his free time trying to get it back. It will prove to be a wild goose chase, just as clearing his friend's name will be.

The Dude's supermarket intro nods to Gould's Marlowe while setting up key themes of aggression, deficient rationales, and institutional corruption. It also gives a good sense of the Dude's antiestablishment preferences. Aesthetically, the scene acknowledges Altman's influence on the Coens' inventive use of music. The Muzak version of "Tumbling Tumbleweeds" borrows a technique from Altman and introduces the conspicuous role music will play. The switch from music expressly for the audience's ears to an in-scene element that the Dude can hear nods to *The Long Goodbye*, which interweaves different styles of the same John Williams' song throughout, to connect the various plot strands, characters, and motifs. Each style, from jazz to flamenco to Muzak, adds texture to the scene and comments on the action therein.

Some of the Coens' biggest tributes to Altman have more to do with this kind of cinematic ingenuity than plot. Take Altman's innovative casting as an example. Marlowe isn't the only sacred cow Altman tips over, and pollution isn't L.A.'s only feature with a chokehold on the city. *The Long Goodbye* satirizes the movie capital. Choice swipes include the gatekeeper who is more interested in performing poor movie star impersonations than in doing his job. Then there's the dog Marlowe almost hits. He calls it Asta, the same name of Nick and Nora Charles's fox terrier in W. S. Van Dyke's *The Thin Man* (1934), based on the Dashiell Hammett novel.

But *The Long Goodbye*'s biggest knock at Hollywood is likely its casting. With the notable exceptions of Gould, who had worked with Altman in M★A★S★H, and veteran actor Sterling Hayden, who plays Roger, the movie stars an eclectic mix of famous personalities without a lot of movie experience. European cabaret singer Nina Van Pallandt is Eileen Wade. New York Yankee pitcher Jim Bouton—who gained notoriety with his 1970 tell-all book *Ball Four*—plays Marlowe's Judas, Terry. *Rowan & Martin's Laugh-In* regular Henry Gibson is the crooked doctor. Director and sometime TV actor Rydell (who would later receive an Oscar nomination for directing *On Golden Pond*) is a sadistic gangster. Acting rookie Arnold Schwarzenegger makes his second screen appearance as one of Rydell's heavies.

Lebowski's casting innovation involves musicians. There's country's David Lee Gilmore, a Texas son and member of the Flatlanders, who gives body and spirit to modern-day cowboy and pacifist Smokey. Rocker Flea, the Red Hot Chili Peppers's funky bassist, plays a nihilist. Singer-songwriter Aimee Mann, formerly Til Tuesday's diva, sits in as the nine-toed lady nihilist. The tangential music figure Carlos Leon (Madonna's ex) plays Maude's thug. And punk rocker Warren Keith of the U.K. punk band the Adicts plays the funeral director.

In Altman's view nothing can save society from its cesspool of corruption, least of all Hollywood. *Lebowski*'s symphonic reverie offers up a more sanguine outlook, and the Dude revives that otherwise absent virtue that Chandler's Marlowe encompasses. The Dude's L.A. might teem with Reagan-supporting poseurs, rich porn kings, artist wannabes, and the blackest of black, the nihilists, but there are points of light in this noir world—there's the Dude and his counterculture revolt against the establishment. Sure, the Dude takes leave of his sullied L.A. surroundings via dreams, bowling, and a mix of white Russians and joints, but he rises to the task when called upon. Like splotches of Day-Glo against a black backdrop, the Dude is the shining star in his less than stellar universe.

ROCK 'N' ROLL FANTASY IN FLUX

From the opening "Tumbling Tumbleweeds" to "Dead Flowers," music helps sift and shuffle through the sands of time while amplifying the satire's themes. By channeling the past, music offers a nostalgic getaway from a ragged modernity as well as a window into memory. This powerful combination is why "the Dude abides."[58] Such ideas take off from the start.

After the Sons of the Pioneers channel the old West, a Muzak version of the cowboy tune plays in the store. On one level, the bastardized sound is a funny comment on the stultifying effects of commodified art—Muzak is a trademark for music engineered to make shopping pleasant. The other main point here has to do with how easily transferred music and ideas can be. The Muzak rendition launches the important concept of memes—the transfer of cultural information through art. This can be a powerful weapon in a place in need of revolution.

The moment the micturating thugs leave, the screen cuts to black, and Bob Dylan, the counterculture's unofficial poet laureate, summons the Dude. Day-Glo stars stipple the screen, calling up the Dude's time and place—the early 1970s and the bowling alley. In no time, Dylan's Common Man anthem becomes the Dude's theme song. Like "The Man in Me," the Dude will do whatever he is asked. The closest thing to a hero in a place where the term is anachronistic, he will drum up his man within to uncover the faux rich man's crime and in the process revive the ethos of pacifism. Then he'll head back to the lanes.

The Dude's fondness for Creedence Clearwater Revival (CCR) amplifies some of his personality traits. "Run Through the Jungle," for instance, whose war of words likens Vietnam to hell, captures the Dude's antiwar leanings while "Looking Out My Backdoor" italicizes his fondness for vivid imaginings, courtesy of dreams and drugs. More generally, the Dude's love of CCR and its country-inflected rock shows a preference for working-man values.

The Coens and their musical archivist T-Bone Burnett made fantastic song selections that express a constellation of ideas important to the film. Townes Van Zandt's cover of the Rolling Stones's "Dead Flowers" is a good example. Never mind that its placement makes it a touching if irreverent farewell to Donny. Its antiestablishment flavor shines through lyrics that talk about rich people and fancy upholstery. The country-rock feel and its bittersweet nostalgia make it the closing bookend to the opening's traditional country twang.

On the other side of the musical spectrum is music of the Dude's doppelgänger. No rock and roll there. One of the first songs heard at the mansion is Mozart's "Requiem in D minor." What's apparent from the sound is the class and generational differences between the Lebowskis. Atmospherically, it adds weight to the heavy atmosphere exuding from the low-lit room where Lebowski stares moodily into the fire. Such hellish imagery, often a sign of a Coen bad guy, hints that his tears are less strong man crying and more crocodile tears crock. The music, which also subtly adds a layer of mystery through the requiem, has a built-in whodunit. Mozart died before completing the piece, leaving scholars to speculate to this day who commissioned and who finished the composition. Such an incomplete resolution could foreshadow the film's ending.

The operatic "Gluck Das Mir Verblieb" is another piece of formal music emanating from Lebowski's manse. When Brandt equips Dude for the ransom drop-off, the strains of the Erich Wolfgang Korngold piece filling the hall again add a certain gravitas to the scene. The selection also allusively and subtly embroiders the film's preoccupation with dreams. Korngold's opera, about grief, the celebration of life, and imaginative power, tells of a widowed man guilt-ridden over his feelings for a woman who looks like his dead wife. To free his conscience, he kills the woman in a dream. The Dude finds similar escape in dreams.

A smattering of Latin-styled songs acknowledges L.A.'s large Latino presence. Santana's "Oye Como Va" and the Gypsy King's Spanish version of "Hotel California" double as Jesus's unofficial theme songs. The Santana tune plays up his aggressive, perverse sexuality he flouts through hip thrusts, sodomy threats, ball shining, and ball licking. "Hotel California," whose eerie storyline seems to fit Jesus's pederasty and the California setting more broadly, elaborates on his fierce competition with the Dude, who hates the Eagles, the group that wrote the song.

The landlord's dance, scored to Modest Mussorgsky's "Pictures at an Exhibition," a piece composed to accompany an art show, subtly notes the ubiquity of "art" in L.A. There, folks might prefer talking TV as Dude's bowling team does to watching a performance. Culture, the sequence suggests, brims with art, from the ludicrous to the popular to the avant-garde. The Latin-inflected "Mucha Muchacha" by Esquivel, Brazil's space-age pop king, goes well with the bowling alley's Googie architecture. The movie's Gesamtkunstwerk ("total art") features architecture among its medley of melodies, paintings, performance art, and dance. From Treehorn's mod pad, introduced by the haunting "Lujon," appropriately from Henry Mancini's *Mr. Lucky Goes Latin* album, to Lebowski's opulent manse, design is on display. Production designer Rick Heinrichs says buildings are critical to describing Dude and Walter's ties to yesteryear.

We wanted to reference a traditional Los Angeles. We focused on L.A. architecture from the '50s and '60s, not only to establish the feel of the city, but also to comment on the characters of the Dude and Walter, who are anchored in the past in the way they lead their lives. Somehow this architecture even refers back to the Vietnam era—which is so important to Walter and to the Dude.[59]

Relationships to the past define what characters stand for—and what they're running from. At every turn, music and art add often subtle critique and commentary to a scene's dynamics. Walter and Smokey's tiff over the line foul plays over the edgy "I Hate You," a punk song by the Monks, a group of ex-servicemen who got together during the Vietnam War. Maude rebels against her loathsome patriarch through both her art and the music she creates it to. The exotic, syncopated breathing of Meredith Monk's orgasmic-sounding "Walking Song" provides the soundtrack for Maude's naked, swooping paint application, which looks part-Pollack, part-mock ejaculation. That the Dude listens to Captain Beefheart's avant-garde "Her Eyes Were a Blue Million Miles" at the doctor's visit foreshadows his affair with Maude, the avant-garde artist who has sent him there for a full checkup. In other words, the song's subject matter and style in a setting connected to Maude foreshadow their coupling.

The luscious, ludicrous mix of artistic set pieces offsets the Coens' often silly Fluxus art and round out the cinematic commentary on art, war, and politics. If the landlord's dance moderne comes across as absurd as the porn movie, at least the Dude and Walter's plan to visit Larry Sellers offsets the odd performance. In other words, whether it's the plot's twists and turns or the panoply of art, the narrative journey is engaging enough to qualify for Chandler's own definition of a good mystery in which the "solution of the mystery . . . [is] only . . . 'the olive in the martini.'"[60] Put differently, it is the story ride that counts.

Lebowski's integrated music is a sneak preview of *O Brother, Where Art Thou?*, a musical odyssey that explores the nexus of folk traditions and history as cultural storytelling. The songs in both movies owe a lot to the Coens' musical archivist T-Bone Burnett. *Lebowski*, as *O Brother* will do, drops song titles into dialogue, illustrating how influential music is. It's so deeply threaded throughout culture that it is part of our collective unconscious—music is a meme that spreads through society like tumbleweed dropping its seeds. When the Dude learns Bunny is a Knudsen, in questioning how innocence can blossom after her adult experiences, he (mostly) cites the American song, "How You Gonna Keep 'Em Down on the Farm (Once They've Seen Gay Paris)?" but replaces the last couplet with "Karl Hungus," updating yesterday's poetic phrase for 1990s raunch. Jim Croce's line "sometimes you eat the bear and sometimes the bear eats you," from his song "Hard Time Losin' Man," captures the Dude's "up and down, gutters and strikes" karmic philosophy.[61] It also plays up the country-and-western motif.

Nearly all the songs tie in to a main motif, and often that is Hollywood. Bunny's theme song, "Viva Las Vegas," is from an Elvis Presley movie. The Dude's drunken rendition of the *Branded* theme song harks to TV Westerns. All in all, though highly original *Lebowski* finds inspiration in erstwhile stories.

A RETROSPECTIVE

Lebowski is a buddy picture that crackles with originality even as it retreads a good deal of earlier Coen, Chandler, and Altman material. As usual, dreams are an integral part of the Coens' landscape. The Dude's first oneiric trip comes courtesy of one of Maude's heavies. It follows that he chases her in his dream, which acts like a crystal ball to his upcoming adventure.

The Dude flies over Los Angeles at night. The cityscape is reminiscent of the opening shot of the city, and his Superman pose referentially taps the idea of the heroic. When he spots Maude flying on an Oriental rug, magic carpet rides come to mind. Such a sight might also spring to mind the episodic *Book of One Thousand and One Nights*, the Middle Eastern epic that celebrates the power of stories. The flying Persian rug also links to the imminent Gulf War. Coen fans might connect the Dude's rug pursuit to *Miller's Crossing*'s case of the missing "Rug," which wasn't much of a case at all. Rugs, it seems, don't just tie the room together; they can tie stories together. When gravity suddenly sends the Dude freefalling a la Norville in *The Hudsucker Proxy*, the bowling alley fortunately provides safe landing. But to his surprise he is suddenly a much smaller man facing down a giant bowling ball. It rolls toward and engulfs him, making him one with the ball. Here, a subjective camera takes on the tumbling orb's perspective, and we see the world through finger holes until the ball hits the pins and the Dude awakes. The dream presupposes that he will chase his rug around the city, escape threats, and then see things in a new light.

The gutter-balls dream is also subtly premonitory. Maude's bowling-attired Valkyrie, a mythological maiden who chooses which heroes are to be slain, preludes Donny's death outside the lanes, after faltering at the pins. He did not understand the ongoing battle (he was busy bowling when things were explained), and his death seems avoidable. In fact his passing is symbolic of young soldiers needlessly dying in an unnecessary war. The easy transfer of ideas from the waking world to the realm of sleep points to the power of memes.

Coen film references reinforce the power of myth and movies. When Treehorn spikes the Dude's white Russian, his face-first fall into a glass table mirrors the unsuccessful suicide attempt of the executive who meets the new Plexiglass window with his face. In another *Hudsucker* nod, Harry Bugin, who played the silent sign-painter, is again a character of few words—a former TV writer, he is now silent in an iron lung. Da Fino, played by Jon Polito, a mob boss in *Crossing*, is the Dude's sleuthing brother in arms. He serves up a host of in-jokes, the first harking back to *Blood Simple*'s detective through the vintage VW Bug. *Crossing* allusions pepper his conversation with the Dude, whom he complements for playing one side against the other (like Tom in

Miller's Crossing). Their semantic quarrel over the Dude's relationship to Maude subtly harks back to Tom's strained relationship with his moll.[62]

Lebowski also cannibalizes from Hitchcock. The initial case of mistaken identity borrows from the situation that thrusts *North by Northwest*'s ad man (Cary Grant) into a world of intrigue. The scene at Treehorn's spoofs the 1959 thriller, which deals with spies, lies, and an innocent man unjustly accused (like the Dude). The Dude's attempts to learn about Treehorn by lightly rubbing his pad of paper to see what he wrote is the same tactic Grant's character employs to discover information about a spy. The Dude is less successful. His pencil rubbing reveals that Treehorn had drawn a naked, aroused man. Along with the Dude's Ralph's card, this dirty picture is what the Malibu cop finds in his pockets—a situation also lifted from *North by Northwest*. After Grant is liquored up and booted from a rich man's party, the police pick him up and do not believe his story. Similarly, Treehorn drugs the Dude, the police pick him up, and don't believe a word he says. The kicker is that in the 1990s scenario, they also abuse him.

In sewing so many story lines and details from songs, movies, and Chandler stories, *Lebowski* keeps life, culture, and the narrative ball rolling on, so to speak. Just as the movie opens with allusions to Westerns, the Stranger closes the picture with the idea of rebirth. Showing the resilience and import of the narrative and more broadly of art, the movie quotes with zest and keeps the Common Man's revolution alive. As in *Blood Simple*, *The Big Lebowski* shows that it's the same old song when it comes to war politics in the United States, whether it is the 1960s or the 1990s. Thankfully, the Dude is around to revive the idea of values, such as peace and love.

WRAP: "CUI BONO" AND UNSUNG HEROES

You say you want a resolution? Well, you know *Lebowski* is more about revolution. The Dude figures out Lebowski's crime, but there is no consequence to the charge. Lebowski denies it, and the Dude goes bowling. It's up to the viewer to decide what happens to Lebowski, and so the movie's very form mimics its theme about ongoing struggles. While underscoring the idea that yesterday's conflicts are still around, the film suggests art can at the very least expose them.

The movie is, in a word, subversive. A bit loose like its shabby hero, it seems to roll out a random, comedic noir adventure. But between the lines— and directly within them—it's as radical as its main character. Despite its jokes and loopy dance numbers, the movie spotlights corrupt power, ill-waged war, and phony rationale. *Lebowski* retells the universal battle between corrupt haves and have-nots with a new spin on it—the bowling-loving Dude. At the heart of its film noir send-up, Busby Berkeley stylings, and bowling ballet lies a cinematic memorial to the unsung heroes of the 1960s and 1970s, who helped bring change to America, even if L.A. shows a lot more work needs to be done. Yesterday's counterculture, as personified by the Dude, is still fighting the good fight when called to, and yesterday's Day-Glo folk heroes who stood up to overreaching authority are as indelible on the American spirit as the cowboy—and the Dude.

NOTES

1. *Fargo* almost had a separate new life after the movie, too, but a TV series starring Edie Falco with Kathy Bates directing never got past its pilot.
2. Roger Ebert, "*Lebowski* Big on Fun," *Chicago Sun-Times*, March 6, 1998, 37. Dowd's work includes *Gandhi, Hoosiers, The Blair Witch Project,* and *Kissing Jessica Stein.*
3. William Preston Robertson, *Lebowski: The Making of a Coen Brothers Film* (New York: W.W. Norton & Co., 1998), 39–40.
4. *The Big Lebowski*, DVD, directed by Joel Coen (1998; Universal City, Calif.: Universal Studios Home Entertainment, 2005).
5. *The Big Lebowski*, DVD.
6. *The Big Lebowski*, DVD.
7. *The Big Lebowski*, DVD.
8. *New York Times* reporter Neil Sheehan quoted in Daniel Patrick Moynihan's *Secrecy* (New Haven: Yale University Press, 1998), 31.
9. *The Big Lebowski*, DVD.
10. Robert G. Kaiser and David Ottaway, "Oil for Security Fueled Close Ties," *Washington Post*, February 11, 2002, A-1.
11. *The Big Lebowski*, DVD.
12. *The Big Lebowski*, DVD.
13. Megan E. Abbott, *The Street Was Mine* (New York: Palgrave Macmillan, 2002), 6.
14. *The Big Lebowski,* DVD.
15. *The Big Lebowski*, DVD.
16. Robert Warshow, "Movie Chronicle: The Westerner," in *Film, Theory, Criticism*, eds. Gerald Mast, Marshall Cohen, and Leo Braudy (New York: Oxford University Press: 1992), 455–58.
17. *The Big Lebowski*, DVD.
18. *The Big Lebowski*, DVD.
19. *Miller's Crossing*, DVD, directed by Joel Coen (1990; Beverly Hills, Calif.: 20th Century Fox Home Entertainment, 2003).
20. *The Big Lebowski*, DVD.
21. *The Big Lebowski*, DVD.

22. *The Big Lebowski*, DVD.
23. *The Big Lebowski*, DVD.
24. *The Big Lebowski*, DVD.
25. Whittled down from eight when one couldn't be found, the Seattle Seven were Chip Marshall, Mike Abeles, Joe Kelly, Jeff Dowd, Susan Stern, Mike Lerner, and Roger Lippman.
26. Roger Lippman, "Looking Back on the Seattle Conspiracy Trial," 1990, terrasol .home.igc.org/trial.htm (accessed March 15, 2006).
27. Raymond Chandler, *The Big Sleep* (1939; repr., New York: Vintage Crime, 1992), 9.
28. Peter J. Rabinowitz, "Rats Behind the Wainscotting: Politics, Convention and Chandler's *The Big Sleep*," in *The Critical Responses to Raymond Chandler*, ed. J. K. Van Dover (Westport, Conn.: Greenwood, 1995), 124.
29. *The Big Lebowski*, DVD.
30. Chandler, *The Big Sleep*, 13.
31. Molly Haskell, *From Reverence to Rape* (New York: Holt, Rinehart & Winston, 1975), 208.
32. *The Big Sleep*, DVD, directed by Howard Hawks (1946; Burbank, Calif.: Warner Home Video, 2000).
33. *The Big Lebowski*, DVD.
34. *The Big Lebowski*, DVD.
35. *The Big Lebowski*, DVD.
36. Jean-Loup Bourget, "Social Implications in the Hollywood Genres," in *Film, Theory, Criticism*, 471.
37. *The Big Lebowski*, DVD.
38. Chandler, *The Big Sleep*, 8.
39. Elizabeth Zimmer, "J. Hoberman on Busby Berkeley," *Dance in America: Busby Berkeley: Going Through the Roof*, www.pbs.org/gperf/busby/html/behind.html (accessed June 5, 2004).
40. *The Big Lebowski*, DVD.
41. *The Big Lebowski*, DVD.
42. *The Big Lebowski*, DVD.
43. *The Big Lebowski*, DVD.
44. *The Big Lebowski*, DVD.
45. Umberto Eco, *Six Walks in the Fictional Woods* (Cambridge, Mass.: Harvard University Press, 1994), 61.
46. *The Big Lebowski*, DVD.
47. Richard Corliss, "That Old Feeling: When Porno Was Chic," *Time*, March 29, 2005, www.time.com/time/columnist/corliss/article/0,9565,1043267,00.html (accessed March 15, 2006).
48. *The Big Lebowski*, DVD.
49. *The Big Lebowski*, DVD.
50. Raymond Chandler, *The Long Goodbye* (New York: Vintage [Crime Series], 1992), 378.

51. Chandler, *The Long Goodbye*, 195; *The Big Lebowski*, DVD.

52. Chandler, *The Long Goodbye*, 81.

53. *The Big Lebowski*, DVD.

54. *The Long Goodbye*, DVD, directed by Robert Altman (1973; Santa Monica, Calif.: MGM, 2002).

55. Recognizing how major an alteration of both the ending and the iconic Marlowe character were, Altman had his contract stipulate that the studio could not change his final edit.

56. Patrick McGilligan, *Robert Altman, Jumping Off the Cliff* (New York: St. Martin's Press, 1984), 363.

57. *The Long Goodbye*, DVD.

58. *The Big Lebowski*, DVD.

59. From the production notes.

60. Gene D. Phillips, *Creatures of Darkness: Raymond Chandler, Detective Fiction, and Film Noir* (Lexington: University Press of Kentucky, 2000), 2.

61. *The Big Lebowski*, DVD.

62. The TV show *Veronica Mars*, starring Kirsten Bell as a teenage detective fighting small-town corruption, often alludes to this semantic quarrel between Da Fino and the Dude as well as other *Lebowski* moments. Besides sharing themes, the persistent allusion might come courtesy of the show's executive producer Joel Silver, who was a Coen collaborator on *The Hudsucker Proxy*.

· 𝒮 ·

O Brother, Where Art Thou?: A Song

From left to right, Tim Blake Nelson, George Clooney, and John Turturro perform "a powerful air." (Credit: © Buena Vista Pictures Buena Vista Pictures/Photofest)

"You gotta be a little tolerant, George. All these poor folk know is the legend."

—Ulysses Everett McGill (George Clooney)

"Songs have been the not-so-secret weapon behind every fight for freedom, every struggle against injustice and bigotry."

—Edgar Yipsel "Yip" Harburg, lyricist, *The Wizard of Oz*

PREVIEW

Fargo's Best Screenplay Oscar cinched what fans, critics, and industry folk already knew: The Coens are master raconteurs. But when the bluegrass-drenched O Brother, Where Art Thou? scored five Grammys, discord rippled through the music world.[1] Some wondered how the retro soundtrack could do well without a modern stroke. Others said it couldn't fix the record industry's warped distribution system, warning that Alison Krauss wouldn't suddenly blanket the airwaves.[2] Such backlash didn't ice O Brother's red-hot music sales. The Coens and their music guru T-Bone Burnett had orchestrated nothing short of an American roots music revival. The theme of that success—folk art has staying power—carried beyond awards and CD sales to the box office, even as the odd odyssey vexed viewers into wondering, oh brother, what art thou?

Pivoting around folklore, the Coens' curious movie opens on the phrase, "O muse, sing in me." These words from Homer, the Greek poet who crafted the epic *The Odyssey*, acknowledge the key role song will play while setting the scene for grand allusions. The very title *O Brother, Where Art Thou?* is lifted from Preston Sturges's 1941 satire *Sullivan's Travels*. It is the same name of the high-handed social epic that his movie-director hero wants to make but never does because he realizes the high value of lowbrow humor. Using these primary references as a cornerstone, the Coens' film builds into a cinematic mosaic that cherry-picks plots, methods, and themes from a slew of stories to make a singular, biting social drama that defies categorization.

With music in almost every scene the Depression-era fable *O Brother, Where Art Thou?* is part nouveau musical—a rhapsody in blues and old-time music that riffs on America's most subjugating and liberating moments. It's also part road picture—a Sturges-inspired social drama that trains a cockeyed look at America's variegated personae. It's a myth that travels back roads to re-form historical figures into hysterical (and hysterically funny) Coen caricatures. It's an inventive inquiry into political and spiritual roots. It's an awakening—a cultural rebirth—stringing together motifs from prison movies, adventure quests, and epic poetry. Ultimately, it's a harmonic voyage and a satirical investigation into America's past.

REVIEW

Loosely structured around *The Odyssey*, the movie traces the journey home of escaped con Ulysses Everett McGill (George Clooney). Just as the Greek Odysseus (Ulysses to the Romans) travels home to wife Penelope, Everett repairs to reunite with wife Penny (Holly Hunter). The stock-in-trade of both heroes is their cunning. Everett cons his fellow cons—the simpleton Delmar O'Donnell (Tim Blake Nelson) and the contrarian Pete (John Turturro)—by promising them a share of the stolen loot buried in his hometown if they escape with him. The catch? They must get it before its hiding place is flooded. This incentive is a pinchbeck.

There is many an adventure before and after Everett's ruse is discovered, but they begin and end on railroad tracks. The trio first meets a blind handcar driver (Lee Weaver II) whose lack of sight and wealth of foresight are reminiscent of *The Odyssey*'s oracle, Tiresias. They next visit Pete's cash-strapped cousin, Washington Hogwallop (Frank Collison), who cuts off their chains and helps them but then tries to turn them in to the authorities for reward money.

The cons evade capture, and religion seeps into the plot. Pete and Delmar get baptized with singing Baptists who resemble Homer's Lotus Eaters. After a wash for heaven, the cons have a brush with hell when they befriend Tommy Johnson (Chris Thomas King), a guitarist who has traded his soul for talent a la legendary bluesman Robert Johnson. They form a band and make what becomes a hot record for some hard-to-come-by cold cash. Unbeknownst to them their song spreads like wildfire on the radio, the medium of choice for Governor "Menelaus" Pappy O'Daniel (Charles Durning) whom the boys meet outside the station.[3] He's about to stump on-air because the campaign of upstart rival Homer Stokes (Wayne Duvall) is upstaging him.

Soon, three sultry, singing river nymphs (Christy Taylor, Mia Tyler, and Musetta Vander) dazzle the cons.[4] Like the Sirens who tried to kill Ulysses with song, the ladies are bad news. When Everett and Delmar awake from a strange sleep to find Pete gone and his clothes splayed on the rocks, Delmar thinks he has been ensorcelled into a toad. They learn later that, like Wash, the women simply turned him in for the reward. This need for currency is a current throughout, as few people have much of it. George "Baby Face" Nelson (Michael Badalucco) is a notable exception. The bank robber has more than he needs but prefers fame to fortune. The cons learn this after they befriend him, join him on a heist, and finally see him elated to get caught.

Throughout, the cons play a deadly hide-and-seek game with the law. Chief among the otherwise amorphous lawmen is the authoritarian Sheriff Cooley (Daniel von Bargen). Two other powerbrokers threaten the trio: Stokes and Dan Teague (John Goodman in his fourth Coen role), both Klansmen. Things come to a head at a political rally when Everett's band unveils itself as the group behind the highly popular tune "A Man of Constant Sorrow." Stokes tries to intervene, but the crowd prefers good music to bigotry. Pappy quickly allies himself with the musicians, exonerating and ultimately hiring them.

After exposing a crooked politician, getting a job, and winning back Penny, Everett embarks on a final quest to retrieve her wedding ring from their old homestead. There, despite the governor's pardon, the vengeful lawmen are ready to dole out capital punishment. Suddenly a deluge—the government flooding—pours in and saves them. They swim to the surface and in a floating desk they find a ring, but like the other "treasures" they have found, it's not the one they were seeking. Everett and his displeased wife trail off into the sunset bickering. The movie fades out on the blind seer, pumping his way down the railroad tracks.

CHAIN REACTIONS

Before the train tracks recede into the final frames, Everett and Penny walk with their children in tow tethered together like so many links in a chain. This wrap-up image of the family cortege bookends the opening chain-gang shots. Both visuals depict interconnectedness. Whether it's a line of shackled cons, a reconnected family, or a community united at a political rally, the film accentuates that people are tied to each other's well-being—like it or not. Complementing actual physical chains are cultural links—often stretched and distorted through the Coens' sardonic lens. These include myth, history, cinema, literature, and music, the most powerful force. Railroads also squeeze into the conceit. Signifying the era's main geographical connector, this symbol of Manifest Destiny taps America's mythology while crisscrossing cultural and temporal boundaries to reconnect to Homer.

The blind handcar driver launches a prophetic narrative when he divines the government flood: "You'll see a cow on a roof."[5] His prediction weds Greek oracles to U.S. history and Christian rites. By the time his cryptic forecast comes to fruition, baptisms, federal revitalization programs, and a song have pooled together to stop unjust hangings and turn the tide on racial attitudes. In this way, the Coens' picaresque yarn threads snippets from *The Odyssey* into its nexus of narratives, making the Greek poem a main link in the conceptual chain. As Homer's epic drew on the fecund subject of Greek history, *O Brother* puts American history on display.

The Odyssey, which recounts Ulysses' journey home after the ten-year Trojan War, is a collection of stories originally sung by traveling performers called rhapsodes (literally, "stitchers-together of songs"). The poem, along with its companion piece *The Iliad*, which chronicles the decade-long war, is a rich example of the oral tradition.

> [*The Odyssey* and *Iliad*] were probably fixed in something like their present form before the art of writing was in general use in Greece; it is certain that

they were intended not for reading but for oral recitation. . . . The[ir] poetic organization . . . suggests that they owe their present form to the shaping hand of a single poet, . . . who selected from the enormous wealth of
the oral tradition and fused [it to] original material to create . . . the *Iliad*
and *Odyssey*.[6]

Odyssey tie-ins inform the film's narrative modes and the playful Homeric
homage stresses how stories—especially oral, musical ones—can be instructive,
regenerative, and unifying.

Music kick-starts the Coens' Mississippi folk odyssey. First, rhythmic
hammer hits and singing play over a black screen. Then Ulysses Everett is sum-
moned via Homer: "O muse, sing in me, and through me tell the story of that
man skilled in all the ways of contending . . . A wanderer, harried for years on
end." The passage hints that like *The Odyssey* Everett's tale will be peripatetic
and will unfurl historical highlights. Structurally, *The Odyssey*'s narrative patchwork is a fitting design template for *O Brother*'s own e pluribus unum tale,
which also retreads history—specifically, America's long, hard road to racial
equality.

Homer's account of the wily warrior's tussles with angry gods and monsters brought ancient myths to life and synthesized Trojan War history. In so
doing, his epics became the basis for education and culture, and ultimately his
telling of the war—the defining moment of Greek history—unified a disjointed society.[7] *O Brother* similarly uses American legends—like bluesmen
dealing with the devil—and often ugly historical artifacts, such as chain gangs
and lynchings, to explore the difficult journey to civil rights, one of America's
defining movements. Instead of rhapsodes, radio broadcasts of Everett's song
blanket the region, uniting a people alienated by race and class. "A Man of
Constant Sorrow," a rough translation of the name *Odysseus* and thus an epithet for the Coens' and Homer's hero, becomes an anthem of acceptance and
freedom. Music and storytelling are chains that connect—and empower.

Other broad *Odyssey* strokes pop up in the Coens' film, including themes
of loyalty, power, and creativity. Allegiance to family and countrymen is a
lodestar for both heroes, who display trickster talents, such as creative camou-
flage, to breed success. Everett's hillbilly masquerade recalls Ulysses' beggar disguise. Homer's hero dresses down to fool his wife's aggressive suitors. Incog-
nito, he enters Penelope's contest set up as a last resort to ward off the
unwanted men. The beggar alone can hit a target with Ulysses's (his own) bow.
Similarly, Everett goes undercover to win back Penny from her beau. Like
Ulysses drumming up his ace marksman skills, Everett in hillbilly togs plies his
musical talents to woo back his wife. (The band's beards also wink to the loopy
Marx Brothers who don silly whiskers to hide in their 1935 hit, *A Night at the
Opera*.) Everett's spoils are personal and political. Akin to Ulysses besting his
rivals and eventually giving birth to a national identity, Everett dazzles the

crowd, outperforms the politicos, and in the process brings freedom to his corner of the South.

Like *The Odyssey*'s historical view—though with the Coens' idiosyncratic "caricaturro"—highlights of and low points in U.S. history percolate into Everett's journey. Taking on the tough subjects of race, class, and religion, the movie mythologizes America's past, casting it as a comic hootenanny that imputes all players in its rich, at times troubled, legacy. Much of this strain borrows from Sturges, who inspired *O Brother*'s title, message, and method and is thus a main link in its chain. What Homer does for touting narrative power, Sturges does for the cinematic, and what *Sullivan's Travels* says about comedy, *O Brother* expresses about music.

Sturges, as the title *Sullivan's Travels* would suggest, owes a great debt to *Gulliver's Travels*, satirist Jonathan Swift's wandering, satirical epic of 1726. Heavy on comedy, the sharp satires by Swift, Sturges, and the Coens veil their core social critiques with a mixture of slapstick, realism, and fantasy. Taking a critical look at movies and their role in culture, Sturges packed political satire into an adventure tale. With Sturges as a muse, the Coens dissect the trouble spots of poverty, racism, and penal farms.

In *Sullivan's Travels* when Joel McCrae's lowbrow, hotshot filmmaker John "Sully" Sullivan wants to make a highbrow movie about the poor titled *O Brother, Where Art Thou?* the rich Sully must first find out how the other half lives. Though he ultimately shelves the social drama in favor of comedy, his excursion down uneasy street makes political statements about poverty and race. *O Brother* recapitulates these themes and adds its own about democracy.

The Coens' movie-theatre scene, where Everett vents to Delmar about women, recalls the stirring turning point in *Sullivan's Travels* in which Sully realizes the elixir properties of comedy. That scene, set in a black church on movie night, begins with the minister welcoming lost souls in the form of a white chain gang. The treatment of race—blacks helping whites—was audacious for the 1941 film when studios tended to cast blacks in subservient roles. On seeing a cartoon uplift the audience, Sully grasps the import of humor on the human condition. This revelation dovetails with the idea that popular art, like movies, can help overcome racial divisions.

While the Coens' film pursues similar themes, their Sturges-inspired movie-theatre scene carries a very different, more serious message, about subjugation.[8] When lawmen burst into the theatre, Everett and Delmar fear getting caught, but then, as in *Sullivan's Travels*, a chain gang shuffles in. When the movie restarts, however, the value of entertainment is not vindicated. Instead, an armed guard's order to "Enjoy yer pikcha show!" rehashes the abuse from the initial chain gang scene, where guards yell out, "Watch your line" and "No break!"[9] It's not until the town-hall scene, the other tribute to Sturges's makeshift theatre scene, that institutional oppression is beat. With Everett's discovery of music's mobilizing powers comes the conclusion that art for the masses—specifically music—can be a potent societal force. The exuberant reception of "Man of Constant Sorrow" shows that blacks and whites can mix in harmony. Like comedy, music is a unifying cultural product—and a most democratic art form.

O Brother examines the have-nots' struggle to participate in a democracy whose chain of command wants to keep them down—and out. Everett's first words to Pete and Delmar, spoken just after they fail to hop on the train as a unit, resonate with the title's question and speak to the importance of solidarity: "Jesus, can't I count on you people?"[10] His question illuminates their symbiotic relationship. The phrase "O brother, where art thou?" is never spoken, but its spirit is ever present. Depicted is a society whose survival depends on the strength of linked individuals standing up against elite power. Music and storytelling are key building blocks for such unity.

Everett and company personify a work-in-progress democracy, and their interactions illustrate their critical role in politics. "Who elected you leader a this outfit?" Pete asks at the start, challenging Everett's self-appointment and injecting political overtones.[11] Their attempts to settle the issue with a vote fail. Pete and Everett each choose "yours truly," while Delmar's humorous "I'm with you fellas" acknowledges group power—puts the public in "republic."[12] Such sticking together will be imperative to their success.

Near the end, leadership issues resurface. Everett suggests posing as the band to enter the rally, but Pete again dissents: "Who elected you leader?"[13] He then cites a laundry list of trouble Everett's direction has led them into. If this were a one-man story, Everett would now go it alone. But unlike Homer's Ulysses, who alone survives, the Coens' democratic hero thrives on group strength. He admits mistakes but implores his friends to stay. In the next shot the "hillbillies" use the working-class portal—their disguises and class status offering a unified front. Inside, they turn a political tide, and their personal democracy broadens to influence.

Everett epitomizes a truly democratic hero, an average citizen who is part of a powerful collective—the electorate. He is empowered by his friends, and when problems arise, all are liable by definition. Regardless of class, race, or station, everyone shapes a democracy's triumphs and shortfalls. Hence, the satire takes aim at the whole lot—from two-faced religious zealots to bigoted politicians to cruel lawmen. Even Everett must atone for his shortcomings as family man and citizen. By tweaking the era's tagline "Brother, can you spare a dime?" to "O Brother, Where Art Thou?" the movie challenges a free society. Bound to each other in a democratic system, only together can folks shake off societal shackles like poverty and racism.

John Turturro (top), George Clooney, Chris Thomas King, and Tim Blake Nelson figure out how to sneak into the invitation-only political rally. (Credit: © Buena Vista Pictures Buena Vista Pictures/Photofest)

In *O Brother*'s satirical rendering of 1930s America, times are tough, but authorities are tougher. Addressing society ("o brother"), the film wonders where are the protests when the real bad guys—not those in jail but those in charge—abuse power. In effect, the Soggy Bottom Boys are a working-class bloc that challenges the status quo. As their adventures add up to problems requiring manmade—political—solutions, a new chain emerges: questioning. Building from the title, the movie is a Socratic discourse on capitalism, family, friendship, and civics.

"EVERYBODY'S LOOKIN' FOR ANSWERS"

While Homer is the Coens' acknowledged muse, Socrates is their ghost muse. Starting with its title, the film presents a series of questions that uncover harsh truths about American history's back pages. The resounding solutions echo Coen themes that run through all their movies: Art has unifying powers, and have-nots must band together to beat the haves.

Everett's odyssey is an answer quest. The first three lines of dialogue are all queries, and soon questions become a means to packaging social issues in personal ones. The cons riddle the blind seer with queries, which he answers with riddles: "Mind if we join you?" "Work for the railroad?" and "Do you have a name?" are met with "Join me," then the cryptic "I work for no man" and "I have no name."[14] While giving him a sense of awe, his "No man" reply echoes a Homeric epithet, implying that knowledge of stories can boost percipience.

When Ulysses is held captive by the Cyclops, the clever hero deploys the name "No Man" to gain advantage. Ulysses' men blind their one-eyed enemy with a burning stake—an act alluded to in *O Brother*'s Klan scene—causing him to cry out in pain. When his shouts grab his neighbors' attention, they come to his aid and ask what's hurting him. His strange reply—"No Man"—befuddles them and they leave. Facing just a blind Cyclops, Ulysses' men sneak out.

In disclosing that he works for "No Man," the driver reveals in code through the pseudonym that he works for Ulysses. In fact, he provides the cons with an underground railroad of sorts. He also helps introduce racial themes. "I have no name" is a powerful comment on the black experience: Imported to America as slaves stripped of individualities and names, African Americans even decades after emancipation found themselves steeped in an identity crisis abetted by prejudice and worse. Racial equality is one answer the men seek.

Variations on the line "Everybody's looking for answers" give shape to the film's leitmotif of inquiry.[15] Everett christens the phrase, which is subsequently intoned around key themes of fidelity, liability, spirituality, and faith. When he guesses that Cora has run off to find answers, there is a subtext to his observation. We don't know it yet, but he is rushing home to stop his spouse from running off. His odyssey-seeking domestic unity will expand into political unity.

Issues of fidelity resurface when Pete learns Everett filched a watch from his backstabbing cousin. Despite Washington's betrayal of them and their own collective theft of his car, Pete is miffed at Everett's perfidy. The inscription on the watch to be pawned for a new car clues Pete in to Everett's theft: "To Washington Bartholomew Hogwallop, from his loving Cora. Amore fidelis." Singing Baptists distract them from a fight, but ideas of loyalty are in the air.

Just as awareness of Homer and history adds meaning to the blind driver's "No Man" claims, knowing the inscription's full citation adds layers of irony. On one level, the phrase is funny, for Cora has proved not "faithful in love" ("*amore fidelis*"). But the passage from which Cora's scrap is plucked packs a bigger wallop: "I say as an expert, no one is faithful in love."[16] This episode adds a poignant footnote to the film's Depression setting, when money often strained relationships.

Cousin Wash's turncoat actions beg the question "O cousin, where art thou?" and prefigure a familial disloyal streak. Later, Pete betrays his friends—when coerced. To avoid the noose, he blurts out Everett's plan. The scene typifies how authorities pit have-nots against each other to keep them down. Guilt-ridden over his forced betrayal, Pete makes it up by warning his friends, or at least trying to. Ultimately, the cons' alliance trumps the authorities' wedge work. Everett and Delmar rescue Pete, the trio saves Tommy, and the quartet accidentally stages a populist revolt. The answer to infidelity foisted on citizens by tyrannical powers is solidarity.

Spousal constancy is a similar matter. When it comes to family, Penny puts her girls first: "I gotta think about the little Wharvey gals. They look to me for answers!"[17] Her betrayal of Everett is like Wash's, which he defends in survival terms: "They got this here Depression on; I got to do for me and mine."[18] In Penny's view, her provider role supersedes fidelity to a husband, who, when it comes to bringing home the bacon, would rather be a ham. Everett didn't go to jail for a bank heist; he went for impersonating a lawyer. When she sees him dressed as a hillbilly, she thinks he's up to his old tricks. She needs a breadwinner and thinks that Everett can't cut it, but Vernon can.

Echoing one of *Barton Fink's* nuisances ("wall drip"), her suitor's name is a Coen in-joke, and this Waldrip bothers Everett about as much as the smelly goop annoys Barton.[19] In fact, when Everett meets Vernon T., sensing he has dipped into his Dapper Dan stash, Everett sniffs him—as Barton smells the wall goop—before asking if he's "Waldrip." The *Fink* connection might tip Coen fans that Vernon is not the bona fide she thinks he is. Even for those who don't infer the phonetic *Fink* link, Vernon is hardly a paragon of faith. As one of Stokes's political pawns, Penny's fiancé is a cog in a corrupt system. *O Brother's* landscape is littered with such seeming nice guys who are monsters underneath, moral gargoyles with roots in myths and Bible stories.

Religion figures prominently in Everett's answer quest, where goodness and faith go up against evil and false prophets. A wolf in sheep's clothing, Big Dan Teague peddles "Truth" with empty rhetoric: "Folks're lookin' for answers and Big Dan Teague sells the only book that's got 'em!"[20] With tastes less mandarin than marauding, the Bible salesman gorges himself on their food and then unveils himself as a snake-oil seller. Another fat-cat crushing the little-guy for a bigger piece of his American pie, the gluttonous sophist is Homer's socially outcast Cyclops retooled for civil society. No longer living on society's fringes, the Coens' monocular brute is a community pillar who catechizes the cons with theft and violence: "It's all about money, boys! Atsy answer! Dough re mi!"[21] This hooded ogre worships the mighty dollar—an idolatry dangerous to a democracy, which, in order to survive, must extinguish such false profiteering.

In his salesman role, Dan is cousin to another large Coen character with a "gift for gab" and a propensity for violence: Charlie Meadows (aka *Fink's* Madman Mundt also played by Goodman and alluded to in *The Hudsucker Proxy*).[22]

Both Dan and Charlie twist and turn biblical phrases into self-serving piffle before cruelly attacking innocents. Both are branded by fire.

Throughout the Coen oeuvre, fire often represents hell and perniciousness, and water goodness. *O Brother*'s destructive fire and renewing water symbolically render the Christian code of "doing unto others as you would have them do unto you." Torches and a burning cross trim the Klan rally along with the Confederate flag. When the Color Guard is unmasked, Everett and his gang flee and javelin the racist totem into the mob. Dan catches it just before it pierces his skull, preventing a full reenactment of Homer's Cyclops' blinding. But the save is short-lived. Seconds later the burning cross crushes him. In effect, fire snuffs out fire. Later, water will douse Cooley's fiery fascism, once and for all.

Hellish imagery and darkness surround the authorities and their perverse agenda. As they try to smoke the cons out of a barn, their torches accidentally ignite their ammunition car, exploding the profuse firepower brought for the small job. Lightning bolts punctuate Pete's torture at the hands of the law. Flames flicker in the mirrored glasses of Cooley who personifies the "white man with mirrors for eyes" devil that Tommy describes.[23] The name Stokes literally means fueling a fire. At the Klan rally, dressed in red and flanked by fire, the Klan wizard embodies the folkloric devil Everett describes. Such imagery and deviant behavior align the power elite with the fallen angel whose thirst for power crowned him king of hell.

But water soon surges in as the opposing force. The clash is visualized during the campfire portion of the "I'll Fly Away" montage when flames engulf a newspaper with a headline about the upcoming flood. Corrosive fire is the power at the moment, the visual implies, but the flood's forecast indicates the situation is fluid. To save Tommy, the trio fights fire with fire, smiting Dan with a burning symbol of hate. The Soggy Bottom Boys politically capsize Stokes, and the actual flood wipes out Cooley. Together, Everett's men free Ithaca from its devils.

Synthesizing the connection between water and Everett is Christianity, America's bedrock religion and another potent solution tossed into the answer quest. He derides his friends' baptism ("I guess hard times flush the chumps").[24] Yet, later, facing what looks like sure death, the self-proclaimed skeptic turns to prayer and dives in deep. Though he quickly writes off his religious turn, insisting the force majeure saved them, the fact is he too was a "chump," for a moment anyway. He was literally flushed out of his tightest spot yet and plunged into a new era. It is a government flood, yes, but its perfect timing and symbolism introduce doubt—and its counterpart faith. Though Everett scoffs theological answers, his actions affirm Christian ethics. He stands by his brothers and treats them as he would like to be treated.

AWAKENINGS—OR "NO MAN'S" ARC

The plot hangs on a government project aimed at bringing electric power to the rural setting. With events poised at such a cultural crossroads, Everett glee-fully forecasts: "Out with the old spiritual mumbo-jumbo, the superstitions and the backward ways. We're gonna see a brave new world where they run everyone a wire and hook us all up to a grid."[25] Yet this new era cannot shake a Christian influence that has spurred many of America's big cultural shifts. The words "power and light" are both literal and figurative. It's not just electricity bestowed on this mythic Mississippi. Underscoring the wrangle between rationality and belief in the divine, the phrase "power and light" adds Christian values of brotherhood to the film's political palette.

O *Brother's* before-the-flood opening, when cows on a roof are prophesied, is the stuff myths are made of. The ensuing story of race, class, and justice is one of revival, awakening—and apocalypse. As in the Bible, where God prepares for a new world by cleansing the old sinful one with a cataclysmic flood, O *Brother's* waters allow for salvation and regeneration. As the valley is purged of evil, circular objects like pomade cans, banjos, tire swings (in a nod to *Night of the Hunter*), and a Victrola horn float by Everett, symbolizing unity and renewal. The life-buoy coffin furthers the idea of rebirth by referencing *Moby-Dick*, in which the quest's sole survivor clutches a coffin and thus lives to tell his story of good and evil and great unknowns.

The film crystallizes the problem that Mississippi's broken institutions need purifying. Cooley's savagery, Stokes's demagoguery, and Big Dan's bigotry endanger this democracy's principles of equality and justice for all. In the past, such crises have sparked what historian William G. McLoughlin calls great awakenings: "The most vital and yet most mysterious of all folk arts . . . [occur in] periods of cultural revitalization that begin in a general crisis of beliefs and values and extend over a period of a generation or so, during which time profound reorientation in beliefs and values takes place."[26] Charismatic reformers have instigated these shifts by reshaping common thought. In effect, Everett leads O *Brother's* great awakening.

Everett's social movement is one of brotherly love. Thus, he resembles early twentieth-century reformers who interpreted Christianity not in terms of individual salvation but with respect to a "brotherhood of man" in which people are "spiritually and ethically united to [their] neighbor."[27] These philosophers, scientists, sociologists, and theologians believed "the conflict of labor and capital brought into prominence a vast number of social problems whose solution requires the united efforts, each in its own sphere, of the church, the state, and of science."[28] A fictional sibling to these reformers, Everett bears witness to faith through his actions despite his denials.

Everett, as much a street philosopher as a con artist, prefers science to religion, or so he says. The facts on the ground say different. When he pitches his band as singers of "songs of salvation to salve the soul," he could be working a wheedle, but his plug recognizes the influence of Christianity on the day's music.[29] Depression-era radio performers often included a "song of hope and inspiration" on each program, and recording artists like the Carter Family recorded both secular and sacred tunes.[30] Everett's own song mentions "God's golden shores."

At different points Everett shows belief in prophesies, magic, and God. He first reveals a less rational side when he talks of foresight compensating for the blind's lack of eyesight. He backpedals only when Pete asks about the seer's prediction of finding a different treasure. Still, his initial endorsement of clairvoyance chalks up a brief victory for belief over rationality.

The conflict between rational worldviews and belief in unknowns fits into the Coens' frequent exploration of belief and knowledge. A bit like *Barton Fink*'s mosquito, *O Brother*'s toad helps pit Everett's rationalism against Delmar's belief. In *Fink*, if we believe mosquitoes do not exist in L.A.'s desert town, we must rethink what's flying about biting Barton's face. When considered with the dream references, a logical conclusion is that we are viewing a dreamscape.

O Brother's use of an animal to flesh out the conflict differs from *Fink*'s but they have similar philosophical roots: Like the mosquito, the toad illustrates the power of belief. In time, Delmar's Pete-is-a-toad theory is squashed but not before Everett's certitude wavers. He flinches when Big Dan kills the toad because it's possible that it was his friend. Doubt cuts both ways—it can turn believer or atheist into an agnostic. Seeing Pete in the flesh doesn't rule out Everett's imperfect rationality. He squints for a better look and asks if Pete has a brother. Though his question must be taken in the context of his overall lying, he is more agnostic than atheistic, as his heartfelt prayer under the noose most vividly shows. Facing death in front of an open grave, he turns not to his fellow man this time but to a divine power. He asks God for forgiveness, apologizes for his errors, and requests deliverance, all the while betraying emotional depth lacking until then. Like an answer to his prayer, a flood of biblical proportions sets him free.

Here the Coens' fiction draws from the apocalyptic tradition of Christianity, which historian Ernest Lee Tuveson defines as "always [having] in view as the true and only solution to the world problem the inauguration of a new heaven and a new earth."[31] The flood is the destruction needed for the new age, whose way has been paved by Christian symbolism, mythical prognostications, and state promises. The deluge that delivers the boys from evil and washes Cooley away is a government action, but its timing also makes it an answer to his prayers. Seeing a cow on a roof, as predicted, again upsets Everett's rational worldview.

The flood's historical roots lie in government-sponsored projects like the Tennessee Valley Authority, which reshaped large swaths of the economically ravaged South. President Franklin D. Roosevelt's revitalization initiative was often heralded in religious language: "A Promised Land, bathed in golden sunlight, is rising out of the grey shadows of want and squalor and wretchedness down here in the Tennessee Valley these days."[32] Set at such a watershed moment, *O Brother* merges history, Christianity, and myth to sing the South's entry into a new age of technology and social change. With the government improving conditions for the poor and Everett holding it to task, Everett helps turn Mississippi into a Promised Land.

Woven into the film's Christian ideals are the purifying effects of water, which works wonders even before the flood. "The Good Old Way (As I Went Down to the River to Pray)"—which tellingly exchanges the traditional song's "valley" for "river"—interrupts Pete and Everett's argument over the stolen watch, preventing a fight. Pete's and Delmar's baptisms help them shed their criminal ways. Everett's cavils help conceal the efficacy of these spiritual turns, but it cannot drown out the aftereffects.

Though he pooh-poohs religion, he too dips into Christian waters. For one, he calls his band the Soggy Bottom Boys, which refers to their baptisms and prophesies their deliverance.[33] His own sobriquet, a bizarre choice for a rationalist, also incorporates water. In dubbing himself Jordan Rivers in a story that deals with healing wounds initially inflicted by slavery, Everett taps a potent Judeo-Christian symbol. Never mind that the river is where Jesus was baptized; the Jordan is a symbolic gateway to freedom. After forty years in the desert Joshua led the enslaved Israelites into Israel via the Jordan River. Everett's is a similar story: He leads outcasts enslaved to a corrupt system to a place of opportunity for all. Early on, Everett tells Delmar that "even if [the baptism] did put you square with the Lord, the State of Mississippi is more hard-nosed."[34] The climactic government flood takes care of this snag. In rooting evil from the Delta, Everett is a savior, helping break a new dawn for the disenfranchised, one of equality for all.

THE LAW AND THE PROFITS

The cadence of hammer hits starts things off with a beat as forced as the labor. It is steady, for sure, but its rhythm captures the singers' backbreaking work. Adding to this sonic weight is a dust-bowl landscape and then the first view of oppression. Black and white images show armed white men lording over fettered criminals building a railroad. From the look of things the laborers are all black. The mounted guards and their merciless "no break" and "lift your hammer higher" directives fill in the picture of corrupt power.[35] Then, there is a fade to black. The next shot fades in on a related scene: Everett's trio running away from a work gang.

The connection between the first two scenes is immediate. More subtle are the differences. For one, "Big Rock Candy Mountain" is stylistically distinct from "Po' Lazarus." Also, the scenes are shot differently—the first in black and white and sepia, the second in color, and a full fade to black separates the two. Still, the chain gang backdrop to the escape sure looks like the initial group, whose song vatically describes Everett's ensuing ordeal. What is crystal clear from the get-go is their shared plight and fight. The opening montage sets the tone for blurred color lines, a situation carried on through the ongoing muddle over the trio's race.

The three main characters are white, but folks keep mistaking them for black. Just as strange, their complexions change. Outside the radio station, for example, their faces, especially Delmar's, are exceedingly white, apparently an effect of the dust bowl. At other times, as when they break Pete out of the work farm and spy on the Klan, their faces are dark. At WEZY, they initially pose as black singers because Everett thinks that's their best shot with the station operator Mr. Lund (Stephen Root). Despite a swift recantation to old-time music, Lund later remembers them as "colored." Such a mix-up is not limited to the blind. A Klansman unmasking the trio at the rally mistakenly observes, "The Color Guard is colored!"[36] They're not, but no one says differently. Stokes blames the use of "the Confed'it flag as a missile" on "miscegenation" and gripes that "these boys is not white."[37] But his message falls on deaf ears. People want the song—a testament not to his false monochromaticity but to America's multicultural heritage.

Throughout, the film shows how music, like truth, can set people free. "Po' Lazarus" not only makes the men's work more palatable, the song also defies their circumstances, personifies their collective, and allows them vicarious escape. Not a spiritual as the name Lazarus might suggest, the song is a work chant that lionizes a crafty fugitive wanted "dead or alive" by abusive lawmen. "[It] sets forth in stark and unforgettable language the essential tragedy of the black man as his condition used to be in the South," wrote John Lomax, who rediscovered and recorded the song.[38] "Po' Lazarus" is a lens on Everett's adventure and the vindication of justice over tyranny. The song's myth records the history of the law's lawlessness, sets the record straight post facto, and thus educates the masses about abuse of power. It also resurrects Lazarus, a bit like his biblical namesake, by making him a hero.

The historical basis for prisoner mistreatment and overarching power can be found in the film's reference to Parchman Farm, a Mississippi penitentiary infamous for its degradation of prisoners, especially blacks. Dubbed "Destination doom" by William Faulkner, Parchman was built by the racist governor James Kimble Vardaman to train black men to treat whites deferentially and provide business with cheap labor.[41] This emblem of abusive power was an extension of America's slave past, showing that, decades after its abolishment, the roots of slavery were still strong in the form of cheap labor and unjust punishment. That Parchman is the trio's prison subtly furthers their racial ambiguity, for the bulk of its inmates were African American.[39] When Everett spots Pete on the chain gang near Parchman, his question, "[Does] Pete have a brother?" revives the title question—where is Pete's kinsman?[40] Everett and Delmar provide the answer when they free him from the work farm. A fuller resolution comes down the line with pardons, job offers, and integration.

Another powerful symbol of tyranny and an outgrowth of slavery is the chain gang, which in the film is transformative. Both *O Brother*'s music and its chain gangs help track the societal progress from exploitation to integration. Though no whites are obviously visible on the opening gang, the escaping cons in the following scene forge a link. About midway through, there's a definite mingling of the races. The group of black and white cons singing "Tom Devil" (an actual Parchman recording) reflects the historical reality that chain gangs were one of the few integrated southern institutions during the Depression.[42] The final speed bump on Everett's long road to freedom incorporates another integrated work force. The gravediggers toiling next to the homey tire swing voice the hard-knock experience of disillusioned folks who seek deliverance, "both physical and spiritual," as historian Melvin Dixon explains, "beyond the reach of the moral, if not the political, authority."[43] A blend of black and white musical styles, "Lonesome Valley" underscores Everett's need for self-reflection.[44] After the flood grants his freedom, the final "chain gang" puts a closing spin on the symbol—Everett walks through an integrated town, now chained to his family.

PRISON BREAKS AND SLAVES TO THE SYSTEM

The conceit of the chain is multifaceted. Not only does it turn a punitive symbol into a civilizing one, but also it embraces a raft of prison film connections. In addition to borrowing from the devil and Lazarus sheriff, Sheriff Cooley's amalgam of tyranny comes courtesy of *Cool Hand Luke*'s Boss Godfrey (Morgan Woodward). Drawn from writer Donn Pearce's prison experiences, Stuart

Rosenberg's 1967 film castigates a penal system whose forms of punishment far outweigh the crime. Paul Newman's Luke is a petty criminal and unfaltering nonconformist who escapes his draconian prison farm with fellow inmate Dragline (George Kennedy, in an Oscar-winning role). When Luke is caught, he refuses to give up or in and mocks the captain with his own (now famous) line, "What we've got here is a failure to communicate." The sadistic boss (a model for Cooley) takes the bait and shoots him dead.[45] Despite this physical defeat, Luke's spirit lives on. Pearce's gospel of Luke turns tragedy into victory by demonstrating the healing powers of myth. Dragline resurrects Luke through his tales of a man who could not be broken. Thus, stories become regenerative and empowering, and art becomes a change agent. This theme runs through a number of *O Brother*'s prison allusions including *The Defiant Ones*.

Stanley Kramer's 1958 movie begins with convicts chained together. As in *O Brother*, the chains transform from tokens of bondage to symbols of brotherhood. Kramer—who continued to forge a reputation for social dramas with *Look Who's Coming to Dinner* (1967) and *Judgment at Nuremberg* (1961), which took on issues of racism and anti-Semitism, respectively—made a film in pre–Civil Rights America that deals with prejudice and injustice. "Joker" Jackson (Tony Curtis) and Noah Cullen (Sidney Poitier) are forced to rely on each other when they escape a chain gang. Poitier's ghost also surfaces when Everett talks of "the lilies of the goddam field," the title of the 1963 film (sans expletive) that earned Poitier—and African Americans—an Oscar first. By the end, Joker and Noah's cooperation of necessity turns into comity.

The arc of Everett's symbiotic relationships parallels Joker and Cullen's, and *The Defiant Ones* episodes patched into *O Brother* reinforce thematic connections. Everett and Pete's fight on the hill after Everett's confession mimics Jake and Noah's wrestle and hill tumble. The gun-toting boy who takes the cons home to his mother, who nurses Joker back to health, is at different turns the mirror opposite or dramatic echo of the Coens' father-son Hogwallop sequence. In both subplots, an abandoned spouse raises a child alone, a family member wants to join the cons, and betrayals mark the climax. In Kramer's film, Joker is set to escape with the mother but when she sends Noah into the swamps, he dumps her for betraying his friend. Rejiggering these pieces, the Coen film has a single dad do the double-crossing and his son trying to join the cons.

While both movies are escape odysseys, both also champion racial harmony. The early scene where Pete cannot make it onto the train is like the opposite of the climactic *Defiant Ones* scene. At the movie's end an unfettered Noah makes it onto the train bound for freedom, but he cannot pull Joker onto it. The powerful, earlier image of black and white hands gripped together is trumped only by Noah's sacrifice to choose his friend and sure

John Turturro (left), Tim Blake Nelson, and George Clooney escape their chain gang. (Credit: © Buena Vista Pictures Buena Vista Pictures/Photofest)

capture over freedom. Sticking together is a powerful antidote to systematic, sadistic subjection.

Like the socially relevant works of Kramer and Rosenberg—which are exceptions, not the rule—*O Brother* spotlights subjects seldom tackled head-on in popular culture. It also demonstrates the ability of art to effect social change. Though not nearly as groundbreaking as the 1932 *I Am a Fugitive From a Chain Gang*'s role in Georgia's abolishment of its chain gangs, *O Brother*'s Grammy wins show the power of art over commercialism. This might have been an unintended consequence, but certainly the film's generous solutions to social issues make it a "relevant" work. Along these lines, the film also adds up to a lesson in civics.

O Brother rips wide open what John Adams called "love of power—which has been so often the cause of slavery." The triumvirate of Big Dan, Cooley, and Stokes shows how slavery lingers in the so-called free world. Stokes claims to offer a new brand of politics, trotting out a little man he says he serves, but his sermons of hate and exclusion delivered under cover of night and hood are old school. Plus, his "servant of the little man" moniker is reversed. The Little Man (Ed Gale) is Stokes's helper, not the other way around. In short, Stokes wants the power of the people so he can lord power over people. Stokes, a demagogue who needs to be ousted, is a composite of corruption with flair.

One prototype is Huey Long, the flamboyant governor of and then U.S. senator from Louisiana. Long was a populist reformer who decried corporate control of government and helped workers gain organizing rights. But his power-hungry appetite and a reputation for corruption got him killed. His colorful character has made him prime fodder for fiction. Randy Newman's 1974 song "Kingfish" conjures Long through his nickname. Walt Disney's cartoon duck Huey was named after him.[46] Of importance to *O Brother* is Robert Penn Warren's Willie Stark, the Long-based character in Warren's Pulitzer Prize–winning novel *All the King's Men*, which Robert Rossen turned into an Oscar-winning film in 1949. Echoes of Long and his "Sweep them out of office!" cries can be heard in the Coens' homage in which the populist Stokes vows to "Sweep this state clean!"

Stokes's political props—a broom and a midget—brush up against another sweeping reference: a famous musical involving broomstick and a land of little folk. *O Brother's* narrative mélange incorporates an extensive homage to *The Wizard of Oz* (1939). To start with, black-and-white overtures begin both colorful fantasies. Then there's Stokes's Little Man and his broom.[47] Both films also work in the recurring visual of companions walking a long road trip. Dorothy's famous recitation from *Oz*, "There's no place like home," is a sentiment echoed in *O Brother's* final line, "my immortal home," from "Angel Band."

The political readings attributed to *Oz* over the years provide another connection. As in *O Brother*, *Oz's* enchanting journey home encompasses a vision of a better America. Lyricist E. Y. Harburg, who penned the earlier hit "Brother, Can You Spare a Dime," wrote *Oz's* lyrics and a good deal of its dialogue, weaving politics throughout. In 1970, Harburg told the audience assembled at the 92nd Street Y in New York City that the songs from *The Wizard of Oz* reflect President Franklin Roosevelt's "sunny leadership."[48] For example, the Tin Man's tune "If I Only Had a Heart" is a musical translation of FDR's Good Neighbor Policy. The Cowardly Lion's song about having nerve echoes President Roosevelt's famous line, "The only thing we have to fear is fear itself." And "Over the Rainbow," Harburg explained, mirrors the glow "that this one man's humanity cast over the nation."[49]

O Brother also taps the progressive politics found in L. Frank Baum's original story. As historian Henry M. Littlefield argues in "*The Wizard of Oz*: Parable on Populism," Baum's tale was an allegory for William Jennings Bryan's failed Populist movement. In this reading, the Scarecrow represents the farmer, the Tin Man the workers, the Cowardly Lion Bryan himself, and Dorothy a "Miss Everyman."[50] The story delivers hope through Dorothy's selflessness in choosing to return to her dreary home instead of staying in the lush Oz.

If such a reading shows that there's a little Dorothy in Everett, *O Brother* shows Pappy possesses some political wizardry. Among other *Oz* topics, *O Brother* riffs on wizards in toto. Delmar plants the seeds of magic solutions when he thinks Pete has been turned into a toad: "We gotta find some kind of wizard [that] can change him back."[51] Though Delmar has no idea that the Sirens were merely more have-nots forced to turn an escaped con in for reward money, he is right in thinking they need a way out from under the authorities' wicked witchy ways. As in the movie *Oz*, the answers will be political.

The first wizard to appear in *O Brother* is Stokes's Grand Wizard. Part Busby Berkley in its choreographed twirls, part Triumph of the Will in its depiction of ritualized hatred, the Klu Klux Klan scene is haunting. It's also an inversion of the Baptism scene. Both begin with music that prevents a fight, but the Klan scene features fire and the song "O Death" instead of water and a song about prayer. The KKK sequence also spoofs *Oz*'s "March of the Winkies," in which the guards march in military formation outside the witch's castle where Dorothy is prisoner. The Klan's odd routine is much darker, though, for the

Some of *O Brother, Where Art Thou?*'s politics have roots in *The Wizard of Oz*. (Credit: MGM/Photofest © MGM)

hate group stepping in time to the beat of bigotry is reality based. Like the real Klan's infiltration of Southern politics in the 1920s, the Coens' Klan guns for political gains and holds Tommy captive because of his skin color. The cons infiltrate the Klan to save Tommy using tactics the *Oz* trio employs to rescue Dorothy: dressing up as guards and joining their ranks. After they free their friend, both heroes make way for more expansive freedoms. Dorothy's accidental dousing of the witch kills her and reverses the evil spell that had enslaved her minions. Similarly, water leads to Cooley's demise which in turn finally liberates Everett from a slavelike chain-gang system. The Coens' allusive wizardry continues into the other rally sequence where the popular Soggy Bottom Boys spur Pappy's comeback and their inclusive agenda rubs off on him. Here he becomes like *Oz*'s wizard bestowing awards on Dorothy's friends (a scene written by Harburg). In calling Everett and company his "brain trust," Pappy also borrows an FDR phrase that references his efforts to bring America's top collegiate talent to Washington to solve the problems of the Depression.

Political solutions and figures are key components of Everett's odyssey. Pappy is inspired by a host of politicians who helped shape America's racial legacy. His historical namesake—W. Lee "Pappy" O'Daniel—was a Texas governor and U.S. senator who posed as a hillbilly and made campaign promises he never kept. A flour magnate with a radio show, he sang with the Hillbillies and the Light Crust Doughboys and famously refused to vote against the poll tax, a voting requirement in parts of the South that disenfranchised blacks. Another wellspring for Pappy is Jimmie Davis, "Louisiana's Singing Governor," who campaigned with—and by some accounts wrote—"You Are My Sunshine." Like Pappy, Davis had a mixed racial record. Though not considered a hard-core racist, he signed segregation bills giving school boards authority over what to do when Washington ordered the admission of black students.[52] Eventually, he helped desegregate, becoming an agnostic reformer like Pappy who takes advantage of the poor reception to Stokes's racism and accepts integration as a matter of political expediency.

For Everett and friends integration is more natural than segregation. Throughout, though not unaware of skin color, the trio does not let it affect their interrelations—they are effectively color blind. Early on, when they meet the blind handcar driver, no "boy" or "sir" is tossed around, despite the fact that the setting is decidedly racist country. Instead they genially call him "grandpa" and he calls them "my sons," producing a familial, "o brother" sensibility. The trio teams up as easily with Tommy as George. The main difference is they have more in common with Tommy—and their music venture winds up paying more handsomely than their crime spree.

The inability of authority figures like Stokes to see that Everett, Pete, and Delmar are white helps unify these have-nots into an alliance undivided by a color line. People brought together by hard times and made to suffer harsh treatment have bigger things to worry about than color. Like "Po' Lazarus," the trio is focused on survival. The cons' constant dodge of the noose helps create a close affinity between them and the African Americans whose history is stained by the horrific crime of lynching. *O Brother* shows a kinship between disenfranchised folk, who, regardless of color, share the goal of escaping oppression, and music is what often sets them free.

RHAPSODY IN BLACK AND WHITE AND BLUES

While the movie allusions tend to focus on the law and its unjust chokeholds, *O Brother's* in-story songs often hook into other main themes—such as religion, faith, poverty, and especially freedom. Soulful music courses through nearly every scene, becoming another primary chain and a freeing agent. The result is a newfangled musical, where characters sing and occasionally dance. It's not Rogers and Hammerstein. It's Coen and Coen . . . and T-Bone Burnett.

Joel Coen calls the movie "a valentine to the music" in the soundtrack's liner notes. "Music became a very prominent feature very early on in the [script]writing, and it became even more so as we went along," he explained.[53] Avoiding clichés, the selections from America's diverse songbook directly play on the film's main themes. The weave of tunes spanning several decades gives *O Brother* charm and staying power while defining the setting's strife and joys. But then, ever since *Blood Simple's* upbeat murder cleanup accompaniment helped add the neo to the noir, the Coens' exceptional musical choices have been a stylistic hallmark.

Thematic relevance and an organic plot fit are prime factors for the Coens' music tracks. In *Raising Arizona* Ed's choice of the murder ballad "Down in the Willow Garden" to soothe her son after a nightmare subtly—and riotously—impugns her maternal instincts. *Barton Fink* uses Stephen Foster's "Old Black Joe," about a slave seeking release, as a centerpiece for Hollywood slave Bill Mayhew. *The Hudsucker Proxy's* "Memories Are Made of This" underscores its panoply of old movie references. *Fargo* introduces the perpetually trapped Jerry Lundegaard with Merle Haggard's lyrics about big city freedom. And before *The Big Lebowski* cranks up its rock-and-roll fantasy, the cowboy-inflected "Tumbling Tumbleweeds" sets in place nostalgic underpinnings with a wink to L.A.'s frontier days. With the notable exception of "Danny Boy" in *Miller's Crossing*, the Coens' music avoids the obvious while amplifying themes spot-on.[54]

Music is so embedded in *O Brother's* story line that song titles filter into dialogue. Big Dan's pun of "Dough, Re, Me" references Woody Guthrie's song about money's undue power as well as *The Sound of Music*. Homer Stokes, who wants to preserve white culture and heritage, ironically alludes to Louis Jordan's jivey "Is You Is or Is You Ain't My Baby?" British rock and roll great Led Zeppelin, a group steeped in American blues, gets an obvious plug with Sheriff Cooley's "stairway to heaven." In the next breath, he quotes a famous funeral hymn from about a hundred years earlier: "We Shall All Meet By and By." The casual, at-times ironic, song-dropping demonstrates the staggering effect music has on culture—it crosses geographic boundaries, crisscrosses time periods, infuses everyday life, and reflects the zeitgeist.

Song is *O Brother's* ultimate connector, as the opening work song and the "O muse, sing in me" line suggest. From there, Everett's journey examines American mores through the interplay of music and society. As he and his band of brothers find common ground among their fellow man, mixed musical styles emerge that alternately poke fun of, reflect on, and offer hope for society. Ultimately, song, like comedy in *Sullivan's Travels*, helps produce racial healing and proves more generally to be a powerful, vital antidote for society's ills. It lifts people's burdens, bridges racial and other divides, and reflects the life force of culture.

The opening uneven playing field between haves (the law) and have-nots (the laboring cons) is divided by race and class. Its rhythms are too. The ballad's brutal authoritative vendetta—a story line imitated in the plot—communicates that the deplorable system in place would make anyone, in the words of Marvin Gaye, want to holler. Archivist Lomax elaborates:

> In most societies the individual can look to organized authority as in some sense beneficent or protective, . . . But increasingly, the laborers of the Deep South, floating from camp to camp, often from prison to prison, came to feel that they had nowhere to turn. There was, as usual in black tradition, a musical response. It came in the sudden emergence of the lonesome holler, and later the blues, notable among all human works of art for their profound despair.[55]

The blues come a bit later in *O Brother*, too, first with the black handcar driver and then more full on with Tommy. His "Hard-Time Killing Floor Blues" (performed by actor Chris Thomas King) sketches the contours of the conditions he and his fellow drifters face: "Times is harder than ever been before/And the people are driftin' from door to door/Can't find no heaven."[56] As with "Po' Lazarus," *O Brother's* blues set the stage for racial and class issues and provide comfort and escape until the divide is bridged.

The division of labor depicted in the emblematic chain gangs sets in place the key struggle between Capital and Labor, which informs so much of Everett's adventures—and the authorities' abuse of power. Sturges invokes the political battle in over-the-top strokes at the start of *Sullivan's Travels*, but as both his film and *O Brother* make clear the grotesque abuse of Capital over Labor in the name of capitalism needs fixing. Satire is the main method of attack, and *O Brother's* buoyant title sequence announces that mordant modus operandi.

The whimsical "Big Rock Candy Mountain" paints *O Brother's* hobo Neverland in utopian hues that belie widespread privation: "In the Big Rock Candy Mountain, all the cops have wooden legs/And the bulldogs all have rubber teeth and the hens lay soft-boiled eggs."[57] By sugarcoating the hobo life's hardships with tantalizing lies, Harry McClintock's 1928 song offers up in substance and feel a sneak preview of Everett's manipulations. The stolen money awaiting the cons is just as fantastic. Their gullibility paints them—especially the goofy, innocent, neophyte Delmar (who confesses in the movie theatre he's a virgin)—as "punks."

> Many of the old-time hoboes took along with them everywhere a "punk"—a younger tramp who, according to the rules of the road, had to wait on his master hand and foot, to die for him if required. Many of these boys were lured away from their farms and small towns by tales as fanciful as that told in this favorite hobo chantey, "The Big Rock Candy Mountain."[58]

The song also points to money woes, a main source of *O Brother's* conflict.

Economic issues are humorously echoed at the campaign rally. As Everett tries to impress an unimpressed Penny with his latest employment scheme—posing as a dentist—the Soggy Bottom Boys perform "In the Jailhouse Now."[59] The backdrop is perfect. In the vein of "The Big Rock Candy Mountain," Jimmie Rodgers's song about "Ramblin' Bob who used to steal gamble and rob" drolly describes a rogue like Everett, who, short on money and willpower, has fun but ends up behind bars.[60] Penny's whole reason for the divorce is that she doesn't need a jailbird husband; she needs a reliable provider. Everett's musical skills solve this problem.

As the trio's quest gains speed, music develops the plot, elaborates the themes, and charts societal change. Where the first two songs illustrate largely divergent musical styles, many subsequent selections illustrate a cross-pollination of influences. The blend of blues, bluegrass, "old-time," and Appalachian mountain music—all sounds of the American South—underscores both racial and social harmony in a diverse culture. Even in the days of segregation "white and black traditions certainly interacted, both in musical styles, as well as instruments—whites borrowed blues and banjos from blacks; blacks borrowed ballads and fiddles from whites."[61]

Ultimately, equal rights and job opportunities are antidotes to the hard times codified in the movie's songs. When Everett sings his theme song, the exuberant reception to "A Man of Constant Sorrow" represents the tipping point on racial attitudes and the opportunity for decent employment. Like Sully noting the importance of comedy through the cartoon, Everett discovers music can free society from unjust shackles, thanks in large part to records and radio.

RADIO DAZE

One way *O Brother's* musical odyssey integrates the capitalist struggle is through the technology behind the music. As Penny and Everett promenade through the mixed-race town in the final scene, the words "power and light" displayed on a building come into view. The phrase nods to dueling forces in this mythic land. But does "power and light" refer to electricity or the divine or both? This double-entendre is integral to the movie's enlightenment tale, which both echoes and confounds Everett's gleeful exclamations of a new age of reason. Though similar to the eighteenth-century movement in which science trumped long-held religious beliefs, *O Brother's* new era finds that science, through radio and recording technologies, is a double-edged sword.

Like the duality of the "power and light" phrase, Everett's "brave new world" remark carries a conflicting message that reflects the words' original meaning and their famous dystopian borrowings. Though electricity and music are predominantly positive forces, the technology associated with them cuts two ways. On the plus side, the new science that sends Everett's song and its inclusive message far and wide reflects the utterance of Miranda in Shakespeare's *The Tempest* who is awed by mankind's potential. But there's a hint of warning associated with the media, too, which captures Aldous Huxley's use of the phrase to question technology's throttlehold on his novel's futuristic society. In other words, like any power source technology can be used for good or bad and can easily be abused.

Like music radio can be a powerful force for good. Its calming effect on everyday life is first witnessed in the Hogwallop parlor when the three cons join cousin Wash to relax and listen to "You Are My Sunshine" on the Pappy O'Daniel Flour Hour. The short scene sets up the film's potent blend of music, radio, and politics, shining a positive light on the medium and its valuable, relaxing entertainment. But the dichotomy between Pappy's personal and public personas casts a shadow on this new high-tech world. When he refuses to shake hands with the quartet outside of the radio station ("We ain't a one-at-a-timing it here—we mass communicatin'!"), his endorsement of broadcast at the expense of personal contact points to a potential problem.[62]

Though not abominable, Pappy is two-faced. On air and on stage, his public face is that of a kindly, gentle unifier. In private he is a quick-tempered, son-bashing, self-serving politico who stands for little more than wanting to sell his flour and win another term. He thinks Stokes is au fait and considers himself old news, but he actually has a leg up on his contender, at least technologically. He's got the airwaves and the public's ear. Nowhere is this more apparent than when the folks at the rally protest Stokes's rant by unplugging him. Finally, they see him in the light that his radio call letters had earlier cast him in: WFAK. He's a fraud posing as new blood. Pappy, on the other hand, sees the future when it's staring him in the face. Though unable to create his own platform, he proves adept at grabbing another's. He rides the Soggy Bottom Boys' coattails, latching onto their message of inclusion and spirituality. In one breath, he publicly pardons the boys, calling himself "a f'give and f'get Christian."[63] In the next, he harshly orders them to sing his campaign song, revealing his less savory private side.

Pappy claims solidarity with the town hall audience, but really he belongs to the moneyed class. There are just two views outside lower-class environs; both belong to Pappy. In one, he sits on the verandah of a sprawling mansion that's probably a plantation; in the other, he sups at a French restaurant. This latter scene begins several tables over from Pappy's, where Everett and Delmar try not to look like fish out of water. Thanks to their recording proceeds they are enjoying steaks, not horsemeat or gopher. Little does Pappy know that these have-nots who keep crossing his path will save his floundering campaign; he doesn't even notice their presence here. Big Dan does and descends on them like a bird of prey. Butting in on their first good meal in ages, he promises them rewards but is really just out to steal their scarce food and money.

O Brother ties class-busting into the new era's mixed bag of technological progress. Rather than recapitulating eighteenth-century France's intellectual, middle-class movement, the Coens' enlightened age means better conditions for the disenfranchised. We see this through the steady struggle—and survival—of the have-nots despite powerful forces against them.

Mr. French's power play is another example of exploitation in the "powered" radio age. With a name directly tied to the Enlightenment era, French joins a growing number of haves out to exploit the boys for personal gain. His reasons are economic: "That record has just gone through the goddamn roof . . . Hot damn, we gotta find those boys! Sign 'em to a big fat contract!"[64] Lund in fact has already gypped them with their paltry payment. Though Everett thinks he has pulled one over on the blind man by adding phantom band members, the extra twenty dollars they get could hardly surpass the potential profits of a hit record.

The "Constant Sorrow" recording sketches the plusses and minuses of the way roots American music was distributed through rural settings in radio's early days. Record producers and radio operators like Lund would advertise for talent, record the musicians who responded, play their records, and usually get compensated far and above the musicians' pay. The Carter Family and Jimmie Rodgers, for instance, whose songs are featured in the film, both answered Ralph Peer's cattle call to record in Bristol, Tennessee, in July 1927. The deal was simple: They were paid $100 to play music. Johnny Cash called those recordings "the single most important event in the history of country music."[65] And yet the influential musicians didn't get a fair cut.

O Brother shows that ironically the ramifications of such recordings were a mixed bag. While they preserved America's vibrant musical heritage, the marketing of the old-time, mountain music left the field wide open for exploitation. Though Peer started out splitting publishing rights with "the Carters, who were diligent song collectors," eventually he took all the copyrights and publishing for himself.[66] Peer's fictional counterparts are Lund and French.

A relevant sidebar to this injustice is the amends the Coens made in securing rights for music in the movie. Research into the chain-gang singers who performed "Po' Lazarus," which was recorded by Lomax at a Mississippi Penitentiary in 1959, turned up James Carter, who was alive and living comfortably and crime-free in Chicago. The producers tracked him down so they could pay him royalties that began flooding in from the film's hot soundtrack.[67]

The movie tracks the growing popularity of "Constant Sorrow" in the "I'll Fly Away" montage. As the boys travel the countryside toward Ithaca, their song visually portrayed with a spinning-record overlay covers much farther ground, reaching cities as far away as Mobile. A woman (played by Gillian Welch, who sings on this track as well as on "Nobody but the Baby") discovers the song is so popular, it's been sold out. Such popularity reflects how technology propelled the careers of acts like Rodgers and the Carters, the Soggy Bottom Boys' models.

> Sales were good. . . . But a real change in their fortunes came in 1938 when Peer did a deal with a border radio company. . . . [The Carters] performed twice daily on the radio station XERA, broadcasting a strong signal from Coahuila, Mexico, that could be heard all the way across America.[68]

The film captures how radio changed the South, turning homespun music into DJ-spun gold, with mixed results. Ultimately, *O Brother* portrays music, recording technology, and radio broadcasts as significant social forces that can upset political careers and propel society into a new age despite some negative accompaniments. Song is a mighty folk art that works in tandem with other powerful forces such as spirituality, art, myths, and legends.

"ALL THESE POOR FOLK KNOW IS THE LEGEND"

Showing how art can give a sagging democracy a well-needed boost, *O Brother* also probes the perennial Coen theme: What is a man? Everett fancies himself a paterfamilias, but Penny sees his jail time as a shirking of parental duties. Forced to become provider for and protector of their children, Penny dignifies his desertion in a folksy fiction of a railroad accident.[69] Thus, Everett's quest involves reviving his manhood by way of brotherhood and fatherhood.

In locating his true worth as a man, Everett must shed his many false skins of Negro singer, bank robber, dentist, and hillbilly. He does this, bit by bit, correctly describing his group's racial mix to Lund, confessing to the boys about the real reason for his escape, and finally excelling in his musical and

George Clooney (Ulysses Everett McGill) stands up for his paterfamilias rights in front of Holly Hunter (Penny) and their child before he gets kicked out of the Woolworth's. (Credit: © Buena Vista Pictures Buena Vista Pictures/Photofest)

leadership ability. When the first strains of "Constant Sorrow" electrify the crowd, he starts to see he is not a musical charlatan. He's got something with the music thing. The song leads to legitimate employment—the key to his family reunion. As head of the family, he is a big man in his family's eyes, but in the film's vernacular he is the little man's true servant—a brother and a political reformer. In these roles he finds salvation and deliverance from those who mistreat him, and boosts the stature of his fellow have-nots.

The Coens' working-class "heroes" are often little guys who strive to find the man within and often fail to see their super-sized archenemies posing as "friends." When it comes to *Barton Fink*'s "Burly Man," the writer sees only a friendly neighbor not a serial killer. "What makes a man?" the Big Lebowski asks the Dude, who is about to become the fall guy in the rich man's kidnapping scheme. "What kind of a man are you?" Big Dave inquires of Ed Crane just before he tries to strangle him in *The Man Who Wasn't There*. In each case "big" does not just apply to size and name; it refers to societal standing and malevolent character. In Coen lands, size counts—and "little" men are generally the good guys.

George is a good little guy trying to be a big bad guy. A kinder, gentler version of his historical namesake who killed for kicks, this latter-day Baby Face guns down cows. Like the men in *The Odyssey* who off Apollo's golden cattle, the Coens' cow-killer gets the death penalty. But unlike Ulysses' crew, George welcomes the execution. His whole criminal raison d'etre is to rise above his despised nickname—a height he attains through the maximum penalty: "These little men finally caught up with the criminal a the century," he proudly yells. "I'm on top of the world! I'm George Nelson and I'm feelin' ten feet tall!"[70] While the detail of the electric chair layers more (darker) meaning onto the phrase "power and light," his lines echo James Cagney's famous last words in *White Heat* (1949), ironically yelled just before he is blown to bits: "Made it, ma! Top of the world!"[71] George's giddy welcome of death skewers the desire for celebrity and the concomitant culture of nihilism that puts individual, money, and fame above the collective.

Everett's accidental fame, on the other hand, is the thread that allows him to retie the marriage knot. But he must first lose his ego and discover that human connections, such as friends and family, are more important than hair gel. Everett's hair-care obsessions playfully reveal a deep vanity and a feminine mystique. Everett's need for perfect hair is a running joke that has him not only on the lookout for Dapper Dan pomade but also donning a lady's hairnet while on the lam. This peculiar gender-bending lumps Everett in with other male Coen characters who have a flair for the feminine. *The Big Lebowski*'s Dude wears his long hair back in a barrette. Hi is feminized by his colorful, flowery shirts in *Raising Arizona*, where the smell of pomade is also in the air. That movie's bounty hunter tracks escaped con brothers (one played by Goodman) by following the scent of their pomade left at a gas station. In *O Brother*, twice Goodman's Dan senses Everett through smell, at the restaurant and the Klan rally. Everett also senses his hair gel on Waldrip, but part of his journey is to lose his vanity. The freeing flood following Everett's spiritual leap in front of the gallows sweeps away his vanity through the many cans of pomade washed away.

Everett's ability to shed his false selves shows him to be a good guy. Those who don't shake their false appearances are the bad guys. Stokes, for instance, is a wizard who personifies the devil. His wrong-headed ideas of unity through exclusion and elimination are anti-Christian, antipolitical, and evil. As the Klansmen perform their lurid dance, Stokes makes a sinister plea bargain—a real deal with the devil. He not only seeks to be spared by Death in song, when he announces Tommy's lynching, he seems to be exchanging Tommy's life to keep his own.

O Brother's state of affairs regarding the have-nots exposes America's crisis of conscience just before integration. Fear of change is hyperbolized in the fascistic Cooley who peddles in slavery and torture and Stokes whose dark arts he wants to make political. In 1927 journalist Walter Lippman described the era of turmoil fictionalized in *O Brother* like this:

> The evil which the old-fashioned preachers ascribe to the Pope, to Babylon, to atheists, and to the Devil is simply the new urban civilization, with its irresistible economic and scientific and mass power. The Pope, the Devil, jazz, the bootleggers are a mythology which expresses symbolically the impact of a vast and dreaded social change. . . . The mythology of the Ku Klux Klan is a kind of primitive science, an animistic and dramatized projection of the fears of a large section of our people who have yet to accommodate themselves to the strange new social order which has arisen in their midst.[72]

O Brother's devils come in many shapes and sizes. Some are the tyrannical men in charge tormenting innocents; others are more playful, less threatening creatures of folklore. Tommy's tale of musical talent melds different devils and myths. The crossroads exchange has roots in sixteenth-century Germany when scholar and magician Johann Faustus gained notoriety for purportedly trading his soul for knowledge and power. His deal with the devil soon spread through Europe and beyond, inspiring such literary luminaries as Christopher Marlowe, Johann Wolfgang von Goethe, and Thomas Mann to expand on this mythic figure. Centuries later, American blues lore tested Faustian waters, or so it seems—and then the Coens joined in.

The legendary bluesman Robert Johnson, whose surviving recordings contain some of the most soul-wrenching blues ever heard, claimed he owed his guitar skills to the devil. Such a deal is echoed in song titles like "Cross Road Blues," "Me and the Devil Blues," and "Hellhound on My Trail." His seemingly overnight talent kept the lore alive. After years of failing to play well, he returned to his home town after a long stint away—and suddenly he could jam. The myth of the devilish deal spread to other blues musicians and became part of the genre's myth.

> Take your guitar and you go to where a road crosses that way, where a cross-road is. Get there, be sure to get there just a little 'fore 12:00 that night. . . . A big black man will walk up there and take your guitar, and he'll tune it. And then he'll play a piece and hand it back to you. That's the way I learned to play anything I want.[73]

Such bartering of one's soul for talent hardly describes evil—just a different kind of soul music and a lifestyle that goes against the grain of traditional Christian values.

O Brother's real crossroads devil is not black; he is white and comes in multiple forms: Big Dan, Stokes, and Cooley—the mirror-eyed sheriff with bloodlust. Like the "Po' Lazarus" sheriff, he would just as soon kill as capture the small-time crooks and sees no difference between "the prison farm or the pearly gates."[74] Tommy, on the run from bigots who will kill him because of his race, and Everett, on the lam because of his chain-gang escape, must help each other to beat the odds stacked against them. Like Joker and Cullen, their cooperation will pay in lifesaving dividends. Everett's trio saves Tommy from a lynching. Tommy's music helps Everett find himself as working man and family man. Jordan Rivers and the Soggy Bottom Boys stanch the flow of rampant corruption. And the flood—representing strong government action while seeming biblical—apocalyptically frees society from tyranny. Tommy and Everett become working-class heroes, folk legends who change—and save—the world. The final scene answers the question of "O Brother, Where Art Thou?" with images of a unified diverse democracy—an integrated town borne from the state's power and light show. It's an American legend of biblical proportions.

WRAP: AFTER THE FLOOD

Chains transform from tokens of an exploitative penal system into a positive symbol of democracy in the Coens' mythologized South. Everett and his friends go from surviving together to thriving as friends, squashing the vicious authority figures and their ineffective methods. Everett's music unifies the once segregated culture. Politics and folk art demonstrate that the power of democracy can topple out-of-control, over-controlling corrupt powers. Music, movies, and good stories can be both entertaining and freeing. As with *The Odyssey*, folk tales can educate and unify—as well as entertain.

NOTES

1. Ralph Stanley won Best Male Country Vocal Performance for his searing version of "O Death." "I Am a Man of Constant Sorrow" earned its performers Dan Tyminski, Harley Allen, and Pat Enright a Best Country Collaboration statue. The soundtrack nabbed Best Album of the Year and Best Compilation Soundtrack. And, last but not least, T-Bone Burnett, the man behind the music, won Producer of the Year. The documentary *Down From the Mountain*, codirected by D. A. Pennebaker, chronicles a concert of *O Brother*'s music and musicians.

2. Neil Strauss, "The Country Music Radio Ignores," *New York Times*, March 24, 2002, 2-1.

3. Homer's Menelaus is the husband of Helen of Troy, whose face launched a thousand ships and who was abducted by the Trojans, prompting the Trojan War.

4. The vocal parts are sung by Emmylou Harris, Alison Krauss, and Gillian Welch.

5. *O Brother, Where Art Thou?* DVD, directed by Joel Coen (2000; Burbank, Calif.: Walt Disney Video, 2001).

6. Maynard Mack et al., eds., *The Norton Anthology of World Masterpieces*, 4th ed., vol. 1 (New York: W.W. Norton & Company, 1979), 8.

7. While *The Iliad* recounts the ten years of the war, *The Odyssey* traces Odysseus's decade-long journey home after it. The English word *odyssey* derives from Homer's poem.

8. Rob Content, Tim Kreider, and Boyd White, "Review: *O Brother, Where Art Thou?*" *Film Quarterly* (Fall 2001): 43.

9. *O Brother, Where Art Thou?*, DVD.

10. *O Brother, Where Art Thou?*, DVD.

11. *O Brother, Where Art Thou?*, DVD.

12. *O Brother, Where Art Thou?*, DVD.

13. *O Brother, Where Art Thou?*, DVD.

14. *O Brother, Where Art Thou?*, DVD.

15. *O Brother, Where Art Thou?*, DVD.

16. The line comes from the poem "Elegies II," by the Roman writer Sextus Propertius, line 34.3–4. The full Latin reads: "Expertus dico, nemo est in amore fidelis."

17. *O Brother, Where Art Thou?*, DVD.

18. *O Brother, Where Art Thou?*, DVD.

19. Some have suggested this character name also likely alludes to Howard Waldrop, a Southern writer whose romans a clefs include the novella "A Dozen Tough Jobs," which recasts Hercules' trials into a 1930s Mississippi setting.

20. *O Brother, Where Art Thou?*, DVD.

21. *O Brother, Where Art Thou?*, DVD.

22. *O Brother, Where Art Thou?*, DVD.

23. *O Brother, Where Art Thou?*, DVD.

24. *O Brother, Where Art Thou?*, DVD.

25. *O Brother, Where Art Thou?*, DVD.

26. William G. McLoughlin, *Revivals, Awakenings, and Reform* (Chicago: University of Chicago Press, 1978), xiii.

27. McLoughlin, *Revivals, Awakenings, and Reform*, 172.

28. McLoughlin, *Revivals, Awakenings, and Reform*, 169. These reformers included John Dewey and William James, scientists like Walter Lippmann, humanitarians Jane Addams and Lillian Wald, sociologist Thorstein Veblen, and theologians Washington Gladden, Harry Emerson, and Richard T. Ely.

29. *O Brother, Where Art Thou?*, DVD.

30. Wayne W. Daniel, *Pickin' on Peachtree* (Chicago: University of Illinois Press, 1990), 199.

31. Ernest Lee Tuveson, *Redeemer Nation* (Chicago: Midway, 1980), vii.

32. This is a letter to Roosevelt's close advisor, Harry Hopkins, from journalist Lorena Hicock. From "Lorena Hickock Reports on the State of the Nation," June 6, 1934, www.newdeal.feri.org/tva/lorena1.htm (assessed March 17, 2007).

33. The name sounds like it is also linked to the Foggy Bottom, an integrated district in 1800s Washington, D.C., that was also home to the gas and power industry.

34. *O Brother, Where Art Thou?*, DVD.

35. *O Brother, Where Art Thou?*, DVD.

36. *O Brother, Where Art Thou?*, DVD.

37. *O Brother, Where Art Thou?*, DVD.

38. This reading belongs to American music archivist John Lomax, who discovered and recorded several versions of the song, including the one in the movie. Alan Lomax, *The Land Where the Blues Began* (New York: Pantheon, 1993), 233.

39. The real penal colony housed such blues luminaries as Son House and Bukka White, who preserved its legendary abuses in songs like "Parchman Farm Blues" and "Midnight Special."

40. *O Brother, Where Art Thou?*, DVD.

41. Content, Kreider, and White, "Review: *O Brother*," 43.

42. Marie Gottschalk, *The Prison and the Gallows* (New York: Cambridge University Press, 2006), 51.

43. Melvin Dixon, *Ride Out the Wilderness* (Chicago: University of Illinois Press, 1987), 17.

44. John A. Lomax and Alan Lomax, *Folk Song: U.S.A.* (New York: Times Mirror, 1975), 419. Actually a quintet, the gospel group the Fairfield Four became popular in the 1940s thanks to a hit radio show.

45. *Cool Hand Luke*, DVD, directed by Stuart Rosenberg (1967; Burbank, Calif.: Warner Home Video, 1997).

46. As for Disney's other animated waddlers, Dewey was named after New York governor Thomas Dewey and Louie after animator Louie Schmitt.

47. Ed Gale, who plays The Little Man, shares the last name of *Oz*'s Dorothy, itself a reference to the windy force that prompts her dream. Other actors whose names either deliberately or strangely play on their roles or a thematic thread include *Blood Simple*'s Nancy Finger, *Miller's Crossing*'s Marcia Gay Harden, and *O Brother*'s Daniel Von Bargen.

48. From a transcript of Harburg's 92nd Street Y appearance, generously provided to the author by Yip's son Ernie Harburg.

49. From Harburg's 92nd Street Y performance.

50. Henry M. Littlefield, "*The Wizard of Oz*: Parable on Populism," *American Quarterly* 16, no. 1 (Spring 1964): 47–58.

51. *O Brother, Where Art Thou?*, DVD.

52. Richard Severo, "Jimmie Davis, Louisiana's Singing Governor, Is Dead," *New York Times*, November 6, 2000.

53. T-Bone Burnett; *O Brother, Where Art Thou?*; various artists, *Lost Highway* CD, 2000.

54. David Morgan, *Knowing the Score* (New York: Harper Entertainment, 2000), 65.

55. Alan Lomax, *The Land Where the Blues Began*, 233.

56. Skip James, "Hard-Time Killing Floor Blues" (1931) (T-Bone Burnett, *O Brother, Where Art Thou?*, CD).

57. Harry McClintock, "Big Rock Candy Mountain" (T-Bone Burnett, *O Brother, Where Art Thou?*, CD).

58. Lomax and Lomax, *Folk Song: U.S.A.*, 324.

59. Tim Blake Nelson sings in "In the Jailhouse Now," but Pat Enright, not John Turturro, is the soundtrack's actual yodeler. George Clooney, singer Rosemary Clooney's nephew, trained to sing "Man of Constant Sorrow," but Dan Tyminski ended up doing the vocals.

60. Jimmie Rodgers, "In the Jailhouse Now" (Carrie Anita Rodgers Court: 1962, 1990) (T-Bone Burnett, *O Brother, Where Art Thou?*, CD).

61. Blues historian Pete Lowry quoted in Daniel, *Pickin on Peachtree*, 7.

62. *O Brother, Where Art Thou?*, DVD.

63. *O Brother, Where Art Thou?*, DVD.

64. *O Brother, Where Art Thou?*, DVD.

65. Fiona Sturges, "Pop: Back to the Old Country," *Independent*, November 22, 2002, 16. Johnny Cash was the son-in-law of Sara Carter's cousin, Maybelle.

66. David Hinckley, "Patronage or Pillage?" *New York Daily News*, July 28, 2002, 16.

67. Bernard Weinraub, "An Ex-Convict, a Hit Album, An Ending Fit for Hollywood," *New York Times*, March 3, 2002.

68. Sturges, "Pop: Back to Country," 16.

69. This detail provides another *Sullivan's Travels* tie-in. When Sully is sent to do hard labor, none of his influential friends come to his aid because they think he was killed by a train.

70. *O Brother, Where Art Thou?*, DVD.

71. *White Heat*, DVD, directed by Raoul Walsh (1950; Burbank, Calif.: Warner Home Video, 2005).

72. Walter Lippman, "The Causes of Political Indifference Today," *Atlantic Monthly* 139, no. 2 (February 1927): 265–67.

73. As told by Rev. Ledell Johnson, brother to musician Tommy Johnson (no relation to the Coens' character), to Peter Guralnick, *Searching for Robert Johnson* (New York: Plume Penguin, 1989), 18.

74. *O Brother, Where Art Thou?*, DVD.

· 9 ·

The Man Who Wasn't There: A Flying Saucer

Wisps of aliens and flying saucers (like Francis McDormand's elliptical perfume bottle) creep into the movie to capture and expose the post-war's zeitgeist of anxiety and dread. (Credit: USA Films/Photofest © USA Films)

"There is no 'what happened.' Looking at something changes it."

—Freddy Riedenschneider (Tony Shalhoub)

"As I was undressing to go to bed, I remembered again the burning sensation I had felt on my left side while I was undergoing the profound 'initiation' in the saucer. I glanced down and saw

277

what appeared to be a circular 'burn' about the size of a quarter
on my left side directly below my heart. The outer rim of the circle was red, inflamed and slightly raised as also was a small dot in
the center of the circle—the symbol of the hydrogen atom. I re-
alized they had impressed that mark upon my body to convince
me beyond all doubt of the reality of my experiences in the cold
light of the coming days."

—Orfeo Angelucci, *The Secret of the Saucers* (1955)

PREVIEW

*T*he Coens' ninth film was spawned on the set of *The Hudsucker Proxy*. A
poster of period haircuts on one of *Proxy*'s sets had lodged itself under the Coens' collective thinking cap, and more than a decade later *The Man Who Wasn't
There* emerged.[1] The film, which earned Joel Coen a third Best Director prize
at Cannes, marks the filmmakers' first black-and-white piece and their fifth
stab at crime fiction.[2]

Inspired by the novels of James M. Cain, this Coenesque neo-noir could
screen as easily at the Museum of Modern Art as at the local multiplex—for
it is a pataphysical exercise in modernism. After Beethoven music, black-and-
white photography, and a man's lackluster life kick-start the noir, the story advances gently into illogical territory. Though it revisits the familiar Coen terrain of a crumbling American Dream and metaphysics, it also branches into
uncharted areas where unidentified flying objects—and the notion of the collective unconscious—act as gateways into the modernity's multifarious unknowns. With certainty out the window, flying saucers become totems of
doubt in the dark comedy's fugue of transcendence.

REVIEW

The Man Who Wasn't There begins just before small-town barber Ed Crane
(Billy Bob Thornton) decides to change his life around—a decision with disastrous outcomes. Bored with his nine-to-five job in a Santa Rosa shop owned
by his brother-in-law Frank (Michael Badalucco), Ed tries his hand as a venture capitalist. He partners with out-of-town entrepreneur Creighton Tolliver
(Jon Polito), who needs seed money for his new dry-cleaning business. The
barber gets the funds by blackmailing his wife's boss and lover, "Big Dave"
Brewster (James Gandolfini), a department store mogul by marriage. Anony-
mously, Ed threatens to expose the affair if Dave doesn't fork over $10,000.

Tracing his cash back to Ed, Big Dave sets up an after-hours meeting with the cuckold. Ed has just returned home from a family party with his wife Doris (Frances McDormand), who is passed out drunk. Ed meets Dave at his office at Nirdlingers department store, the family business of Dave's wife Ann (Katherine Borowitz). Dave insinuates that Ed's blackmailing has destroyed Dave's chances of opening his own annex and making Doris comptroller of it. Questioning the barber's ethics and manhood, Dave lunges at Ed, who, in self-defense, grabs a cigar knife from Dave's desk and sticks it into his neck. The poke is a death-dealing blow.

Ironically, Doris is charged with Big Dave's murder. For her defense, Ed hires Freddy Riedenschneider (Tony Shalhoub), an expensive attorney from Sacramento with an excellent reputation. As Freddy explores alternate theories for the best defense, Ed comes clean that he killed Big Dave. Doris is stunned to learn of both her husband's knowledge of her affair and his part in the murder. Freddy, however, dismisses it. He decides to go for the blackmailing angle to establish reasonable doubt scientifically with Werner Heisenberg's "uncertainty principle." But he never gets to try this out on a jury because Doris kills herself before the trial begins.

Her suicide devastates Frank, so much that he stops working and starts drinking heavily. This forces Ed, the perfunctory hair-cutter, to become "first chair." He hires on another barber to help with the heads and is dismayed that the new barber chats as much as Frank. Narrator Ed, so he tells us during his incessant voice-over, doesn't like to talk or entertain.

For solace, Ed visits Rachel "Birdy" Abundas (Scarlett Johansson), the teen daughter of Ed's friend Walter (Richard Jenkins), a local lawyer. Ed likes to listen to her piano playing and becomes so taken with her musical skills that he tries to arrange for lessons with a top-notch music teacher in Sacramento. The unimpressed Jacques Carcanogues (Adam Alexi-Malle) turns them down. On the ride home, in a move that seems out of character, Birdy makes a sexual advance toward Ed, which causes a car crash. When he wakes from his coma, he is arrested for the murder of Tolliver, who had disappeared after receiving Ed's money.

Ed now hires Freddy for his defense, but after his brother-in-law attacks him in the courtroom, the judge declares a mistrial and Ed cannot afford Freddy a third time. So he hires Lloyd Garroway (George Ives), who advises him to plead guilty in hopes of avoiding the death penalty. The strategy fails, and Ed is sentenced to death. From prison, Ed makes another confession: A men's magazine is paying him to tell his story. The night before he is executed, he dreams he walks out of his cell and into the prison yard where a spaceship hovers. The next day, as he muses about an afterlife, the executioner pulls the electric chair switch. The film draws to a close as the electricity surges and the screen is gradually overexposed until it is completely white.

SHEAR FICTION

The Man Who Wasn't There is a modernist film, so leave your expectations of traditional narrative at the door. In its self-conscious story of ironic transcendence, the film subversively uses film noir tropes to create a feel of alienation and anomie that help cover up its core, self-referential joke. Uncertainty reigns so supreme in the modern world, the film suggests, that the very plot is suspect.

The revelation comes at the end with the magazines scattered on the desk in Ed's cell. Like "the reveal" in *The Usual Suspects* (1995), when the camera scans the clippings from which Kevin Spacey's character concocts his canard, Ed's magazines in *The Man Who Wasn't There* propound his "journalistic" confabulation. Cover lines like "I was abducted by aliens" and "After 10 years of married life, I discover I am an escaped lunatic!" explicate the kind of strange fiction-as-fact his men's magazine publishes. For instance, while the tabloid *Wonder* playfully capitalizes on the expansive notions of doubt, the magazines *Muscle Power* and *Stalwart* tie into the thematic thread of masculinity—a frayed concept in the movie's modernity. In short, the final reel reveals what Freddy has suggested all along: "There is no 'what happened.'"[3] It's all made-up entertainment, a fabulous story ride illustrating that doubt rules the modern world.

The signs for such perfidy are abundant throughout, and important dichotomies, motifs, and disconnects established early on hint at the expansive joke. First off, there are inconsistencies in Ed's narration. "I worked in a barbershop," he explains in voice-over, "but never considered myself a barber."[4] True, the statement announces his deep disaffection. But it also points to one of several disconnects between narrator and physical Ed. Namely, he is a barber, like it or not.

Later on, similarly facetious commentary delivers healthy servings of self-consciousness and duplicity: "As Doris said, 'We were entertaining.' Me, I don't like entertaining."[5] Yet at the end he admits he is selling his story for its entertainment value—five cents a word, in fact, so he's gone on a bit to up his pay. It's a funny line because it calls into question whether any of what he has related has happened at all, never mind with remuneratively beneficial flourishes. Why increase profit margins just before one is exterminated? The detail of his payment calls into question whether or not, in fact, he is really stewing in his own juice or juicing up the story.

Finally, there is his priceless comment, "Me, I don't talk much."[6] While this is true of his physical presence, his statement flies in the face of his narrating persona who in fact trucks in talk to tell his tale. By the end, the double-entendres become doublespeak. Ed's whole story is precisely about what he says it is not—talking and entertaining for his reading audience. Such disjunctures are important clues pointing to the film's modernist slant.

Ed is the main storyteller, but the film teems with raconteurs. Some, like Frank, are relatively harmless, incessant talkers—mere competitors for the narrating Ed. Others dabble in truth-stretching or outright lies to hide things they would prefer be kept secret. Their storytelling and misrepresentations inform Ed's milieu, of which he is a part even though he often feels like an outsider. The flying saucer motif comes to represent his alienation as well as the culture's collective unconscious in which dreams, fears, and explanations are all bundled up in unprovable, fantastic details.

After Ed kills Dave and Doris is charged with the murder, his wife Ann visits Ed late at night with a far-out yarn. It's a marvelously spooky scene that heightens the strangeness of her vignette; both her story and the ambience capture the undercurrent of dread in sleepy Santa Rosa. On a personal level, her account of an alien-visitation camping trip is an outrageous excuse for why she and Dave no longer have sex. Forget something as mundane as an affair—Ann attributes Big Dave's lack of affection to otherworldly mischief. Later, Ed will dream up his own UFO story just before the state sends him into the great unknown of death—which is also, self-consciously, the story's afterlife. The UFO symbolizes an uncertainty so all-encompassing that, like Ann's strange tale, everything Ed has told us is open to debate. Thus the peace he finds through his storytelling is our chaos.

If Ann's yarn rockets uncertainty into the cosmos and the realm of conspiracy theory, her husband's storytelling is grounded in plausibility. Despite his "holding down the porch" battle lingo and his claims of being a combat hero, it turns out he had a desk job during the war.[7] This detail makes the weapon that Ed uses to kill him not a spoil of war but a simple cigar cutter and his "Arnie Bragg" cannibalism story, used to mock his wife's cooking, just fantastic "bragging."

Doris is a liar out of necessity: She must hide her affair. Though she tosses Ed a "love ya, honey," she treats him more like a handmaid than a husband, asking him for a shave and a "zip."[8] Well before Ed admits their marriage is sexless (like Ann's), we see there is no romantic flicker between them, never mind a fire. Doris's lively interactions with Dave tell a different story. She laughs at his stories and enjoys dishwashing with him. It turns out, though, that her fidelity to Big Dave comes with the price of making her numbers lie. Cooking her otherwise pristine books—creating fiction from figures—undoes her financial freedom.

When Freddy arrives to help beat Doris's murder rap, his strategic borrowing of Heisenberg's uncertainty principle not only aims to seed the jury with doubt but also pokes holes in Ed's story. After all, Heisenberg's theory suggests that just looking at something (like a movie) changes it, and so when Ed's story doesn't add up in the end, we can chalk it up not just to fictional mischief but also to a modern quandary. Forget the riddle about whether or not a tree falling in the forest with no one around makes a sound. Here we have people watching a tree fall in a forest and their observation affecting its trajectory. Modernity would have it that nothing definitive exists, suggests *The Man Who Wasn't There*—at least in the realm of fiction.

Ed, the official story guide, gets the last word, but his words and truth are just as fuzzy as everyone else's. He is, after all, writing a tabloid tale with all the fantastic fixings of fiction. Like the jury's consideration of Doris's and Ed's trials, the film viewer should acknowledge the thread of doubt's supremacy. Ultimately, the film suggests the truth is not out there, at least not necessarily so. But lies and stories—with all their humor, drama, mystery, and occasional salaciousness—are everywhere. Fabrications are the movie's universal "truth"—and unknowns are hallmarks of modern times.

"HE IS YOUR REFLECTION"

As if exemplifying Heisenberg's idea that observing something changes its trajectory, the film becomes more and more iffy the more it follows its main character. With lying and yarn-spinning such common actions among Ed's contemporaries, there is little to suggest that Ed is above the practice and lots to suggest he too is prone to being two-faced. After all, there are two of him.

A bit like Hi and his *Raising Arizona* "twin," Ed's dual forms indicate his trapped feelings as the barber and his need for freedom. Physical Ed is immured by his life while narrating Ed holds his ticket to freedom. Here again is the theme of the double, which in this film probes the dual meanings of "bound"—namely, the predicament of being tangled up in something and the process of bounding away from it.[9] A small clipping on the barbershop wall amplifies this need for escape: "Lend me 15 minutes a day, and I'll prove I can make you a new man."[10] Ed's story does just that on a different time schedule. It transforms him from a disaffected barber to a man who finds peace. In the end, Ed gets a shave rather than gives one, and he does not have to remind people who he is and what he does. He moves from observer to observed, and, when the prison onlookers watch him settle into the electric chair, it is apparent he has transcended his barber persona. The guards unchain him, and, freed from his coiffeur existence, he bounds for a world unknown. In other words, his story sets him free.

While his liberation provides the climax, the bulk of the story explores the barber manqué cooped up in his measly existence, dissatisfied with his life in Santa Rosa, the same small-town backdrop for Alfred Hitchcock's *Shadow of a Doubt* (1943). That movie also explores the double motif but through two characters named Charlie. Teresa Wright plays a niece who slowly discovers her favorite uncle's (Joseph Cotton) deep, dark secret: He is a serial killer. What's clear is her abhorrence of his hideous actions. What is murkier is their uncanny connection throughout. The movie ends on Uncle Charlie's funeral, where the praises heaped upon him make clear that the town is ignorant of his murderous doings and true nature. Ed's double is not a niece or uncle but himself.

When Freddy tells the jury that Ed "is your reflection," there is more to his postulation than simply that Ed is a middle-class Everyman whose existential quandary applies to the barber's peers, the jury.[11] Freddy's reflection comment acknowledges Ed's duality. Visually, mirrors expand on his double, as does light. On the one hand, mirrors magnify the notion that Ed represents his modern society advanced by technology but bogged down by malaise. But mirrors also point to Ed's split self: the ho-hum barber and the plotting, murderous criminal.

Mulling over the prospect of partnering with Tolliver, Ed's split self is sculpted first by the lighting, then in a mirror shot. Standing in profile in the bathroom's threshold, Ed considers dry cleaning. In this first of two shots, half of him is shown, fully lit, features distinguishable, with a look of deep thought about him. A cut from the opposite angle shows his other half in dark shadow, completely featureless. In this framing, he wonders if he should even contemplate going into business and whether or not Tolliver is as he appears to be: "Was I crazy to be thinking about it? Was he a huckster, or opportunity, the real McCoy?"[12] After debating Tolliver's own duality, he enters the bathroom to give Doris a shave, and two Eds appear: his second self, reflected in the mirror, as if visualizing his good and bad sides. His internal deliberations continue, as he counters thoughts that the idea is crazy with the possibility that such "instinct [has] kept me locked up in the barbershop, nose against the exit, afraid to try turning the knob."[13] Thus he acknowledges his thinking has up to now trapped him.

While creating a noir feel, shadows and light, as the bathroom scene demonstrates, also hint at a secret side of things—a seedy, shady, criminal side. This dualism is intimated right from the start when the opening credits appear in dual form: The white letters have a drop shadow behind them. In addition to this duality, the gray and white image of the iconic barber pole recalls the traditional red and white pole whose colors represent blood and bandages, respectively. Barbers advertised their surgery and bloodletting services by hanging rags outside their shops. The Coens' opening pole shot also advertises: It shows how a mundane pole can symbolize bloody business and that one symbol can denote dual meanings.

After the credits, as the camera moves slowly toward and then down the pole, the narrating Ed spells out his existential quandary of being but not considering himself a barber. This line offers another peek at his duality. In one view, he is a barber who simply wants to get ahead and chooses to commit a crime to do so; in another, he is a jealous husband, whose crime will strike at the heart of Doris's two loves: her job and her lover. The viewer's task, like that of the jury, is to decide which view is real: what is presented as real versus what could be.

The opening shot also tellingly incorporates a mirror, suggesting hidden, nonapparent views hold sway. Following the credits, the camera tilts down from the barber pole to the shop's door, where the figure of a man approaching the shop is reflected. As he enters, we see both his physical form and the mirrored image. The detail is odd and subtle. As Ed introduces himself through his voice-over, a man appears onscreen, but despite appearances this is not Ed. Instead, the man is just a random customer—a reflection of the Santa Rosan society, perhaps, but strangely not our first-person narrator. This detail shows an initial disjunction between Ed's voice and what we see. Only after three minutes of narration and two men's introductions (including barber Frank's) do we finally meet the physical Ed, who then mentions he doesn't talk much. Of course, that's all he has done up to that point. A sliver of Ed can be spotted in his station's mirror as he cuts the hair. Soon his split self becomes abundantly more apparent.

An important part of the visual landscape, mirrors allude to the hidden self. Doris's round mirror, for instance, appears in her introductory scene above her vanity. Her first shots show her dressed in a slip, primping in front of an off-screen mirror as she tries on new Nirdlinger's purchases. Ed's understated but scathing portrait of her makes it clear that Doris is part of his unpropitious life. Indeed, she may be vain, but she is hoping to impress Dave not Ed. Later, before the Christmas party, she fixes her hair in front of it (not unlike Verna primping in the ladies' room in *Miller's Crossing*). When Ed enters the shot and takes a drag off of her cigarette, their physical forms give way to their reflections, visualizing first the apparent then the hidden.

When Tolliver makes a pass at Ed, a round mirror on his wall suggests his closeted, gay side. Like his baldness he prefers to conceal under his "rug," he keeps his homosexuality under wraps except with people and in places he deems safe—such as with Ed in his hotel room. In other words, the mirror represents characters' secret side. With Doris that side is her affair. For Tolliver it is his homosexuality. For Ed his secrets are his blackmail crime and perhaps other sides of himself he prefers not to show, like his softer, feminine side.

Opposite Doris, the numbers cruncher who likes the determinacy of figures, is Ed, a narrator, writer, and purveyor of the less determinate symbols

Mirrors often symbolize the double. Here, as in *Miller's Crossing*, Billy Bob Thornton's Ed and Frances McDormand's Doris both have secret sides to hide. (Credit: USA Films/Photofest © USA Films)

called words. While Doris likes things black and white, Ed is a bit looser with the facts, preferring shades of gray. His church joke is an early example of this. After introducing Doris in the context of their Napa home, he goes on to describe him and Doris as churchgoers. The image of the crucifix corresponding to this description makes us believe one thing, but the "usually Tuesday night" payoff and the bingo game visuals right our initially wrong impression.[14] Thus, entertainment, not spirituality, draws them to church. A deceptively minor point in the murder mystery that follows, the church detail sets up the kind of deception in which Ed is fluent. His words do not always immediately give the true picture.

Ed plays hide and seek with his talk, reflecting the title's built-in ambiguity. Just as Freddy attempts to do with the jury, Ed manipulates words to confound significance and breed doubt. We can safely assume that Ed is the "the man who wasn't there," but the title begs the question, how is he not there? The film offers up multiple meanings.

On a basic narrative level, Ed is a man not there because he has secrets and considers himself a ghost. He is a man not there because no one recalls the barber, a workingman, "second chair" nobody. Gradually, he reinvents himself, becoming a killer, then a writer whose story replaces the unremembered man with a tragic, misunderstood figure, the central player in a dark drama. On a self-conscious level, Ed is a man not there because he is a fictional character who does not exist in three-dimensional form but rather in words and pictures that make up cinematic and literary narratives. As a narrator, he is perhaps more conscious of this special nonbeing than others, and admits as much when he reveals, "It seemed like I knew a secret—a bigger one even than what had really happened to Big Dave, something none of them knew . . . Like I had made it to the outside, somehow, and they were all still struggling, way down below."[15] He makes it to the outside of the story, unlike the other players, because he has special narrative status as chief storyteller (read fact manipulator).

On a homoerotic level, Ed is a man not there perhaps because his latent desires for another man are considered womanly. This could be the kind of secret "he didn't want and no one to tell them to anyway."[16] After all, he talks of Tolliver being "gone . . . like a ghost."[17] Then later, he considers himself a ghost, too: "It was like I was a ghost walking down the street" and "I sat in the house, but there was nobody there. I was a ghost."[18] And finally, there is his fear that he is "turning into Ann Nirdlinger, Big Dave's wife."[19] Throughout, Ed is identified as separate from the rest of the town, and that distinction ties into the alien motif. Extraterrestrials and spaceships are Ann's secret, but they come to represent the wider unknown that is stitched into the film's narrative fabric. The modern world is full of X factors, as is Ed.

ALIEN NATION OR ALIENATION

Ed portrays himself as an alien, an outsider in his own life. He's a shadow of a man, going through the motions of existing but hardly living. The movie opens on the minutiae of Ed's personal anomie: his life. He works in a "dump," plays second fiddle to his first-chair brother-in-law, and is out of tune with the rest of society. He doesn't command a lot of respect about town. In fact, few people remember or recognize him without his smock. Divorced from his barber role, he is indeed a man who isn't there. And even when people recall he is the barber, most disparage him via his job. Such treatment makes one wonder if others' perceptions contribute to his disaffection with his second-chair station in life.

Tolliver is one person who shows no sign of recognition when Ed knocks at his hotel door. Ed has to spell out their relationship despite their formal introductions made a short time before during the haircut. Standing awkwardly in the portal, neither quite in or out of the room, as if mocking his life, Ed reintroduces himself haltingly (not unlike the duplicitous Jerry Lundegaard in

Fargo): "I'm, uh, Ed. . . . Ed Crane. . . . I'm, uh, I'm—the barber."[20] Ed's occupation finally sparks Tolliver's recollection. He didn't recognize Ed without the smock, he says by way of apology. When Ed explains that he is interested in becoming a dry-cleaning partner, even as Tolliver is pleased to receive the offer, he chuckles at the unlikelihood of the funding coming from a barber. Such disrespect for Ed's line of work does not stop Tolliver from a veiled proposition.

After the men team up in a business partnership, the idea of a sexual partnership arises. Tolliver's subtle come-on to Ed momentarily breaches Modern Man's masculinity—or at the very least questions his sexuality. Interestingly, as authors Vincent Brook and Allan Campbell point out, Ed "not only discerns the 'pass' instantly but turns it down with surprising nonchalance—especially for a small-town 'straight' male in the United States of the late 1940s. Moreover, he proceeds to consummate their business deal rather than reject 'the goddamn pansy.'"[21] This and other evidence suggests that sexuality may be a prime alienating factor for Ed, whose androgynous name, Ed (think *Raising Arizona*) might provide another cryptic hint.

The screenplay's foreword advances the gay theory. Roderick Jaynes (aka Ethan and Joel Coen) introduces the published screenplay by waxing on about how the film's title came to be. His jocular account cruises through a smattering

Jon Polito shows his "rug" and exposes his pate to Billy Bob Thornton at the barbershop before coming on to him at the hotel. (Credit: USA Films/Photofest © USA Films)

of allegedly considered titles, two of which could allude to Ed's possible repressed homosexuality. "Pansies Don't Float," Jaynes thankfully notes, was puta-
tively a discarded working title.[22] The amusing title may provide insight by way
of innuendo into Ed's malaise. After all, titles tend to refer to a main character
or topic, not secondary ones. So rather than referencing Tolliver's underwater
burial site, perhaps the humorous title points to a gayness below the surface, sub-
merged beneath apparent meanings.[23] Certainly, there is much in the film that
insinuates the possibility. Film critic Stuart Klawans collected the evidence in
his review for *The Nation*.

> [Ed] goes to visit a gay man in a cheap hotel, because he can't stop think-
> ing about . . . dry cleaning. He visits the in-laws with his heavy-drinking
> wife and hears the classic question, Why haven't you two ever had children?
> He runs into a high school girl to whom he's formed a sentimental attach-
> ment and turns shy—not to her, but to her boyfriend. These may be some
> of the reasons why, twice in the picture, people shout at the barber, "What
> kind of a man are you?"[24]

Among the film's dealings in uncertainty, it well may be that Ed wishes
to repress the crimes that he can somewhat admit to, and the homosexuality
he cannot. Though he leaves the details of his sex life veiled, he unveils some
possibly telling tidbits. To wit, he and Doris do not have sex; Ed won't
"prance" at the possibility that Doris and Dave are having an affair; he isn't the
"he-man" Big Dave is; he kills Dave with a small, woman's weapon, as the gay
Mink does in *Miller's Crossing*; he refuses Birdy's sexual come-on.

The screenplay's preface also notes that the title *The Man Who Wasn't All
There* didn't make the final cut. This possibility supposedly became a choice
because the title without the word *all* had already been taken.[25] Indeed, *The
Man Who Wasn't There* is a 1983 film starring Steve Guttenberg, so the introduction contains at least a scrap of truth. The tentative title containing the
word *all* suggests that something is missing, and Ed's story leaves wide open the
possibility that what could well be absent from his life is the part of a man that
likes women.

When Birdy is talking with a boy after the music concert, Ed horns in on
her conversation with a hint of jealousy. The conversation between the three
of them is awkward, and Ed's inability to talk much strains it more. Ed, not
Birdy, is acting strange. The question is, of whom is he jealous, Birdy or Tony
(Nicholas Lanier)? There is awkwardness between Ed and the boy. Is the barber jealous of him instead of Birdy? Does she actually come on to him later
and he rebuffs her because he is gay? The men's magazine for which he is writing is a muscle mag, and Ed is forever trying to shed his image of himself in a
smock. It could be that like working in a barber shop but not considering him-

self a barber, he has a gay persona without admitting to himself he's a homosexual.

Ed feels like an outsider among his fellow Santa Rosans. Homosexuals represent one class of threats to accepted societal "norms" in the small town. Tolliver is the apparent example of this, but the piano teacher, whom Ed seeks out, could be another example. Though not explicitly labeled a "pansy" like Tolliver, Jacques's mannerisms on top of his artistic profession imply an effeminate if not quite homosexual persona. And it is after his encounter with Jacques that Ed describes Birdy's sexual advance on him. Since we see everything through Ed's eyes, her come-on, unsubstantiated by other indications that she is sexually interested in him, is questionable. In fact, it could be Ed's artistic license to inject a hetero-normative bit of sexuality, and yet he fends off her advances. Instead of sex, her come-on leads to a car accident whose UFO imagery ramps up the rampant uncertainty.

Regardless of his ambiguous sexual preference, Ed is consistently discriminated against. At the bank, for instance, when Frank tries to loop him into his conversation with the loan officer, the man asks about Ed's credentials. The bank officer wants to know his name and his stake in the business. "He's a barber," Frank explains, working in both Ed's professional and familial status. "Second chair, not an owner. . . . He's family, he's my brother-in-law."[26] The officer isn't interested in talking with him, implying on all counts that Ed is a loser. Classism is at work here. Such slights on his career amount to chauvinism against the non-owning workingman. Modern Man, the movie suggests then, is the classic have-not, now an alien in America's postwar "boom" society, where entrepreneurs and industries hold promise for the future and where white men are becoming lost in the country's multiculturalism.

Tied to classism is the film's most apparent alien invasion touching down on postwar America: the rise of immigrants. In Santa Rosa, outside forces are infiltrating from both urban areas and faraway countries. These influences are bringing often unwanted cultural changes. For example, Santa Rosa's home-grown lawyer Walter tells Ed that Big City crimes call for Big City lawyers. "Nobody around here has any experience with this kind of, er . . . And I hear they're bringing a prosecutor up from Sacramento."[27] To match his sophistication, Ed hires Sacramento attorney Freddy Riedenschneider. Later, when Freddy's expensive tastes dry up Ed's funds, the court appoints Lloyd Garroway from San Francisco as Ed's new lawyer.

Fancy products and tastes are associated with such outside forces. Ed, in another sign of his own foreignness, tells Big Dave he gets his barber smocks from a specialty store in Sacramento. Out-of-towner Tolliver brings his dry-cleaning idea along with an expensive toupee made by Jacques of San Francisco. Another French transplant named Jacques is the San Franciscan piano teacher. Freddy stays at the Metropole, an antiquated word for metropolis. His Turandot suite is named for an Italian opera. He eats at Da Vinci's restaurant. All these add up to an expansive European invasion of—and increasing influence on—American life.

Immigrants, especially Italians, surround Ed at home and work. While we don't know his lineage, his wife's background and family define his existence. For example, he works at Guzzi's, the barbershop built from Doris's father's sweat and tears. Her brother Frank is Ed's boss and first chair to Ed's second. Working for his wife's family puts him in the same boat as Big Dave, who wants to open an annex to have a little something of his own slightly apart from his wife's business. The common chord is a somewhat emasculating or at least disempowering effect that working women and "aliens" have on these white males from the 1940s.

The film shows a slow assault on established power and traditional roles. Not only are "dames" a force in the workplace now, but also other aliens are popping up in the once homogenous Santa Rosa. Language cannot quite stanch the flow of immigrants but it can put them in their place. Prejudiced put-downs punctuating the film's patois—"wops," "pansies," "Japs," "Nips," and "Heinies"—are linguistic power grabs and reactions to the nonstop acculturation evident in Da Vinci's restaurant, the Metropole hotel, and the Turandot suite.

Ed is thus an Everyman estranged—personally, professionally, and possibly sexually. His isolation captures the zeitgeist of postwar America and symbolizes a growing unease in the country—and Santa Rosa in particular. This setting was chosen to hark back to *Shadow of a Doubt*'s sleepy, provincial nook, which Hitchcock chose, according to biographer Donald Spoto, to show that "in our securest settings, right in our own dining room, wickedness can sprout like malignant weeds."[28]

In the Coens' movie, doubt's shadows still lurk on the home front but in its postwar setting they are less objectified than in *Shadow of a Doubt*, Hitchcock's personal favorite among his own films.[29] Ed's internal struggle is intimated through an uneasy, unsure malaise—a hidden, unnamed tension befitting the times. Though the defeat of Nazism is implicit in the Coens' 1948 setting, palpable threats still lurk—they are just less visible, less tangible. Uncertainty abounds. "It says here Russia exploded the A-bomb," Frank says, "and there's not a damn thing we can do about it."[30] As unknown forces start to creep into daily life, disquiet grips the nation's unconscious—the cold war heats up paranoia, *Life* magazine lifts the lid off Roswell, and traveling salesmen talk up the "washing without water" mysteries of dry cleaning.[31]

Tied to global fears are people's personal misgivings, failures, and disenchantments. It may be boom times in retail, but it's a bust for individuals like

Ed. Other disaffection is more personal still. Walter, for instance, tries to out-run the loss of his late wife through genealogical research and hard-drinking. Doris, who likes her job but wants something more, also takes to the bottle—and another man's bed. Big Dave lies about war experiences he never had and has an affair with his employee, promising her a piece of his wife's business.

After Dave is murdered, Ann visits Ed late at night to tell him a tale. Unsure just what Ann knows, Ed eyes her as cautiously as he had Big Dave. With her face partly hidden under her mourning veil, she tells Ed she knows Doris had nothing to do with her husband's death. She goes on to recount a camping trip with Dave during which she saw a spaceship full of little creatures take her husband aboard their craft. The biggest difference between pre- and postabduction Dave, she explains further, is that after the experience he stopped touching her.

Her predicament prior to Dave's death is very similar to Ed's minus the UFO bit. She, like him, is estranged from a two-timing spouse. But rather than finger the culprit and pinch him where it hurts as Ed does to both Dave and Doris by taking away their planned annex, she points to extraterrestrial forces. Is the spaceship story a scapegoat for her own inability to recognize or see her husband's infidelity? Or does her belief in a fantastic experience show a preference for the unknown? Maybe she'd rather believe a far-out tale than the truth. Whatever her reasons, her outlandish alien invasion story captures the malaise scratching at the surface of a not-so-squeaky-clean Santa Rosa where infidelities, lies, and other uncertainties loom large.

"MYTHING" IN ACTION

Depicted in *The Man Who Wasn't There* is a society undergoing a sea change in demographics, social mobility, and social order. Uncertainty abounds in such conditions, and central to this pervasive doubt is the UFO. Well before Ann uncorks her story about alien abductions, the motif has secured itself in the physical environment on a near "subliminal" level, Dennis Gassner suggests in the production notes. Doris's perfume bottle, for example, is in the shape of a flying saucer. The ceiling fixtures in Nirdlinger's hang like upside-down saucers. The sconces in the Cranes' living room cast light in triangular formations mimicking the beam of light from a spaceship, a shape well known from pop culture references and Jung's idea of a collective unconscious.

Though the modern myth of UFOs dates back to the late 1800s, around the time dirigibles took to the skies, sightings became prevalent in the late 1940s and early 1950s when Roswell became a household name and people like Orfeo Angelucci wrote books about abductions (*The Secret of Saucers*). So intriguing are these narratives that while they do not substantiate alien life, they capture a kind of spiritual longing and continue to pique the curiosity of scientists and scholars. Psychologist Dr. Carl Jung saw in Angelucci's book that the lure of UFO stories is akin to human yearning to embrace or fear the unknown.

> In the threatening situation of the world today, when people are beginning to see that everything is at stake, the projection-creating fantasy soars beyond the realm of earthly organizations and powers into the heavens, into interstellar space, where the rulers of human fate, the gods, once had their abode in the planets. . . . Even people who would never have thought that a religious problem could be a serious matter that concerned them personally are beginning to ask themselves fundamental questions. Under these circumstances it would not be at all surprising if those sections of the community who ask themselves nothing were visited by "visions," by a widespread myth seriously believed in by some and rejected as absurd by others.[32]

The movie's flying saucers offer both representations of the unknown and an alternative spirituality. It is a modern myth linking bits of science in the technological age to strands of meaning-seeking beyond this known world.

Skimming Ed's dissatisfied life is a just-under-the-surface dread. Despite having a home and a job, he doesn't like his status quo. Reflecting both his sense of failure and the unease emerging from Russia's acquisition of the atomic bomb, the UFO lore expresses the duality of advancement and potential annihilation. That is, as we become technologically more powerful, the belief that potent forces lurking somewhere out in the heavens far beyond our scope, ken, and capabilities can cast a dark cloud of dread over modern times. Rather than use the dreamscape that is so integral to the Coens' films, the filmmakers mine the myth of flying saucers to locate and explore the collective unconscious—ideas shared and understood innately by people across cultures. In this way, the American lore of UFOs becomes a polestar in the movie's dance with enlightenment.

Ed is skeptical of Ann's abduction story but in the end he too is freed by a flying saucer. He walks out of his open cell door and into the prison yard. There, a saucer hovers casting its triangularly shaped, telltale beam of light down on the yard. The vision is a dream, symbolizing the realization of Ed's quest for escape.

The foundation for the strange sighting that gives him momentary release—prior to his more thorough liberation via the electric chair—is built in stages, both visual and narrative. On the image front, adding to the subtle saucer shapes dotting the Cranes' living room and Nirdlinger's department store is the conspicuous saucerlike flood of conic light that bathes Freddy as he unleashes his presumed winning strategy: Heisenberg's uncertainty principle. Together tapping the unknown, sight and sound present a picture of reality where certainties no longer hold court. In fact, things are so unsure that Freddy cannot even recall whether the man behind the theory is a Fritz or Werner.

In becoming a beacon of light for the lawyer, Werner Heisenberg's uncertainty principle becomes a tongue-in-cheek "pataphysical" construct. That is, it is a scientific theory woven into a work of art offering up an imaginary solution in a way that mimics and parodies modern scientific methods. Freddy is not interested in Ed's confession that he committed Big Dave's murder, and the blackmailing angle that titillated the attorney has now lost its luster. Replacing both Story A and Story B is subatomic theory, the variable Freddy thinks just right for the courtroom equation of reasonable doubt. Like *O Brother, Where Art Thou?*, the expressionistic *Man Who Wasn't There* probes the uncertainties of subjective truths in a post-Enlightenment age—here the specific time period is the dual-sword era of the advent of quantum physics.

This scientific course that Freddy and the Coens trod is a path worn by other absurdist artists in a similar quest to clutch something beyond the physical and metaphysical realms. It is a playful avenue aimed at showing that life in the modern era is not as certain as was previously thought—science too has its illogical bits. Artist Marcel Duchamp, a pioneer in cubism and ready-mades, for example, appropriated pataphysics in a piece that uses non-Euclidean geometry to poke fun at France after it introduced the metric system.[33] The Coens trot out Heisenberg's theory for their cinematic exploration of "facts" in a courtroom drama where uncertainty by way of reasonable doubt is the cornerstone of a defense team's strategy. Freddy's preferred arguments turn deeply ironic when, despite the film's intense focus on it, doubt is the main element missing from Ed's dealings with the judicial system. Without it, Ed becomes the ultimate alien booted out of the known world into the uncertain realm of death. By the end, the satire slyly casts a shadow of doubt on a draconian judicial system that could dole out so final and certain a punishment as the death penalty in a world as subjective and uncertain as ours.

FLYING THE COOP

But if doubt is missing in the courtroom where Ed's fate is determined, it is abundant in his musings at the film's conclusion, delivered in tropes that suggest alien abduction. "I don't know where I'm being taken. I don't know what waits for me, beyond the earth and sky," he says, adding that he is not scared.[34] He wonders if there will be less uncertainty in the place he is going to and, adding more grist to the possibility that he is gay, he imagines being able to tell Doris things he hasn't been able to express to her here.

From the start the barber seeks a way out of his existential lock. He doesn't like being the barber, so the opportunity presented in the dry-cleaning venture might be a way. It's not just employment, though, from which he needs release. A hen-pecked husband whose wife is cheating on him, he needs a way to stop the discord of his marriage, too. Early on, he admits to finding peace at church, and the ending plays on the idea of a heavenly if not quite a religious deliverance. Birdy's piano music also offers release, and art sprinkled throughout the film explores catharsis. Escape is also intimated through a linguistic patchwork of bird references.

A background conversation in the barbershop is a sonic complement to the *Life* article that Ed peruses. As he leafs through a spread on UFO sightings at Roswell, there is an off-screen colloquy about an "Early Bird special." The men's difficulty remembering the term calls even more attention to it. Tolliver tells Ed that what has brought him to town is "a goose, friend. I was chasing

The music of Scarlett Johansson's character Birdy offers Ed Crane escape. (Credit: USA Films/Photofest © USA Films)

a wild goose."[35] At different places, the term "fly-by-night" is flown into the soundtrack. Tolliver first uses it to defend the legitimacy of his business to Ed. "This is dry cleaning," Tolliver insists, "this is not some fly-by-night thing here!"[36] Ed echoes the phrase, trying to convince himself that Birdy, whose piano teacher is Mrs. Swan, is no fly-by-night musician.

Ed's name, much like his character, works on a split level. On the one hand, crane references a wading bird, which intimates his need for flight. On a more allusive level, Crane recalls Marion's surname in Hitchcock's *Psycho*. Ed, like Marion, wants to flee his present situation, but money is an obstacle. So, like Marion, Ed chooses crime to overcome that hurdle. In Marion's case it is stealing money from her boss; in Ed's case it is blackmailing his wife's boss. In both instances, these shortcuts temporarily unbind the characters from money-pinched existences until their plans backfire with fatal consequences.

After Marion steals money to solve her romantic problems, she has a change of heart, but it comes too late—she has crossed paths with a psycho killer whose personal demons instruct him to kill her. In Ed's case, his ill-gotten dry-cleaning funds tear down his barriers to freedom, but his flight from barberdom is short-lived. Big Dave won't let him flee, but Dave's offensive—launched in pursuit of his own freedom—backfires too. After Ed kills Big Dave and Doris kills herself, Ed becomes first chair at work and turns his attention to the aptly named Birdy.

Ed first talks to Walter's daughter Rachel, who prefers her nickname "Birdy," at the Christmas party where she is off by herself playing the piano. Drawn toward the music, he is also likely attracted to her isolation and likes the fact that she actually recognizes him. Eventually, like the puff from a cigarette, Birdy's music wafts across his senses and brings him the peace he has trouble finding elsewhere.

After Ed's hopes of being a silent dry-cleaning partner vanish along with Tolliver, Ed hatches another money-making idea: managing Birdy's musical career. This pie-in-the-sky plan starts to reveal Ed's cracks. The first time they chat she tells him that she is not particularly fond of music. The apathy of the fledgling pianist does not matter much to Ed, however, because his desires have little do with her and everything to do with him. "I could afford to charge less than the usual manager," he says in voice-over, "not having to put up a big front like a lot of these phonies. And I could be with her, enough to keep myself feeling OK."[37] Thus, his management offer would give him a better job, get him out of his barbershop grind, and perhaps have a hetero-normative effect on him through a Lolita-like relationship.

Ed arranges for her to have an audition, but the exclusive teacher finds her playing ordinary. He tries to convey to Ed that while she hits notes accurately, her playing lacks heart. Ed is dismayed, but Birdy reiterates that she's not interested in music as a career. On the car ride back to Santa Rosa, she verbally thanks him for setting up the audition and then offers to show her appreciation sexually. When Ed fends off her advances, he drives them off the road and Crane and Birdy actually fly. As they soar together in slow motion, Ed ponders time and the mysteries of hair. Then he dreams.

Though sleep is often a form of escape, Ed's dream is a recapitulation of his life as a barber. While he sits passively, Doris aggressively dismisses a salesman who tries to sell a modern driveway to the man of the house. Inside, she pours herself a drink and then she and Ed sit on opposite ends of the couch. Ed starts to say something, but she cuts him off and tells him she's all right. When he awakes, Officer Persky (Christopher Kriesa) and Officer Pete Krebs (Brian Haley), who had told him about Doris's arrest, now charge him with murder.

Both times Ed encounters the detectives he is coming out of sleep. In the first instance, he is snoozing at work; in the second, he is awaking from a coma. As they do the first time around when they gripe about getting such a dull assignment, they provide comic relief. "Are you awake?" Persky asks, thus initiating silly banter and confusion over whether Ed is conscious or asleep. "His eyes are open," Persky goes on. Taken together, the two lines recall both *Barton Fink*'s "I'm awake now . . . My eyes are open" lines and the exchange between Tom and Tad in *Miller's Crossing* when Tom grouchily tells Tad, "I am awake," and Tad counters, "Your eyes were closed."[38] Tom finishes the conversation with "Who're you going to believe?" and then gets up. Paralleling the detectives' confusion over levels of consciousness is the viewer's understanding of the story.

The Man Who Wasn't There, *Miller's Crossing*, and *Barton Fink* all deal with limits to knowledge and the expanse of belief and how easily the latter can be taken for the former. In *Barton Fink*, much of what we see is the activity in Barton's head. But without many of the signs that normally indicate someone is dreaming, we can easily mistake our belief for knowledge and muddle through the surreal film. *Miller's Crossing* also explores the realms of uncertainty even choosing to end without revealing motive. *The Man Who Wasn't There* echoes these themes. Here, both the collective unconscious, as probed in flying saucer imagery and alien visitation stories, and dreams have the power to give flight and to frighten—again, it's the duality of bound.

A boy swimming at a waterhole finds Tolliver's car, says Ed, as we see a boy glide underwater toward the vehicle. Tolliver's body sits in the driver's seat, his toupee still loosely attached but sticking straight up from his head, swaying in the currents. The visuals allude to Charles Laughton's surreal *Night of the Hunter* (1955), in which a wife's body is found underwater similarly positioned in her car. The Coens' scene is ironic in that Tolliver's business plan of washing without water ends up being all washed up for him and Ed anyway. (The article in *Life* suggests that someone is pursuing dry cleaning.) These kinds of neo-noir twists play off of Laughton's nightmarish fairy tale and self-consciously layer in irony and humor. Ed douses his American Dream when he kills Big Dave, turning it into a nightmare with a bit of help from Dave who has killed Tolliver. Like UFOs and technology, dreams can be freeing or confining—and confusing.

Freddy describes the facts surrounding Ed's involvement in Tolliver's murder as the "chaos of modern art."[39] Though Ed claims to be innocent of everything save a little blackmail to fund his silent partnership, Ed's narration paints in layers of confusion. A telling line conjures up revenge: "I knew the ten grand was going to pinch [Big Dave] where it hurt, but Doris was two-timing me and I guess, somewhere, that pinched a little too."[40] His remark is fleeting, but it acknowledges jealousy, and in the end Doris's and Dave's deaths placate such feelings. Such admission pokes holes in Ed's blamelessness. Later, he strikes a similar chord when the prosecutor argues that Ed is a master manipulator and Ed concurs that "some of [what the attorney argued] was close to being true."[41] In the end, Freddy's postulation that "the facts had no meaning" along with Ed's own mixed-up version of things serves up reasonable doubt to the viewer.[42] Whose is the real story—Freddy's, the district attorney's, Ed's—is impossible to tell. There is reason to question them all. Thus, Freddy's comment to the jury that the closer they look, "the less sense it would all make," applies to the film audience, too.[43] The film puts the act of observation on trial and concludes that visual knowledge is deficient at best.

MODERN TIMES

The film's dark portrait of 1940s Santa Rosa shows times are a-changing, with lots of conflict between the old and the new. Part of this is shown through the transformation of the middle class to the consumer class—modernism means "buy," a difficult prospect for the likes of a barber. Dave talks about good times for retail. Nirdlinger's throws a Christmas "push" party. Ed talks about his modern conveniences—a gas hearth, garbage grinder, and icebox. In his dream, a traveling salesman hawks a tar driveway to replace the old-fashioned peastones. Spending is au courant, and purchasing power signifies rank.

Freddy is introduced at Da Vinci's restaurant, ordering a gigantic meal of poached eggs, steak, flapjacks, potatoes, juice, coffee, prairie oysters, and fruit salad. Freddy makes clear that Ed is buying, but he orders nothing for himself. The obstacle of money is obvious. Freddy's explanation of his legal bill makes his feast look like a tiny midnight snack. Freddy's upper-class consumerism stretches Ed's means, ultimately doing him in.

Like the other major characters, Freddy is depicted in front of a mirror, but rather than suggesting duality, the image denotes vanity. Even his mirror's irregular shape, distinct from Ed's rectangular one and Tolliver's and Doris's round ones, is showy and fancy. Freddy's tastes in food and design are upper crust. The art associated with him is also elite. Freddy stays at the Metropole in the Turandot suite. The high art of Italian opera contrasts with the film's Italian working-class immigrants, characterized by Doris and Frank—Ed's family.

Throughout, music points to contrasts and tensions between the Old World represented by formalism and the New World and its emerging free form. The opening piano strains set a formal tone, a tenor that establishes an old-fashioned feel to a place on the cusp of change. It also cues us to the cross-pollination of noir and melodrama that will occur. At the Christmas party the clash between tradition and modernity comes across through the counterpoint of jazz and classical music. The chaos of modernity is visualized at the Nirdlinger's dance party where dancers swing and twist to the modern beat of jazz. Ed observes these movers and shakers, and then he retires upstairs to where Birdy sounds out a different meter, one that is marked by formalism. Framing the film is a Beethoven piano trio that subtly alludes to Ed's love triangle. The formal, classical framework belies the chaos of "modern art" that is Ed's story.

Ed is Modern Man adrift in a modernity he can't quite come to terms with. His imperfect marriage, representing the new age, is sharply contrasted with the traditional familial bonds portrayed at the wedding reception. The disparity between the new and old ages is drawn in loosening family ties. During the celebration of marriage Ed and Doris feel like fish out of water. She copes by getting drunk and Ed, feeling distant and invisible and as out of place as ever, simply observes. But in the midst of it all, Doris's relative Constanza (Rhoda Gemignani) commends Ed's occupation: "Barber, right, it's a good trade."[44] With the rest of the world snobbishly looking down on the blue collar workingman, the Italian aunt sees good in it. It is the only positive comment regarding his job. Their lack of children, however, is not so good. Constanza's reprimand of their childless marriage implicitly casts doubt on Ed's masculinity through the implication that he is unable to get her pregnant.

Ed and Doris are childless adults who tend to their jobs and other (sexual) affairs, but not so much to each other. The modern family as exemplified by the Cranes is a sharp departure from the traditional representation of the many aunts, uncles, and cousins running about at the family picnic. The tight-knit, multigenerational group of immigrants expresses a joie de vivre missing in Ed and Doris's life—and from Santa Rosa in general. The reception and its pastoral setting—one of the few upbeat slices of life in the entire film—provide a stark contrast to Santa Rosa's enveloping gloom.

If Ed is Modern Man, Frank is Family Man. Riding the pig, playing with the children, and winning the pie-eating contest, Frank enjoys the social institution of family. Such familial commitment sets up his no-holds-barred legal help for Doris. "This is what family is for, Ed. This is when you come together," Frank says.[45] To get her the best defense possible, he mortgages the shop. Despite such brotherly love and assistance, though, strangely, we never see brother and sister interact. Even at the picnic, they are barely in the same frame together, never mind engaged in a conversation. It's a bizarre disconnect that questions Ed's reliability as a narrator—along with Frank's pie-eating trophy that seems a bit much for such a reception. In the end, Frank's family ties break him, and one is left to wonder if such an end is simply just desserts for the man the narrator pegs for a blabbermouth. At length, all of Ed's nemeses are broken by the end.

Doris is the opposite of Frank when it comes to family. She doesn't like her Italian roots and wants to distance herself from them. Her ambitions and upward mobility may offer an explanation as to why. She "hates wops," she tells Ed.[46] They represent the old ways, and she's a modern woman. She cannot stand looking backward, preferring to move forward, onward, and upward. Thus, she enjoys Big Dave, who offers her the chance of escape—both professionally and domestically. She is Modern Woman, after all, someone with a career who loves what she does. But Big Dave's tawdry secrets and lies will dash her hopes for the high life.

A number-cruncher who loves her job, Doris is a working woman in an age when females, especially wives, were encouraged to leave their wartime posts and return to their kitchens and families. Though her real-world contemporaries in large numbers eagerly did, Doris does not. A pragmatist, she likes her job both for the precision and freedom it offers. That freedom is intellectual (she's a mathematician), sexual (she is sleeping with her boss), and practical (it gives her buying power). When we first meet her, she is opening a Nirdlinger purchase presumably purchased with her 10 percent discount. Doris represents a new breed of wives and women: a thinker, worker, and buyer. Her strength and independence collapse, however, after her arrest. When she is whisked away from her comfortable world of certainties, she sinks in the quicksand of unknowns.

MODERN MANQUÉ

Over the course of the film, the formalism, most strongly expressed by the Beethoven music, gives way to Ed's modern art of confusion. Subtle cracks spread through his story like alien tendrils wrapping round him. His experience models the societal structures that are starting to collapse in the Modern World—such as traditional gender roles. Twice Ed is asked, "What kind of man are you?" Freddy suggests Ed is Modern Man, and that implies, the film suggests, a diminishing masculinity.

Most of the modern males in Ed's story, not just the "pansy" Tolliver, lack virility. Sure, when Big Dave thinks the gay dry cleaner has crossed him, the bigoted bombast makes sure the dry cleaner's wild entrepreneurial goose chase ends in a cooked goose scenario. But despite killing Tolliver and having a macho epithet, Big Dave is not all the he-man Ed supposes him. Dave's weapon, for instance, is a dame's knife, which Dave uses on cigars but Ed uses for murder. Indeed, when Ed and Big Dave fight to the finish, the barber is the victor. While a Nirdlinger partygoer believes he has seen Ed in ladies' wear, at the Cranes' dinner party, Big Dave actually wears an apron. While doubt abounds, possessing both feminine and masculine traits is a clear duality in *The Man Who Wasn't There*.

In spite of the fact that Ed and Dave are drawn as opposites and even adversaries, the two husbands have more in common than Ed lets on. For instance, though Dave lies about his macho war exploits, his actual desk job puts him closer to Ed's 4-F status than his faux war stories. Like Ed, Big Dave has his job courtesy of his wife, a fact reflected in the names of both workplaces. Nirdlinger's department store like Guzzi's barbershop incorporates each wife's maiden name. In short, both men strive for independence through business ventures of their own. Dave wants to open "Big Dave's Annex" while Ed sees potential satisfaction in a silent partnership in "Tolliver's" dry-cleaning store.

Ed has women problems even before Tolliver shows up. He is married to a "lovable bitch," as McDormand describes her, who wants to be with someone else.[47] After Tolliver walks into Guzzi's for a haircut, exposing to Ed his baldness under his wig, Ed starts thinking about Tolliver's proposition of cleaning without water. Later, as he lathers up and shaves Doris's leg, silently performing his obligatory, depilatory tasks, his mind is abuzz with thoughts of dry cleaning.

Ed acts on those thoughts and extorts money from Big Dave, effectively killing several birds with one stone. The cash gives him an in with Tolliver's enterprise, which will allow him to untether himself from his wife's family business and his humdrum barber job. Furthermore, he robs Doris of the comptrollership Dave was going to award her with in his new store. Thus, Ed squashes Doris's career plans and sends ripples of discord into her and Dave's relationship. Put differently, Ed's move offers as much an opportunity to change the dynamics of his marriage as his job. Blackmailing Dave undercuts Doris as both a sexual being and a workingwoman. Thus, Ed's actions could be those of an *homme* fatale.

Ed admits thinking that Doris "and Big Dave were a lot closer than they let on" and later that the affair pinched.[48] Since Ed takes Dave's money rather than fighting him over the affair, Big Dave wonders what kind of man Ed is. The implication is that such a tactic is more feminine than manly. Later, Frank poses the same question to Ed, "What kind of a man are you?"[49] He, too, forgoes waiting for an answer and attacks Ed. The incident causes Ed's mistrial, which in turn leads to Ed's death sentence. The sequence of events begs the question, what is Frank so bent out of shape about? As posed by Big Dave, who has found out that Ed is his blackmailer, the question makes sense. But what has Frank discovered about the kind of man Ed is? The answer to that question is left unresolved.

With so much uncertainty pervading the events of the story, it's interesting to note that Ed's initial voice-over is quite precise. In the opening narration, for instance, eight numbers are trotted out for the viewer. After the camera shows the barbershop is street number 43, Ed complains that Frank's chattiness might be interesting to an eleven- or twelve-year-old, but not to an adult. On the wall behind Frank's station is the ad asking for "15 minutes a day" to become a "new man." He goes on to describe the shop physically— 200 feet square with three stations but only two barbers—then he explains it took Frank's father, Guzzi, thirty-five years to save enough money to buy the place. Later, when they have to sign the shop over to the bank to pay Freddy, Ed says it took Frank's father thirty years. This discrepancy, granted it is not a script error, shows Ed can be capricious with the facts.

Returning to the question of gender and the movie's central question about Ed's breed of manhood, we see at the end that Ed's makeover peaks, along with his feminization, when his legs are shaved at his execution. The reversal is notable. The barber receives a shave rather than gives one. And it's not his face removed of hair, it's his legs—a woman's place for a shave. Ed is such a "deeply closeted gay man," as *The Nation*'s Klawans surmises, that he is unable to admit it to himself, but his absurdist story reveals snatches of his feminized persona.[50] Borrowing from noir styles, *The Man Who Wasn't There* cleaves closely to science fiction themes of alienation and sexuality. Nontraditional gender roles and deviant sexual behavior abound in science fiction, from mandatory promiscuity in Aldous Huxley's *Brave New World* to the sympathetic treatment of homosexuality in Theodore Sturgeon's *The World Well Lost*, and group marriage in Robert Heinlein's *Stranger in a Strange Land*.

The way Ed spells things out, he and Doris are polar: Doris deals with numbers whereas Ed is the word man. He claims to talk little but as the narrator, he is all-talk. In the end, we also discover he's a writer—or at least, he's penning his story for a magazine. From the onset, at least this one point is crystal clear—he uses an awful lot of words, including numbers, to tell his tale.

Ed and Doris are visually wedded at a bingo night at a local church. Ed is not crazy about the game, but for Doris, bingo is like heaven on earth. She plays with multiple cards and pays strict attention to each one as the number-letter combinations are called out. Making the numbers work is one of Doris's main means of satisfaction. Ed's satisfaction, on the other hand, comes through manipulating words. He too cooks the books, so to speak, to score a paycheck from the men's magazine and alleviate both his money and masculinity problems.

RAISING CAIN

Literature specifically and art more broadly are presented as escape routes, and, as often happens in Coen films, this thematic track is aroused in dialogue. In telling the jury, "You may look at these lines and see only the chaos of a work of modern art," Freddy gives away the film's own dabblings in modernism.[51] Words are the paint that Ed uses to create artistic mayhem, and thus all kinds of literary references make a showing.

Tony Shalhoub introduces the jury to "Modern Man" by way of the uncertainty principle and modernism. (Credit: USA Films/Photofest © USA Films)

Readers of hardboiled writers like James M. Cain and Raymond Chandler—"poets of the tabloid murder," as Edmund Wilson called them—might recognize some of the movie's proper names.[52] For instance, the name of Tolliver's hotel is a small Chandler homage: The Hobart Arms is the name of Phillip Marlowe's apartment house in *The Big Sleep* (a story referenced in *The Big Lebowski*). Another nod to these dark poets comes via Freddy Riedenschneider's last name, an appellation used in author W. R. Burnett's novel *The Asphalt Jungle*, subsequently a 1950 film noir directed by John Huston. Nirdlinger, the family name of Big Dave's wife, comes from the femme fatale in Cain's *Double Indemnity*. In the film version of the novel the Nirdlinger character's name was changed to Dietrichson, a name close to the medical examiner's Diedrickson surname in *The Man Who Wasn't There*.

The crime fiction these loose referential strands point to informs Ed Crane's character and his story. "Cain's stories nearly always had as their heroes schlubs—losers, guys who were involved in rather dreary and banal existences—as the protagonist," said Ethan Coen. "Cain was interested in people's workaday lives. . . . We took that as a cue."[53] In addition to prompting the film, literature is an important narrative focus that helps give it a modernist bent.

Depicted is a late 1940s society that has not yet embraced—or been engulfed by—TV and instead is enraptured by printed words. Not a TV or even a radio can be spotted in the Cranes' living room—but a *Collier's* sits atop a pile of magazines. Where *Fargo* spotlighted an image-saturated society plastered with televisions, *The Man Who Wasn't There* portrays a reading culture. Frankie learns from the paper the Russians have the bomb. Doris is immersed in her magazine during her bath. As Ed strangely questions why people cut their hair, a natural part of themselves, the eyes of the little boy who is under Ed's scissors remain glued to the pages of his *Dead-Eye Western*.

The magazines and newspapers filling the screen are more than mere window dressings. They are clues to Ed's mode and method—he is a modernist painter, swirling words around his canvas to approach the experimentation, freedom, and unpredictability of modern art. A close look at the *Life* article on Roswell and UFO sightings, for instance, brings the widespread narrative havoc briefly to the surface in black and white. Rather than excerpts of strange, first-hand abduction stories like Ann's, the article is plastered with repeated illogical words and phrases, all pointing to indeterminacy. Here are a few examples: "widest possible latitude is being allowed to more carefully assess all salient points," "given questions regarding result determination," "theories have been advanced which suggest a combination of causes and effects," and "imponderable absolutes provide a foundation for examination of forays into these realms."[54] Like Ed's entire narrative and Ann's conspiracy theory, the *Life* snippets above all else push uncertainty and absurdist touches to the fore.

Literary references abound throughout the film. Doris keeps then cooks the books. Ed describes the judge who sentences him to death as "going by the book."[55] When the medium Ed visits describes a wife far different from the one he has described, he says disgustedly, not sarcastically, that "she was reading me like a book."[56] This idiom is used to imply that one understands precisely what another is doing. If Ed has been truthful, his tone and phrase applied to the medium do not quite compute, prompting the inference that maybe she is telling the truth and Ed has created a false depiction of her. Such mayhem abounds in Ed's experimental art.

The many internal stories, which would normally advance a plot, here create pandemonium—or experimentation, if considered artistically and stylistically. Ed does not need to include Frank's nonstop persiflage about catching fish or when to choke an engine, but he does, despite his disparaging remarks about gabbers. Ed needs their words to tell his story. Rather than create a unified whole, as traditional literature would warrant, the many internal story strands foment discord, supporting Freddy's theory of knowing less the more one looks and Ann's statement about knowledge being a curse.[57] Both ideas fall under modernist thought.

Another way modernism enters the film is through the disruption of time. The first of these occurs when Doris is passed out drunk after the wedding reception. After Ed takes her into the house and helps her to the bed, narrating Ed begins to tell the story of how they met on a double blind date. His recollection is interrupted when Dave calls him requesting a meeting. What follows is a jumble of time—a rather strange occurrence for a narrator who should have control over the story. This disjuncture is another pataphysical device that unmoors us from certainty. Ed momentarily abandons his first-date story and goes to the store. After killing Dave he returns home, takes the spot on the bed he had occupied before the call, and resumes his story. He includes the emasculating detail of Doris asking him to marry her and concludes with: "We knew each other as well then as now."[58] While such a statement might prompt the viewer to recalibrate his knowledge of the narrator, certainly, such a narrative interruption should give us pause.

The other main example of disrupted time—an attribute of modernism—ties into the idea of missing time associated with aliens, UFOs, and abduction stories. When Ed and Birdy get into the car accident—and the two birds finally fly—he explores philosophical notions of time: "Time slows down right before an accident, and I had time to think about things. I thought about what an undertaker had told me once—that your hair keeps growing, for a while anyway, after you die."[59] On the one hand his observations reveal an obsession with hair from someone who doesn't fancy being a barber. His musings on time that capitalize on uncertainty also recall his earlier ruminations on hair as one of life's mysteries. During the accident Ed picks up on this strand and again ponders what makes it grow before going on to link it to the soul. "I thought, what keeps it growing? Is it like a plant in soil? What goes out of the soil? The soul? And when does the hair realize it's gone?"[60] From there, he moves on to the uncertain realm of dreams.

The irony of his subsequent dream about Doris is that it recapitulates his unsatisfying life with her. She is as unpleasant in the dream as she was in the movie's "real" parts. And she reveals nothing to him about the afterlife. It's another piece of the modernist puzzle that gets us no closer to understanding and gives us more unknowns.

The more we look, the more it seems that Ed's story veers toward modernist pulp fiction. Contrasted with the traditionalism and formalism of Beethoven's piano sonatas and Mozart's arias that blanket the soundtrack are the disjointed story lines in dingy hotel rooms, a teenager's bedroom, and a prison cell. Each individual story strand looks like the kind of narrative fodder from the pulp pages that gave the crime genre its pulp fiction name—the cheap paper that the books were printed on. Yet, the little details that don't match or add up in the end, the gaggle of liars that round out his story, the tangents into skepticism and alien saucers, and the string of murders that his story touches off all point to an elaborate tale Ed spins for the men's magazine—modern, absurdist art.

What kind of man is Ed Crane? Ed is an alien among his fellow Santa Rosans who spins a yarn about getting ahead by leaving his scruples behind. His change is forecast ever so subtly in the newspaper clipping on the mirror at Ed's station. It is the type of advertisement found in the back pages of the kind of magazine he is writing for. Picturing a man whose crooked leg contributes to an effeminate stance of a pinup girl, the ad boasts, "I'll prove I can make you a new man!" This is precisely what Ed's story does. It transforms him out of his existential angst and into a new man, one who gets his legs shaved instead of shaving others', and one who finally bounds away from this world we know.

Toward the heavens, away from his drab existence as barber, Ed can become the guy from the title—"a man who wasn't there," a fictional character in a sensational men's mag article. He throws off the trappings of his middle-class existence for a story as sensational—and lurid—as one that might grace *Muscle Man* or *Wonder* and achieves life-everlasting at least in readers' imaginations. Unloosing himself from his barber role ironically propels him into the ultimate freedom and unknown—death.

In his final analysis, Ed says he achieved an understanding at the end of the road that he hadn't been able to find along the way. "While you're in the maze, you go through willy-nilly," he tries to explain, "turning where you think you have to turn, banging into dead-ends. . . . But get some distance on it, why, all those twists and turns are the shape of your life."[61] Such weavings also form the shape of a plot—and create the texture of his artwork. It is modernist metafiction—it's nothing but nothing about itself.

WRAP: UNIVERSAL TRUTHS

As with many of the Coens' films, the universal truth pursued in *The Man Who Wasn't There* is the power of lies—or fiction by way of doubt. Freddy implores the jurors to question the prosecutors' "facts" because, he argues, the modern world is too disordered for "facts." Jumping off Heisenberg's theory about not being able to measure the path of a subatomic particle without influencing it, the film suggests that even things at the atomic level, too, might not be as clear-cut as we think—like narratives and art. Thus, the film becomes modern art.

The announcement that we are in deep tongue-and-cheek land comes early, when Ed confesses he is a churchgoer—on Tuesday nights for bingo. It's a game of chance that perfectly weds the oil-and-water couple: numbers cruncher Doris and Ed who's a one-time scribbler. Her numbers and his letters collide in the film like a game of chance—or bingo.

Once again, *The Man Who Wasn't There* sets up a dialectic between knowing and believing. The film lures us into believing what we think we know and then throws a monkey wrench into such "knowledge" by Ed's final admission that he's telling his story to a men's mag. So what is the truth? Ed finds peace through telling his narrative. His redemption comes from giving form to the twists and turns of experience. Truths can be carved from lies.

The power of the story is once again the alpha and omega in Coen land. The narrator is a one-time writer who pens for a sensational magazine. In the end, Ed's story throws off the determinate for the indeterminate. Like all his story's characters, Ed disappears into the great unknown, thus fully taking on the persona of a man who isn't there. He becomes the work of art he has created, slipping into the great aesthetic unknown of characters postdrama. "The greatest trick the Devil ever pulled," says a character in *The Usual Suspects*, "was convincing the world he didn't exist."[62]

NOTES

1. Coen won in a tie with David Lynch for *Mulholland Drive*.
2. The film was actually shot on color stock and then desaturated in postproduction.

3. *The Man Who Wasn't There*, DVD, directed by Joel Coen (2001; Universal City, Calif.: Universal Studios Home Entertainment, 2002).

4. *The Man Who Wasn't There*, DVD.

5. *The Man Who Wasn't There*, DVD.

6. *The Man Who Wasn't There*, DVD.

7. *The Man Who Wasn't There*, DVD.

8. *The Man Who Wasn't There*, DVD.

9. Karl Miller, *Doubles: Studies in Literary History* (New York: Oxford University Press, 1985), 10–14.

10. *The Man Who Wasn't There*, DVD.

11. *The Man Who Wasn't There*, DVD.

12. *The Man Who Wasn't There*, DVD.

13. *The Man Who Wasn't There*, DVD.

14. *The Man Who Wasn't There*, DVD.

15. *The Man Who Wasn't There*, DVD.

16. *The Man Who Wasn't There*, DVD.

17. *The Man Who Wasn't There*, DVD.

18. *The Man Who Wasn't There*, DVD.

19. *The Man Who Wasn't There*, DVD.

20. *The Man Who Wasn't There*, DVD.

21. Vincent Brook and Allan Campbell, "'Pansies Don't Float'—Gay Representability, Film Noir, and *The Man Who Wasn't There*," *Jump Cut: A Review of Contemporary Media*, no. 46, www.ejumpcut.org/archive/jc46.2003/brook.pansies/index.html (accessed July 20, 2006).

22. Ethan Coen and Joel Coen, *The Man Who Wasn't There* (New York: Faber & Faber, 2001), vii.

23. Brook and Campbell, "'Pansies Don't Float'—Gay Representability, Film Noir, and *The Man Who Wasn't There*."

24. Stuart Klawans, "Static Electricity," *The Nation*, December 6, 2001, www.thenation.com/doc/20011224/klawans (accessed July 21, 2006).

25. Coen and Coen, *The Man Who Wasn't There*, ix.

26. *The Man Who Wasn't There*, DVD.

27. *The Man Who Wasn't There*, DVD.

28. Donald Spoto, *The Art of Alfred Hitchcock* (New York: Anchor Books, 1992), 124.

29. From the production notes for *The Man Who Wasn't There*.

30. *The Man Who Wasn't There*, DVD.

31. *The Man Who Wasn't There*, DVD.

32. C. G. Jung, *Flying Saucers: A Modern Myth of Things Seen in the Sky* (Princeton, N.J.: Princeton University Press, 1979), 14.

33. Jonathan Williams, "Pata or Quantum: Duchamp and the End of Determinist Physics," *Tout-fait*, issue 3, (2000), www.toutfait.com/issues/issue_3/Articles/williams/williams.html (accessed January 21, 2006).

34. *The Man Who Wasn't There*, DVD.

35. *The Man Who Wasn't There*, DVD.

36. *The Man Who Wasn't There*, DVD.
37. *The Man Who Wasn't There*, DVD.
38. *Barton Fink*, DVD; *Miller's Crossing*, DVD.
39. *The Man Who Wasn't There*, DVD.
40. *The Man Who Wasn't There*, DVD.
41. *The Man Who Wasn't There*, DVD.
42. *The Man Who Wasn't There*, DVD.
43. *The Man Who Wasn't There*, DVD.
44. *The Man Who Wasn't There*, DVD.
45. *The Man Who Wasn't There*, DVD.
46. *The Man Who Wasn't There*, DVD.
47. From the production notes for *The Man Who Wasn't There*.
48. *The Man Who Wasn't There*, DVD.
49. *The Man Who Wasn't There*, DVD.
50. Klawans, "Static Electricity."
51. *The Man Who Wasn't There*, DVD.
52. William Preston Robertson, "Prince of Darkness," *Guardian*, April 15, 2001, film.guardian.co.uk/features/featurepages/0,,472454,00.html (accessed January 5, 2006). Robertson has done voice work for the Coens. In *Blood Simple*, he is the radio evangelist. He also does various voices in *Raising Arizona*, *Miller's Crossing*, and *Barton Fink*.
53. From the production notes for *The Man Who Wasn't There*.
54. *The Man Who Wasn't There*, DVD.
55. *The Man Who Wasn't There*, DVD.
56. *The Man Who Wasn't There*, DVD.
57. *The Man Who Wasn't There*, DVD.
58. *The Man Who Wasn't There*, DVD.
59. *The Man Who Wasn't There*, DVD.
60. *The Man Who Wasn't There*, DVD.
61. *The Man Who Wasn't There*, DVD.
62. *The Usual Suspects*, DVD, directed by Bryan Singer (1995; Santa Monica, Calif.: MGM, 1999).

• *10* •

Intolerable Cruelty and *The Ladykillers*:
Spoils or Oh Brothers, Where Art Thou?

Intolerable Cruelty and *The Ladykillers* are the first two films directed by the Coens from material created by others. Both deal with the pitfalls of greed. In *Cruelty* George Clooney and Catherine Zeta-Jones want to nail each other's assetts. (Credit: Universal Pictures/ Photofest © Universal Pictures)

In *The Ladykillers* Tom Hanks (right) plucks blasted bills out of the air, joined by (from left, clockwise) Tzi Ma, Ryan Hurst, and J. K. Simmons. (Credit: Touchstone/Photofest © Touchstone Pictures)

> Marylin Rexroth: They bought Massey's argument. If I lied or cheated and was with Rex only for his money, then he shouldn't have to give me any.
> Sarah Sorkin: Well, that makes no sense. Why else would you put in all those years?
>
> —from *Intolerable Cruelty*

> "Think of the riches, Lump, that you and I alone shall divide! Recall the dream of wealth untold that first drew you to this enterprise!"
>
> —Professor Dorr (Tom Hanks) from *The Ladykillers*

> "The man who cannot laugh is not only fit for treasons, stratagems, and spoils; but his whole life is already a treason and a stratagem."
>
> —Thomas Carlyle, *Sartor Resartus* (1831)

PREVIEW: SPOILS OR OH BROTHERS, WHERE ART THOU?

*S*ince breaking onto the cinema scene in 1984, the Coen brothers have established themselves as connoisseurs of the visual, who produce a film about every two years. Less known is that in between feature filmmaking, they keep their creative muscles toned with side projects. They executive-produce friends' features, such as Terry Zwigoff's 2003 *Bad Santa*, starring Billy Bob Thornton, and even dabble in advertising. Football fans who tuned into the 2002 Super Bowl likely saw a Coen-produced ad for tax prep company H&R Block. "We felt this commercial was relevant to our filmmaking style," said Joel Coen, who added (presumably) facetiously, "We have always been fascinated with the mysteries of the tax code and with the people who struggle so mightily to plumb its depths."[1] In the spot, which incorporates a snippet of the Beatles' "Tax Man," a man reads, in an excruciating monotone, various pieces of the tax code from an enormous tome reminiscent of Mussburger's appointment book and the number cruncher in *The Hudsucker Proxy*.

Script doctoring is another regular gig for the brothers. They did uncredited rewrites for *Bad Santa*, for instance.[2] Two other jobs that began as rewrites turned into directing projects: *Intolerable Cruelty* (2003) and *The Ladykillers* (2004). After originating nine idiosyncratic films, the Coen brothers, known for heavy borrowing, finally turned to adoption. *Cruelty* and *Ladykillers* became the first two movies directed by the Coens from material originally written by others. The original *Cruelty* script was written by Robert Ramsey and Matthew Stone. *Ladykillers*, on the other hand, is an update of—and vast departure from—the Oscar-nominated William Rose screenplay that Ealing Studios produced in 1955 with the redoubtable Alec Guinness in the lead role. Spurred by box office darlings George Clooney in *Cruelty* and Tom Hanks in *Ladykillers*, the Coens' two comedies performed very well for Coen films, drawing $35 million and $39.8 million, respectively, in domestic receipts. But the question is, after twenty years of helping shape America's arty independent cinema, are the Coens testing the waters of the mainstream or are they diving in headfirst?

PREVIEW: *INTOLERABLE CRUELTY* (2003)

Intolerable Cruelty made the rounds before landing in the Coens' directing hands. The brothers had taken up the screenplay years earlier, as a rewrite job for Universal Studios. In the late 1990s, a stream of directors considered taking on the project, including Andrew Bergman (*Striptease*, 1996; *Honeymoon in Vegas*, 1992), Joe Dante (*Gremlins*, 1984), Ron Howard (*A Beautiful Mind*, 2001; *Apollo 13*, 1995), and Jonathan Demme (*Philadelphia*, 1993; *The Silence of the Lambs*, 1991). In 2002 Demme dropped the project. When Clooney took the lead, the Coens signed on to direct.

Cruelty weds Cupid and cupidity to yield a screwball comedy, humorously dissecting the business of divorce and the sport of lawyering while cutting a scathing portrait of Los Angeles glamour. Like *Barton Fink* and *The Big Lebowski* before it, the movie skewers L.A., depicting it here as a town corrupted by money lust. Mixing slapstick, black humor, and the Coens' inventive dialog, *Cruelty* takes aim at love in a land of TV and other surface attractions.

REVIEW: *INTOLERABLE CRUELTY*

An opening infidelity between two minor characters—Bonnie (Stacey Travis) and Donovan Donaly (Geoffrey Rush)—sets the tone for the rest of the movie: Stinking rich Hollywood is awash with infidelities and divorce proceedings, the art and craft of its denizens. Divorce is the cash cow of protagonist Miles Massey (Clooney) and the hoped-for ticket to independence of his arch rival, Marilyn Rexroth, coolly played by Catherine Zeta-Jones. Miles is a top-notch litigator adept at getting his clients the most bang for their buck when their marriages hit the skids. His prize creation, "the Massey prenup"— the subject worthy of an entire semester at Harvard Law—is the key weapon for (broken) family lawyers.[3]

Serial cheater Rex Rexroth (Edward Herrmann) hires Miles after his sexcapade is videotaped by private detective Gus Petch (Cedric the Entertainer). Despite Rex's bad behavior, he wants his wronged wife Marilyn to get nothing in the divorce. Miles eagerly accepts the challenge and sticks to his guns after meeting—and falling for—Rex's wife. Keeping his libido in check, he destroys her in court. Marilyn's lawyer, Freddy Bender (Richard Jenkins, in his second Coen role), easily convinces the court of Rex's infidelity, but Miles hauls in Heinz, the Baron Krauss von Espy (Jonathan Hadary). He reveals that Marilyn had secured his help to find a philandering husband. His testimony leaves Marilyn with nothing to show for her separation.

Marilyn, displeased with losing, plots revenge, taking a page out of her divorced friend's play book and aiming for Husband Number Two. Julia Duffy's Sarah Sorkin is Marilyn's best friend and the epitome of the Beverly Hills divorcée set. She lolls about a sprawling mansion with her peptic ulcer, living a bloated existence of money but starved of love.

Miles thinks he might have a shot at Marilyn when she visits his office after the divorce. She has actually come to request his prenup. At her wedding, her new husband, oil tycoon Howard D. Doyle (Billy Bob Thornton), eats the prenup, declaring he completely trusts his new wife. Miles is impressed with Marilyn's brilliant move. Soon after, she divorces Howard, and Miles, who is still taken with her and assumes she is filthy rich, woos her. Their romance leads to matrimony and, thus, a signing of a prenup. On their wedding night, she rips it up, exposing her money to her new hubby. Really, she is double-crossing the love-struck attorney for his fortune. She in fact is dirt poor, having hired an actor to play the part of her rich, oil-tycoon husband.

After discovering her scheme, to save professional face, he hires a hit man to kill her. But then her first real and really rich husband Rex croaks, making her loaded. When Miles learns of her change of fortune, he tries to stop hit-man Wheezy Joe (Irwin Keyes) but can't reach him. So he and his right-hand man, Wrigley (Paul Adelstein), set out to stop the murder. It turns out they're too late—Marilyn has discovered their plot and doubled their offer to Wheezy Joe, who now is looking to kill *them*. They are fortuitously saved when the asthmatic killer mistakes his gun for his inhaler and draws his last breath with a shot to the mouth.

At their divorce negotiations, Marilyn and Freddy prepare for the final killing: the money. But when Miles offers up reconciliation, Marilyn rips up the prenup, and the two reunite. The movie ends on a new TV show hosted by voyeur-extraordinaire Petch, who introduces couples destroyed by infidelities caught on film. So while Cupid's arrow sends Miles and Marilyn into each other's arms, the satire's arrow cleaves romantic notions in two, making marriage and greed the primary targets of this modern screwball comedy.

LOVE IS A BATTLEFIELD

The title *Intolerable Cruelty* suggests the viciousness of the satirical attack on modern love. Revenge, lies, and violence are the tactics of cutthroat adversaries waging war in a movie where Cupid's bow and arrow are the first line of offense. Launching the title sequence is a cartoon Cupid shooting a dart. The projectile soars past the credits for Clooney and Zeta-Jones and into a heart, breaking it in two. Such visual foreshadowing, we soon find out, points less to the idea of broken hearts than to a deconstruction—if not the destruction—of romance and the divorce industry.

The rest of the credit sequence, designed by frequent Coen collaborator Randall Balsmeyer, strews the battlefield of love with iconic clip art of cupids and yesteryear's lovers. "We thought that the best way to set up the story would be to start with a reminder about the myth of true love and marriage as an institution that's forever," said Balsmeyer.[4] With Elvis's "Suspicious Minds" driving home the point with lyrics about being trapped in love, the animated cut-outs of old-fashioned love turn cheeky. The punch line comes at the end of the sequence. What looks like a love letter unfurls to reveal a legal document: the all-important prenup, both armor and ammunition for spouses-to-be who want to protect themselves and their stuff should love last shy of forever.

A matrimonial ambulance chaser, Miles has a vested interest in spousal "cruelty." His goal is to make a killing in the monetary sense, and his main weapon is his prenuptial agreement. Put differently, Miles reaps the spoils from the battlefield of love. As his tailored suits, sports cars, and multiple houses indicate, he thrives on others' romantic losses. Fortunately, he is unburdened by morals, so he can command the courtroom like a general and decimate his opponents with wild, fictional versions of events: For instance, he suggests that a cheating wife claim abuse when none has occurred. In the end, we are supposed to believe that somehow love has miraculously warmed the cockles of his otherwise cold, money-grubbing heart. His transformation from cutthroat misanthrope to true love is one bitter pill for the viewer to swallow.

More than just an attack on romance, the movie is a feisty if uneven assault on Los Angeles nihilism, something of a recurring theme in the Coen canon. *Cruelty's* black "romantic comedy" is set in a land where romance is dead, greed is flourishing, and savage business practices are de rigueur. Beverly Hills is an incubator for naked cupidity and a hotbed of selfishness. It is where Marilyn and her girlfriends marry for money and Miles and Wrigley choose murder over losing their jobs and reputation. Were the movie a more straightforward, conventional romantic comedy, the Coens might well be out of their element, for their films tend to favor violence over sex (*Miller's Crossing*), intimation and cutaways over hot and steamy romantic encounters (*Blood Simple, Barton Fink*), and psychedelic fantasy and practical procreation over old-fashioned love (*The Big Lebowski*). The possible exception is Marge and Norm in *Fargo*, whose domestic bliss offers a powerful counterpoint to the movie's otherwise bleak moral landscape. But exposing broken institutions is a Coen specialty, so satirizing today's commodification of love is prime Coen material—and where *Cruelty* excels.

The Coen brothers' films routinely probe the cracks in America's social systems. *Raising Arizona* and *O Brother, Where Art Thou?* cast doubt on the effectiveness of our penal system. *The Big Lebowski* questions the politics of war. *The Man Who Wasn't There* looks at our justice system and its hypocritical treatment of doubt. And *Barton Fink's* satire peels back the glamour of Hollywood's studio system to reveal a frightening workplace akin to slave labor. *The Hudsucker Proxy* takes aim at corporate America and the greed incorporated in Big Business. Avarice is a core subject of many Coen films and a vice, their movies show, to which both haves and have-nots are prone. *Cruelty*, set in a location thematically close to *Fink's*, pinpoints the pricks of love characterized by rapacity. Here, it's often the haves wanting more and fighting down and dirty for it. *Cruelty* is a fiduciary battle of the sexes that has little to do with romance or sex. It's a war of the worlds of spouses and attorneys fighting over a stash of cash.

Violence is both a cause and effect of *Cruelty*'s broken hearts. The opening scene sets the bloodthirsty tone for the sorry state of affairs—emphasis on affairs—in the Coens' solopsistic L.A. It all starts with the bellicose-titled song, "The Boxer," accompanying TV producer Donovan's drive home. In his bedroom, he discovers his wife's infidelity and naturally seeks revenge. But his gun is no match for the weapon she uses: his own daytime Emmy statue. The jab foreshadows one of the other prongs of the movie's satire: the television industry. The sleazy soap producer getting pricked with his status symbol smacks of poetic justice. Also, in Beverly Hills, a place overflowing with money and celluloid, it is no surprise that he drops his gun for his camera and shoots Polaroids of his backside for evidence in his now imminent divorce case. Taking pictures of his buttocks' puncture wounds kicks off the self-conscious touches to the L.A. dream factory—and his own touché to his cheating wife.

While Donovan and Petch use cameras as their secret weapons, Miles launches his petards with fighting words. For instance, he describes his career goals as the "ultimate destruction of your opponent."[5] He speaks in battle tropes, telling Donovan's wife Bonnie to "draw up a picture of your husband's net worth, a map of enemy territory."[6] Similarly, he invites Rex to make his office his "war room for the duration of the campaign."[7] What Ivan the Terrible, Attila the Hun, and Henry VIII all have in common, he explains to Wrigley, is not an article for a middle name but a lust for ultimate victory. "They didn't just win," Miles tells Wrigley moments before attacking the wronged "sex slave" Mrs. Gutman. "They destroyed."[8]

Miles tends to delegate when it comes to dirty work. He has Wrigley take pictures of Marilyn's date book and ultimately hires a hit man to kill Marilyn when he cannot figure out any other way to stop her from ruining him. But in the courtroom he is the star, and compromise and niceties are not parts of his legal strategy. After all, he's interested in one thing: making a pecuniary killing. But his hard heart becomes suddenly warm when he meets Marilyn, and her own stealth campaign to beat him at his own game threatens not just Miles's personal fortune but his law firm's reputation. When it looks like his foray into romance means a blow to Massey, Myerson, Sloan & Guralnick, the lawyers push aside the law and turn to crime. In fact, they only call off the hit after learning that Marilyn does have some money they can plunder, thanks to Rex who never changed his will nor lost his penchant for young women and trains.

As much as the court is a battlefield, it is also a stage on which Miles performs brilliantly. A primo storyteller, befitting a denizen of Beverly Hills, he engages his clients and the other courtroom spectators with often dramatic

Paul Adelstein, Edward Hermann, and George Clooney, from left to right, fire off their opening salvos in a divorce case. (Credit: Universal Pictures/Photofest © Universal Pictures)

fantasies. The first case establishes the cynicism at the heart of his courtroom performances. It begins during a trial in progress with Miles holding a side conversation with Wrigley. Between them sits their client, the supererogatory respondent (character actor Royce D. Applegate, uncredited). While his client's wife is recounting her sexual humiliation on the stand, Miles is outlining his midlife crisis woes—he has too many cars and houses so he's not sure where to spend his money. The juxtaposition between Miles's rude self-absorption, his client's impassiveness, and the wife's deadpan delivery of salacious details is biting. When it's time for Miles to address the court, he clobbers the poor wronged woman with a "David and Goliath" story about her tennis pro. Here we see the film's title—"intolerable cruelty"—applies as much to the lawyers as to the unfaithful husbands and wives.

As he so rudely spells out in court, Miles is bored with his job. He takes on Rex's provocative, all-or-nothing case because it offers a real challenge and a merciless finale: He must disprove the reality of the husband's blatant infidelity caught on videotape. His interest in the case is piqued further when he meets and is smitten by the luscious Marilyn, a worthy contender. She is to marriage what Miles is to divorce: They are both "carnivores." Following the official divorce meeting between the Rexroths, Miles applies some version of "don't ask, don't tell" to the law and takes his client's wife out for dinner, furthering what appears to be romantic interest. Before we learn that the date is merely a decoy for Petch to do some picture-taking, we witness a dinner that shows, while they are not yet lovebirds, they are birds of a feather—no-holds-barred, win-at-all-costs players who deal in matrimony for wealth and independence.

At dinner, Miles orders them both steaks, setting in motion a meat-eating conceit the two will carry throughout the scene. When he double-checks on her status as a carnivore, she picks up on the bald double-entendre and runs with it: "You have no idea. . . . You may think you're tough, but I eat men like you for breakfast."[9] As in *Miller's Crossing*, where multifarious animal references help define a Hobbesian setting of presocietal anarchy, *Cruelty's* verbal landscape is strewn with critter metaphors. Marilyn elaborates to Miles that she plans to "have [her husband's ass] stuffed and mounted" so that her "lady friends [can] come over and throw darts at it."[10] When Miles concludes she is a "man-hater," she wittily retorts, "People don't go on safaris because they hate animals."[11] Savannah or jungle, *Cruelty* is loaded with fauna.

In addition to her strategic duplicities, Marilyn employs attack dogs. Her Cujo-like rottweilers chase her cheating husband Rex away from the house and into his car. Her standard poodle bites Miles's hand in the Las Vegas elevator. The baron's more froufrou pet, Elzbieta, is not an attack dog. But when the baron insults the cheating husband, Rex—a satyriasis with a canine appellation ("Rex, sit," he is told in court)—assaults both the baron and his chichi lap dog.[12] Animals peppered in conversations serve as social ranking. Before the ink is dry on her divorce papers Marilyn's girlfriends describe the eligible bachelor they want her to meet in piscine terms. Their talk begins by describing what he does. First he is in fish. Then, emphasizing his net worth, they amend that characterization with the explication that he is fish. Finally, Sarah indicates that he is top of the line: "He's tuna," she trumpets.[13] Miles, on the other hand, is a schnauzer in Marilyn's view, until her friends correct her impression. Eventually Miles (and then Marilyn) becomes a "sitting duck," as he tells the ancient head of law firm Herb Myerson (Tom Aldredge). To save face, Miles hires Wheezy Joe who needs to know who the "pigeon" is.

While Marilyn and Miles talk safaris over dinner, the lawyer is already on the hunt. He invites her out not so much as a libidinous litigator but as a sneaky attorney who lures Marilyn away from her house so Petch can play both sides of the fence. That is, Miles hires the same videographer who videotaped her husband in flagrante delicto, to get the dirt on her. In the stills Petch takes of her address book, Miles finds Marilyn's "Tensing Norgay," his term for a person who helps someone achieve something great (like Mt. Everest climber Edmund Hillary's sherpa). As it turns out, Marilyn's marriage was anything but fair and square. Before tying the knot with Rex, she had gone man-hunting. The Baron von Krauss Espy testifies to the fact, proving that she married for money and was going for broke to land a divorce settlement that would be her passport to easy street. Miles nails her ass, in the parlance of the movie, preventing her from nailing her husband's. But this is only Round One, and Rex is only Marilyn's first spouse, an anomaly in her circle. In Round Two, Marilyn will trump Miles, who will fall for her lead-ons as surely as she fell for his decoy date.

"GOD IS DEAD"

Marilyn's friends, whom we meet poolside where Sarah holds court, are part of the divorce set, Beverly Hills's burgeoning social class. The uproariously unflattering portrait of this lounging elite puts a spotlight on the region's prevailing materialism. If husbands are routinely unfaithful cads or sexual perverts, women are financiers of sorts looking for "venture capitalist" husbands. Relationships in general are tenuous among these sybaritic women, whose focus is directed first and foremost on themselves. Claire (Kiersten Warren) is so self-absorbed that, as her friends chat, she examines her breasts as if considering a tune-up. She snaps out of her self-involvement with a guilty coughing fit when Ramona Barcelona (Mia Cottet) complains of trouble catching her "careful" husband cheating. Their priorities are further exposed when they try to set up a meeting time and they discover that between body wraps, hair appointments, therapy, and facial injections, they are too busy pampering themselves to make time for others. With everyone's self-interests so front and center, the line "God is dead" extends beyond Las Vegas and its no-fault divorces into Beverly Hills country. God is certainly missing from these ladies' lives, as well as from Massey, Myerson, Sloan & Guralnick.

Religion is a Coen staple that finds some form in each of their movies. Hell, for example, usually crops up metaphorically to designate wickedness, and fire routinely designates something evil is afoot. In *Blood Simple*, Marty and Visser's murders and double-crosses create a manmade hell visually alluded to by the fiery incinerator behind the bar. *Raising Arizona* features Hi's doppelgänger, a biker whose entrance and exit are marked by flames and who represents Hi's lust for crime. Corporate hell is the setting of *The Hudsucker Proxy*'s Big Business satire in which embers from sinister Sid's cigar set a fire that leads to the advancement of the force of good, Norville. *Barton Fink*'s blazing Hotel Earle reinforces the cruelty that can visit finks who inform on the wrong guy and who won't listen to cries of help from neighbors. In *O Brother*, while the innocuous devil of myth gives Tommy his musical chops, the movie's true villains—the Law and the Klan—do their dirty work with torches, burning crosses, and explosives until they are conquered by a government flood of biblical proportions.

Cruelty's hell is probably most in synch with that in *The Big Lebowski*, also set in Los Angeles, a place on whose door nihilism knocks loudly. In *Lebowski*'s 1990s L.A., "the smut-business" is mainstream, crooked porn kings are part of the establishment, art asymptotically approaches meaninglessness, and reality is hard to spot. Nihilists who "believe in nothing" but money terrorize the main character and his buddies, to the point of killing one of them over pocket change. *Cruelty*'s nihilistic tendencies similarly arise from a perverted belief in, if not quite worship of, material wealth, the alpha and omega of the Beverly Hills crowd. Before love makes a late—and rather weak—entrance in *Cruelty*'s final reel, L.A. is a place where prenups have replaced foreplay, good divorce settlements beat out good marriages, and love of money has uprooted romance. In other words, Beverly Hills—a heaven for avarice—is hell, and the beautiful creatures that inhabit the derelict locale are its comely devils.

Our introduction to this lowly place comes not via the main character or his antagonist but by way of a trio of double-crossed lovers: Bonnie Donaly, Mr. Gutman, and Rex Rexroth. They are minor demons in a universe controlled by the devilish Miles. He has the power to make or break the fortunes of the spouses who call on him for legal advice. In *Cruelty*'s cosmos help from Miles is akin to profane, not divine, intervention.

First burned is soap producer Donovan Donaly, an aging TV producer who blasts Simon and Garfunkel from his sports car. He arrives home to discover wife Bonnie interested more in the pool boy—we learn rather latish that they don't have a pool—than in her higher-on-the-food-chain spouse. Humorously, neither Donovan nor the pool boy seems like a great catch. Donovan garners little sympathy as the cuckolded husband wielding a gun. The young pool boy fares no better when he cries at gunpoint (think *Miller's Crossing*'s Bernie Bernbaum) and claims impotency, as if he would have chosen a tête-à-tête with Bonnie over a vial of Viagra. Ironically, Bonnie, the one most in the wrong, is the most likable, perhaps because she defends her lover by attacking his attacker with a daytime Emmy statue. She makes her getaway in her husband's Jaguar, "The Boxer" blasting from the stereo, as Donovan snaps photos of his buttocks for evidence of her betrayal and attack. This detail sets up the "nail your ass" theme and the overall opening establishes that this type of spousal backstabbing is the norm. Soon we will see it is Miles's bread and butter.

Miles's reputation as master of matrimonial massacre precedes him. When Marilyn's friends learn he is Rex's lawyer, they describe his expertise through the story of Muriel, a second wife who went up against Miles in divorce court and is now a McDonald's manager. It is hard to determine which is funnier, the fast-food detail or the fact that the woman must actually now work. Miles may be good at his job, but he and the divorce industry are also the brunt of caustic critique. Miles is self-centered. He is introduced via his vanity and obsession. In a close-up of his teeth illuminated blue, he talks on the phone with his secretary (Wendle Josepher, who has many TV credits) as he gets his teeth whitened. Several scenes later, in a quick take inside his office, Miles reveals how low he will go to win when he considers, with no compunction, depriving a special-needs boy of special-ed classes.

Though Miles's contumely is often despicable, his boss Herb is the epitome of darkness, a grotesque human specimen married to the job. Herb shows us the dark side of a life that has no meaning outside of its occupation. He is the monster that Waring Hudsucker feared he would become if he didn't unchain himself from such a destiny by flying out the office window to begin again. The horror-movie feel to Herb's scenes, one of which is a nightmare, gives the sense that the law firm is one of the movie's visions of hell where God is dead, as Nietzsche famously stated. Ironically, the practice of law in *Cruelty* is as devoid of legalities as marriage is devoid of love. Herb speaks of the law in religious, almost matrimonial terms, espousing a course of action that distinguishes between thought and deed: "We serve the law. We honor the law. And sometimes, we obey the law. But this is not one of those times."[14] Actually, lawfulness is never honored or served, and Miles's legal ken is questionable. Though successful, the Nietzsche-quoting Miles evidences a lack of knowledge when he keeps citing "Kirshner" during his meeting with the Rexroths. Freddy finally points out the case only applies in Kentucky.

The magazine *Living Without Intestines* slyly suggests Herb is someone living without the guts to apply morality to his work. Whatever law it is that they serve is not apparent in the firm's ethics, fairness, or general business practices. Fittingly, it is Herb who all but orders Marilyn's murder, which, of course, represents the greatest legal stretch the lawyers will make to ensure their professional standing. But though God may be dead in these environs, irony and comedy are not, and it is in the context of black humor that the murder-for-hire and other legal loopholes are explored.

COURT AND SPARK

Next to love and its stings and arrows, the law is the target of *Cruelty*'s barbs. If not a favorite subject of the Coens', legal issues get a lot of play in their work. Excluding movies that merely count criminals among their main characters still leaves *Raising Arizona*; *Miller's Crossing*; *O Brother, Where Art Thou?*; and *The Man Who Wasn't There*. These films explicitly tackle various aspects of jurisprudence, usually on some level of corruption or ineffectiveness. Here in *Cruelty* Miles and fellow attorneys baldly demonstrate that law is usually beside the point in the practice of their profession.

A spate of infidelities, offset by a playbook that twists facts, amount to an extended indictment of our judicial system. Bonnie, for instance, is obviously the cheater in her marriage. Yet when Miles gets her case, he makes clear that his plan of attack will be based on creativity and pure fiction. Despite all the evidence against her, including her own admission of an affair, Miles suggests that she is the real victim, conjecturing that Donovan slapped her around. She protests at every false claim he makes, but that doesn't affect his narrative. He even self-edits as he imagines the purely imaginary events, one bettering his previous choice.

> [Your husband] was at the time brandishing your firearm, trying in his rage to shoot an acquaintance—friend of long standing. . . . But if not for your cool-headed intervention, his tantrum might have ended this schmoe's life and ruined his own. As for the sexual indiscretion which he imagined had taken place, wasn't it in fact he who had been sleeping with the pool man? . . . Am I going too far here?[15]

The humorous critique of the divorce industry takes aim at all involved: lawyers, spouses, and their friends. Miles's competitor, Freddy Bender, is no better than Miles—it is obvious his primary goals are winning and getting paid. This is best evidenced through his revisionist history of the hit man, which follows the looseness of the law that Miles applied to Bonnie: "Nobody hired anyone to kill anyone. . . . Apparently, from what I can gather, a burglar broke into your house . . . intending to loot the place, uh, repented, became despondent over his lifestyle and shot himself."[16] Wrigley might seem a tad more above board than Miles or Freddy, questioning Miles's dinner-date decoy so Petch could steal into Marilyn's house. But he is a Miles in-training. Like Myerson he too lacks the guts to follow the law and soon helps hire a killer.

Marilyn's friends are rich, bored divorcées, who could be called career exes or men-hunters looking for their next victim. In their world, it is not just God that is dead; sex is, too. "Getting laid is financial Russian roulette," Sarah explains later on, and so she goes without.[17] Whether too much of it or too little, sex is a problem for the movie's characters—and it may be a problem that dogs the whole movie.

Cruelty crackles with quick, smart dialog modeled after screwball comedies like *Adam's Rib* (1949), *The Palm Beach Story* (1942), and *The Awful Truth*

Catherine Zeta-Jones and Julia Duffy lounge during a break from their battle of the sexes. (Credit: Universal Pictures/Photofest © Universal Pictures)

(1937). As *New York Times* film critic Elvis Mitchell put it, the movie is "a minor classic on the order of competent, fast-talking curve balls about deception and greed."[18] The battles of the sexes in and out of court fuel *Cruelty*. In fact, sparks fly more when Marilyn and Miles try to top each other's wits and court strategies than when they are amorous. So while some of their gender jousts hark back to the screwball classics, the film's acerbic look at love alongside today's sexual mores makes even the smartest dialog lack romantic luster after its first crackles. In other words, it's funny but empty.

When Miles serves up sweet talk about her beauty at their first dinner, Marilyn quotes Shakespeare to retort: "Dismiss your vows, your feignéd tears, your flattery/For where a heart is hard they make no battery." Again, though more disguised, she pulls out language of the hunt. Her hard-hearted lines come from the bard's "Venus and Adonis," a long poem deriving from the Greek myth. The story tells of the goddess of love lusting after the gorgeous young Adonis, who is more interested in hunting with his buddies than frolicking with her. The poem is a dialog between the two would-be lovers, who verbally parry over the competing forces of romance in the form of eroticism and friendship. Strutting his knowledge of verse, Miles rebuts her comeback with Christopher Marlowe: "Who ever lov'd that lov'd not at first sight?" This phrase is from "Hero and Leander," a poem about another set of Greek lovers, who conducted an affair by night under their families' radar. Though their penchant for Elizabethan poetry unites them, the words also serve as double-crossing weapons.

Miles quotes her Shakespeare lines in a strange attempt to impeach her during the Rexroth trial.[19] Her retort by way of Marlowe's love-at-first-sight lines leads to her downfall. Though she claims to have loved Rex from the start, we learn that he was merely her gold-digging target. This kind of back-and-forth, love-hate relationship is a stamp of the great screwball comedies, but the Coens do such a good job at grounding the plot in a loveless, godless hell, that it's difficult, if not downright impossible, to believe that love could win out. Miles and Marilyn can talk the talk through romantic verse, but walking the walk is a different story. *Cruelty* is like a throwback to the golden screwballs but with an overdose of acid and bile.

Unlike the classic screwball comedies of the 1930s and 1940s, where romance was evident under lovers' pointed barbs, *Cruelty* lacks the foundation on which to build Miles and Marilyn's romance. The Coens' crisp focus on skewering the divorce industry and Beverly Hills types leaves no room for love to breathe, let alone blossom. As film critic David Edelstein put it:

> The glibness exhausts you, and the Coens are emotionally so far outside their subject that *Intolerable Cruelty* is finally no different from most of the other dumb slapstick spoofs that pass for screwball comedy these days. The reason that many of us still treasure *The Lady Eve* (1941) and *Adam's Rib* (1949) after 50-plus years is that the people who wrote them were serious about exploring the issues of constancy and trust, and the jokes allowed them to raise the stakes in ways that most non-comic dramatists don't dare. The Coens are too armored by irony to take those kinds of risks. Cupid would need a rocket launcher.[20]

The Coens are enamored of irony but lacking in amour. George Cukor's *Adam's Rib* helps illuminate this difficulty.

The name *Miles Massey* may well be a minor tribute to this Cukor comedy, for *Adam's Rib* was based on the real divorce between actors Adrianne Allen and Raymond Massey. The Cukor film traces the course of a perfect partnership between married attorneys that nearly implodes when the two face off in court over an attempted murder. The foundation of their true love firmly established at the start allows for their ultimate reunion.

The movie pits strict, letter-of-the-law interpretations against liberal, heart-of-the-law ones, and examines true love by probing sexual mores and gender stereotypes. All of these subjects intersect at the main characters' relationship, which is pushed to its limits. Real-life lovers Spencer Tracy and Katharine Hepburn play the sparring attorneys who are keenly aware that each risk they take in court potentially jeopardizes their domestic bliss. In other words, the stakes are enormous both in and out of the courtroom. But unlike the wife (Judy Holliday) on trial for attempting to kill her abusive husband (Tom Ewell), Hepburn and Tracy's relationship is rock solid enough to survive a contentious courtroom battle.

By contrast, when Miles and Marilyn suddenly decide they are meant for each other, there is no basis on which to believe this change of heart, for heart is missing throughout. *Cruelty* spends so much time showcasing its titular subject that there is little room for romance to fit, and where it does turn up, it's not so believable or powerful. As Ben Walters writes in *Sight and Sound* about the final act, "When . . . the plot degenerates into a slapdash slapstick caper (pegged on a secret will and an asthmatic assassin), there's little to do but sit back and roll with the sight gags with increasingly contrived plot points of dubious motivation piling up against each other, emotional engagement isn't an option."[21]

Today's sexual mores present a hurdle for romantic comedies. Because sex is so prevalent in today's culture, finding clever, funny ways to broach what used to be an awkward, even taboo subject poses a challenge to modern filmmakers. In the past, romantic comedies used the uneasiness surrounding sex to fuel humorous situations. *The Major and the Minor* (1942), *Kitty Foyle* (1940), and *It Happened One Night* (1934) often spark from the liberties the films take with the established social—and sexual—order. Even under the Production Code, Hollywood's strict rules that governed what could and could not appear on film between the 1930s and 1960s, these movies presented electric situations that traded on pushing the limits of sexual propriety. In *It Happened One Night*, for example, much of the tension between madcap heiress Claudette Colbert and Clark Gable's newsman, who hopes to get an exclusive on the runaway daughter, derives from the bedroom they must share posing as husband and wife to avoid detection. The conflict intensifies as they develop feelings for each other and wish their pretend relationship were real.

With sex so much more open in today's society, *Cruelty*'s daring—like so many contemporary sex comedies—isn't so much bold as it is raunchy. Though there is some slapstick, *Cruelty*'s jokes tend to be verbal, but with heart so paltry in this land of self-love, it's tough to believe when a flame dimly appears. During their vaguely titillating dinner conversation when Marilyn tells Miles she wants to nail her husband's ass and mount it on her wall, Miles responds that they're looking for the same thing—"an ass to mount."[22] Then she tells him not to look at hers. The joke is, would such an instruction stop him? No, what would prevent him from lusting after her is his conceit, his cutthroat lawyer practices, and his love of money—traits that leave little room for love or even lust. In the end *Cruelty* is heavy on comedy but light on substance, especially when it comes to romance, which is all but eclipsed by an intense focus on "cruelty."

O BROTHER AND BEYOND

While *Cruelty* doesn't quite measure up to other Coen brothers' wholly original scripts, it displays some of their special touches. Most notably, it continues the fraternal filmmakers' practice of including a smattering of self-referential allusions. Foremost among these is a running homage to their cinematic song-fest, *O Brother, Where Art Thou?*, in which Clooney also stars.

Clooney is one of the main reasons the Coens signed on to direct *Cruelty*. "George Clooney, who we got to know on *O Brother*, read it and said he was interested in doing it if we were interesting in making it," Ethan Coen said.[23] Joel Coen elaborated: "With someone like George playing [leading man] Miles Massey, you suddenly see it could be a lot of fun."[24] Part of this fun arises from the way Clooney's Miles arouses his previous persona of Ulysses Everett McGill.

Ulysses Everett's gift of gab certainly carries over to his lawyer character in *Cruelty*, as does an obsession with his looks. Rather than fixate on his hair, like Everett, Miles focuses on his teeth. He is introduced talking a blue streak with his secretary while getting his teeth whitened. Before meetings, he does a quick check in on his dentition. Such a detail humorously characterizes Miles's fondness for himself. His vanity, like his powerhouse reputation, precedes him. And his teeth are the perfect feature for a carnivore.

A somewhat more veiled tribute to Clooney's previous Coen vehicle is the Socratic exchange between Miles and Marilyn on their first dinner date. Their question-filled conversation implicitly acknowledges a mode prominent in *O Brother*, a movie that features Clooney as a trickster convict whose creativity and cunning help him outrun vengeful lawmen. At the fancy restaurant while Miles himself is in trickster mode, luring Marilyn on a date so he can retrieve information from her house, he answers Marilyn's queries with questions—and vice versa. Their inquisition by candlelight culminates with an exasperated Miles wondering, "Don't you ever answer a question?" to which Marilyn responds, "Do you?"[25]

The most recondite reference to Clooney's *O Brother* character can be spotted in the Las Vegas setup shot. Just below the Caesar's Palace sign is a billboard welcoming Miles's group: the National Organization of Matrimonial Attorneys, Nationwide, or NOMAN for short. This is a clever tribute to both

Homer's *Odyssey*, in which "No Man" is a pseudonym for Ulysses, and *O Brother*, which applies the same epithet to Ulysses Everett. (See chapter 9 for more details.)

Names are important in Coen films, so it is a multilayered joke when Miles advises Wrigley to "start with the silly names" in his search for Marilyn's Tensing Norgay. From *Raising Arizona*'s McDunnoughs (which sounds like "dunno") to *Fargo*'s grim Grimsrud and normal Norm Gunderson, to Riedenschneider, Ulysses Everett, Delmar, Norville, Jesus, Hudsucker, Mussburger, and Lebowski, Coen movies present a spectrum of funny names. *Cruelty* is no exception. Choice names include Bonnie and Donovan Donaly, Ollie Olerud, Freddy Bender, Doyle Oil's Howard Doyle, and the two pieces des resistance: Sarah Batista O'Flanagan Sorkin and Heinz, the Baron Kraus von Espy. The judge's name Marva Munson is the name of the main antagonist in their following film *The Ladykillers*. And finally there is the "dog," Rex Rexroth.

In addition to referencing Clooney films, *Cruelty* also nods to other Clooney vehicles and similarly themed movies. Marilyn's smooth entrance to the casino in her red dress recalls a similar move by Julia Roberts in *Ocean's Eleven*, which also starred Clooney. The "love" speech Miles delivers to the attorneys gathered in Sin City is a take-off of Michael Douglas's blistering "greed" speech in *Wall Street*. And infidelity and a blurring of reality and fantasy come through *Cruelty*'s small *Mulholland Drive* tribute, David Lynch's 2001 surreal movie that tied with *The Man Who Wasn't There* for the Palme d'Or at Cannes. As if modeled after the scene in *Mulholland Drive* in which a husband returns home to find a workman's vehicle in the driveway and his wife with another man, Donovan discovers his wife's infidelity in a sequence shot and edited similarly to Lynch's. The Coens certainly did not invent self-referential moviemaking, but it is certainly a hallmark of their work and their cribs usually contain thematic tie-ins.

Dovetailing with its excoriation of the divorce industry is *Cruelty*'s critique of American television and voyeurism (which are thematic concerns in *Fargo* and *Blood Simple* as well). *Cruelty* looks at the insipid nature of reality TV and takes aim at its producers who hunt out people's private problems to display for public consumption and personal profit. Mixing one part of *Fargo*'s passive-viewing cautions with two parts of *Blood Simple*'s voyeuristic tendencies, *Cruelty* "nails" American TV's "ass," to use the film's patois.

Petch follows the footsteps of *Blood Simple*'s Peeping Tom PI Visser. Petch has a penchant for catching couples in flagrante delicto. As he tells Miles when he delivers him the 35mm film of Marilyn's address book, Petch prefers salacious videotape to still photography. His preference smacks of voyeurism. Indeed, he excitedly screens a new sex-in-the-office video for his football pals. His fondness for hidden cameras and their forbidden fruit sets up the movie's final rib: "America's Funniest Divorce Videos." Here, in a vague and poor homage to *Network*'s (1976) brilliant TV satire, *Cruelty* takes one last jab at the public's taste for prurience. The reality-cum-game show weds the opening infidelity to professional success, but as a coda to the lackluster romantic comedy it too fizzles instead of sizzles.

WRAP: LOVE OF MONEY

Cruelty's view is dark and cynical even as it closes on the bright lights of a TV set. Beverly Hills is awash with profits from people's misfortunes. If the divorce industry isn't frothing at the bit to seize a jilted lover's assets, then maybe a sleazy TV producer is salivating for a juicy voyeur video. From undercover videographer to game-show host, Petch has just the right credentials to make it in TV land: no ethics. The final scene harks back to the even darker view of television as a cultural inebriate portrayed in Sidney Lumet's cutting satire, *Network*. In *Network*, the evening news hour is transformed into a carnival act complete with a soothsayer and gossip columnist before becoming a shooting gallery to oust the once star anchor.

Things are not quite as blistering at the end of *Cruelty*, but the gist is similar. The sheen of TV land and Petch's upbeat persona pick up where Miles and his law firm left off. Donovan, who got nailed by both his Emmy statue and Miles's courtroom wizardry, is back on top, thanks to Marilyn's wiles. She engages his help to get back at Miles, and in the process helps him out of his economic backslide resulting from his wife Bonnie's divorce settlement. It is through him she gets a terrific actor to play her second husband. In the end his partnership with Petch promises riches from others' infidelities. The final scene masks the exploitation of matrimonial mayhem so engagingly that it might just look like a happy ending instead of a perverse statement on a society replacing love with schlock.

PREVIEW: *THE LADYKILLERS* (2004)

After years of unofficial remakes and postmodern cribbing, the Coen brothers finally produced an official remake. Naturally, they would be drawn to a film from England's Ealing Studios, famous for its black comedies and clever crime capers. But the fact that the script stemmed from a dream that screenwriter William Rose had might make it even more appealing to oneiric filmmakers like the Coens, who for the first time officially share credit on both directing and producing. Previously Joel has been credited with directing and Ethan with producing, but in reality both have codirected and coproduced all their films.

Though much is different from the original *Ladykillers*, the Coens' version retains parts of the 1955 version's satirical core but hardly any of its understated tones. Both the subject matter—crime as cure and money as cure-all—and to some extent the treatment also hew closely to other Coen works, such as *Blood Simple, Raising Arizona,* and *Fargo.* And thanks to its setting and religious content, there is some common ground with *O Brother, Where Art Thou? The Ladykillers* captures elements of the quintessential Coen cocktail in its dark, comedic morality tale concerning oddball characters with a lust for lucre and a penchant for violence. But some of the remake's cruder slapstick and toilet humor replace much of the wicked fun and quiet intelligence found in the more unassuming Ealing Studio production.

REVIEW: *THE LADYKILLERS*

As a gospel tune sets a religious tone, the opening credits roll next to a giant bridge under which a trash barge passes. The landscape broadens into a sleepy town in the Deep South, and an angry Marva Munson (Irma P. Hall) trudges to the police station to lodge a complaint. Before she can carp about her neighbor's loud hip-hop music, she has to wake Sheriff Wyner (George Wallace), who politely listens to her before "returning" to work.

Back at home, Professor G. H. Dorr (Tom Hanks) shows up at her door, wanting to rent a room in her boarding house, conveniently located near a casino. He moves in, and his friends visit under the pretense that they are musicians needing to practice. The basement becomes their "practice room" and criminal headquarters from where they can launch a heist. Dorr masterminds a plan to build a tunnel to the casino. Joining him in this endeavor are explosives expert Garth Pancake (J. K. Simmons), dumb jock Lump Hudson (Ryan Hurst), the General (Tzi Ma), and the casino worker and inside man Gawain MacSam (Marlon Wayans).

As the team builds a tunnel, a boom box plays their practice pieces. Whenever Marva visits them, they halt their work and run to their instruments so that by the time she comes down the stairs, they are poised as if in mid-rehearsal. Marva suspects nothing, but tensions flare in the group, especially between Gawain and Pancake, who invites his girlfriend Mountain Girl (Diane Delano) to join the group without asking. Their rivalry continues throughout the caper.

Once the tunnel is complete, they put their plan into action. Gawain works from the inside, while the others pack the cash and move it into Marva's basement. The heist is a success. Gawain mends the casino wall, and Pancake's bomb destroys their trail. But when the explosives go off, Marva, whom the men have tried to send off to a concert, is startled, and the group's slow unraveling begins. Professor Dorr tries to downplay her questions about the ruckus, barely succeeding when Pickles the cat runs out of the house with one of Pancake's fingers, a casualty of the blast. They recover Pickles, and Marva goes to her music outing, but all is not well.

Pancake wants a bigger cut of the loot not only because his girlfriend helped out but also because he is down one digit. No one agrees. Then, Marva discovers the money. When the men try to explain away the cash with a variety of excuses, she doesn't buy any of them, so they decide they must get rid of her. They draw straws and tough-guy Gawain gets the short one. But upstairs he finds he cannot bring himself to shoot her. When he returns to the lair, mission unaccomplished, he and Pancake fight and Gawain winds up dead. The gang dumps his body over the bridge onto a garbage barge passing below.

Pancake, still miffed about his lost finger, tries to steal the money, but en route to the getaway car, he is struck with irritable bowel syndrome. This stops him dead in his tracks and allows the men, who have discovered his betrayal, to catch up to and kill him and Mountain Girl. They dump the bodies, again over the bridge, onto a trash boat below. Next, the General tries to kill the old lady in her sleep but dies trying. They take his body to the bridge too.

Finally, just Dorr and Lump are left. Lump, dismayed that the professor deems him doltish, pulls a gun on Dorr and quotes from the original movie, "Who looks stupid now?"—a line also used in *Blood Simple*. He pulls the trigger only to discover the chamber is empty. Moments later, he is knocked over the bridge onto the boat passing below. An overly self-pleased Dorr smirks at this turn of events moments before he soars over the bridge when a dislodged gargoyle falls from the bridge and strikes him.

With all the men now dead, Marva goes downstairs again to find the money. Unsure where Dorr and his friends have gone, she concludes that they reconsidered their crime and ran away. She returns to the police station to turn the money over, but the police do not buy her crazy story. Believing he is humoring her, the sheriff tells her to keep the cash. She selflessly decides to donate the money to charity and sends fat weekly checks to Bob Jones University.

FINDERS, KEEPERS, LOSERS

The Ladykillers begins in the heavens, and then focuses on earth. The camera tilt is a forecast. From a flock of birds flying, the opening shot moves to a bridge gargoyle, its face contorted in a scream. A black bird flies into view and lands on the head. The shot moves to a bird's eye view above the bridge under which a trash barge emerges. By the end of the credit sequence, in just under two minutes, the movie has given advance notice of the plot's arc: There will be some to do about God, some comically Gothic elements, and a view toward hell.

Such a prophetic opening is familiar Coen territory and, like *Barton Fink* and *O Brother, Where Art Thou?*, *The Ladykillers'* introduction also gives a sneak preview of the finale. In this case, at the end a raven like the one in the opening alights on a gargoyle, knocking its stone head off its perch and onto Professor Dorr. The professor sails over the railing and onto a passing garbage scow's heap of trash, effectively following the camera's initial trail. Having engaged in nefarious deeds, Dorr, like his fellow thieves, travels a final voyage from earthly existence to waste removal. The movie's final shot is a reversal of the opening: It moves from the garbage scow en route to the island of trash, and then tilts up toward the sky. Such visual bookends evoke the hybrid idea of Christian karma.

The movie's often tongue-in-cheek religious elements, along with a change in setting, mark notable departures from the original. Other touches, such as the darkness at the door when the charlatan professor arrives, are truer to the original. As in the Coens' update, in director Alexander Mackendrick's original, when the professor (Alec Guinness) arrives at the boarding house of Mrs. Wilberforce (Katie Johnson), his silhouette and the minor theme on the soundtrack hint that trouble is nigh. Gothic sensibilities inform both films, but the original sticks with the secular kind while the update adds religious touches. In both films, the deep irony is that the bad men reap what they tried to sow when it comes to killing the old lady.

The Coens add a mix of divine and profane elements to their irreverent remake and elevate the Gothic influence. Such changes help to Americanize the satire while also complicating it, leading many a critic to wonder why. "The Coen brothers have given us the most perplexing oddity of their career: a weirdly pointless remake of the 1955 Ealing classic, transplanted from postwar London to the modern Deep South," wrote Peter Bradshaw in the *Guardian*, a paper often partial to the Coens' work.[26] And it wasn't just the British being protective of their own. Despite decent box office receipts, American critics generally found it "never lives up to its promise," as *Rolling Stone's* Peter Travers put it.[27] Even the *New York Times* review, which acknowledged some inventive sparks, called it "a bit of a throwaway."[28]

One reason Mackendrick's film works so well is the unlikely foil to Guinness's weird, snaggle-toothed professor. Katie Johnson's Wilberforce is a vulnerable, unsuspecting, at times annoying old lady, given to occasional kvetching. It is her character and dead-on performance, alongside Guinness's

Alec Guinness and Katie Johnson in Alexander Mackendrick's original *Ladykillers*. (Credit: Touchstone/Photofest © Touchstone Pictures)

marvelous gargoyle, that power much of the brilliant comedy. Indeed, several critical turning points stem from her actual incorporation into the crime, which in the original is an armored car heist. In Mackendrick's version, the gang engages Mrs. Wilberforce's help in transporting the stolen money they left as luggage at the train station. So, directly under the noses of the police who are searching for criminals trying to flee the town, an elderly Brit least likely to have committed the crime strolls in and picks up the stolen loot. Clueless about the men's affairs, she slowly carts the money home, the bandits agonizing over her indirect route.

Once she discovers their crime and threatens to tell the authorities, the stakes shoot up. Before they decide that the only way to get away scot-free is by killing her, they turn her pointed finger around and tell her she's just as culpable as they since she moved "the lolly"—a word that sounds especially funny coming from her mouth. Suddenly, their ethical dilemma becomes hers. In one of the most hilarious scenes, after they scare her temporarily into not telling the authorities lest she be arrested too, a completely flustered Wilberforce tries to get rid of a policeman at the door. Acting suspicious, frightened, and very much unlike her normal self, she parrots what the gang has told her to say, using their jargon like "buzz off." Such nuances and her great contrast with the thieves are priceless, ironic gems missing from the Coens' version.

Still, Hanks and especially Hall, who won the Jury Prize at Cannes, get props for turning out great performances. And just to listen to the Coens' dialogue can be sheer joy. Writing what they know—which is the U. S. of A.—the Coens move the action to the American South. As Charles Taylor wrote in Salon.com, "The Coens have come up with a good funny idea in realizing that the only contemporary American equivalent to proper old Victorian pensioners are the righteous black church ladies who . . . are quick to tut-tut anything that reeks of disrespect to them."[29]

Despite the good equivalent, the two female leads are worlds apart, and the cultural shift is huge. Stronger, louder, and much bulkier than the diminutive Mrs. Wilberforce and her quiet eccentricity, Marva Munson is less vulnerable and much saucier. In fact, the Coens' movie exchanges the original's British reserve for saucy American bombast, a detail pointed to in the relocated Saucier, Mississippi, setting. Besides a more impertinent tone across the board—except from the peculiar, disingenuously polite professor—other major differences include a casino burglary over a truck heist, beefed up roles of the four supporting thieves, and an explicit if not quite neat battle between good and evil. Greed is the primary sin here, and materialistic appetites buy folks a one-way ticket to the dump. In the end, the movie suggests, perhaps it might just be better to leave one's wallet in El Segundo.

THE GOLDEN CALF

The Ladykillers is a tongue-in-cheek, roguish morality play that takes a look at the destructive capabilities of mammon. The first scene introduces wisps of the economic problems plaguing a town that's a little too sleepy—the snoring sheriff is soundly asleep at the proverbial wheel. A scan of the sheriff's office reveals a cell door open and its unused key gathering cobwebs, indicating there's not too much crime in Saucier. But the next visual clue questions whether that's the case or not. A campaign sign suggests the law might just be too lazy to catch any criminals: "Help reelect Sheriff Wyner. He is too old to go to work."[30] Asleep on the job, the sheriff is about to be deaf to Marva's prophetic warnings. She comes in steaming about her neighbor but warns danger is about to disrupt their world.

Marva's loud entrance wakes up the sheriff, and in high dudgeon she reports a noise problem with the "hippety-hop" music blaring from her neighbor's new blaster. Though she grouses about the sonic pollution, her meandering conversation broaches ever so mischievously the movie's satirical target: capitalism run amok. The song her young neighbor insists on blasting, she details, is "I Left My Wallet in El Segundo," a 1990 hip-hop tune by the group A Tribe Called Quest. Thus begins the connection between hip-hop music and a lust for lucre. This link is forged during Gawain's first scene, set in the casino, and is scored to the hip-hop beat of "Another Day, Another Dollar" emanating from his boom box. The gold dollar-sign necklace he sports furthers the pecuniary theme. Later, after they have taken the money while Gawain patches up the hole in the wall, the El Segundo tune plays.

Besides subtly launching an affiliation between money and hip-hop, Marva's opening tirade touches on issues of race and religion. The problem is that her speech heads in so many directions that her hilarious detours—along with the authorities' patronizing attitude toward her—easily crowd out these thematic nuances. When she describes her neighbor's music, she shows her outrage over the hip-hop genre's use of the word *niggaz*.[31] Lumping together Jesus Christ, Martin Luther King, and the odd-man-out Montel, she decries such a civil-rights setback. She is so upset that though she vows to say the dreaded word only once as a reference she utters it a second time to drive home her indignation. For reinforcement, she tells the authorities that the songs are also upsetting her dead husband Othar. Such hilarity alongside serious issues like racism might lead us away from the scene's larger thematic tie-in of avarice. Her wanderings into religious territory, though, provide a bit more insight into the matter of greed.

Before she leaves, Marva warns the sheriff about being tried and found wanting. "Don't want that writing on the wall," she says.[32] He agrees with this offhandedly but she loses him with her next line that sounds like "many, many" something. It's difficult to catch her drift unless one knows Aramaic—or the Bible: "Mene, mene, tekel, upharsin" (Daniel 5:25). She exits raging against the "feast of Belshazzar," allusively launching a lightning-quick assault on blasphemers and moneygrubbers.

Like *Barton Fink's* incorporation of the King Nebuchadnezzar story, *The Ladykillers* draws on a narrative from the book of Daniel as a warning. Marva fleetingly mentions the story of the downfall of Belshazzar, the last Babylonian king whose demise was foretold in a strange graffito scribbled by a magical hand. The words appeared in the midst of an extravagant celebration the king was throwing for his lords during which he served wine out of golden goblets meant for the temple. Daniel alone can decipher the coded message: "It has been counted and counted and weighed and divided."[33] He goes on to explain it: God is angry at both the desecration of sacred objects and Belshazzar's generally bad, impious leadership, and the message is a prediction of the king's imminent downfall. That night, Persian invaders ransack the Babylonian kingdom, and Belshazzar is killed. Belshazzar's punishment for his greed and bad behavior cryptically augur what's in store for the professor and company.

Chances are that Marva's prophecies, unknown even to herself, go undetected by her fellow Sauciers as well as the audience. So in the first church scene the preacher fills in the gaps, spelling out the situation more clearly. After a rousing gospel number—gospel being the primary alternative to hip-hop—the minister talks of Moses coming down from Mt. Sinai with the Ten Commandments. Upon seeing the godless, golden-calf worshipers, he smites them. "To smite," explains the minister, "is to go upside the head because sometimes, brothers and sisters, that's the only way."[34]

The rest of his sermon connects thematic strands that the camera and Marva have dangled, namely bad deeds that will send one crashing down onto a trash heap. He talks of a civilization in decline that worships earthly things and

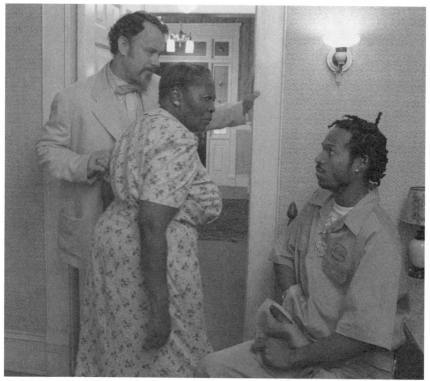

Tom Hanks tries to bridge the generation and communication gap between Irma P. Hall's old-school landlady and Marlon Wayans's hippety-hop bad boy. (Credit: Touchstone/ Photofest © Touchstone Pictures)

offers up smiting as a solution "to stop that decline and scramble back up to the face of the almighty God."[35] Not long after he conjugates the verb *smite*, Marva puts his preaching into action, smacking Gawain upside the head for talking about oral sex. More potent smiting follows among those who worship the golden calf. The professor and his gang are so destructively selfish that there's no need for the sheriff or minister to even get involved, for they end up smiting themselves in an effort to take out their perceived enemy: Marva.

As with Fink's dead-on forecasting, pretty much everything the minister lays out regarding sinners happens to the bumbling thieves. The preacher instructs against "worshippin' that golden calf, that earthly trash on that garbage island! That garbage island in that shadowland way outside the kingdom a God!"[36] In other words, those who worship money and other material things end up in a godless place on a garbage island, "where scavenger birds feast on the bones of the backsliding damned."[37] Sometimes the birds even help effectuate the downfall.

SOUTHERN-FRIED GOTHIC

Professor Dorr is the ringleader of the "backsliding damned," all of whom become food for the trash heap's scavenger birds. Unbeknownst to Marva, Dorr is her nemesis, the "stranger in our midst" who pretends to befriend her while really exploiting her, her house, and even her love of gospel.[38] Where Marva represents good, however imperfect, the garrulous professor personifies waywardness. The film plays with spookiness, Edgar Allan Poe, and Dorr's devilish aversion to the church, but his fatal flaw is his avarice with more than a soupçon of conceit.

Certainly, there is an overlay of a battle between good and evil. After getting along superficially the church-going Marva and the Poe-reciting professor lock horns over their vastly different worldviews when it comes to stealing money. Their failure to see eye-to-eye drives Dorr and his gang to attempt the ultimate sin of killing. But greed, not some intrinsic evil, is at the root of the motives, while Gothic elements create background dread where humor is never too far away. As in *Barton Fink*, a host of horror cues momentarily tease us away from the real meat of the satire: the worship of earthly things.

The gang of hoods in her basement wants cash and they devise a way to steal it from the gold mine that is the nearby casino. Like Belshazzar's feast, the casino represents the profane. It is emblematic of civilization in decline. It is a place for worshipping money. But evil floats into the picture in more storied ways, too, with a host of ghostly trimmings.

The Gothic blitz begins in the first minute with the gargoyle's appearance juxtaposed with the heavens. Next, a black bird, like an envoy of Poe, flies in. Soon comedy makes an entrance. Marva's house is a trove of comic-gothic items. Othar's portrait changes expressions, adding silly commentary to the ongoing action, a la the portrait gag in *Sullivan's Travels* (1941). Professor Dorr's shadowed entrance is preceded by flickering candles, as if a mysterious, dark breeze announces his presence. Marva's cat Pickles, whom she often calls "Angel," fears the professor, suggesting they are of opposite moral persuasions. And there's the root cellar whose dirt walls the professor likens to the crypts and catacombs of "the cinquecento." All in all, a host of familiar horror story details fill out the movie's "evil" side.

Running counter to these forces is the church-going Marva. While the professor's gang toils in the basement, blasting through its earthen walls, Marva praises the Lord and lifts her voice to heaven with gospel music. Unlike Mrs. Wilberforce's opposition to the original thieves, which is characterized by frailty and vulnerability, Marva's contrast comes through her moral rectitude and strong personality. Here is a woman who tries to live right. A miniature of Da Vinci's Last Supper hangs in the spare bedroom, and she regularly writes out checks to charity. Whereas the professor's speech is gilded by orotund erudition of ancient poems, Marva's conversations are informed by the Bible. In addition to quoting from Daniel, she knows about the Israelites' musical instrument, the khalil. She rarely fails to recognize a word, phrase, or point the prolix professor makes. One notable exception is for comic effect when Dorr suggests that in addition to the khalil, perhaps Othar liked to blow the shofar, which she denies as strongly as she might its homophone. Ultimately, she is the real deal, if imperfect. Professor Dorr is a fraud.

The professor is a wolf in sheep's clothing. As his bookish feints reveal, he's less Ph.D. and more, as Marva mishears, Elmer Fudd. His verbosity is sprinkled with mistakes. He misuses the word "cosseted." He introduces himself as a professor on sabbatical from the University of Mississippi in Hattiesburg. The university is actually located in Oxford; the University of Southern Mississippi is in Hattiesburg. While Marva probably should have caught his mistake, we learn later, in the movie's most final ironical twist, that details about schools are lost on her. Professor Dorr tries to assure her that he and his fellow musicians do not play modern music, like the hip-hop she loathes. Insisting that they play church music only, he adds that they play nothing more modern than the Rococo period, an interesting choice, for the highly ornate style was deemed too worldly and inappropriate in the Catholic Church's view.

Modeled after *The Ladykillers'* original professor, Dorr is the type of character the Coens love to create: a con that fancies himself an intellectual. Interestingly, Hanks never saw the original movie prior to filming so as not to imitate Guinness. What separates Dorr from other Coen cons, like *Raising Ari-*

zona's Hi or *O Brother*'s Everett, is his unrelenting belief that he is a cut far above the rest. While greed is his biggest sin, hubris is a close second. (Everett is vain but repents.) Dorr's demise is especially fitting because it checkmates his excessive pride, and is highly ironic, for it caps all the tie-ins to his beloved poet Poe. The Helen of the poem is not quite the unknown woman Dorr suggests. Poe's love poem, "To Helen," is an ode to the ideal woman, written in part about a family friend and in part about the famously beautiful Helen of Troy, whose face launched a thousand ships and sparked the Trojan War. In addition to harking to the Coens' previous film *O Brother*, many of the Poe lines link up with the trash barge the thieves use as a body dumpster: "like those Nicaean barks of yore,/That gently, o'er a perfumed sea,/The weary, wayworn wanderer bore/To his own native shore." Thus, the wayward thieves are borne over waters to the hell described in the minister's sermon and Poe's poem.

At the end, Dorr recites the final stanza, and again the poem connects to the story. The phrase "How statue-like I see thee stand" connotes the gargoyle on the bridge, while the line "Ah, Psyche, from the regions where Are Holy Land!" speaks to the movie's religious dabblings. Following his recitation, the raven, so emblematic of Poe, knocks the gargoyle off its perch and onto Dorr's head, sending him over the railing. His flapping overcoat makes him look like a bird in descent. Bridging the poem's mythical waters of ancient Greece and the movie's own trash heap of material excess, the death of the Poe-reciting professor is comic poetic justice. And Marva, unbeknownst to her, beats him and his entire gang at their own racket.

The professor is the "stranger in our midst" about whom Marva warns in the beginning but does not recognize when he shows up at her door. As in *Barton Fink*, the Coens' bad guy is the "good" character's main confidante. She doesn't even get it when the professor hides under the bed from the sheriff. She becomes most vulnerable when the professor and company try to do her harm just to keep the stolen money. But ironically what they wish on her befalls the professor and company. Their desire to get rich quick is not only what bonds the otherwise misfit team the professor assembled; it is what tears them apart.

The contrast between the professor's materialistic cravings and Marva's spiritual yens speaks to an underlying cultural chink: love of money. The two main musical genres represented in the film explore this defect, as does the dichotomy between Marva's religion and Dorr's secularism: Hip-hop music, which is used to spotlight material excesses, and gospel, whose focus is on less worldly pleasures. Two songs in particular illuminate competing desires in *Ladykillers*' universe: to give versus to get. "Let Your Light Shine on Me" illustrates Marva's aspirations and motivations, while "Another Day, Another Dollar" amplifies what arouses the professor and his gang. These songs help characterize the main difference between protagonist and antagonist. The punch line is that Marva, in trying to live an upstanding, selfless life, ends up supporting an institution blackened by racist controversy. Such misguided but well-intended action can throw our belief systems into check. Here's where there is some Gothic payoff.

In its embrace of the supernatural and the inexplicable, Gothic literature often looks at underlying societal fears caused by disruptions to wide-held beliefs, such as scientific findings upending religious positions. In *Ladykillers*, Gothic details create a foreboding atmosphere, suggesting that the professor spells trouble. On top of this, Marva's own dubious charity calls into question her lifestyle and choices.

Perhaps the satire's sharpest jab at American morality is a potshot at Marva's attempts to live a good, Christian life, especially in relation to charity. Ultimately, the film pokes fun at the strength she derives from her religion. She is justified in smiting Gawain for his uncouth sexual talk, and then she gives to Bob Jones University. For her part, her charitable giving helps reveal the imperfect morality play at work in *Ladykillers*. Creating such a morally divided and conflicted landscape, the Coens take the oh-so-British Ealing movie and Americanize it. But the ultimate twist capitalizes on money. In the original a running gag of an umbrella routinely left behind by the absent-minded Mrs. Wilberforce pays off with her decision to buy a new one—several, in fact—with all the loot she comes to inherit in the end. The Coens leave out the umbrella device and replace it with the running Bob Jones University gag, making the morality play imperfect. Though Marva selflessly gives to charity, her goodwill is in all likelihood misplaced. As the *Village Voice* put it, "Like George W. Bush, she's supposed to be oblivious to the bible school's racist history."[39]

RACES WILD

Though far less politically correct than *O Brother*, *Ladykillers* manages some commentary on America's racial divides. It exploits some stereotypes and bucks others and generally depicts a world where no one gets along. If whites and blacks often view the world differently, blacks from different generations don't understand each other either, and folks of all races face the same temptations and pitfalls when it comes to doing right and wrong.

Marva introduces the racial theme with her outrage over the word *niggaz* in the hip-hop song. The delivery of her complaint, especially when she repeats the abhorrent word she promises to say only once is quite funny, even as her point about the once-derogatory racial epithet is well made. In the 1990s the rap group A Tribe Called Quest, who own the song "I Left My Wallet in El Segundo," addressed the very issue in their tune, "Sucka Nigga," ultimately supporting its use as a form of empowerment or "endearment" earned from "embrac[ing] adversity."[40]

The generational gulf between Marva and young black males is pressed further through her interactions with Gawain. Gawain is the stereotyped, aimless black youth who is a prime candidate for criminal enterprise. He is shiftless, crude, and rude and has just the lack of skills needed to join the professor's motley band of thieves. When Gawain crudely mentions the performance of oral sex in front of Marva—whom, strangely, he later sees as a mother figure—the professor tries to keep the peace by chalking up the remarks to his age and the high libido associated with it. Marva, without missing a beat, retorts, "My youth I was in church, I wasn't walkin' around fiery. Youth ain't no excuse for nothin'!"[41] Fire again connotes corrupting forces, which Marva challenges with her religious convictions.

The real racial sparks fly when the ultra-liberal Pancake tries to get Gawain to straighten up. After starting out on the wrong foot, Pancake tries to smooth things with Gawain by touting his civil-rights efforts. Gawain couldn't care less about his liberal leanings or his activism, and their relationship somehow becomes even more antagonistic—an unsurprising outcome given Pancake's track record. (We first meet him on a TV shoot where he puts a gas mask on the lead dog in a commercial, causing it to die from asphyxiation when Pancake's mouth-to-mouth can't save him.) Gawain and Pancake's antagonism reaches a peak when the talk-tough youth cannot get himself to kill Marva. As they wrestle, Pancake summons the racist Bull Connor, infamous for turning water hoses and attack dogs on civil-rights activists. Shortly thereafter, the gun goes off and Gawain is the victim.

If the film's ironic punch line comes in the form of supporting an institution with a racist reputation, earlier racial commentary, especially in the casino scenes, provides the setup and context. Before racism plays out in the Bandit Queen's den of iniquity, more of Gawain's fiery temperament in the form of sexual harassment gets him fired, and the inside man is pushed out. Gawain tries getting his job back by pulling the race card, a strategy that backfires not because it would constitute fraud but because, as his manager (Stephen Root, who also plays a somewhat racist manager in *O Brother*) points out, the casino employs almost all blacks in its low-paying jobs. The point is obvious, for we have seen Gawain's coworkers. For instance, the large black casino worker, played by Walter Jordan, something of a Coen stock character, is a glutton who works at a place where people's excessive instincts tend more toward money than food. But the idea of gluttony alongside racism is in play. While *Ladykillers* points to some basic problems concerning the races from all sides, the movie also deals primarily with crime and rapacity in a color-blind fashion. Gawain gets his job back by applying Lump's winning strategy: a fat bribe. As elsewhere in the materialistic universe, and especially in the casino, money talks.

STEALING EALING ET AL.

Directing, Coen friend and fellow filmmaker Barry Sonnenfeld once said, is all about decision-making, and the Coens' choice to actually remake such a fine film to begin with might well leave fans wondering, why? As with *Cruelty*, the Coens' work on *Ladykillers* began as a writing job for a remake that Sonnenfeld was slated to helm. "The casting started with Tom [Hanks] actually whom we wanted to work with for some time," said Joel Coen at a 2004 Cannes Film Festival press conference. "Usually when we work on a script we write for specific actors. That wasn't the case with this [because] it started as a writing job, and we came to it as directors only after we were finished with the script."[42]

Just as *Cruelty* presented itself as another opportunity to work with Clooney, directing *Ladykillers* would be a chance to work with leading man Hanks—fresh blood. It turns out the feeling was mutual. "I'm a big fan of *Fargo*," Hanks told reporters at Cannes, adding that what he especially likes about the Coens is their unpredictability. "They'd just done some things I'd never seen before. . . . The fact that . . . you have no idea honestly what's coming means they have some skewed sensibility as filmmakers."[43]

Certainly, *Ladykillers* takes a skewed look at, among other things, race and religion, and steers the original Ealing satire into zany Americana where a Poe-loving imposter meets his match in a Bible-fearing smiter. With a raft of pop culture and literary references along with a boatload of toilet humor, the movie tries to appeal to all manner of viewership. For the toilet-humor crowd, there is irritable bowel syndrome (IBS). For those who like to chortle at sex jokes, there's Gawain and his lewd talk. American Lit–lovers can be entertained by Hanks's orotund recitations. For lovers of irony, there is the final twist of Bob Jones University.

For film lovers, there is, as usual with a Coen movie, opportunity to spot references to other films. While citing the motto for Las Vegas, the professor's "What we say in this root cellar, let it stay in this root cellar" also recalls the prison counselor's chalkboard message in *Raising Arizona*. The cat fetching Pancake's stray finger is reminiscent of the dog in Kurosawa's *Yojimbo* (1961) that tows a disembodied hand. This, in turn, recalls *Miller's Crossing*, which nods to the Kurosawa film and features an alley reminiscent of the one that Pickles trots past en route to dropping Pancake's finger off the bridge onto the garbage barge. The expression-changing portrait, as mentioned earlier, comes from *Sullivan's Travels*, an inspiration for *O Brother, Where Art Thou?*

Finally, there are all the sight gags, plot points, and dark humor that inspired the remake of Mackendrick's *The Ladykillers*, which earned screenwriter Rose an Oscar nomination for Best Screenplay. Producer Michael Balcon, who helmed the Ealing's production team renowned for its satires, described the studio's films as "comedies about ordinary people with the stray eccentric amongst them—little men who long to kick the boss in the teeth."[44] Such a description could also apply to the Coens' work: Jerry Lundegaard, with a father-in-law complex, and the underdog-who-wants-to-be-top-dog Johnny Caspar spring to mind—and perhaps to a lesser extent, the eccentric caricatures of the 2004 *Ladykillers* carved ever so loosely from the original.

The Coens' admiration for Ealing Studios can be gleaned through small tributes peppering their work. There's the stolen line "Who looks stupid now?" from *Blood Simple*. *The Man Who Wasn't There* borrows a trademark comic touch from Ealing: a final punch line. Ealing Studios' satires tend to end on a scene that transforms the viewer's understanding of the story in its final moments. For instance, in *Kind Hearts and Coronets* (1949), the ultimate freedom of the murderous main character is left hanging when he is called out of his cell to be exonerated but unwittingly leaves behind his confessionary notes. The final scene of *The Man Who Wasn't There* uses a similar plot twist to suggest that everything its main character has told us from his jail cell is fictitious.

Like their demonstrated fondness for America's great cinematic satirist Preston Sturges, the Coens' appreciation for Ealing likely stems from their own predilection for send-ups. Take *The Hudsucker Proxy*, for instance, the Coens' 1994 satire of Corporate America. Like the British studio's bold look at labor and business in *The Man in the White Suit* (1951), which features a lynch mob, a giant bust of the company president, and wall art depicting Capital and Labor, *Proxy* takes swipes at all involved in capitalistic enterprise, using each of these elements.

Moving *The Ladykillers* to the Deep South allowed the Coens to satirize again the pitfalls of capitalism as practiced in a place where too often results trump means. This familiar theme runs through many of the Coens' films, whose American satires expose hypocrisies while pointing to the value systems crumbling behind them—all without getting too moralistic. In broadening the original *Ladykillers'* scope to sketch in arch religious touches that hit below the Bible belt, the wider social view of the Coens' version delivers a setting at odds with itself. If the original British film showed a buttoned-up England easily upset by a group of bungling thieves that only a little old lady can foil, the Coens' film gives us an America fighting for its own soul amid greed, institutions (the gang and casino), and racism (satirically epitomized by Marva's well-intentioned but poor charity of choice).

WRAPS: COEN LITE

Both *Cruelty* and *Ladykillers* hold mirrors up to money lovers. In *Cruelty*, it's the upper class wanting more and doing just about anything to get it. In

Ladykillers, it's a group of lowlifes stealing cash and then trying to kill to keep it. Both films attack societies sharply focused on materialistic spoils without regard for the means, but the caricatures lean too closely to the grotesque. While there is brilliant dialog and funny jokes in both, they are more cookie-cutter Hollywood than the Coens' wholly original work. Whether a trend toward the mainstream or a diversion from their idiosyncratic craft remains to be seen, but hopefully these two movies are mere diversions in a body of work that has pushed the envelope of independent filmmaking.

NOTES

1. "Ad Isn't Taxing for Coen Brothers," *Boston Globe*, January 23, 2002, D-4. Ad is viewable online at www.ifilm.com/?sctn=collections&pg=superbowl2002.

2. Mark Olsen, "Going Commercial but Not Exactly Mainstream," *Los Angeles Times*, December 2, 2003, E-1.

3. *Intolerable Cruelty*, DVD, directed by Joel Coen (2003; Universal City, Calif.: Universal Studios Home Entertainment, 2004).

4. "Intolerable Cruelty," *New York Times*, www.nytimes.com/slideshow/2004/03/28/movies/20040328_CRUELTY_SLIDESHOW_1.html (accessed January 29, 2006).

5. *Intolerable Cruelty*, DVD.

6. *Intolerable Cruelty*, DVD.

7. *Intolerable Cruelty*, DVD.

8. *Intolerable Cruelty*, DVD.

9. *Intolerable Cruelty*, DVD.

10. *Intolerable Cruelty*, DVD.

11. *Intolerable Cruelty*, DVD.

12. *Intolerable Cruelty*, DVD.

13. *Intolerable Cruelty*, DVD.

14. *Intolerable Cruelty*, DVD.

15. *Intolerable Cruelty*, DVD.

16. *Intolerable Cruelty*, DVD.

17. *Intolerable Cruelty*, DVD.

18. Elvis Mitchell, "Film Review: A Lawyer's Good Teeth Help in Court and Love," *New York Times*, October 10, 2003, E-13.

19. Miles also quotes a line from *Julius Caesar* to Rex: "The fault, dear Brutus, lies not in our stars but in ourselves." In *Good Night and Good Luck,* the 2005 biopic of Edward R. Murrow, which Clooney starred in and directed, fellow actor David Strathairn, who plays Murrow, quotes this same line.

20. David Edelstein, "King George vs. Catherine the Great," October 10, 2003, slate.msn.com/id/2089688/ (accessed January 29, 2006).

21. Ben Walters, "Bringing Up Alimony," *Sight & Sound,* November 2003, www.bfi.org.uk/sightandsound/review/1143/ (accessed January 29, 2006).

22. *Intolerable Cruelty*, DVD.

23. Phillip McCarthy, "Cruel Hands," *Sidney Morning Herald*, October 24, 2003, www .smh.com.au/articles/2003/10/23/1066631572748.html (accessed January 29, 2006).

24. McCarthy, "Cruel Hands."

25. *Intolerable Cruelty*, DVD.

26. Peter Bradshaw, "We Woz Robbed: *The Ladykillers*," *Guardian*, June 25, 2004, film.guardian.co.uk/News_Story/Critic_Review/Guardian_review/ 0,4267,1246445,00.html (accessed January 29, 2006).

27. Peter Travers, "*The Ladykillers*," *Rolling Stone*, February 6, 2004, www.rolling stone.com/reviews/movie/_/id/5949541 (accessed January 29, 2006).

28. A. O. Scott, "A Gang of Impostors Vs. One True Lady," *New York Times*, March 26, 2004, E-1.

29. Charles Taylor, "*The Ladykillers*," Salon.com, March 26, 2004, www.salon.com/ ent/movies/review/2004/03/26/ladykillers/index.html (accessed January 29, 2006).

30. *The Ladykillers*, DVD, directed by Joel Coen and Ethan Coen (2004; Burbank, Calif.: Walt Disney Video, 2004).

31. *The Ladykillers*, DVD.

32. *The Ladykillers*, DVD.

33. Columbia Encyclopedia, 6th ed., 2001-2005, www.bartleby.com/65/me/ Mene-Men.html (accessed January 29, 2006).

34. *The Ladykillers*, DVD.

35. *The Ladykillers*, DVD.

36. *The Ladykillers*, DVD.

37. *The Ladykillers*, DVD.

38. *The Ladykillers*, DVD.

39. J. Hoberman, "Dud Simple," *Village Voice*, March 29, 2004, www.village voice.com/film/0413,hoberman,52206,20.html (accessed January 29, 2006).

40. John W. Davis, Ali Shaheed Jones-Muhammad, and Malik Taylor, "Sucka Nigga" (Zomba Enterprises, Inc., Ali Shaheed Jones-Muhammad, John W. Davis, Ma- lik Taylor, and Hub-Tones Music: 1994).

41. *The Ladykillers*, DVD.

42. Cannes Film Festival press conference, May 18, 2004, www.festival-cannes .fr/films/fiche_film.php?langue=6002&partie=video&id_film=4200622&cmedia =5708 (accessed July 18, 2006).

43. Cannes Film Festival press conference.

44. Caroline Westbrook, "Ealing: Home of British Film," August 9, 2002, news.bbc .co.uk/1/hi/entertainment/film/2179330.stm (accessed January 29, 2006).

Appendix: Winks and Nods

*T*he Coens stitch recurrent ideas into their films to spark recognition, acknowledge their influences, and underscore thematic threads. These in-jokes include:

- Circles: often symbolic of rebirth and cultural continuity
- Dreams: pointing to characters' psychologies and extending thematic discourse
- Names: often allegorical
- Russia: often representing a covert threat
- Animals: often emblematic of a character's wild nature
- Regurgitation: not so symbolic, rather a simple bodily function
- Endomorphic men screaming
- Rugs: implying cover-ups or MacGuffins (story plants that engage and mislead)
- Gender twists, especially as incursions into "what makes a man" territory
- Nods to books, authors, films, and maverick filmmakers (writers and directors)

The following is a smattering of choice Coen tidbits.

BLOOD SIMPLE

Russia: Visser's opening voice-over invokes Russia to color Texas as a place for loners. Later, he mentions Russia to countenance his "money simple" decision.

The name *Ray*: In the film's dark universe, Ray is doomed by his name, which means stream of light.

Vomit vamping: Marty throws up after seeing Visser's pictures, after receiving Abby's kick to the groin, and when he appears in her nightmare after Ray has killed him.

Gender twists: Marty to Visser: "This is an illicit romance. . . . For richer, for poorer."

Texas horror: The opening shot's road kill is possibly a nod to Tobe Hopper's low-budget, indie horror film *Texas Chainsaw Massacre*, which opens on a dead armadillo and takes place in *Blood Simple*'s setting.

Hitchcock nod: The theatrical print's title card quotes Alfred Hitchcock: "It is very difficult, and very painful, and it takes a very, very long time . . . to kill someone."

Hammett nod: "Blood simple" is a phrase out of the novel *Red Harvest*, referring to the craziness a murderer experiences after killing.

Literary lights: Crime novels by James M. Cain, such as *The Postman Always Rings Twice*, inspired *Blood Simple*.

Alexander Mackendrick nod: "Who looks stupid now?" comes from *The Ladykillers*.

Dreams: Abby's dreamworld is sometimes mistaken for the film's "reality."

Animals: Marty's mounted moose head suggests his hostile nature. Dead fish, the spoils of Marty's trip to Corpus Christi, far outnumber Visser's body count which is at zero when Marty pays him for murder.

RAISING ARIZONA

Russia: Allusive references to the cold war come from the threatening Leonard Smalls (destroyed in an explosive duel) and from *Dr. Strangelove* references.

Kubrick reference: The P.O.E. and O.P.E. graffiti in the gas station bathroom.

Dreams: Hi conjures the chimerical Leonard Smalls in a nightmare.

Night of the Hunter nod: Hi's line, "It's a hard world for little things," from Charles Laughton's spooky cinematic fairy tale, acknowledges Hi's cryptomnesia.

Literary lights: Leonard Smalls nods to John Steinbeck's Lenny Smalls in *Of Mice and Men*. The name *Snopes* references William Faulkner's low-down, low-class clan. H. I. "call me Hi" McDunnough harks back to Ishmael from *Moby-Dick* and the Bible.

The names *Nathan* and *Dot*: Nathan, meaning "God has given," ties into the idea that the McDunnoughs will have to experience some sort of "gift from God" (the meaning of *Dot*, short for Dorothy) if they are to overcome their childlessness.

***The Hudsucker Proxy* nod:** "Hudsucker Industries" appears on Hi's work togs.

Large men screaming: Gale and Evelle bawl like babies escaping prison and after they realize they have left the toddler behind.

***Blood Simple* nod:** M. Emmet Walsh's gruesome tale about a spherical object in the road winks at *Blood Simple*'s opening image.

Gender twists and manliness: Gale wonders if the androgynously named Ed wears the pants. Where she is masculinized through her gruff manners and police uniform, Hi is feminized through flowery, faux poetic language and his bright-colored Hawaiian shirts. After punching Glen and before stealing the Huggies, Hi tells Ed she has "a man for a husband."

Animals: A pack of angry dogs joins the hunt for Hi after he filches some Huggies.

MILLER'S CROSSING

Large men screaming: The just-tortured Drop Johnson screams as the Dane is whacked.

Hitchcock nod: The fight poster in Drop's apartment features a boxer named Lars Thorwald, also the name of a character in Alfred Hitchcock's *Rear Window*.

Vomit vamping: Tom throws up when Eddie the Dane escorts him to Miller's Crossing.

Gender twists: Men in drag appear in the ladies' room (look for Albert Finney in a maid outfit). Tom is referred to as a "twist" and "mother hen."

Rugs: The theft of the hairpiece of the murdered "Rug" Daniels perplexes Leo not Tom. Rugs and toupees crop up in later films as winks to homosexuality and missing info.

Literary lights: The movie cribs heavily from Dashiell Hammett's *Red Harvest* and *The Glass Key*.

Dreams: Tom's dream of a hat blowing through the woods prefigures his hat toss by the Dane when it looks like Tom's lie of killing Bernie is about to be uncorked. Tom's dream also harks back to *The Glass Key*.

Circles: Before Tom confesses to Leo about Verna, Leo gets up and walks around his desk in a circular pattern. The spray of gunfire from the gangster whom Leo shoots in the window forms a circle. Leo's office features an arced window; Tom's living room is round thanks to bay windows. The ladies' room features circular mirrors.

The name *Mink*: The name of this shady, gay character ties into the anarchy explored in a gangland devoid of rules. An animal name, Mink represents the "cozy as lice," "jungled up" intimate male relationships, so key to the gangster genre.

Animal: A dog with a quizzical expression looks at the dead man in the alley.

BARTON FINK

Vomit vamping: Charlie throws up in Barton's bathroom (offscreen, like Marty in *Blood Simple*) when he spies Audrey's dead body in Barton's bed.

The name *Fink*: Barton's surname refers to the informant role Barton takes on in Hollywood—he becomes a fink.

The name *Mundt*: Charlie's last name is the name of a Republican congressman from South Dakota who served for decades in first the House and then the Senate from the late 1930s to the late 1960s. A strident anti-Communist, he cosponsored a bill to register all Communists. He also cosponsored the Smith-Mundt Act, which both shields Americans from U.S. propaganda aimed at foreign audiences and turns publicly funded government information into a classified weapon.

Large men screaming: Charlie as Mad Man Mundt runs down the hotel hallway screaming, "I'll show you the life of the mind."

Russia: Jack Lipnik is from Minsk.

Circles: When Charlie frees Barton from the bed, a ball from the post conspicuously rolls across the floor.

Animal: Barton's disingenuous line about wrapping fish in the newspaper where his stupendous review appeared circles back to the fishmonger character in his play.

THE HUDSUCKER PROXY

The circle: Norville's ticket to success is the film's predominant symbol. It points to the regenerative effect of folk tales and grassroots storytelling (like movies) on culture.

The names *Sidney J. Mussburger* and *Waring Hudsucker*: These names chosen for two top-guns at the Hudsucker company represent compilations of names from similarly themed movies. These include J. J. Hunsucker from *Sweet Smell of Success* and the eponymous *Hud*, whose title role was played by Paul Newman.

Vomit vamping: When Norville takes Amy to his office, he runs to the bathroom and throws up offscreen after drinking a shot.

Frank Capra nods: Large story chunks are cribbed from *Meet John Doe* and *Mr. Deeds Goes to Town*.

Animals: Norville's talk of reincarnated gazelles and ibexes ties into the circle theme. The Muncie eagle symbolizes the idea of flight, a key trait in the film for creative ideas and inspiring leaders. The chief's remark about wrapping a fish in his newspaper harks to a line in Billy Wilder's scathing film noir *Ace in the Hole*, about an unethical reporter, as well as a disingenuous line in *Barton Fink*.

FARGO

Vomit vamping: Marge starts to throw up at the crime scene, but it turns out that her morning sickness is a false alarm.

The name *Yanagita*: The surname of the odd character Mike Yanagita references a prominent, Japanese cultural historian who looked to folklore, regional dialect, and other grassroots rites and rituals to explore and report on Japan's underreported history.

Hitchcock nod: The curtain-less bathtub recalls *Psycho*.

Kubrick reference: Carl's euphemism for sex—"the old in and out"— recalls a line from *A Clockwork Orange*.

Animal: Babe the Blue Ox references tap the movie's tall-tale mode.

THE BIG LEBOWSKI

Russia: The White Russian is the cocktail of choice for the Dude.

Raymond Chandler nod: *The Big Lebowski* nods *The Big Sleep*.

Robert Altman nods: In addition to paying homage to Chandler, the film pays tribute to Altman's revisionist *The Long Goodbye*.

Dreams: The Dude's *Gutterballs* dream spoofs Busby Berkeley's fantastic choreography that smacked of sexual metaphors and imagery.

Gender twists: The Big Lebowski asks, "What makes a man?" The Dude wears his hair in a barrette.

Large men screaming: Walter, prone to angry outbursts, explodes and goes on the attack at the bowling alley, yelling at Smokey for an alleged line foul.

Circles: There are two main orbs: the tumbling tumbleweed and the bowling ball.

Kubrick reference: Kubrick is invoked by mention of the "In and Out Burger" joint during the dance performance. Jesus thrusts his gloved hand in a gesture reminiscent of Kubrick's antiwar satire, *Dr. Strangelove*.

Hitchcock nod: The Dude's attempt to glean info from Treehorn's drawing spoofs a more successful information-gathering event in *North by Northwest*: Cary Grant discovers info about Eva Marie Saint by penciling over a notepad she just used. The Dude's discovery is markedly different: His pencil etching reveals Treehorn's picture of a cartoon man with an erection.

Rugs: While the Dude's spoiled rug is a precipitating event, Jon Polito's turn as a detective who alludes to *Miller's Crossing*'s plot twists is remindful of Rug Daniels.

Animals: The ferret the nihilists throw in the Dude's bathtub is incorrectly referred to as a marmot. Walter, whose belief in rules shines through his knowledge of rodent ownership in city limits, has no qualms about letting his ex-wife's Pomeranian run around the lanes.

O BROTHER, WHERE ART THOU?

Gender twists and manliness: The paterfamilias wannabe Everett, played by the sexily masculine George Clooney, sleeps in a hair net.

The name *Tommy Johnson*: Tommy's character conjures up the historical bluesman Robert Johnson, whose legend about acquiring his musical skills from the devil is part of blues lore.

***Wizard of Oz* nods:** In its exploration of political solutions to social problems of classism and racism, *O Brother* borrows *Oz*'s incorporation of a wizard symbolic of a politician.

Sturges nod: *O Brother, Where Art Thou?* is the title of the movie that film-director protagonist John Sullivan wants to make in *Sullivan's Travels*.

Circles: The round Dapper Dan pomade can and tire swing are two visual circles. The ring is Everett's final quest to get Penny back. The plot comes

full circle when he finds the wrong ring, and the picture closes on him tied to his family instead of chained to his fellow cons as in the opening.
Animal: In one of many nods to Homer, George kills cows.

THE MAN WHO WASN'T THERE

Gender twists and manliness: "What kind of a man are you?" is a question posed to Ed Crane by Big Dave and then his brother-in-law Frank.

The name *Ed Crane*: The title character's given name implies androgyny and adds to his sexual ambiguity (it can be short for Edwina or Edward) while *Crane* signifies his need to fly from his humdrum existence.

Animal: Birdy, flying saucers, references to the "early bird special" symbolize Ed's need for escape.

Russia: Frank reads the paper and notes that Russia has gotten the bomb.

***Night of the Hunter* nod:** The underwater shot of Creighton Tolliver's dead body in a car recalls the watery grave in Laughton's dark fairy tale of good and evil.

Circles: Key circular items include the doctor's headwear and the rolling hubcap that flies through the air, taking on the appearance of a flying saucer.

Dream: Ed's dream takes off with flying saucer imagery before veering into a mundane domestic scene with his deceased wife.

Rugs: Jon Polito, who plays a gay character, has a toupee like a "whacked" gangster in *Miller's Crossing*.

Hitchcock nod: The film's setting of Santa Rosa was chosen to summon the idea of dread descending on a small town, as delivered in *Shadow of a Doubt*.

INTOLERABLE CRUELTY

Literary lights: Lines from poems by William Shakespeare and Christopher Marlowe are quoted.

Coens nod: The "NOMAN" sign at the Las Vegas convention for divorce attorneys references *O Brother, Where Art Thou?* by way of a Homeric disguise for Ulysses.

Animal: Miles, who is introduced by way of a close-up on his teeth, is a carnivore and thus a good match for the carnivorous Marilyn. Other animal references come in the form of Rex Rexroth, a lothario who is commanded like a dog to sit in court, and a man described as "tuna" for being such a great catch as a husband to divorce.

THE LADYKILLERS

Mackendrick nod: This remake of Alexander Mackendrick's *The Ladykillers* nods to the original with Tom Hanks's introduction.

The name *Marva Munson*: This is also the name of a judge in *Intolerable Cruelty*.

Literary light: Edgar Allan Poe's poem "To Helen" is recited by the professor whose deference to the dark side culminates in his ravenlike ending off a bridge.

Kurosawa nod: The cat trotting Pancake's finger to the bridge is reminiscent of the dog at the beginning of *Yojimbo* carrying a severed hand in his mouth. The alley that the cat passes also recalls *Miller's Crossing*, another movie that references *Yojimbo* (and its influencing *Red Harvest*) by way of Tom's playing both sides.

Animal: Marva Munson's cat Pickles, nicknamed Angel, is repelled by the dark Professor Dorr.

Bibliography

Abbott, Megan E. *The Street Was Mine*. New York: Palgrave Macmillan, 2002.
"Ad Isn't Taxing for Coen Brothers." *Boston Globe*. January 22, 2002. www.ifilm.com/?sctn=collections&pg=superbowl2002
Anderson, John. "Screen's Mercurial Girl Is at It Again." *Los Angeles Times*. March 11, 1994.
Attanasio, Paul. "Brothers in Film Noir: The Complicated Joys of Making *Blood Simple*." *Washington Post*. February 3, 1985.
Ball, Howard. "Downwind from the Bomb." *New York Times*. February 9, 1986.
Barton Fink, DVD. Directed by Joel Coen. 1991; Beverly Hills, Calif.: 20th Century Fox Home Entertainment, 2003.
Behind the Name, www.behindthename.com.
Berczeller, Paul. "Death in the Snow." *Guardian*. June 6, 2003, film.guardian.co.uk/features/featurepages/0,4120,970908,00.html (accessed November 11, 2005).
Bezanson, Walter E. "*Moby-Dick*: Work of Art." *Moby-Dick*. New York: W.W. Norton & Company, 1967.
The Big Lebowski production notes.
The Big Lebowski, DVD. Directed by Joel Coen. 1998; Universal City, Calif.: Universal Studios Home Entertainment, 2005.
The Big Sleep, DVD. Directed by Howard Hawks. 1946; Burbank, Calif.: Warner Home Video, 2000.
Blood Simple, DVD. Directed by Joel Coen. 1985; Universal City, Calif.: Universal Studios Home Entertainment, 2001.
Bourget, Jean-Loup. "Social Implications in the Hollywood Genres." In Mast, Cohen, and Braudy, *Film Theory and Criticism*, 467–74.
Bradshaw, Peter. "We Woz Robbed: *The Ladykillers*." *Guardian*. June 25, 2004. film.guardian.co.uk/News_Story/Critic_Review/Guardian_review/0,4267,1246445,00.html (accessed January 29, 2006).
Braudy, Leo. *The World in a Frame*. Chicago: University of Chicago Press, 1976.
Brook, Vincent, and Allan Campbell. "'Pansies Don't Float'—Gay Representability, Film Noir, and *The Man Who Wasn't There*." *Jump Cut: A Review of Contemporary Me-*

dia, no. 46. www.ejumpcut.org/archive/jc46.2003/brook.pansies/index.html (accessed July 20, 2006).

Brown, Georgia. "Only the Lonely." *Village Voice*. March 1996.

Burnett, T-Bone. *O Brother, Where Art Thou?* Various artists. *Lost Highway* CD, 2000.

Campbell, Joseph. *The Power of Myth*. New York: Doubleday, 1988.

Canby, Vincent. "In Miller's Crossing, Silly Gangsters and a Tough Moll." *New York Times*. September 21, 1990.

Cannes Film Festival press conference, www.festival-cannes.fr/films/fiche_film .php?langue=6002&partie=video&id_film=4200622&cmedia=5708 (accessed July 18, 2006).

Chandler, Raymond. *The Big Sleep*. 1939. Reprint, New York: Vintage Crime, 1992.

———. *The Long Goodbye*. New York: Vintage Crime, 1992.

Cheshire, Ellen, and John Ashbrook. *Joel Coen and Ethan Coen*. Great Britain: Pocket Essentials, 2000.

Clausewitz, Carl von. *On War*. NuVisions Publications, 2004.

Coen Brothers. "Independent Focus: The Coen Brothers." Interview with Elvis Mitchell. Independent Film Channel, 1998.

Coen, Ethan, and Joel Coen. *The Man Who Wasn't There*. New York: Faber & Faber, 2001.

———. *Barton Fink & Miller's Crossing*. London: Faber & Faber, 1991.

Columbia Encyclopedia, 6th ed. 2001–2005. www.bartleby.com/65/me/Mene-Men .html (accessed January 29, 2006).

The Conformist, DVD. Directed by Bernardo Bertolucci. 1970; Hollywood, Calif.: Paramount Home Video, 2006.

Content, Rob, Tim Kreider, and Boyd White. "Review: O Brother, Where Art Thou?" *Film Quarterly* (Fall 2001): 43.

Cool Hand Luke, DVD. Directed by Stuart Rosenberg. 1967; Burbank, Calif.: Warner Home Video, 1997.

Corliss, Richard. "Swede 'n' Sour." *Time*. March 1996.

———. "That Old Feeling: When Porno Was Chic." *Time*. March 29, 2005, www .time.com/time/columnist/corliss/article/0,9565,1043267,00.html (accessed March 15, 2006).

Daniel, Wayne W. *Pickin' on Peachtree*. Chicago: University of Illinois Press, 1990.

Dargis, Manohla. "Too Simple." *LA Weekly*. July 7–13, 2000. www.laweekly.com/ ink/00/33/film-dargis.php (accessed December 30, 2005).

Davis, John W., Ali Shaheed Jones-Muhammad, and Malik Taylor. "Sucka Nigga" (Zomba Enterprises, Inc., Ali Shaheed Jones-Muhammad, John W. Davis, Malik Taylor, and Hub-Tones Music: 1994).

Dawes, Amy. "Chaos and the Coens." *Los Angeles Daily News*. March 15, 1996.

Defoe, Daniel. *Moll Flanders*. New York: Signet Classic, 1981.

Denby, David. "Swede 'n' Sour." *New Yorker*. March 18, 1996.

Derosa, Robin. "Box Office." *USA Today*. March 18, 1996.

Diamond, Neil. "I'm a Believer" (1966).

Dixon, Melvin. *Ride Out the Wilderness*. Chicago: University of Illinois Press, 1987.

Easton, Matthew George. *Illustrated Bible Dictionary*, 3rd ed. Published by Thomas Nelson, 1897.

Ebert, Roger. "*Lebowski* Big on Fun." *Chicago Sun-Times*. March 6, 1998.

———. "*Rashomon*." *Chicago Sun-Times*. May 26, 2002. rogerebert.suntimes.com/apps/pbcs.dll/article?AID=/20020526/REVIEWS08/205260301/1023 (accessed June 24, 2006).

Eco, Umberto. *Six Walks in the Fictional Woods*. Cambridge, Mass.: Harvard University Press, 1994.

Edelstein, David. "King George vs. Catherine the Great." October 10, 2003. slate.msn.com/id/2089688/ (accessed January 29, 2006).

———. "Invasion of the Baby Snatchers." *American Film* (April 1987): 28.

Elliott, David. "Brothers in Fact and Film: Coens' Latest Movie Shows Comedic Bent." *San Diego Union-Tribune*, April 5, 1987.

Emerson, Jim. "That Barton Fink Feeling." 1991. www.cinepad.com/coens.htm (accessed January 1, 2006).

Eyman, Scott. "*Crossing* Straight but Not All That Serious." *San Diego Union-Tribune*. October 19, 1990.

Facets Model Assignment: "Sabre Dance." Music 3824: Music for Elementary Teachers, Allegra Helper, by Juanita Wasatch. April 16, 2002. faculty.weber.edu/tpriest/FacetsMdl_files/Sabre%20Dance.html

"*Fargo*." Box Office Mojo. www.boxofficemojo.com/movies/?id=fargo.htm (accessed December 4, 2005).

Fargo, DVD. Directed by Joel Coen. 1996; Santa Monica, Calif.: MGM, 2003.

Foster, Stephen. "Old Black Joe" (circa 1860).

Fowler, H. W. *A Dictionary of Modern English Usage*. Oxford: Oxford University Press, 1985.

Geffner, David. *MovieMaker*, issue 29, www.moviemaker.com/issues/29/shooting/29_shooting.html (accessed January 1, 2006).

Girard, René. *Deceit, Desire, and the Novel*. Translated by Yvonne Freccero. Baltimore: Johns Hopkins University Press, 1965.

Gothic Keywords. courses.nus.edu.sg/course/ellgohbh/gothickeywords.html (accessed January 27, 2006).

Gottschalk, Marie. *The Prison and the Gallows*. New York: Cambridge University Press, 2006.

Guralnick, Peter. *Searching for Robert Johnson*. New York: Plume Penguin, 1989.

Haggard, Merle, and Dean Holloway. "Big City" (Shade Tree Music, Inc., and BMI: 1981, 1982)

Hall, John W., et al., eds. *The Cambridge History of Japan*. New York: Cambridge University Press, 1988.

Hammett, Dashiell. *Complete Novels*. New York: Literary Classics of the United States, 1999.

———. *The Glass Key*. New York: Vintage Books, 1989.

Harrison, Robert Pogue. *Forests: The Shadow of Civilization*. Chicago: University of Chicago Press: 1993.

Haskell, Molly. *From Reverence to Rape.* New York: Holt, Rinehart & Winston, 1973.

Hayes, John. "Coen Heads: Pitt Attempts a Live Adaptation of the Cult Hit *The Hudsucker Proxy.*" *Pittsburgh Post-Gazette.* November 5, 1999.

Hays Code. www.artsreformation.com/a001/hays-code.html

Hendricks, John, Irving Mills, and Fletcher Henderson. "Down South Camp Meetin'" (Hendricks Music and EMI Mills Music: 1997).

Hillman, James. "Psychology and Alchemy." *Suicide and the Soul.* Dallas: Spring Publications, 1976.

Hinckley, David. "Patronage or Pillage?" *New York Daily News.* July 28, 2002, 16.

Hoberman, J. "Dud Simple." *Village Voice.* March 29, 2004, www.villagevoice.com/film/0413,hoberman,52206,20.html (accessed January 29, 2006).

Holland, Eddie, Brian Holland, and Lamont Dozier. "It's the Same Old Song" (Motown Record Corporation and Jobete Music Co., Inc.: 1965, 1993).

Holt, Linda. "I'm So Prouda You." *Times Literary Supplement.* June 14, 1996.

Hoskyns, Barney. "Sticky Fingers & Exile on Main Street, The Rolling Stones." *Observer.* June 20, 2004 (accessed March 11, 2006).

Hud, VHS. Directed by Martin Ritt. 1963; Hollywood, Calif.: Paramount, 1991.

"*Hudsucker Proxy.*" *Pittsburgh Post-Gazette.* November 5, 1999.

The Hudsucker Proxy, DVD. Directed by Joel Coen. 1994; Burbank, Calif.: Warner Home Video, 1999.

Hunter, Stephen. "Dazzling *Hudsucker Proxy* is a Delightful Echo of Old-Time Flicks." *Baltimore Sun*, April 8, 1994.

"*Intolerable Cruelty.*" *New York Times.* www.nytimes.com/slideshow/2004/03/28/movies/20040328_CRUELTY_SLIDESHOW_1.html (accessed January 29, 2006).

Intolerable Cruelty, DVD. Directed by Joel Coen. 2003; Universal City, Calif.: Universal Studios Home Entertainment, 2004.

James, Skip. "Hard-Time Killing Floor Blues" (1931).

Jung, C. G. *Flying Saucers: A Modern Myth of Things Seen in the Sky.* Translated by R. F. C. Hull. Princeton, N.J.: Princeton University Press, 1978.

Jung, Carl G. *Man and His Symbols.* New York: Anchor Books, 1964.

Kaiser, Robert G., and David Ottaway. "Oil for Security Fueled Close Ties." *Washington Post.* February 11, 2002.

Kempley, Rita. "*Miller's Crossing:* Brutal Beauty." *Washington Post.* October 5, 1990.

King, Larry. "The Barton Fink Anomaly." *USA Today.* September 17, 1991.

Klady, Leonard. "Wacky Movie's Sibling Producers Hit on Hot Formula." *Toronto Star.* April 11, 1987.

Klawans, Stuart. "Static Electricity." *Nation.* December 6, 2001. www.thenation.com/doc/20011224/klawans (accessed July 21, 2006).

Klemesrud, Judy. "The Brothers Coen Bow in With *Blood Simple.*" *New York Times.* January 20, 1985.

The Lady Eve, DVD. Directed by Preston Sturges. 1941; New York: Criterion, 2001.

The Ladykillers, DVD. Directed by Joel Coen and Ethan Coen. 2004; Burbank, Calif.: Walt Disney Video, 2004.

LaSalle, Mick. "*Crossing* Just Another Stylish Mob Film." *San Francisco Chronicle.* October 5, 1990.

Leigh, Danny. "The Silver Age." *Guardian*. December 8, 1999.
Lippman, Robert. "Looking Back on the Seattle Conspiracy Trial." 1990. terrasol
.home.igc.org/trial.htm (accessed March 15, 2006).
Lippman, Walter. "The Causes of Political Indifference Today." *Atlantic Monthly* 139,
no. 2 (February 1927): 265–67.
Lomax, Alan. *The Land Where the Blues Began*. New York: Pantheon, 1993.
Lomax, John A., and Alan Lomax. *Folk Song: U.S.A.* New York: Times Mirror, 1975.
The Long Goodbye, DVD. Directed by Robert Altman. 1973; Santa Monica, Calif.:
MGM, 2002.
"Lorena Hickock Reports on the State of the Nation." June 6, 1934. www.newdeal
.feri.org/tva/lorena1.htm.
Mack, Maynard, et al., eds. *The Norton Anthology of World Masterpieces*, 4th ed. Vol. 1.
New York: W.W. Norton & Co., 1979.
Malmgren, Carl D. "The Crime of the Sign: Dashiell Hammett's Detective Fiction."
Twentieth Century Literature, September 22, 1999, www.findarticles.com/p/articles/
mi_m0403/is_3_45/ai_58926042 (accessed January 7, 2006).
The Man Who Wasn't There production notes.
The Man Who Wasn't There, DVD. Directed by Joel Coen. 2001; Universal City, Calif.:
Universal Studios Home Entertainment, 2002.
Maslin, Janet. "*Blood Simple*, A Black-Comic Romp." *New York Times*. October 12,
1984.
———. "Deadly Plot by a Milquetoast Villain." *New York Times*. March 8, 1996.
Mast, Gerald, Marshall Cohen, and Leo Braudy, eds. *Film Theory and Criticism*. New
York: Oxford University Press, 1992.
McCarthy, Phillip. "Cruel Hands." *Sidney Morning Herald*. October 24, 2003. www.smh
.com.au/articles/2003/10/23/1066631572748.html (accessed January 29, 2006).
McClintock, Harry. "Big Rock Candy Mountain."
McGilligan, Patrick. *Robert Altman, Jumping Off the Cliff*. New York: St. Martin's Press,
1984.
McGrady, Mike. "Colorful Characters in Gangster Land." *Newsday*. September 21,
1990.
McLoughlin, William G. *Revivals, Awakenings, and Reform*. Chicago: University of
Chicago Press, 1978.
Meyerson, Harold, and Ernie Harburg. *Who Put the Rainbow in the* Wizard of Oz? Ann
Arbor: University of Michigan, 1993.
Miller, Karl. *Doubles: Studies in Literary History*. New York: Oxford University Press,
1985.
Miller's Crossing production notes.
Miller's Crossing, DVD. Directed by Joel Coen. 1990; Beverly Hills, Calif.: 20th Cen-
tury Fox Home Entertainment, 2003.
Mitchell, Elvis. "Film Review: A Lawyer's Good Teeth Help in Court and Love." *New
York Times*. October 10, 2003.
Morgan, David. *Knowing the Score*. New York: Harper Entertainment, December
2000.
Moynihan, Daniel Patrick. *Secrecy*. New Haven, Conn.: Yale University Press, 1998.

Mr. Deeds Goes to Town, DVD. Directed by Frank Capra. 1936; Culver City, Calif.: Sony Pictures, 2000.

Munroe, Charlie. "Down in the Willow Garden" (1957, 1972).

Nyman, Jopi. *Men Alone*. Netherlands: Rodopi B.V. Editions, 1997.

O Brother, Where Art Thou? DVD. Directed by Joel Coen. 2000; Burbank, Calif.: Walt Disney Video, 2001.

Olsen, Mark. "Going Commercial but Not Exactly Mainstream." *Los Angeles Times*. December 2, 2003.

Oxford English Dictionary, 2nd ed. 1989. OED Online. Oxford University Press. dictionary.oed.com (accessed August 28, 2006).

Patterson, Nicholas. "Gates of Ethan." *Boston Phoenix*. November 19–26, 1998. www.bostonphoenix.com/archive/books/98/11/19/ETHAN_COEN.html (accessed January 7, 2006).

Peachment, Chris. "Brothers With One Eye." *Sunday Telegraph*. May 26, 1996.

Phillips, Gene D. *Creatures of Darkness: Raymond Chandler, Detective Fiction, and Film Noir*. Lexington: University Press of Kentucky, 2000.

Polito, Robert. Introduction to *The Maltese Falcon, The Thin Man, Red Harvest*. New York: Everyman's Library, 2000.

Pulver, Andrew. "Blood Ties." *Daily Mail and Guardian*. August 20, 1998. www.mg.co.za/mg/art/film/9808/980820-coen.html

Rabinowitz, Peter J. "Rats Behind the Wainscotting: Politics, Convention and Chandler's *The Big Sleep*." In *The Critical Response to Raymond Chandler*. Edited by J. K. Van Dover. Westport, Conn.: Greenwood Press, 1995.

Raising Arizona, DVD. Directed by Joel Coen. 1987; Beverly Hills, Calif.: 20th Century Fox Home Entertainment, 1999.

Robertson, William Preston. "Prince of Darkness." *Guardian*. April 15, 2001. film.guardian.co.uk/features/featurepages/0,,472454,00.html (accessed January 5, 2006).

———. *Lebowski: The Making of a Coen Brothers Film*. New York: W.W. Norton & Co., 1998.

Rodgers, Jimmie. "In the Jailhouse Now" (Carrie Anita Rodgers Court: 1962, 1990).

"The Sabre Dance Man." NPR's *Morning Edition*. June 5, 2003. www.npr.org/templates/story/story.php?storyId=1287262 (accessed January 15, 2006).

Scott, A. O. "A Gang of Impostors Vs. One True Lady." *New York Times*. March 26, 2004.

Sedgwick, Eve Kosofsky. *Between Men*. New York: Columbia University Press, 1985.

Severo, Richard. "Jimmie Davis, Louisiana's Singing Governor, Is Dead." *New York Times*. November 6, 2000.

"Shadowing the Third Man." Turner Classic Movies. www2.turnerclassicmovies.com/thismonth/article.jsp?cid=82840&mainArticleId=93530 (accessed September 25, 2006).

Sharkley, Betsy. "Movies of Their Own." *New York Times*. July 8, 1990.

Simon, John. "*Fargo*: Movie Review." *National Review*. April 22, 1996.

Siskel, Gene. "*Blood Simple* Is Shocking, But With Style." *Chicago Tribune*. March 1, 1985.

Some Like It Hot, DVD. Directed by Billy Wilder. 1958; Santa Monica, Calif.: MGM, 2001.

Spoto, Donald. *The Art of Alfred Hitchcock*. New York: Doubleday, 1992.

Squires, Kathleen. "Magic Markers." *Time Out New York*, April 1–8, 1999.

Stern, Gary. "The Brothers Coen: Two *Noir*-Do-Wells Score With Original *Blood Simple*." *Chicago Tribune*. February 3, 1985.

Strauss, Neil. "The Country Music Radio Ignores." *New York Times*. March 24, 2002.

Sturges, Fiona. "Pop: Back to the Old Country." *Independent*. November 22, 2002.

Sweet Smell of Success, DVD. Directed by Alexander Mackendrick. 1957; Santa Monica, Calif.: MGM, 2001.

Taylor, Charles. "*The Ladykillers*." March 26, 2004. www.salon.com/ent/movies/review/2004/03/26/ladykillers/index.html (accessed January 29, 2006).

Thomas, Kevin. "*Blood Simple* Is Dark Comedy." *Los Angeles Times*. February 28, 1985.

Travers, Peter. "*The Ladykillers*." *Rolling Stone*. February 6, 2004. www.rollingstone.com/reviews/movie/_/id/5949541 (accessed January 29, 2006).

A Tribe Called Quest. "Sucka Nigga." *Midnight Marauders*. Jive: 1993.

"Trickster Tale." Encyclopaedia Britannica. www.britannica.com/eb/article-9073359 (accessed June 20, 2006).

Triplett, William. "Busting Heads and Blaming Reds." January 11, 2000. www.salon.com/ent/movies/feature/2000/01/11/blacklist (accessed January 1, 2006).

Tuveson, Ernest Lee. *Redeemer Nation*. 1968; Reprint, Midway Reprint Series, 1980.

Unsworth, John. "Tom Jones, The Comedy of Knowledge." *Modern Language Quarterly* 48, no. 3 (September 1987). www.iath.virginia.edu/~jmu2m/modern.language.quarterly.48:3.html (accessed January 1, 2006).

The Usual Suspects, DVD. Directed by Bryan Singer. 1995; Santa Monica, Calif.: MGM, 1999.

Walters, Ben. "Bringing Up Alimony." *Sight & Sound*. November 2003. www.bfi.org.uk/sightandsound/review/1143/ (accessed January 29, 2006).

Warshow, Robert. "Movie Chronicle: The Westerner." In *Film Theory and Criticism*, 455–58.

Weales, Gerald. *Clifford Odets, Playwright*. New York: Pegasus, 1971.

Weinraub, Bernard. "An Ex-Convict, a Hit Album, an Ending Fit for Hollywood." *New York Times*. March 3, 2002.

West, Nathanael. *Miss Lonelyhearts & the Day of the Locust*. New York: New Directions, 1962.

Westbrook, Caroline. "Ealing: Home of British Film." August 9, 2002. news.bbc.co.uk/1/hi/entertainment/film/2179330.stm (accessed January 29, 2006).

White Heat, DVD. Directed by Raoul Walsh. 1950; Burbank, Calif.: Warner Home Video, 2005.

Willett, Ralph. "Hard-Boiled Detective Fiction." BAAS Pamphlets in American Studies 23. First published 1992. www.baas.ac.uk/publications/pamphlets/pamphdets.asp?id=23#ch1 (2002).

Williams, Jonathan. "Pata or Quantum: Duchamp and the End of Determinist Physics." *Tout-fait*, no. 3 (2000). www.toutfait.com/issues/issue_3/Articles/williams/williams.html (accessed January 21, 2006).

Williamson, Bruce. "Movies—*Fargo* directed by Joel Coen and written by Joel Coen and Ethan Coen." *Playboy*. April 1996.

Zimmer, Elizabeth. "J. Hoberman on Busby Berkeley." *Dance in America: Busby Berkeley: Going Through the Roof.* www.pbs.org/gperf/busby/html/behind.html (accessed June 5, 2004).

Filmography

BLOOD SIMPLE (1984)

Writers: Joel Coen and Ethan Coen
Directors: Joel Coen, Ethan Coen (uncredited)
Producers: Ethan Coen, Joel Coen (uncredited), Daniel F. Bacaner (executive), Mark Silverman (associate)
Cast (in order of appearance): John Getz (Ray), Frances McDormand (Abby), Dan Hedaya (Julian Marty), M. Emmet Walsh (Private Detective aka Loren Visser), Samm-Art Williams (Meurice), Deborah Neumann (Debra), Raquel Gavia (Landlady), Van Brooks (Man from Lubbock), Señor Marco (Mr. Garcia), William Creamer (Old Cracker), Loren Bivens (Strip-bar Exhorter), Bob McAdams (Strip-bar Senator), Shannon Sedwick (Stripper), Nancy Finger (Girl on Overlook), Rev. William Preston Robertson (Radio Evangelist–voice), Holly Hunter (voice on Meurice's answering machine, uncredited)
Director of Photography: Barry Sonnenfeld
Production Design: Jane Musky
Costume Design: Sara Medina-Pape
Original Music: Carter Burwell
Film Editors: Roderick Jaynes (aka Joel and Ethan Coen), Don Wiegmann
Sound Editors: Skip Lievsay and Michael R. Miller
Casting: Julie Hughes and Barry Moss
Production Companies: River Road Productions, Ted and Jim Pedas and Ben Barenholtz at Circle Releasing
Principal Shooting Locations: Austin, Hutto, and Round Rock, Texas

361

Budget: $1.5 million
Running Time: 96 minutes

RAISING ARIZONA (1987)

Writers: Ethan Coen and Joel Coen
Directors: Joel Coen, Ethan Coen (uncredited)
Producers: Ethan Coen, Joel Coen (uncredited), James Jacks (executive), Mark Silverman (coproducer), Deborah Reinisch (associate)
Cast: Nicolas Cage (H. I. "Hi" McDunnough), Holly Hunter (Edwina "Ed" McDunnough), Trey Wilson (Nathan Arizona Huffhines Sr.), John Goodman (Gale Snopes), William Forsythe (Evelle Snopes), Sam McMurray (Glen), Frances McDormand (Dot), Randall "Tex" Cobb (Leonard Smalls), T. J. Kuhn Jr. (Nathan Arizona Jr.), Lynne Dumin Kitei (Florence Arizona), Peter Benedek (Prison Counselor), Charles "Lew" Smith (Nice Old Grocery Man), Warren Keith (Younger FBI Agent), Henry Kendrick (Older FBI Agent), Sidney Dawson (Ear-Bending Cellmate), Richard Blake (Parole Board Chairman), Troy Nabors (Parole Board Member), Mary Seibel (Parole Board Member), John O'Donnal (Hayseed in the Pickup), Keith Jandacek (Whitey), Warren Forsythe (Minister), Ruben Young ("Trapped" Convict), Dennis Sullivan (Policeman in Arizona House), Dick Alexander (Policeman in Arizona House), Rusty Lee (Feisty Hayseed), James Yeater (Fingerprint Technician), Bill Andres (Reporter), Carver Barns (Reporter), Margaret H. McCormack (Unpainted Secretary), Bill Rocz (Newscaster), Mary F. Glenn (Payroll Cashier), Jeremy Babendure (Scamp with Squirt Gun), Bill Dobbins (Adoption Agent), Ralph Norton (Gynecologist), Henry Tank (Mopping Convict), Frank Outlaw (Supermarket Manager), Todd Michael Rodgers (Varsity Nathan Jr.), M. Emmet Walsh (Machine Shop Ear-Bender), Robert Gray (Glen and Dot's Kid), Katie Thrasher (Glen and Dot's Kid), Derek Russell (Glen and Dot's Kid), Nicole Russell (Glen and Dot's Kid), Zachary Sanders (Glen and Dot's Kid), Noell Sanders (Glen and Dot's Kid), Cody Ranger (Arizona Quint), Jeremy Arendt (Arizona Quint), Ashley Hammon (Arizona Quint), Crystal Hiller (Arizona Quint), Olivia Hughes (Arizona Quint), Emily Malin (Arizona Quint), Melanie Malin (Arizona Quint), Craig McLaughlin (Arizona Quint), Adam Savageau (Arizona Quint), Benjamin Savageau (Arizona Quint), David Schnei-

der (Arizona Quint), Michael Stewart (Arizona Quint), William Preston Robertson (Amazing Voice–voice)
Director of Photography: Barry Sonnenfeld
Production Design: Jane Musky
Costume Design: Richard Hornung
Original Music: Carter Burwell
Editors: Michael R. Miller, Arnold Glassman (associate)
Sound Editors: Skip Lievsay (supervising), Phillip Stockton, Magdaline Volaitis, Ron Bochar, Bruce Poss (assistant), Marissa Littlefield (assistant), Stephen Visscher (assistant), Christopher Weir (assistant)
Casting: Donna Isaacson and John Lyons
Storyboard Artist: J. Todd Anderson
Baby Wrangler: Julie Asch
Banjo: Ben Freed
Yodeling: John Crowder
Production Company: Circle Films
Principal Shooting Locations: Camelback Mountain, Carefree, Florence, Scottsdale, and Tempe, Arizona; Lost Dutchman State Park; and Tonto National Forest
Running Time: 94 minutes

MILLER'S CROSSING (1990)

Writers: Joel Coen and Ethan Coen
Directors: Joel Coen, Ethan Coen (uncredited)
Producers: Ethan Coen, Joel Coen (uncredited), Ben Barenholtz (executive), Mark Silverman (coproducer), Graham Place (line)
Cast: Gabriel Byrne (Tom Reagan), Marcia Gay Harden (Verna), John Turturro (Bernie Bernbaum), Jon Polito (Johnny Caspar), J. E. Freeman (Eddie Dane), Albert Finney (Leo), Mike Starr (Frankie), Al Mancini (Tic-Tac), Richard Woods (Mayor Dale Levander), Thomas Toner (O'Doole), Steve Buscemi (Mink), Mario Todisco (Clarence "Drop" Johnson), Olek Krupa (Tad), Michael Jeter (Adolph), Lanny Flaherty (Terry), Jeanette Kontomitras (Mrs. Caspar), Louis Charles Mounicou III (Johnny Caspar Jr.), John McConnell (Cop, Brian), Danny Aiello III (Cop, Delahanty), Helen Jolly (Screaming Lady), Hilda McLean (Landlady), Monte Starr (Gunman in Leo's House), Don Picard (Gunman in Leo's House), Salvatore H. Tornabene (Rug Daniels), Kevin Dearie (Street Urchin), Michael Badalucco (Caspar's

Driver), Charles Ferrara (Caspar's Butler), Esteban Fernandez (Caspar's
Cousin), George Fernandez (Caspar's Cousin), Charles Gunning (Hit-
man at Verna's), Dave Drinkx (Hitman #2), David Darlow (Lazarre's
Messenger), Robert LaBrosse (Lazarre's Tough), Carl Rooney
(Lazarre's Tough), Jack David Harris (Man with Pipe Bomb), Jery He-
witt (Son of Erin), Sam Raimi (Snickering Gunman), John Schnauder
Jr. (Cop with Bullhorn), Zolly Levin (Rabbi), Joey Ancona (Boxer),
Bill Raye (Boxer), Frances McDormand (Mayor's Secretary, uncred-
ited)
And featuring the Remarkable Voice of William Preston Robertson
Frank Patterson ("Danny Boy" singer)
Director of Photography: Barry Sonnenfeld
Production Design: Dennis Gassner
Costume Design: Richard Hornung
Original Music: Carter Burwell
Editors: Michael R. Miller, Michael Berenbaum (first assistant), Anthony
    Grocki (assistant), Tricia Cooke (apprentice)
Sound Editor: Skip Lievsay (supervising)
Casting: Donna Isaacson and John Lyons
Storyboard Artist: J. Todd Anderson
Music and End Titles Design and Production: Balsmeyer & Everett Inc.
Production Companies: Circle Films, 20th Century Fox
Principal Shooting Location: New Orleans
Running Time: 115 minutes

BARTON FINK (1992)

Writers: Ethan Coen and Joel Coen
Directors: Joel Coen, Ethan Coen (uncredited)
Producers: Ethan Coen, Joel Coen (uncredited), Ben Barenholtz (execu-
    tive), Ted Pedas (executive), Jim Pedas (executive), Bill Durkin (exec-
    utive), Graham Place (coproducer)
Cast: John Turturro (Barton Fink), John Goodman (Charlie Meadows),
    Judy Davis (Audrey Taylor), Michael Lerner (Jack Lipnick), John Ma-
    honey (W. P. Mayhew), Tony Shalhoub (Ben Geisler), Jon Polito (Lou
    Breeze), Steve Buscemi (Chet), David Warrilow (Garland Stanford),
    Richard Portnow (Detective Mastrionotti), Christopher Murney (De-
    tective Deutsch), I. M. Hobson (Derek), Megan Faye (Poppy Carna-
    han), Lance Davis (Richard St. Claire), Harry Bugin (Pete), Anthony

Gordon (Maitre D'), Jack Denbo (Stagehand), Max Grodénchik (Clapper Boy), Robert Beecher (Referee), Darwyn Swalve (Wrestler), Gayle Vance (Geisler's Secretary), Johnny Judkins (Sailor), Jana Marie Hupp (USO Girl), Isabelle Townsend (Beauty)
And featuring the Golden Throat of William Preston Robertson
Director of Photography: Roger Deakins
Production Design: Dennis Gassner
Costume Design: Richard Hornung
Original Music: Carter Burwell
Editors: Roderick Jaynes (aka Joel and Ethan Coen), Michael Berenbaum (associate), Tricia Cooke (assistant)
Sound Editors: Skip Lievsay (supervising), Anne Sawyer (assistant), Randy Coleman (assistant), Bill Docker (assistant)
Casting: Donna Isaacson and John Lyons
Storyboard Artist: J. Todd Anderson
Production Companies: Circle Films, Working Title Films
Principal Shooting Location: Los Angeles
Running Time: 116 minutes

THE HUDSUCKER PROXY (1994)

Writers: Ethan Coen, Joel Coen & Sam Raimi
Director: Joel Coen, Ethan Coen (uncredited)
Producers: Ethan Coen, Joel Coen (uncredited), Graham Place (coproducer), Eric Fellner (executive), Tim Bevan (executive), Joel Silver (executive, credited as a Silver Pictures production)
Cast: Tim Robbins (Norville Barnes), Jennifer Jason Leigh (Amy Archer), Paul Newman (Sidney J. Mussburger), Charles Durning (Waring Hudsucker), John Mahoney (Chief), Jim True (Buzz), Bill Cobbs (Moses), Bruce Campbell (Smitty), Harry Bugin (Aloysius), John Seitz (Benny), Joe Grifasi (Lou), Roy Brocksmith (Board Member), I. M. Hobson (Board Member), John Scanlan (Board Member), Jerome Dempsy (Board Member), John Wylie (Board Member), Gary Allen (Board Member), Richard Woods (Board Member), Peter McPherson (Board Member), David Byrd (Dr. Hugo Bronfenbrenner), Christopher Darga (Mail Room Orienter), Pat Cranshaw (Ancient Sorter), Robert Weil (Mail Room Boss), Mary Lou Rosato (Mussburger's Secretary), Ernie Sarracino (Luigi the Tailor), Eleanor Glockner (Mrs. Mussburger), Kathleen Perkins (Mrs. Braithwaite),

Joseph Marcus (Sears Braithwaite of Bullard), Peter Gallagher (Vic
Tenetta), Noble Willingham (Zebulon Cardozo), Barbara Ann Grimes
(Mrs. Cardozo), Thom Noble (Thorstein Finlandson), Steve Buscemi
(Beatnik Barman), William Duff-Griffin (Newsreel Scientist), Anna
Nicole Smith (Za-Za), Pamela Everett (Dream Dancer), Arthur
Bridges (The Hula-Hoop Kid), Sam Raimi (Hudsucker Brainstormer),
John Cameron (Hudsucker Brainstormer), Skipper Duke (Mr. Grier),
Jay Kapner (Mr. Levin), Jon Polito (Mr. Bumstead), Richard Whiting
(Ancient Puzzler), Linda McCoy (Coffee Shop Waitress), Stan Adams
(Emcee), Karl Mundt (Newsreel Announcer), Joanne Pankow (News-
reel Secretary), Mario Todisco (Norville's Goon), Colin Fickes (News-
boy), Dick Sasso (Drunk in Alley)
Director of Photography: Roger Deakins
Production Design: Dennis Gassner
Costume Design: Richard Hornung
Original Music: Carter Burwell
Editor: Thom Noble
Sound Editors: Skip Lievsay (supervising), Anne Sawyer (assistant),
Randy Coleman (assistant), Bill Docker (assistant)
Casting: Donna Isaacson and John Lyons
Visual Effects: Michael J. McAlister (supervisor and producer)
Mechanical Effects: Peter M. Chesney
Storyboard Artist: J. Todd Anderson
Title Sequence and Other Cool Stuff Design and Production: Balsmeyer
& Everett Inc.
Production Company: Warner Brothers
Principal Shooting Locations: Wilmington, North Carolina; Chicago
Running Time: 110 minutes

FARGO (1996)

Writers: Ethan Coen and Joel Coen
Directors: Joel Coen, Ethan Coen (uncredited)
Producers: Ethan Coen, Joel Coen (uncredited), Tim Bevan (executive),
Eric Fellner (executive), John Cameron (line)
Cast: Frances McDormand (Marge Gunderson), William H. Macy (Jerry
Lundegaard), Steve Buscemi (Carl Showalter), Harve Presnell (Wade
Gustafson), Peter Stormare (Gaear Grimsrud), Kristin Rudrüd (Jean Lun-

degaard), Tony Denman (Scotty Lundegaard), Gary Houston (Irate Customer), Sally Wingert (Irate Customer's Wife), Kurt Schweickhardt (Car Salesman), Larissa Kokernot (Hooker #1), Melissa Peterman (Hooker #2), Steven Reevis (Shep Proudfoot), Warren Keith (Reilly Diefenbach–voice), Steve Edelman (Morning Show Host), Sharon Anderson (Morning Show Hostess), Larry Brandenburg (Stan Grossman), James Gaulke (State Trooper), J. Todd Anderson (Victim in the Field—as symbol spoofing The Artist Formerly Known as Prince), Michelle Suzanne LeDoux (Victim in Car), John Carroll Lynch (Norm Gunderson), Bruce Bohne (Lou), Petra Boden (Cashier), Steve Park (Mike Yanagita), Wayne Evenson (Customer), Cliff Rakerd (Officer Olson), Jessica Shepherd (Hotel Clerk), Peter Schmitz (Airport Lot Attendant), Steve Shaefer (Mechanic), Michelle Hutchinson (Escort), David Lomax (Man in Hallway), José Feliciano (Himself), Don William Skahill (Night Parking Attendant [also Office Production Assistant]), Bain Boehlke (Mr. Mohra), Rose Stockton (Valerie), Robert Ozasky (Bismarck Cop #1), John Bandemer (Bismarck Cop #2), Don Wescott (Bark Beetle Narrator–voice)
Director of Photography: Roger Deakins
Production Design: Rick Heinrichs
Costume Design: Mary Zophres
Original Music: Carter Burwell
Editors: Roderick Jaynes (aka Joel and Ethan Coen), Tricia Cooke (associate)
Sound Editors: Skip Lievsay (supervising), Todd Milner (assistant), Dan Evans Farcus (assistant)
Dialect Coach: Elizabeth Himmelstein
Casting: John Lyons
Storyboard Artist: J. Todd Anderson
Title Design: Balsmeyer & Everett Inc.
Production Companies: Polygram, Working Title
Principal Shooting Locations: Pembina County, North Dakota; Brainerd, St. Paul, Edina, and Minneapolis, Minnesota
Running Time: 98 minutes

THE BIG LEBOWSKI (1998)

Writers: Ethan Coen and Joel Coen
Directors: Joel Coen, Ethan Coen (uncredited)

Producers: Ethan Coen, Joel Coen (uncredited), Tim Bevan (executive) Eric Fellner (executive), John Cameron (coproducer)

Cast: Jeff Bridges (Jeffrey Lebowski "The Dude"), John Goodman (Walter Sobchak), Julianne Moore (Maude Lebowski), Steve Buscemi (Donny), David Huddleston (Jeffrey Lebowski "The Big Lebowski"), Philip Seymour Hoffman (Brandt), Tara Reid (Bunny Lebowski), Philip Moon (Woo, Treehorn Thug), Mark Pellegrino (Treehorn Thug), Peter Stormare (Nihilist/Uli Kunkel/"Karl Hungus"), Flea (Nihilist), Torsten Voges (Nihilist), Jimmie Dale Gilmore (Smokey), Jack Kehler (Dude's Landlord), John Turturro (Jesus Quintana), James G. Hoosier (Quintana's Partner, Liam), Ben Gazzara (Jackie Treehorn), David Thewlis (Knox Harrington), Carlos Leon (Maude's Thug), Terrence Burton (Maude's Thug), Richard Gant (Older Cop), Christian Clemenson (Younger Cop), Dom Irrera (Tony the Chauffeur), Gérard L'Heureux (Lebowski's Chauffeur), Lu Elrod (Coffee Shop Waitress), Michael Gomez (Auto Circus Cop), Peter Siragusa (Gary the Bartender), Sam Elliott (The Stranger), Marshall Manesh (Doctor), Harry Bugin (Arthur Digby Sellers), Jesse Flanagan (Little Larry Sellers), Irene Olga Lopez (Pilar), Luis Colina (Corvette Owner), Leon Russom (Malibu Police Chief), Ajgie Kirkland (Cab Driver), Jon Polito (Private Snoop Da Fino), Aimee Mann (Nihilist Woman), Jerry Haleva (Saddam), Jennifer Lamb (Pancake Waitress), Warren David Keith (Funeral Director), Asia Carrera (Sherry in *Logjammin'*—uncredited)

Director of Photography: Roger Deakins

Production Design: Rick Heinrichs

Costume Design: Mary Zophres

Original Music: Carter Burwell

Editors: Roderick Jaynes (aka Joel and Ethan Coen), Tricia Cooke (assistant)

Sound Editors: Skip Lievsay (supervising), Kimberly McCord (assistant), Wyatt Sprague (assistant)

Musical Archivist: T-Bone Burnett

Casting: John Lyons

Baby Wranglers: Patti Cooke, Eileen Sullivan

Giggles/Howls/Marmots: William Preston Robertson

Storyboard Artist: J. Todd Anderson

Title Design: Balsmeyer & Everett Inc.

Production Companies: Polygram, Working Title

Principal Shooting Location: California

Running time: 117 minutes

O BROTHER, WHERE ART THOU? (2000)

Writers: Ethan Coen and Joel Coen, Homer (plot chunks)
Directors: Joel Coen, Ethan Coen (uncredited)
Producers: Ethan Coen, Joel Coen (uncredited), Tim Bevan (executive), Eric Fellner (executive), John Cameron (line), Robert Graf (associate)
Cast: George Clooney (Ulysses Everett McGill), John Turturro (Pete), Tim Blake Nelson (Delmar O'Donnell), John Goodman (Big Dan Teague), Holly Hunter (Penny), Chris Thomas King (Tommy Johnson), Charles Durning (Pappy O'Daniel), Del Pentecost (Junior O'-Daniel), Michael Badalucco (George Nelson), J. R. Horne (Pappy's Staff), Brian Reddy (Pappy's Staff), Wayne Duvall (Homer Stokes), Ed Gale (The Little Man), Ray McKinnon (Vernon T. Waldrip), Daniel Von Bargen (Sheriff Cooley), Royce D. Applegate (Man with Bullhorn), Frank Collison (Wash Hogwallop), Quinn Gasaway (Boy Hogwallop), Lee Weaver (Blind Seer), Millford Fortenberry (Pomade Vendor), Stephen Root (Radio Station Man Mr. Lund), John Locke (Mr. French), Gillian Welch (Soggy Bottom Customer), A. Ray Ratliff (Record Store Clerk), Mia Tate (Siren), Musetta Vander (Siren), Christy Taylor (Siren), April Hardcastle (Waitress), Michael W. Finnell (Interrogator), Georgia Rae Rainer (Wharvey Gal), Marianna Breland (Wharvey Gal), Lindsey Miller (Wharvey Gal), Natalie Shedd (Wharvey Gal), John McConnell (Woolworth's Manager), Issac Freeman (Gravedigger), Wilson Waters Jr. (Gravedigger), Robert Hamlett (Gravedigger), Willard Cox (Cox Family), Evelyn Cox (Cox Family), Suzanne Cox (Cox Family), Sidney Cox (Cox Family), Buck White (The Whites), Sharon White (The Whites), Cheryl White (The Whites), Ed Snoderly (Village Idiot), David Holt (Village Idiot)
Director of Photography: Roger Deakins
Production Design: Dennis Gassner
Costume Design: Mary Zophres
Original Music: Carter Burwell
Editor: Roderick Jaynes (aka Joel and Ethan Coen), Tricia Cooke (assistant)
Sound Editor: Skip Lievsay (supervising), Mike Poppleton (assistant), Chris Fielder (assistant), Allan Zaleski (assistant)
Musical Archivist: T-Bone Burnett
Casting: Ellen Chenoweth
Yodeling: Pat Enright
Storyboard Artist: J. Todd Anderson

Title Design and Other Cool Stuff: Balsmeyer & Everett Inc.
Production Companies: Buena Vista Pictures, Working Title, Mike Zoss
    Productions, Studio Canal, Touchstone Pictures, Universal Pictures
Principal Shooting Location: Mississippi
Running Time: 103 minutes

THE MAN WHO WASN'T THERE (2001)

Writers: Joel Coen and Ethan Coen
Directors: Joel Coen, Ethan Coen (uncredited)
Producers: Ethan Coen, Joel Coen (uncredited), John Cameron (copro-
    ducer), Tim Bevan (executive), Eric Fellner (executive), Robert Graf
    (associate)
Cast: Billy Bob Thornton (Ed Crane), Frances McDormand (Doris
    Crane), Michael Badalucco (Frank), James Gandolfini (Dave "Big
    Dave" Brewster), Katherine Borowitz (Ann Nirdlinger), Jon Polito
    (Creighton Tolliver), Scarlett Johansson (Rachael "Birdy" Abundas),
    Richard Jenkins (Walter Abundas), Tony Shalhoub (Freddy Rieden-
    schneider), Christopher Kriesa (Officer Persky), Brian Haley (Officer
    Pete Krebs), Jack McGee (Burns), Gregg Binkley (The New Man),
    Alan Fudge (Diedrickson), Lilyan Chauvin (Medium), Adam Alexi-
    Malle (Jacques Carcanogues), Ted Rooney (Bingo Caller), Abraham
    Benrubi (Young Man), Christian Ferratti (Child), Rhoda Gemignani
    (Costanza), E. J. Callahan (Customer), Brooke Smith (Sobbing Pris-
    oner), Ron Ross (Banker), Hallie Singleton (Waitress), Jon Donnelly
    (Gatto Eater), Dan Martin (Bailiff), Nicholas Lanier (Tony), Tom
    Dahlgren (Judge #1), Booth Colman (Judge #2), Stanley Desantis
    (New Man's Customer), Peter Siragusa (Bartender), Christopher Mc-
    Donald (Macadam Salesman), Rick Scarry (District Attorney), George
    Ives (Lloyd Garroway), Devon Cole Borisoff (Swimming Boy), Mary
    Bogue (Prisoner Visitor), Don Donati (Pie Contest Timer), Arthur
    Reeves (Flophouse Clerk), Michelle Rae Weber (Dancer), Randi
    Pareira (Dancer), Robert Loftin (Dancer), Kenneth Hughes (Dancer),
    Gordon Hart (Dancer), Brenda Mae Hamilton (Dancer), Lloyd Gor-
    don (Dancer), Leonard Crofoot (Dancer), Rita Bland (Dancer), Au-
    drey Baranishyn (Dancer), Qyn Hughes (Dancer), Rachel McDonald
    (Dancer)
Director of Photography: Roger Deakins
Production Design: Dennis Gassner

Costume Design: Mary Zophres
Original Music: Carter Burwell
Editors: Roderick Jaynes (aka Joel and Ethan Coen), Tricia Cooke, David
Diliberto (associate)
Sound Editors: Skip Lievsay (supervising), Alex Soto (assistant), Igor
Nikolic (assistant)
Casting: Ellen Chenoweth
Piano Performances: Jonathan Feldman
Storyboard Artist: J. Todd Anderson
Title Design: Balsmeyer & Everett Inc.
Production Companies: Polygram, Working Title
Principal Shooting Locations: Los Angeles, Glendale, and Pasadena, California
Running Time: 116 minutes

INTOLERABLE CRUELTY (2003)

Writers: Joel Coen and Ethan Coen, Robert Ramsey (story and screenplay), Matthew Stone (story and screenplay), John Romano (story)
Directors: Joel Coen, Ethan Coen (uncredited)
Producers: Ethan Coen, Joel Coen (uncredited), Brian Grazer (producer), John Cameron (coproducer), Sean Daniel (executive), James Jacks (producer), Grant Heslov (coproducer), James Whitaker (coproducer), Robert Graf (producer)
Cast: George Clooney (Miles Massey), Catherine Zeta-Jones (Marilyn), Geoffrey Rush (Donovan Donaly), Cedric the Entertainer (Gus Petch), Edward Herrmann (Rex Rexroth), Paul Adelstein (Wrigley), Richard Jenkins (Freddy Bender), Billy Bob Thornton (Howard D. Doyle), Julia Duffy (Sarah Sorkin), Jonathan Hadary (Heinz, the Baron Krauss von Espy), Tom Aldredge (Herb Myerson), Stacey Travis (Bonnie Donaly), Jack Kyle (Ollie Olerud), Irwin Keyes (Wheezy Joe), Judith Drake (Mrs. Gutman), George Ives (Mrs. Gutman's Lawyer), Booth Colman (Gutman Trial Judge), Mr. Gutman (Royce D. Applegate, uncredited), Kristin Dattilo (Rex's Young Woman), Wendle Josepher (Miles's Receptionist), Mary Pat Gleason (Nero's Waitress), Mia Cottet (Ramona Barcelona), Kiersten Warren (Claire O'Mara), Rosey Brown (Gus's Pals), Ken Sagoes (Gus's Pals), Dale E. Turner (Gus's Pals), Douglas Fisher (Maitre d'), Nicholas Shaffer (Waiter), Isabell Monk O'Connor (Judge Marva Munson), Mary Gillis (Court Reporter), Colin Linden (Father

Scott), Julie Osburn (Stewardess), Gary Marshal (Las Vegas Waiter), Blake Clark (Convention Secretary), Allan Trautman (Convention Lawyer), Kate Luyben (Santa Fe Tart), Kitana Baker (Santa Fe Tart), Camille Anderson (Santa Fe Tart), Bridget Marquardt (Santa Fe Tart), Emma Harrison (Santa Fe Tart), John Bliss (Mr. MacKinnon), Patrick Thomas O'Brien (Bailiff), Sean Fenton (Bailiff)

Director of Photography: Roger Deakins

Production Design: Leslie McDonald

Costume Design: Mary Zophres

Original Music: Carter Burwell

Editors: Roderick Jaynes (aka Joel and Ethan Coen), David Diliberto (associate)

Sound Editors: Skip Lievsay (supervising), Todd Milner (assistant), Dan Evans Farcus (assistant)

Casting: Ellen Chenoweth

Storyboard Artist: J. Todd Anderson

Title Design: Balsmeyer & Everett Inc.

Production Companies: Universal Pictures, Alphaville Films, Imagine Entertainment, Mike Zoss Productions

Principal Shooting Locations: California, Nevada

Running Time: 100 minutes

THE LADYKILLERS (2004)

Writers: Joel Coen and Ethan Coen, based on William Rose screenplay

Directors: Joel Coen, Ethan Coen

Producers: Ethan Coen, Joel Coen, Tom Jacobson (producer), Barry Sonnenfeld (producer), Barry Josephson (producer), John Cameron (coproducer), David Diliberto (associate), Robert Graf (associate)

Cast: Tom Hanks (Professor G. H. Dorr), Irma P. Hall (Marva Munson), Marlon Wayans (Gawain MacSam), J. K. Simmons (Garth Pancake), Tzi Ma (The General), Ryan Hurst (Lump Hudson), Diane Delano (Mountain Girl), George Wallace (Sheriff Wyner), John McConnell (Deputy Sheriff), Jason Weaver (Weemack Funthes), Stephen Root (Fernand Gudge), Lyne Odums (Rosalie Funthes, as Baadja-Lyne Odums), Walter Jordan (Elron), George Anthony Bell (Preacher), Greg Grunberg (TV Commercial Director), Hallie Singleton (Craft Service), Robert Baker (Quarterback), Blake Clark (Football Coach), Amad Jackson (Doughnut Gangster), Aldis Hodge (Doughnut Gang-

ster), Freda Foh Shen (Doughnut Woman), Paula Martin (Gawain's
Mama), Jeremy Suarez (Li'l Gawain), Te Te Benn (Gawain's Sister),
Khalil East (Gawain's Brother), Jennifer Echols (Waffle Hut Waitress),
Nita Norris (Tea Lady), Vivian Smallwood (Tea Lady), Maryn Tasco
(Tea Lady), Muriel Whitaker (Tea Lady), Jessie Bailey (Tea Lady),
Louisa Abernathy (Church Voice–voice), Mildred Dumas (Church
Voice–voice), Al Fann (Church Voice–voice), Mi Mi Green-Fann
(Church Voice–voice), Maurice Watson (Othar)
Director of Photography: Roger Deakins
Production Design: Dennis Gassner
Costume Design: Mary Zophres
Original Music: Carter Burwell
Editors: Roderick Jaynes (aka Joel and Ethan Coen)
Sound Editor: Skip Lievsay (supervising)
Casting: Ellen Chenoweth
Production Companies: Touchstone Pictures, Jacobson Company (un-
credited), Pancake Productions Inc. (uncredited)
Principal Shooting Locations: Los Angeles; Natchez, Mississippi
Running Time: 104 minutes

ADDITIONAL COEN CREDITS

The Evil Dead (1981), directed by Sam Raimi

Joel Coen was assistant film editor.

Crimewave (1985), directed by Sam Raimi

Joel Coen and Ethan Coen cowrote with Sam Raimi.

Down from the Mountain (2000), directed by D. A. Pennebaker, Nick Doob,
and Chris Hegedus

Joel Coen and Ethan Coen were executive producers on this documentary
on the bluegrass-roots concert celebrating the music and musicians featured
in *O Brother, Where Art Thou?*

Bad Santa (2003), directed by Terry Zwigoff

Joel Coen and Ethan Coen were executive producers.

Sawbones (2005), written and directed by Joel and Ethan Coen

The Coen brothers teamed up with longtime collaborator Carter Burwell for this sonic screenplay. Starring the voices of Phillip Seymour Hoffman, Steve Buscemi, Brooke Smith, John Slattery, Marcia Gay Harden, and John Goodman, the piece was part of a show billed as *Theater of the New Era.*

Romance and Cigarettes (2005), directed by John Turturro

Joel and Ethan Coen were executive producers.

Paris, Je T'Aime (2006), multiple directors

Joel and Ethan Coen directed the segment "Tuileries."

No Country for Old Man (forthcoming), directed by Ethan and Joel Coen

The next feature by the Coen brothers is based on a Cormac McCarthy novel.

Index

The Double (Fyodor Dostoyevsky), 44
Double Indemnity. See Wilder, Billy
double motif, 7, 9, 23–26, 43–48, 52,
    57, 186, 210–11, 217–19, 282–83,
    285
Dr. Strangelove or: How I Learned to Stop
    Worrying and Love the Bomb, 61–62,
    224–25, 316, 350. *See also* Kubrick,
    Stanley

Ealing Studios, 311, 327–28, 330, 338,
    340–41

Faulkner, William, 41, 57, 105, 126,
    128, 131, 220, 258, 346
film genres: comedies, 16, 27, 29, 38,
    47, 62, 84, 104, 106, 109, 112,
    118–19, 152–53, 155, 166, 181–82,
    186, 248, 267, 312–14, 321, 323–24,
    328, 331, 336, 341; gangster films,
    70, 73, 78–80, 84, 86, 88, 91, 97,
    271, 347–48, 351; horror films, 2,
    13, 19–20, 106, 113, 117, 119,
    122–24, 128, 199, 320, 335–36, 346;
    musicals, 166, 261; prison movies,
    258–60; Westerns, 39, 96–97, 99,
    214–16, 220, 236, 238. *See also Cool*
    Hand Luke; The Defiant Ones
film noir, 4, 6, 8, 10–11, 13, 17, 19, 27,
    31, 33–34, 106, 122, 128, 155, 199,
    208, 212, 233, 280, 283, 301, 303
Fluxus art, 223–24, 236
folk tales, folklore, and other folk art, xi,
    36, 62, 127, 143, 174, 177, 182, 193,
    195, 200–201, 236, 254, 270,
    272–74, 348–49
French New Wave, 10

Gassner, Dennis, 291, 364–66, 369–70,
    373
Gilliam, Terry. *See Brazil*
The Glass Key, 69–70, 74, 76–77, 81,
    83, 91, 93–94, 347. *See also*
    Hammett, Dashiell
Godard, Jean-Luc. *See Vivre sa Vie*

The Godfather, 78–81, 177
Goodman, John, 17, 39, 63, 105, 116,
    160, 208–9, 214, 216, 245, 252, 272,
    362, 364, 368–69
Googie, 211, 235

Hammett, Dashiell, 2–4, 6, 30, 69–70,
    74–77, 90–96, 128, 134, 208, 233,
    346–47. *See also The Glass Key; Red*
    Harvest
Hanks, Tom, ii, 310–11, 328, 332, 334,
    336, 340
Harburg, E. Y., 243, 261, 263
Hawks, Howard, 145, 220–21
Hays Production Code, 117, 221, 324
Hinduism, 142, 145, 150, 156–58,
    163–65
Hitchcock, Alfred, x, 9, 129, 156, 192,
    226, 238, 282, 295, 346–47, 349–51;
    North by Northwest, 117; *Psycho*, 9,
    11, 26, 30, 191, 295, 349; *Shadow of*
    a Doubt, 9, 25, 156, 282–83, 290,
    351; *Strangers on a Train*, 9, 16, 25
Homer, xi, 128, 244–52, 326, 351, 369
Hud, 154, 349
Hunter, Holly, 36n32, 38, 55, 57, 245,
    270, 361–62, 369
Huston, John, 122, 303

The Iliad. See Homer; *The Odyssey*

Johnson, Robert, 245, 272–73, 351
Judaism, 256
Jung, Carl, 43, 47, 51, 291–92

Kasdan, Lawrence. *See Body Heat*
Khachaturian, Aram, 143, 151–52, 166
Kind Hearts and Coronets, 341
King, Steven. *See* Kubrick, Stanley
Kramer, Stanley, 259–60
Kubrick, Stanley, 61–62, 122–23,
    224–25, 346, 349–50. *See also A*
    Clockwork Orange; Dr. Strangelove or:
    How I Learned to Stop Worrying and
    Love the Bomb